OXFORD WORLD'S CLASSICS

THE OXFORD SHAKESPEARE

General Editor · Stanley Wells

The Oxford Shakespeare offers new and authoritative editions of Shakespeare's plays in which the early printings have been scrupulously re-examined and interpreted. An introductory essay provides all relevant background information together with an appraisal of critical views and of the play's effects in performance. The detailed commentaries pay particular attention to language and staging. Reprints of sources, music for songs, genealogical tables, maps, etc. are included where necessary; many of the volumes are illustrated, and all contain an index.

JOHN JOWETT, the editor of *Timon of Athens* in the Oxford Shakespeare, is Reader in Shakespeare Studies at the Shakespeare Institute, University of Birmingham. He has also edited *Richard III* for the Oxford Shakespeare.

THE OXFORD SHAKESPEARE

Currently available in paperback

The rest of the plays are forthcoming

OXFORD WORLD'S CLASSICS

WILLIAM SHAKESPEARE
AND
THOMAS MIDDLETON

The Life of Timon of Athens

Edited by
JOHN JOWETT

OXFORD
UNIVERSITY PRESS

OXFORD

UNIVERSITY PRESS

Great Clarendon Street, Oxford OX2 6DP

Oxford University Press is a department of the University of Oxford.
It furthers the University's objective of excellence in research, scholarship,
and education by publishing worldwide in

Oxford New York

Auckland Bangkok Buenos Aires Cape Town Chennai
Dar es Salaam Delhi Hong Kong Istanbul Karachi Kolkata
Kuala Lumpur Madrid Melbourne Mexico City Mumbai Nairobi
São Paulo Shanghai Taipei Tokyo Toronto

Oxford is a registered trade mark of Oxford University Press
in the UK and in certain other countries

Published in the United States
by Oxford University Press Inc., New York

British Library Cataloguing in Publication Data

Data available

Library of Congress Cataloging in Publication Data

Data available

ISBN 978-0-19-953744-0

2

Typeset by SNP Best-set Typesetter Ltd., Hong Kong
Printed in Great Britain by
Clays Ltd, St Ives plc

ACKNOWLEDGEMENTS

I OWE thanks above all to Stanley Wells, who has overseen this project with his characteristic wisdom, tolerance, and sure touch. Christine Buckley has averted many errors, and has added more to the intellectual content of the edition than one has any right to expect of a copy editor. Frances Whistler was there from the beginning. She, Judith Luna, and others at Oxford University Press helped to turn a typescript into an elegant book.

Amongst colleagues and friends my gratitude is owed to: Brian Boyd, for urging me to write on the authorship question and commissioning my work for publication in *Words that Count*; Alice Cooley, for information on Bolsover Castle; George Craig, for answering a query about the letters of Samuel Beckett; Tony Dawson and Gretchen E. Minton, the Arden editors of *Timon*, for friendly co-existence; Joy Leslie Gibson, for information on the Young Vic production; Hugh Grady, for kind remarks on a paper that was revised to become part of the Introduction; Roger Holdsworth, for advice and comments when I was working on the play for Middleton's *Collected Works* and since; Trevor H. Howard-Hill, for details of his unpublished work on compositor attribution; Andrea Jackson, for her generosity in providing information on Stratford, Ontario productions; MacD. P. Jackson, for comments on authorship questions, and for encouragement; Russell Jackson, for advice on theatre history and help with German; M. J. Kidnie, for an extraordinarily careful, rigorous, and generous reading of the introduction; Tomonari Kuwayama, for sharing ideas on the play, Ildikó Limpár and Kinga Földvá, for help beyond all expectation in researching Hungarian productions; Stuart Loone, for information about the production in Launceston; Kristin Lucas, for pointing me to Bataille, and much else; Catherine Richardson, for advice on historical matters; Clare Smout, for saving me from a misreading; Martin Wiggins, for valuable suggestions on masques and other matters; Fiona Wilson, for pointing out a Ted Hughes poem; and Akihiro Yamada, for information on the Japanese Shimpa adaptation.

The Education Department of the Royal Shakespeare Company,

Gary Taylor, István Géher and Géza Kállay, and Luciano García García, all stimulated my work by inviting papers relating to it; these were presented at the 1999 Prince of Wales Summer School in Stratford-upon-Avon, the 2002 meeting of the Shakespeare Association of America in Miami, the Stratford–Budapest Post-graduate Conference, and the 14th SEDERI conference in Jaén in 2003. Linda Woodbridge invited me to submit the Miami paper to appear in *Money and the Age of Shakespeare*.

Jim Shaw, Kate Welch, and other staff of the Shakespeare Institute Library have been, as ever, outstanding in their efficiency and helpfulness. I am grateful also to Library Assistants who have undertaken research tasks: Kelley Costigan, Emma Harper, Eleanor Lowe, Will Sharpe, and others. Staff of the Shakespeare Centre Library have capably and actively enabled my work on the Royal Shakespeare Company archives. Jo Elsworth and others helped me to make the most of a long and intensive day's work at the Bristol Theatre Collection. Marilyn Halperin of the Chicago Shakespeare Theater responded with enthusiastic generosity to enquiries and provided photographs reproduced as Illustrations 2 and 3a. Elizabeth McGrath of the Warburg Institute located the woodcut reproduced as Illustration 1. Zsuzsa Koncz provided a copy of her photograph reproduced as Illustration 6.

The academic staff and students of the Shakespeare Institute have constituted a stimulating intellectual environment for my work. They have repeadedly provided a sounding-board for work in progress, and made available the considerable fund of knowledge they collectively hold. I mention in particular the students of my MA special topic on *Timon of Athens*, Middleton, and early modern culture, alongside whom I learnt much about the play.

My children David and Hannah Jowett were the middle of humanity and a constant delight, saving me from *Timon* daily. A special thank-you to Hannah for numbering the first typescript.

JOHN JOWETT

CONTENTS

Contents

LIST OF ILLUSTRATIONS

ILLUSTRATIONS are reproduced by permission of the Shakespeare Birthplace Trust unless otherwise noted.

INTRODUCTION

It is no coincidence that Shakespeare's least loved play is about a misanthrope. *Timon of Athens* presents a man who expresses unmatched savage vehemence against the whole of humanity. It does not seek out a warm place in the affections of its readers. Nor does it seem to be designed to have popular appeal in the theatre. This play reaches into extreme areas of experience that are usually absent from everyday life, and are avoided by what Timon's critic Apemantus calls 'The middle of humanity'.

Some critics have speculated that Shakespeare abandoned the play before it reached the stage, perhaps in a state of personal or artistic crisis. This view has influenced many readers, and has encouraged theatre practitioners to adapt the text freely. It has a mythical truth, in that it speaks eloquently of how the play has both fascinated and troubled its readers. What has become increasingly clear in recent years is that many of the apparent peculiarities of the text do not reflect Shakespeare's disordered intellect or dissatisfaction with his own work, but instead result from his writing the play in collaboration with another dramatist, Thomas Middleton.[1] The printers of the 1623 Folio text were evidently working from a manuscript that lacked some finishing touches and that was written in two hands. The oscillation between harsh but comic satire and vehement rage results in part from the shifts between Middleton and Shakespeare.

The present edition is the first to locate the play firmly within a context of collaboration between Shakespeare and Thomas Middleton. This issue depends on evidence that needs presenting in some detail, and is therefore postponed until the end of this introduction. The conclusion, however, is not postponed: Middleton will be a key point of reference. Shakespeare concentrated on the opening, the scenes dealing most fully with Timon himself, and the conclusion.[2] *Timon of Athens* follows a highly Shakespearian structure in its shift

[1] For accounts of Middleton's life and work, see Gary Taylor, 'Life of Middleton', in *Collected Works*, and John Jowett, 'Thomas Middleton', in *A Companion to Renaissance Drama*, ed. Arthur F. Kinney (Oxford and Malden, Mass., 2002), pp. 507–23.

[2] Later, Shakespeare similarly contributed the substantial opening scene, parts of the main plot, and the final scene, in collaborating with John Fletcher on *Two Noble Kinsmen*.

The following table gives a schematic summary of Middleton's contributions to *Timon of Athens*, as elaborated in the Introduction and commentary. In reading this table, allowance should be made for the fluidity of the collaborative process, and for the presence of passages where exact attribution is insecure, inappropriate, or impossible.

Scene	Middleton's contribution
Sc. 1	0.3 (Mercer), 38.1–42 (?), 276–86
Sc. 2	entire scene
Sc. 3	none
Sc. 4	various passages
Sc. 5	entire scene
Sc. 6	entire scene
Sc. 7	entire scene
Sc. 8	entire scene
Sc. 9	entire scene
Sc. 10	entire scene
Sc. 11	opening (to 25 or 38?), 64–8 (??), end (from 105)
Sc. 12	none
Sc. 13	touches in 1–29, all from 30
Sc. 14	456–535; touches elsewhere; perhaps part transcription
Sc. 15	none
Sc. 16	none
Sc. 17	10–13 (?)

Figure 1: Middleton Passages

from the life of the social elite in the city to the natural world of the woods or heathland, a pattern found in plays such as *A Midsummer Night's Dream* (another play set in ancient Athens), *As You Like It*, and *King Lear*. Middleton evidently assumed responsibility for about one-third of the play (see Fig. 1). Co-authorship studies show that he wrote the banquet scene (Sc. 2), the central scenes with Timon's creditors and Alcibiades' confrontation with the senate, and most of the episodes figuring the Steward. The play's abrasively harsh humour and its depiction of social relationships that involve a denial of personal relationships are Middletonian traits, drawing on his excellence in the genre of city comedy. To identify Middleton's hand is not to dismiss the supposedly weaker sections as having been written by an inferior dramatist. *Timon of Athens* is all the more interesting because the text articulates a dialogue between two dramatists of very different temper, sometimes finding rapprochement, sometimes writing in contestation. Seen in this way, it emerges a more compelling and understandable work.

Of course, the question of who wrote what cannot always be answered with clarity, and in any case is often not the most important question to ask. Parts of this introduction will unfold with little or no reference to it. Moreover, the play departs from Shakespearian patterns in ways that are not dependent on Middleton's contribution. As a tragedy it is anomalous because the titular hero fades into an anticlimactic death off stage. As a depiction of social life it is deeply abnormal because it almost entirely excludes women and children. As a drama it resorts to the remarkable and apparently untheatrical device of having almost a third of its action made up of the single sequence in which Timon, statically dwelling in the woods, is visited by a succession of Athenians. By such means the play develops as an extreme drama with its extreme view of life. These are some of the traits that lead us into the work that Algernon Charles Swinburne melodramatically described as 'a poem inspired at once by the triune Furies of Ezekiel, of Juvenal, and of Dante'.[1]

The fringe of Shakespeare's achievement is a place in touch with agony, and subjected to fierce, dangerous, and sometimes unpleasant emotion. It is a place where art makes few compromises. Some readers will decide to leave it alone. Those who engage with it can expect to be disturbed and challenged. But the play has attracted many admirers and has often surprised audiences with its power as a work for the stage. Quite apart from its innovative features, it encompasses astonishing moments of theatre, scenes of incisive humour, glimpses of unexpected tenderness, and passages containing some of the most enthralling, if shocking, dramatic verse that Shakespeare wrote. These are fragments of what *Timon of Athens* is not, a popular play.

Date of Composition

Shortly before *Timon of Athens* was first published in the Shakespeare First Folio, the publishers formally secured their entitlement to the text. It was one of sixteen previously unpublished plays that were entered in the Stationers' Register on 8 November 1623. No earlier document mentions it or relates to it. In order to determine the date of composition, attention must focus on the internal evidence of the text, and on its relationship to its sources.

---

[1] *A Study of Shakespeare* (1880), p. 215.

The following discussion leads towards a suggested date of early 1606.

The story told in *Timon of Athens* of self-exclusion from society and the play's angry mood show particular affinities with *King Lear* (1605–6) and with *Coriolanus* (1608?). Much discussion of the date of authorship has centred on the question of whether it was written close in time to one or the other of these plays. Shakespeare drew on Plutarch's 'Life of Marcus Antonius' for *Julius Caesar* (1599) and again for *Antony and Cleopatra* (1606?). When writing *Coriolanus*, he would have found the 'Life of Alcibiades' paired with that of Coriolanus. Both of these 'Lives' mention Timon, and so it is possible to imagine Shakespeare encountering the figure as he revisited Plutarch when working on the late Roman plays. On this basis, E. K. Chambers is often followed in assigning the play to 'between *Coriolanus* and *Pericles* in 1608'.[1]

There are, however, no secure foundations to this dating. Shakespeare had studied Plutarch's 'Marcus Antonius' for *Julius Caesar* before 1600, and he mentions 'critic Timon' as early as 1594–5 in *Love's Labour's Lost* 4.3.168; he would have found an account of Timon based ultimately on Plutarch in William Painter's *The Palace of Pleasure*, the main source for *All's Well That Ends Well* (1604–5); furthermore, he may have been revisiting Plutarch with *Antony and Cleopatra* in mind some time before actually writing that play or *Coriolanus*. What is really striking about the 'Life of Alcibiades' is how meagre its influence is on *Timon of Athens*. And what is striking about the case for the 1608 date is the lack of any firm evidence to support it.

There is, moreover, an important consideration that weighs heavily against any date after mid-1608. A play printed in the First Folio would have been written for the King's Men, the company to which Shakespeare belonged, and the company that owned his manuscripts and after his death brought them to the stationers. Seen in this context, the absence of act divisions in the Folio text give an immediate clue as to the play's date. They suggest that it was written before the company began performing with act intervals, a change introduced as a result of their occupancy of the Blackfriars Theatre in August 1608. Act divisions were essential for staging at the Blackfriars as an indoor playhouse, as there had to be

[1] *William Shakespeare*, 2 vols. (Oxford, 1930), i. 483.

a break in the performance while the candles were replaced. Though a pretheatrical text such as is printed in F might hypothetically have been left for the divisions to be marked into a transcript at a later date, the intractable difficulties in dividing the play into five meaningful sections (see pp. 9–11) suggest that this is not the explanation here. This is a play written without regard to a performable five-act structure, and with no sign that performance at the Blackfriars was a consideration.

A large measure of importance must be attached to evidence arising from internal stylistic tests of the sections attributed to Shakespeare. This evidence again leans strongly away from 1608 and towards a date several years earlier. MacD. P. Jackson, after analysing Shakespeare's share in a test examining the distribution of rare vocabulary, placed the play at 1604–5.[1] Gary Taylor's test of colloquialisms in verse places the Shakespearian portion between *All's Well That Ends Well* (*c*.1604–5) and *Macbeth* (1606). *Lear* produces anomalous results in this test, and so is effectively out of the picture. However, Taylor's two separate examinations of rare vocabulary in the Quarto *History of Lear* find that *Timon of Athens* was written either immediately before or immediately after that play. The proximity of date is confirmed by both tests independently, and if anything is reinforced by the tests' inability, between them, to establish a sequence.[2] These investigations strikingly converge in suggesting that *Timon of Athens* was written in 1604–6. They weigh firmly against any date later than mid-1606.

As with other aspects of the play, the play needs to be placed in the sequence of Middleton's writing as well as that of Shakespeare. Holdsworth, looking at the Middleton material from the point of view of Middleton's dramatic works, similarly concluded that the play most convincingly fitted 1604–6. The strongest stylistic parallels are with plays written in this period. The creditor scenes in *Timon of Athens* display a species of dramatic writing Middleton had perfected in plays such as *A Trick to Catch the Old One* (1605). Holdsworth notes that the significant verbal parallels between the Middleton section of *Timon of Athens* and Middleton's other works show a stronger association with those written a few years before 1608. In so far as *Timon of Athens* is an experimental subspecies of

---

[1] *Studies in Attribution: Middleton and Shakespeare* (Salzburg, 1979), p. 155.

[2] *Textual Companion*, p. 128.

tragedy, it can be associated with Middleton's other experiments in the genre at this time: the small-scale and intense domestic drama of *A Yorkshire Tragedy* (1605), or the violent *sprezzatura* of *The Revenger's Tragedy* (1606).[1] It also happens that these two last-mentioned plays were both written for Shakespeare's company, the King's Men. There is no other period of Middleton's career when a collaboration with Shakespeare on a tragedy would be more likely.[2]

Where within this period should *Timon of Athens* be placed? In unpublished notes Holdsworth has pointed out the probable influence on the play of *Two Most Unnatural and Bloody Murders*. This pamphlet was entered in the Stationers' Register on 12 June 1605 in anticipation of its being published, and is the main source of Middleton's *A Yorkshire Tragedy*, which was probably written soon after it appeared.[3] In the pamphlet, the eventual murderer Walter Calverley indulges in profligacy that is described in phrases echoed in the language of *Timon of Athens*.[4] On this account, the play cannot have been written before June 1605.[5]

In view of the date of *Bloody Murders*, it is significant that there is a probable reference to the Gunpowder Plot, discovered on 4 November 1605. At 7.31–3 Timon's Servant refers to 'those that under hot ardent zeal would set whole realms on fire'. The reference could be to religious zeal in more general terms; but the comment is extraneous to the dramatic situation, and this strengthens the case for its being a topical allusion.[6] It remains unclear how closely an allusion to the Gunpowder Plot would affect the later limit of the play's date of composition. The Plot was remembered by Middleton (who clearly wrote this scene) many years after the

---

[1] For Middleton's authorship, see MacD. P. Jackson, pp. 33–40.

[2] However, Middleton also wrote *The Lady's Tragedy* for the King's Men in 1611. His adaptation of *Macbeth* was probably undertaken after Shakespeare died, or at least had retired from the London theatre.

[3] On the authorship of *A Yorkshire Tragedy*, see MacD. P. Jackson, *Studies in Attribution*, pp. 43–53, and Jonathan Hope, *The Authorship of Shakespeare's Plays* (Cambridge, 1994), pp. 124–6.

[4] See commentary to 1.42, 4.1–5, and 8.13.

[5] These considerations (along with the linguistic evidence) effectively rule out Sandra Billington's case, on the basis of a reference to a play about Timon of Athens in John Marston's *Jack Drum's Entertainment* (1600), for an earlier date still: 'Was *Timon of Athens* Performed before 1604?', *Notes and Queries*, 243 (1998), 351–3. See pp. 19–20 for suggestions of an earlier Timon play.

[6] Soellner notes that Coleridge thought the passage 'so *nolenter volenter*, by the head and shoulders' that it might be an interpolation (p. 203).

event, as it was by many other writers. Despite these reservations, the consistency between this likely allusion to the most startling event of King James's reign and the recollection of another sensational event of 1605 in the echo of *Bloody Murders* suggests that very late 1605 may not be far off the mark.

There are some reasons for postponing the date further to early 1606. This would still accommodate the influence of the Calverley pamphlet and an allusion to the Gunpowder Plot (the perpetrators were convicted on 27 January 1606 and executed on 31 January), and it would be consistent with other possible topical allusions. King James's Timonesque generosity in gift-giving had been especially evident in the celebrations of the marriage of the Earl of Essex to Lady Frances Howard that culminated in Ben Jonson's masque *Hymenaei*, performed on 5 January 1606. James's reliance for financial relief on the Members of Parliament, an equivalent of the play's senators, was a matter of public comment in the months that followed. In early 1606 Parliament voted to grant funds to the King and then debated whether to increase its subsidy. It is at this time, according to *OED*, that the noun *supply* began to be used in this context, and the sense is used in *Timon of Athens* at 3.27.

Finally, *Timon of Athens* has a close if enigmatic relationship with Jonson's satiric and in some ways Lucianic comedy *Volpone*, in which the main character exemplifies the accumulation of wealth as surely as Timon represents its loss. The King's Men performed *Volpone* in about mid-March 1606.[1] Though both are set far from London, the two plays depict city states and share strong elements of city comedy. In particular, they present extravagant and absurd pictures of the obsession with gold. Gold is centrally thematic to *Volpone*. In Volpone's opening soliloquy he ritualistically worships it: 'Good morning to the day; and next, my gold! | Open the shrine that I may see my saint'. The trio of self-interested creditors in the middle scenes of *Timon of Athens* corresponds with the trio of avaricious would-be male heirs to Volpone. The beast fable of *Volpone* and the bounty-hunters named after raptors and corvines relate to the widespread theme of bestiality and to the specific animal fable at 14.328–45 in *Timon of Athens*. With *Timon of Athens*'s theme of expenditure and loss, and *Volpone*'s theme of acquisition and

---

[1] *Volpone*, ed. Parker, pp. 7–8.

accumulation, it would seem that one play was written partly as a response to the other. The reference to parasites as 'flies' in *Timon of Athens* at 4.167 is a possible recollection of *Volpone* (see commentary). Furthermore, given the success of *Volpone* on stage and the uncertainties as to whether *Timon of Athens* was performed at all, it would be more secure to assume that *Volpone* was the originator. It is just possible that Shakespeare, who as a theatre company sharer would have known about Jonson's play even before it was finished, planned *Timon of Athens* as a companion piece.

Thus there are strong reasons based on the play's language for accepting the 'early' dating of 1604–6. Within that span a date before June 1605 looks highly improbable, a date before November 1605 looks unlikely, and spring 1606 offers the most plausible date of composition. Whether *Timon of Athens* was finally staged we do not know. The Folio's list of the King's Men's principal actors claims that 'all these Playes' were performed by them, but then the Folio preliminaries wrongly present all the plays in the volume as written by one hand only, and are not necessarily to be accepted at face value. The play can therefore be placed with more confidence within the authorial œuvres than within the sequence of productions staged by the King's Men.

Setting aside *King Lear*, the preceding play in Shakespeare's output would have been *All's Well*, assuming the Oxford dating for that play of 1604–5, and this accords well with the influence of its source text. If *All's Well* came earlier, *Timon of Athens* would be closer in date to *Othello*. It is evidently closest of all to *King Lear*, the Shakespeare play with which it has the strongest affinities of plot, style, and philosophical disillusionment—so close, indeed, that it is impossible to be sure which was written first. In 1606 Shakespeare went on to write *Macbeth* and perhaps also *Antony and Cleopatra*. *Timon of Athens* belongs to the most magnificently productive phase of Shakespeare's tragic writing.

Middleton, born in 1580, was sixteen years younger than Shakespeare, and at a relatively early stage in his career as a dramatist. Of his extant plays, the short and trenchant *A Yorkshire Tragedy* would probably have come most immediately before. Here the authorial chronology is strikingly consistent with the influence upon *Timon of Athens* of the source for Middleton's immediately preceding play. The comedy *The Puritan Widow*, played by the Children of Paul's, and *The Revenger's Tragedy* are the plays most likely to have followed.[1] It is at about this time too that he wrote the lost tragedy for the Children of the Queen's Revels called *The Viper and Her Brood*. Middleton was a writer in transition, moving on from city comedy to tragedy, affiliated to no one theatre company, writing for boys' companies and the adult King's Men alike.

The Structure of a Theatre Work: Acts and Scenes

If the dramatists left the play in some ways incomplete, it is clear that they were nevertheless working to a clear overall plan for the play's structure, and that this structure was unconventional.

The play has a starkly formal, simple, and echoic division into two parts. The first part of the play is set entirely in the city. The second part revisits the city briefly, but Timon's own journey to the woods outside Athens is irreversible, and most of the action focuses on him. Each of these two main sections coalesces around a major sequence of action. Scs. 1–2 present Timon apparently at the height of his prosperity surrounded by various friends and seekers of favour. Sc. 14 is an ironized pageant of these same figures visiting Timon in his abjection.

But there are some complicating factors. The plot-line suddenly bifurcates in Sc. 10 with the banishment of Alcibiades. It is significant that this split of focus happens in the middle of the play just before Timon breaks with his friends and leaves Athens. The consecutive scenes of Alcibiades' banishment, the mock banquet with which Timon punishes his false friends, and Timon's departure are the central hinge of the entire play. By the end, Timon is dead, and the action switches over to the Alcibiades plot before the play comes to a close. This is, then, a carefully patterned sequence of dramatic action that might be summarized as falling in five phases:

(a) Timon in prosperity, centring on an ensemble scene of banqueting, masquing, and munificent gift-giving (Scs. 1–2);
(b) Timon in debt, represented most typically in short, fragmented, and satirical scenes showing separate creditors (Scs. 3–9);
(c) The turn from Athens, which entails the division of the play into two plots, with the senators acting as authority figures in

[1] This is the chronology in Middleton, *Collected Works*. The language and prosody are particularly close to *Revenger's*. For the latter, see p. 136.

relation to Alcibiades, but as humiliated self-servers in Timon's mock banquet (Scs. 10–13);

(d) Timon in the woods, an attenuated ensemble scene broken into separate encounters, with Timon static, the visitors coming to him and departing in turn (Sc. 14);

(e) Alcibiades and Athens, leading to an ensemble in which the dead Timon is remembered (Scs. 15–17).

There are suggestions here of a five-act structure, a framework that would have been familiar to Middleton from his work for the boys' theatre companies where act intervals were always observed. Yet, apart from the first, these five sections do not correspond with the act divisions that appear in most editions. The Folio was printed without act breaks. Nicholas Rowe in 1709 inserted breaks after the scenes identified in this edition as Sc. 2, Sc. 4, and Sc. 12; the final break came after 14.457, at the beginning of the episode of the Steward's visit to Timon. The first three of Rowe's breaks proved uncontentious and were accepted by subsequent editors. The last is more problematic. Edward Capell adjusted it by placing the beginning of Act 5 after 14.536, the entry of the Poet and Painter (see Fig. 2). Though editors have followed this arrangement with few modifications, it is entirely arbitrary.

This Edition	Capell	Variations
Sc. 1	1.1	
Sc. 2	1.2	
Sc. 3	2.1	
Sc. 4	2.2	
Sc. 5	3.1	
Sc. 6	3.2	
Sc. 7	3.3	
Sc. 8	3.4	
Sc. 9	3.4 continued	3.5
Sc. 10	3.5	3.6
Sc. 11	3.6	3.7
Sc. 12	4.1	
Sc. 13	4.2	
Sc. 14, ll. 1–536	4.3	
Sc. 14, ll. 537–650	5.1	
Sc. 14, ll. 651–763	5.2	5.1 continued
Sc. 15	5.3	5.2
Sc. 16	5.4	5.3
Sc. 17	5.5	5.4

Figure 2: Act and Scene Divisions in Other Editions

Act divisions confuse the play's structure because, unlike many of Middleton's plays, but like all of Shakespeare's plays written to this date, *Timon of Athens* was not designed to be performed with act breaks. *Timon of Athens* is particularly resistant to the editors' act divisions. The second half presents an unbroken stretch of action showing Timon's life in the woods from beginning to end. This is the passage of over seven hundred lines identified as Sc. 14 in this edition. It splits into cleanly separated episodes, but the over-all continuity of theatrical experience is remorselessly stretched, producing a rigorously self-contained sub-drama. The scene forms the core of the play, and could virtually be performed as a separate entity.[1] Act divisions impose a structure of action that is alien to the play and disrupt its startlingly inventive form. That is why, despite the convenience offered by a standard act-scene-line refer-encing system, the eighteenth-century act divisions have been rejected in this edition.[2]

Early Staging: Possibilities

In 1606 the King's Men's single playhouse was the Globe. A few critics have urged that the play's experimental qualities reflect a script written for a more socially elite venue. For Bradbrook, *Timon of Athens* was performed in spectacular fashion at the indoor Black-friars theatre. Yet there is no staging requirement that singles this play out as different from other Globe plays, the most likely date falls before the King's Men began to perform at the Blackfriars, and the absence of any provision for act breaks tells against indoor performance. The first and last objections also hold also for Honigmann's suggestion that this play and *Troilus and Cressida* were both written for one of the Inns of Court. The following dis-cussion will therefore assume that the play was written for the Globe. Attention will be addressed to performances such as the text anticipates, without implying any judgement as to whether that expectation was fulfilled.

---

[1] Episodes entitled 'Alcibiades and his Army', 'Some bandits', and 'The Senators of Athens' were performed as a sequence in George Wilson Knight's 'This Sceptred Isle' at Westminster Theatre in 1941.

[2] See scene headnotes in the commentary for traditional act–scene numbers. For discussion of continuity within this edition's Sc. 14, see commentary note to 14.536.1.

Though *Timon of Athens* perhaps requires further adjustment for the stage, the text as it stands is largely performable, and it conforms with the staging facilities of the public theatre. Despite the flamboyance of the masque in Sc. 2, there is no requirement for elaborate staging such as the descent from the 'heavens' in plays such as *Pericles* or *Women Beware Women*, even though such effects were well within the resources of the Globe Theatre.

The masque is, however, a spectacular drama within the play. The Folio stage directions, elsewhere usually restrained, are here detailed, even overloaded. The direction for the masquing ladies' entry demands that they appear '*with lutes in their hands, dancing and playing*' (2.126.1–2). When the ladies take partners with the guests they dance '*a lofty strain or two to the hautboys*' (2.140.3–4), confirmation that off-stage musicians contribute to the musical effect. Hautboys are unusually formal instruments for a dance, and they suggest an effect of exalted ceremony, perhaps to the extent of parody or satire.

The effect of the episode depends largely on costume, and one would guess that a Jacobean production would have been as lavish as possible in this respect. We know from Philip Henslowe's *Diary* that large sums of money were spent on gowns. Nevertheless, the resources of the commercially oriented public theatre would have fallen well short of the spending lavished on court masques, which were notorious for their extravagance. A good impression of how an Amazon might be dressed in these unstraitened circumstances can be gained from Inigo Jones's design for Penthesilea, queen of the Amazons, in Jonson's *Masque of Queens* (1609).[1] The overall effect is feminine, but Penthesilea wears a sword and an extravagantly plumed helmet. A transparent bodice leaves little to the imagination as to her gender. This last detail, of course, could scarcely be followed in the public theatre, where women's roles were played by boy actors. But the combination of the martial and the female would otherwise readily be imitated, and something approaching the effect of a masque costume might have been achieved with a more modest expenditure.

It is at least possible that the masque is absurdly excessive to the extent that it incorporates a show of the Five Senses as well as Amazons. The Cupid says, 'The five best senses acknowledge thee

---

[1] See Stephen Orgel and Roy Strong, *Inigo Jones*, 2 vols. (1973), I.140.

their patron' (2.119–20). Middleton's *Triumphs of Truth*, ll. 354–8, describes a tableau of the five senses with their 'proper emblems' of an eagle (sight), a hart (hearing), a spider (touching), an ape (tasting), and a dog (smelling). Such properties could be carried, or depicted on shields bearing emblematic motifs (as in the 1578 Masque of Amazons performed for Queen Elizabeth and the French ambassador). But there is a practical difficulty here. As the ladies carry '*lutes in their hands*' and also dance, portable properties would be almost impossible to manage. The senses might alternatively be indicated by motifs on their costumes. These could be either emblems as mentioned, or the organs of the senses, as with Queen Elizabeth's gown in the 'Rainbow' portrait attributed to Isaac Oliver, or Shakespeare's Rumour '*painted full of tongues*' in the Induction to *2 Henry IV*.

This assumes that the Cupid's line signifies that the ladies represent the five senses. However, the parallel with *Triumphs of Truth* may well be misleading. The Cupid is instead more likely to indicate that 'There' at the banquet the senses 'rise' from the table, whereas here and 'now' the Amazons more modestly 'come' to feast only one sense, the 'eyes'. This seems true to the text (except in that the music appeals to the hearing), it eases the potential overloading of effect in the masque, and it avoids what would be an unusually high requirement for six boy actors: the five senses plus Cupid.[1]

Despite the borrowing of style from the court theatre where money was no object, the scene's impression of high living would depend on an audience's imaginative response to the costumes. When Renaissance audiences saw wealthily dressed men seated at a table as in Sc. 2, they would have understood that the rear wall of the stage represents the wall of a banqueting room in a palace or great house, a place of ostentatious wealth that is set apart from the rest of the world by that wall. In Sc. 8 a door in the rear of the stage stands for a door in Timon's house: 'What, are my doors opposed against my passage?' demands the enraged Timon. As he leaves Athens, the wall at the rear of the stage represents, as by convention, the city wall, and a door in it the city gates. Perhaps the same door was used, in order to correlate Timon's house and Athens as equivalent enclosed spaces. Timon again draws attention to the physical structure of the theatre: 'Let me look back

---

[1] But see commentary to 2.122.1.

upon thee. O thou wall . . .' (12.1). At this liminal moment Athens is still in sight, and in the Shakespearian theatre the wall at the rear of the stage will inevitably be the wall at which Timon looks back. Now the wall encloses the city itself, and the on-stage vantage is from outside. The movement is from inside to outside, from bound-aried community to wilderness.[1] Timon's words make neutral ele-ments of the theatre structure resonate with significance at the key moment of transition. This dependence on words makes the equa-tion of stage wall and city wall contingent and temporary.

In Sc. 14 Timon calls on the 'blessèd breeding sun' (14.1), the earth, the gods, and the 'clear heavens' (14.28), and the 'Common mother' earth again (14.178). To translate this statement into theatrical terms appropriate to the Globe, the actor, alone on stage, gestures towards the structures of the theatre building: not now to the wall at the rear of the stage and the door in it through which he has entered, but to the 'wooden O' through which daylight pours into the amphitheatre, and to the platform of the stage on which he stands. The stage floor now represents part of an undefined and formless space, a space that lacks correspondence with physical architecture. Its signifying boundary is internal, the edge of the trap that represents the hole in the ground when Timon digs.

The grand vocatives of Timon's soliloquies in this passage shape out the physical structure of the building as though the audience heard on behalf of the building, and yet as though human beings were absent. It is significant, surely, that Timon invokes almost every element of the theatre building (and the sky above it) *except* the yard and galleries where the audience is placed. When Timon rhetorically savages the populace of Athens, the audience stands for that populace as citizens and as members of humanity, but only obliquely and not, typically, by way of direct address. Athens is supposedly elsewhere, behind the stage, beyond the galleries that surround the stage and the walls that hem in the theatre, as though the city walls had reversed their curvature to enclose the outside world.

The staging of the city wall is repeated when Alcibiades besieges the city in the final scene. The senators' position on the battlements is represented by the actors' appearance on the upper acting space

---

[1] For Timon's self-expulsion from the city, see Illustration 4, where Timon defies dark and classically monumental city walls.

or balcony above and behind the main stage. Their stage entry through the door after 17.65, which is a location exit from the city, enigmatically harks back to Timon's departure from Athens in Sc. 12. In the long scene between these crucial moments of entrance on stage and exit from Athens, Timon's gold is dug from a hole that would be represented by a raised trapdoor in the middle of the stage. Timon's cave, presumably at the rear of the stage, might have been a solid stage property or a gap to the rear of the stage between curtains. When the soldier in Sc. 16 finds Timon's tomb he perhaps draws back the same curtains to reveal the monument.

In the banquet scene and elsewhere, jewels may have glittered by the light of torches, and music would have lent further suggestions of courtly magnificence and the 'magic of bounty'. Except in the masque, the King's Men might have been more interested in suggesting a Renaissance style of richness by using costumes readily available to them than in imitating the garb of ancient Athens, though stage directions for '*Senators*' and the '*Old Athenian*' of 1.111.1 conceivably point to an element of historical costume. Throughout, simple properties signify potently and often emblematically: the painting and manuscript in the opening scenes; Apemantus' root and Timon's casket of jewels in Sc. 2; Flaminius' empty box in Sc. 5; the muffle over the Steward's face in Sc. 8; the covered dishes with steaming water and stones in Sc. 11; the rich clothing Timon strips off in Sc. 12; the spade, earth, gold, and roots in the woods; the epitaph, and the impression the soldier takes from it, at the end of the play.

As for the actors and their roles, the Folio text does not correlate the anonymous speaking lords, the similar senators, and the named 'friends' of Timon: Ventidius, Lucius, Lucullus, and Sempronius. However, it is clear from 9.8 that Lucius, Lucullus, and Sempronius are among the guests in Sc. 11, and clear also on account of inconsistencies in the stage directions and speech-prefixes of Sc. 11 that the lords and senators who attend Timon's feasts, receive his gifts, and refuse to lend him money, are overlapping groups or even exactly the same men. Whether the First Lord in one scene is the same figure as the First Senator in another, and, if so, whether he equates with one of the named friends, are questions of directorial choice in the theatre. Similar issues surround the numbered but unnamed servants of Timon and the named servants Flaminius and Servilius. The text in general terms encourages such equations to be made, yet leaves it difficult to determine a self-consistent system in any detail (see notes to 11.0.2 and 11.1).

The play as it stands requires a minimum of about thirteen adult men; this would impose some awkward doubling, and in an actual staging a few more men may have taken part. In addition, several boys are needed for the masque in Sc. 2 (see note to 2.119–23). Mute actors are required as lords and soldiers. There are a few opportunities for the doubling of speaking parts in a way that might be significant on stage. The Thieves in Sc. 14 conveniently and logically double with the lords Lucius, Lucullus, and Sempronius (or Ventidius). As has been apparent in some modern productions, the boy actors playing whores Phrynia and Timandra in the same scene would quite probably already have appeared as two of the ladies in the masque of Sc. 2. Of the King's Men's principal actors, the laconic comedian Robert Armin, who was probably the Fool in *Lear*, might have been most suitable to play Apemantus. Timon itself is a role that must surely have been written for Richard Burbage, the King's Men's most famous actor, who is believed to have been the original performer of all Shakespeare's major tragic roles.

Plutarch and Lucian

Timon was well known as the type of misanthropy long before the play was written.[1] Both Seneca and Montaigne mention him as such. Several English writers working before the play also refer to him, including Robert Greene. A cluster of brief references appearing in the years 1600–6 include John Weever's *Faunus and Melliflora* (1600), in which Timon is a miser rather than a spendthrift; John Marston's *Jack Drum's Entertainment* (1601), in which a Page offers, ironically, to 'be as sociable as Timon of Athens'; John Beaumont's *Metamorphosis of Tobacco* (1602), in which the 'odious beast' Timon 'would have turned jester at each solemn feast' had he known tobacco; William Warner's *Albion's England* (1602), in which intriguingly, Timon is compared with Robin Hood; the same author's *A Continuance of Albion's England* (1606), in which a 'land-stripped' gentleman 'grew thenceforth shy of women, and a Timon unto men'; and Craig Alexander's *Poetical Essays* (1604), in which

[1] For discussion of classical and early modern accounts of Timon beyond the immediate sources, see Bullough.

Timon is ruined by overspending and the addressed prince is urged to be the 'stone' to drive off parasites. Timon was therefore a figure of some literary currency when our play was written, perhaps partly in response to the source-play *Timon* discussed below.

The dramatists drew most immediately on two classical texts, Plutarch's *Lives of the Noble Grecians and Romans* and Lucian's *Dialogues*. They were evidently influenced also by two texts in English, William Painter's *The Palace of Pleasure*, which contains a passage on Timon translated from Plutarch, and the anonymous comedy *Timon* (see pp. 19–22), which is loosely based on Lucian. None of these offers a sustained source; the play's dramatic structure, language, and many of its plot details are original.

As noted above, Shakespeare was in a position to have been drawn to the story of Timon when he was writing *All's Well* (1604–5). The source for that play is the thirty-eighth 'novel' or novella in Painter's *Palace of Pleasure* (1566). The twenty-eighth 'novel' is entitled 'Of the strange and beastly nature of Timon of Athens, enemy to mankind, with his death, burial, and epitaph'. A fuller chapter heading goes on to identify the key features of the Timon myth: 'All the beasts of the world do apply themselves to other beasts of their kind, Timon of Athens only excepted, of whose strange nature Plutarch is astonied in the "Life of Marcus Antonius".' Perhaps Shakespeare's reading of this account returned him to the 'Life of Marcus Antonius' in Plutarch's *Lives*, as translated by Sir Thomas North and published in 1579.[1] Painter's account of Timon is an indirect and slightly elaborated translation of a passage in Plutarch's 'Life of Marcus Antonius'.[2] Shakespeare had used North's version in writing *Julius Caesar*. In this, the full text, Plutarch digresses from his main narrative when he tells how Mark Antony, after his defeat at Actium, withdrew to an island. There, according to North's marginal note, he 'followeth the life and example of Timon Misanthropos' (see Appendix B). In summarizing Timon's life, Plutarch claims to draw on accounts of Timon, now lost, in Plato and the comedies of Aristophanes. His brief narrative includes anecdotes that associate Timon with the

---

[1] This supposes that *Timon of Athens* was written before Shakespeare returned to the 'Life of Antonius' when working on *Antony and Cleopatra*. See the discussion of date on pp. 3–9.

[2] Painter's source is Pedro Mexía's *La silva de varia lección* (1540), trans. into French by Claude Griget (1552).

military commander Alcibiades and with Apemantus, who 'was much like of his nature and conditions, and also followed him in manner of life'. He relates that Timon taunted Athenians to hang themselves on his fig-tree, and that he was buried after his death by the seashore. Words from an epitaph written by Timon before his death and another by the poet Callimachus are quoted.

These particulars are mostly to be found in Painter's translation as well as North's. The dramatists, particularly Shakespeare, make much of the little detail both versions contain. The description of Timon's grave at 14.749–52 most closely recalls Painter's *Palace of Pleasure*: 'By his last will, he ordained himself to be interred upon the sea shore, that the waves and surges might beat and vex his dead carcass'. But the title Timon chooses for himself—'Misanthropos' (14.53)—comes from North. At least one of the dramatists was aware of the 'Life of Alcibiades' in North's Plutarch, and the names given to six minor roles are drawn from the 'Life of Marcus Antonius', and so are Latin instead of Greek: Lucius, Hortensius, Ventidius, Flavius, Lucilius, and Philotas.[1]

Despite its certain debt, the play owes surprisingly little to the 'Life of Alcibiades', which offers a much fuller account of the history surrounding the play's events and, potentially at least, a source for the plot-line showing Alcibiades' revolt against Athens. In Plutarch, Alcibiades is banished not for overstepping the mark in pleading for clemency on behalf of his soldier, but for mocking the holy mysteries of Ceres and Proserpina. Though he attacks Athenian forces, he does not aim to destroy the city of Athens itself. Marginal notes in North's Plutarch provide a slight cue for Alcibiades' appearance in the play with two prostitutes, one of whom is called Timandra. In North the reader finds a comment on '*Alcibiades' dishonesty* [i.e. sexual promiscuity] *and wantonness*', and a note that '*Timandra the courtesan buried Alcibiades*' after his death.[2] The dramatists—or perhaps only Shakespeare—may have done no more than merely skim the notes of this 'Life'; they may have read the text little if at all.[3]

---

[1] As noted by Honigmann. Ventidius is associated with both Shakespeare and Middleton, the others mainly with Middleton.

[2] The notes appear on sigs. T1^v (p. 218) and V3^v (p. 234).

[3] One possible exception is the last page, which mentions that 'Some hold opinion that Lais, the only famous courtesan, which they say was of Corinth ... was his [Alcibiades'] daughter'. This might inform the allusion to Corinth as a place of prostitution at 4.68 (and perhaps frequented by Alcibiades; see 4.80).

The other main classical source is the *Dialogues* of the Greek satirist Lucian of Samosata (AD 125–180). Desiderius Erasmus' Latin translation of 1528 was used as a school text. The *Dialogues* were also available in Italian and French translation. However, the reference to 'Plutus' at 1.279 recalls Plutus as in the Greek and Latin, who is differently named in the Italian or French, as 'Richezza' or 'Richesse'.[1] Erasmus' well-known translation is therefore the most likely source.

Lucian tells of Timon's spectacular fall from prosperity. However, the dialogue does not show Timon as he lived in Athens; he is placed only in the 'desert corner' where he digs for a living. This part of the story corresponds to the play's Sc. 14, and Lucian's satirical account of Timon's friends as they process one by one to visit him informs the scene's structure (see Appendix B). Some passages recollect Timon's earlier and more prosperous days. As Timon explains, 'To come to myself, that have set so many Athenians afloat, of miserable beggars have made them wealthy men, and succoured all that craved assistance at my hands, nay, rather poured out my riches by heaps to do my friends good; yet when by that means I grew poor and fell into decay I could never be acknowledged by them, nor they once so much as cast an eye towards me who before crouched and kneeled unto me, and wholly dependent on my beck.' Timon's gift to enable his servant Ventidius to marry recalls Timon in Lucian, who remembers that the parasite Philiades 'had from me a whole lordship, and two talents I gave his daughter to her marriage'. Any dramatists taking on the challenge of constructing a full play on Timon for the early modern stage might be grateful to seize on such details, and from them develop an account of the events that led to Timon's downfall. By such means Timon can be translated: no more simply a byword for an extreme condition, but a biographical figure who lives through time and goes through experiences that determine his later solitary life and death.

The comedy *Timon* probably offered the dramatists further help. As early as 1584 William Warner suggested that Timon was the subject of a play, writing 'let the Athenian misanthropos or manhater bite on the Stage'.[2] If Timon was biting on the stage in the

---

[1] Bullough, p. 239.

[2] 'To the Reader', in *Pan his Syrinx*, entered in the Stationers' Register on 22 September 1584.

1580s, this version is potentially a dramatic source for *Timon of Athens*. Evidently, however, the play in question is not the academic comedy known simply as *Timon* that is extant in manuscript, which was probably written at a later date. The relationship between the two extant plays is not readily discerned. *Timon of Athens* and the comedy *Timon* might hypothetically derive from a lost earlier version independently.[1] It is possible, alternatively, that the academic comedy was written after *Timon of Athens*, and was itself influenced by the Shakespeare–Middleton play.[2] But James C. Bulman has argued persuasively that the comedy is a source for *Timon of Athens*. Disputing earlier suggestions that, as an academic play, it would have been performed at Oxford or Cambridge, he posits that the comedy was written for an audience of law students at a London Inn of Court soon after 1601.[3] This view of the provenance finds some support in Bradbrook's observation that Gelasimus fancifully plans to fly through the zodiac on Pegasus, as Pegasus was the emblem of the Inner Temple. And Timon's resolution to return to 'the city' when he lays aside his misanthropic role in the Epilogue, though it refers most immediately to Athens, might metatheatrically invoke a London setting to its audience.

Shakespeare's *Twelfth Night* had been performed at the Middle Temple in 1602, and Middleton's father-in-law Edward Marbeck had strong connections with the London legal establishment; Middleton's *Masque of Heroes* would be written for the Inner Temple in 1619. Assuming that Bulman identifies the provenance and date correctly, either or both of the dramatists could have seen the comedy on stage in London not too long before they wrote their play, and perhaps within a relatively short time of Shakespeare's reading of Painter.[4] Like Painter's account, the English comedy *Timon* could have drawn attention to the story of Timon as presented in its own source text, and so prompted the dramatists to look to another Greek writer of the early Christian era, in this case Lucian.

---

[1] As argued by Staunton in his edition, and G. A. Bonnard, 'Note sur les sources de *Timon of Athens*', *Études Anglaises*, 7 (1954), 59–69.

[2] Bullough, pp. 234–5.

[3] 'The Date and Production of *Timon* Reconsidered', *Shakespeare Survey* 27 (1974), 111–27.

[4] If the comedy were, notwithstanding Bulman's case, slightly earlier in date and performed at Oxford, Middleton could have seen it there while a student at Queen's College in 1598–1601. But the Jonson echoes make this unlikely.

The comedy, like *Timon of Athens* itself, hinges on a scene in which Timon exposes his false friends by entertaining them with a mock banquet of food Timon throws at his guests in rage: painted imitation artichokes in the comedy, steaming water and probably stones in *Timon of Athens* (Sc. 11). The comedy turns around the structural emphasis of Lucian's dialogue, dealing in considerable length with Timon's life in Athens, and reserving Timon's life as a digger for shorter treatment in the later scenes. Now the story of how Timon came to be a misanthrope dwelling in the woods becomes the central dramatic focus. A foolish and generally comic figure, he loses his wealth not through prodigality but because his ships are wrecked. The play fleshes out the account by having Timon fall in love with a mercenary woman called Callimela ('I loved Timon rich, not Timon poor'), and introducing the figure of the faithful Steward, here called Laches. Laches realizes:

> So are my master's goods consumed. This way
> Will bring him to the house of poverty
>
> (ll. 1283–4)

—and resolves:

> Well, howsoever fortune play her part,
> Laches from Timon never shall depart.
>
> (ll. 1289–90)

So, like Kent in *King Lear*, he follows Timon to the wilds in disguise.[1] When Laches reveals himself Timon allows him to stay and dig alongside him, provided that he keeps at a distance. A change of heart is on the way, for Timon does not kill himself at the end of the play, but relents:

> A sudden change my fury doth abate.
> My heart grow mild and lays aside its hate.
>
> (Epilogue; ll. 2620–1)

This is a more conclusive ending than Lucian provides, and it confirms the play's genre as comedy.

To summarize, the episode in *Timon of Athens* set in the Athenian

---

[1] Irrespective of the order of composition of the two plays in the Shakespeare canon, the comedy could be one source for this strand in *King Lear*, though Kent is based mainly on Perillus in the source play *King Leir*, and the treatment of the Steward in *Timon of Athens* seems to be mostly by Middleton.

woods is a point of intersection between passages in the two classical sources: Lucian's account of the procession of hangers-on who visit Timon when he finds gold, and Plutarch's brief anecdotes about Timon's meetings with Alcibiades and Apemantus during his solitary life. It is likely that both dramatists had read a version of Lucian's dialogue. Lucian not only underlies the plotting, but also suggests the tone of sardonic comedy that informs, in particular, Middleton's contribution to the play, and is a possible influence on the animal imagery that is so persistent in *Timon of Athens*. Shakespeare, exclusively, develops the material found in the 'Life of Marcus Antonius'. The lack of debt to the 'Life of Alcibiades' may reflect, in part at least, Middleton's unfamiliarity with Plutarch. The academic comedy *Timon*, perhaps recalled from performance, provided little in the way of specific language or moment-by-moment dramatic content. Evidently Timon's fall from prosperity in some respects echoes the comedy, which supplied the figure of the loyal steward and the device of the mock banquet.

None of these sources establishes the intense pessimism of Timon's view of life after he leaves Athens as it is shown in the Shakespeare–Middleton play. But the authors may have been aware of other texts describing Timon. For instance, Pierre Boaistuau's description of Timon in *Theatrum mundi* may have suggested how the legend of Timon can be placed within the serious and pessimistic Christian traditions of *contemptus mundi, vanitas*, and the decay of the world.[1] As Ralph Soellner comments, 'The pride and deceit of merchants, the amassing of gold and silver, the spread of luxury, the eruptions of war, the increase of murder, treason, fraud, covetousness, usury, and theft—all indicated to him [Boaistuau] that the apocalyptic predictions of the ancient philosophers were being fulfilled' (p. 213).

Ultimately the play belongs to a far larger and more complex textual field. The play interacts with texts such as Ovid's *Metamorphoses*, Cicero's *De amicitia*, Edmund Spenser's *Faerie Queene*, John Lyly's *Campaspe*, Thomas Nashe's *Christ's Tears Over Jerusalem*, and

---

[1] Trans. John Alday (1566?; repr. 1581). Soellner (p. 213) and Bullough (pp. 295–7) reprint short passages. Soellner also discusses Richard Barckley's *A Discourse of the Felicity of Man* (1598; repr. 1603) and Heinrich Cornelius Agrippa's *De vanitate artium et scientiarum* (1530; trans. James Sanford as *Of the Vanity of Arts and Sciences*, 1569), which are important texts in the *contemptus mundi* tradition, but which do not discuss Timon. For Agrippa, see commentary to 2.128–30.

Stephen Gosson's *Ephemerides of Philao*. More generally, the play's textual field encompasses the whole Renaissance myth of Timon;[1] the literary and theatrical tradition of Diogenes and the cynic; the tropes of city comedy, of Shakespearian tragedy, and of court masque; Renaissance discussions of art, of ancient Greece,[2] of friendship and homosociality,[3] of misogyny, of misanthropy, of patronage, of the city,[4] of money and credit, of disease; and much more besides.

Satire and Tragedy

Timon of Athens is a play that spans various dramatic genres. Somewhere in the background lie morality plays. In *Everyman*, for example, Everyman is summoned by Death, is abandoned by his friends, learns that his treasure is 'thy damnation' (compare 5.44, 5.49, 14.42, and 14.164), and faces death accompanied only by Good Deeds.[5] The divestment of worldly goods, the abandonment by friends, the moralization of wealth, and the lonely last journey to death all recur in *Timon of Athens*. Robert Wilcher sees a schematic genre division between the first half as morality play and the second half as satire.[6] Yet moral tableaux and satire are to be found throughout the play. If anything, it is the element of tragedy that emerges as the play moves forward, though not to the exclusion of all else. What is most immediately evident in the play's most extensive source material is the satirical dimension. What is most conspicuous from the play's placement in the Shakespeare Folio is

[1] Willard Farnham, *Shakespeare's Tragic Frontier* (Berkeley and London, 1950), pp. 64–7; Harry Levin, 'Shakespeare's Misanthrope', *Shakespeare Survey* 26 (1973), 89–94.

[2] T. J. B. Spencer, *Fair Greece, Sad Relic: Literary Philhellenism from Shakespeare to Byron* (1954); Spencer, '"Greeks" and "Merrygreeks"', in Richard Hosley, ed., *Essays on Shakespeare and Elizabethan Drama in Honor of Hardin Craig* (1962), pp. 223–33; and Robert S. Miola, 'Timon in Shakespeare's Athens', *Shakespeare Quarterly*, 31 (1980), 21–30.

[3] See the discussion of Cicero's *De amicitia* on p. 69 and of Alcibiades on pp. 70–1.

[4] See Gail Kern Paster, *The Idea of the City in the Age of Shakespeare* (Athens, Georgia, 1979).

[5] Eric Rasmussen, 'Shakespeare's Use of *Everyman* in *Timon of Athens*', *American Notes and Queries*, 23 (1985), 131–4.

[6] '*Timon of Athens*: A Shakespearian Experiment', *Cahiers Élisabéthains*, 34 (1988), 61–78.

its claim to be a tragedy. It is on these genres that the following account focuses.

The word 'Lucianic' refers to a scoffing satire, and Apemantus as a Diogenes figure (see pp. 76–7) recalls a related mode of classical satire. Early uses of the word *Timonist* meant simply 'man-hater', but by the late 1630s, in the wake of two editions of the Shakespeare Folio, it had clearly come to signify a particularly bitter species of satirist:

> In this fantastic and ridiculous habit Time gives me leave to play the fool and make a fool both of the time and myself too. And fooling in this censorious age is a fashion that some of your wits will vouchsafe to walk in. Your Timonist, or, as we call 'em, Time-ist, is your only man, for he is allowed, or at least takes allowance, to rail at authority, gird at government, and, under pretence of striking at petty abuses in others, begets and generates greater in himself.[1]

These lines accurately identify the Timonist with theatrical playing, and specifically with the role of the fool, recognizing that he assumes the fool's licence to rail and 'gird at government', and that by doing so he inflicts damage on himself.

Timon of Athens is grounded in satire and yet is not straightforwardly satirical. Much the same can be said of its relation to tragedy. The inclusion of *Timon of Athens* with the Tragedies in the First Folio, though helpful in some ways, is also misleading on account of both the problems in the Folio's three-way division of Shakespeare's plays into comedies, histories and tragedies, and the circumstances in which this particular play found itself classified as a tragedy.

If the Folio editors had included a section of, for instance, 'Tragicomedies' they might have produced a generically more coherent volume. John Fletcher, writing an epistle 'To the Reader' in *The Faithful Shepherdess* (published *c*.1609), described tragicomedy as a form that brought some characters close to death without any of them actually dying. *Timon of Athens* breaks with Fletcher's understanding of the term because in this play Timon indeed dies. But the intermixing of serious themes with satire and comedy gives the play a tragicomic complexion; moreover the Timon of the academic play had relented at the end, and *Timon of Athens* may play with

---

[1] *The Wasp*, ed. J. W. Lever, Malone Society Reprints (1976), ll. 1074–82.

the expectation that this Timon will do likewise, in accordance with the pattern of tragicomedy. The play would have found a good place in a differently structured Folio alongside *Measure for Measure* and *Winter's Tale* as well as *Troilus and Cressida* and *Cymbeline*.

In the absence of a fourth category of this kind, there was no better place for it than in the tragedies, for it is certainly not a comedy or an English history play. However, *Troilus and Cressida* was originally planned to appear where *Timon of Athens* is printed, and so the position of the play in the volume reflects a perception of an entirely different play. It says little about *Timon* itself beyond that the Folio editors considered that it would not look conspicuously inappropriate in the Tragedies section.

The Folio title is enigmatic: not *The Tragedy of Timon of Athens*, on the model of every other play in the Folio tragedies, nor even *The Life and Death of Timon of Athens*, on the model of history plays such as *King John* and *Richard III*, but simply *The Life of Timon of Athens*. The 'Life and Death' formula may have been avoided because Timon's death is not presented on stage, which is in itself a sign that *Timon of Athens* is an unusual member of its group.

Yet it is only an extreme example of the hybridization of genre that typifies the whole of early modern drama and is particularly conspicuous in the field of tragedy in the very years when the play was written. Ranged alongside other plays such as Shakespeare's *Troilus and Cressida*, Jonson's *Sejanus*, and Middleton's *Revenger's Tragedy*, *Timon of Athens* can be seen as part of a collective attempt in the early years of the seventeenth century to experiment with tragedy by infusing it with an ethos of anti-heroism and deep scepticism.[1] Satire and comedy are part of that ethos.[2]

Generic intermixture is found throughout *Timon of Athens*, but varies in complexion from scene to scene, partly in accordance with the pattern of authorship, partly in accordance with a linear development as the play progresses. Despite the foreshadowings of disaster, the early scenes are largely compatible with the world of city comedy. So too, for all its heartless self-interest, is the treatment meted out to Timon when he seeks aid from his friends. As a new species of comedy, usually based in London, city comedy

---

[1] In the background lies the example of Marlowe in plays such as *The Jew of Malta*.

[2] Oscar James Campbell, *Shakespeare's Satire* (1943); Alvin Kernan, *The Cankered Muse* (New Haven, 1959).

satirized the social mores of city artisans, merchants, and gentry. It was the pre-eminent speciality of Jonson and Middleton. In plays such as *A Trick to Catch the Old One*, Middleton shows the callousness of life driven by the desire for sex and money, and the strange deformation of humanity that can be produced.

In the opening scenes of *Timon of Athens* Timon appears as the symptomatic centrepoint of the society to which he belongs. He is the patron of sycophants, the host to parasites. Without Timon, his false friends would have nowhere to go, no one with whom to be what they are. He generates the world in which he and they live. An intermittent chorus of criticism surrounds him. It flows from the Poet and Painter, and then, more reliably, Apemantus, and then, more reliably still, Timon's Steward. In the early scenes it is they rather than Timon who enjoy a rapport with the play's audience. The dramatic device of Apemantus' commentary on the masque as the masquers dance in Sc. 2 typifies a play that is fiercely analytic in its social satire.

As the play moves forward, social analysis yields to subjectivity of experience. Timon, who remains reticent in the early scenes, becomes angrily eloquent in response to his self-inflicted misfortune. Shakespeare fully meets one expectation of tragedy by writing language that resounds with what the Renaissance rhetorician Thomas Wilson calls the 'grand style', the style associated with princes, high passion, and tragedy.[1] Its devices are 'great words' (exotic, Latinate, neologistic diction), 'vehement figures' (including grammatical features such as the use of high-pitched vocatives), 'metaphors', 'stirring sentences' (meaning 'extravagant propositions'), and 'amplification' (through synonym, descriptive phrase, and adjective). In her study of the grand style, Sylvia Adamson gives an example from *King Lear*:

> You sulphurous and thought-executing fires,
> Vaunt-couriers to oak-cleaving thunderbolts,
> Singe my white head; and thou all-shaking thunder,
> Smite flat the thick rotundity of the world,
> Crack nature's mould, all germens spill at once
> That make ingrateful man.

(9.4–9)

[1] Sylvia Adamson, 'The Grand Style', in *Reading Shakespeare's Dramatic Language*, ed. Sylvia Adamson, Lynette Hunter, Lynne Magnusson, Ann Thompson, and Katie Wales (2001), 31–50; p. 32.

Lear's experience of ingratitude, his flight to the desolate country-side, and his self-exposure to the elements can all be compared with Timon. Indeed the equivalent moment of self-expulsion from society is rhetorically similar:

> Let me look back upon thee. O thou wall
> That girdles in those wolves, dive in the earth,
> And fence not Athens! Matrons, turn incontinent!
> Obedience fail in children! Slaves and fools,
> Pluck the grave wrinkled senate from the bench
> And minister in their steads! To general filths
> Convert o'th' instant, green virginity!

(12.1–7)

Both these speeches respond to personal suffering by furiously demanding the destruction of humankind. Both speeches use extravagant apostrophe along with all the devices of the grand style. But the use is ironic, in that they express the loss rather than possession of authority. Both require the human voice to become an instrument that is outrageously expressive. The audience might respond with both pity and astonishment. The anguish is unquestionable, and both figures are caught in an overwhelmingly powerful process of transition that will lead eventually to the grave.

In the case of Lear, the apostrophes are reworkings of his earlier regal imperatives. In the case of Timon they are equivalent to his performative utterances of gift-giving, in that they assume what is now a fictitious power, and in that they will a change in estate to the people to whom he refers.[1] Samuel Taylor Coleridge gave some impression as to how *Timon of Athens* is and is not *Lear*, describing it as 'a *Lear* of the satirical drama, a *Lear* of domestic or ordinary life'.[2] His comment is borne out in these key passages where the plays run in closest parallel. The passions and the linguistic and rhetorical devices through which they are communicated are similar, but the addressees and hence the register of the passages are crucially different. Lear addresses the elements, seeing them as

[1] See Karen Newman, 'Cultural Capital's Gold Standard: Shakespeare and the Critical Apostrophe in Renaissance Studies', in *Discontinuities*, ed. Viviana Comensoli and Paul Steverns (Toronto, 1998), 96–113. Newman notes that Timon's gift-giving tends to be performative in that it is executed through promissory words, 'I'll pay', 'I will send his ransom' etc., rather than physical transfer of the gift, though the jewels at the end of Sc. 2 are an exception.

[2] *Coleridge's Criticism of Shakespeare: A Selection*, ed. R. A. Foakes (1989), p. 170.

manifestations of the gods; Timon addresses the visible wall and the unseen people of the city, humanity 'high and low' (l. 40).

The access to the grand style and the passions of tragedy does not mean that satire evaporates at this point in the play. Rather, instead of permeating the play through other characters' commentaries on Timon, it is now expressed primarily in the worldview of Timon himself as a critique of the society he has left. And the satire darkens from social comedy to an unremittingly negative view of human nature. The process of the play is to extract Timon from his community and constitute him as a peculiar variant of a Shakespearian tragic figure. The satirical content of Timon's outbursts stands uneasily between social critique and symptom of the speaker's obsessively anguished mind.

Now Shakespeare invokes an imaginable but absent world of beneficent and respected authority presided over by a metaphysical order. It is against this idea of order that Timon pitches his destructive call 'And yet confusion live'. Similar negations of the metaphysical are to be found in *Troilus and Cressida*, *King Lear*, and elsewhere in Shakespeare's works.[1] Timon's journey from the civic and political world to the wilderness is also shared with Lear. Lear's tragedy will eventually involve the loss of a loved one, his daughter Cordelia. This return to human fellowship, to love and loss, is something that Timon rigorously denies himself. Timon will never return—unlike the forest-goers in Shakespeare's romantic comedies, and in some ways even unlike Lear. Timon continues to talk obsessively about Athens, but his speech is always an act of aggressive repulsion, pushing Athens away, stripping its tenacious filth off him, and flinging it back so as to keep his distance.

He is perhaps a scapegoat for the shortcomings of Athens who, in Gail Kern Paster's words, 'remains the most expressive symbol of his city'.[2] He is also a man who forcibly confronts areas of knowledge that his society represses, a mind on the edge of madness, a voice of wild vision and extreme emotion, a figure with no destiny other than death. His speeches are of insecure register. They swerve between incoherent rage, pungent satire, high passion, lyrical ecstasy, and the pathos of exhaustion.

[1] The positive image that Timon negates is essentially the order described in E. M. W. Tillyard's *The Elizabethan World Picture* (1943).

[2] *Idea of the City*, p. 102.

Much of this is, again, true of Lear too. In other respects Timon stands apart from the Shakespearian tragic hero. Above all, his death is off-stage and obscure. It is not associated with any task, any grand act, victory or defeat. Confuting suggestions in the play's imagery that Timon is a Christlike figure, his death does not produce any clear signs that the world he lived in is symbolically renewed, or that there will be socio-political change.[1] All this is symptomatic of a play that scales the heights of tragedy only to reveal them as strange, bleak, and without the comfort of catharsis.

Misanthropy

From an early modern point of view, misanthropy was a beast-like state. The received view as expressed by Aristotle was that the solitary man is not properly a human at all. Shakespeare may have known a translation of Aristotle's *Politics* published in 1598, where the famous passage defining the civic nature of human existence read: 'he that cannot abide to live in company, or through sufficiency hath need of nothing, is not esteemed a part or member of a city, but is either a beast or a god'.[2] Francis Bacon was to paraphrase Aristotle neatly by saying 'Whosoever is delighted in solitude is either a wild beast or a god', a suitable epigram for *Timon of Athens*.[3] In the Aristotelian tradition social organization was an essential aspect of human behaviour, so the antisocial man was an anomaly and a contradiction.

The depiction of Timon as bestial, as current before *Timon of Athens* was written, draws on this tradition. Sir John Beaumont in 1602 called Timon 'that odious beast'.[4] Painter had gone even further: aware that even animals have social organization, he opened his account of Timon with the words 'All the beasts of the world do

---

[1] Any change is intiated at the end of the play by Alcibiades, before news of Timon's death arrives. For the dubious validity of the promised reform of Athens, see commentary notes to 17.21–9, 31, 34–5, and 85.

[2] *Politics*, trans. from French [by J.D.?], with commentary (1598), 1.2. Shakespeare's possible familiarity with the translation is discussed in F. N. Lees, '*Coriolanus*, Aristotle, and Bacon', *Review of English Studies*, NS 1 (1950), 114–25.

[3] 'Of Friendship', in *Essays*, ed. John Pitcher (1985), p. 138. The essay is not in the first edition of 1597. The manuscript version of 1607–10 includes a variant of the essay that lacks the quotation from Aristotle.

[4] *Metamorphosis of Tobacco*, E1ᵛ.

apply themselves to other beasts of their kind, Timon of Athens only excepted', adding 'he was a man but by shape only; in qualities he was the capital enemy of mankind, which he confessed frankly utterly to abhor and hate'. Robert Burton later observed that those who indulge in destructive solitude 'do frequently degenerate from men, and of sociable creatures become beasts, monsters, inhuman, ugly to behold, *misanthropi*; they do even loathe themselves, and hate the company of men, as so many Timons, Nebuchadnezzars, by too much indulging to these pleasing humours, and through their own default'.[1] In all these accounts, Timon puts himself beyond common humanity. The repeated references to beasts in Sc. 14 draw on and contribute to this tradition.

To name that extreme bestial is to see only one part of the picture. The Aristotelian solitary man might also be a god, or at least, in the words of the anonymous English commentator in the 1598 version of Aristotle's *Politics*, someone of 'a certain heroical and divine virtue'.[2] It is part of the play's distinctive reworking of the Timon myth to find in him suggestions of a kind of mania that relates to religious experience as well as a bestial savagery.

Yet if Timon touches on the bestial and the divine, he is presented as human too, and therefore he unboundaries our sense of what it might mean to be human.

Giving and Sacrifice

The 1969 production of *Timon of Athens* at the Balustrade Theatre in Prague, directed by Jaroslav Gillar, was staged at the time of the 'invited' occupation of Czechoslovakia by the Soviet military. Contemporary Absurdist theatre works had been banned, and the production was a suppressed cry of political protest in its own right. One account captures vividly the anguish provoked by but coming from beyond political and military oppression: 'In the second half, Timon came forward with a roar, his back to the audience. The gate fell, cutting him off from the city forever. After delivering his curse, he turned around; his hair and beard were now white, and he had a fierce, insane stare. He appeared as a saint in the desert, a

---

[1] *Anatomy of Melancholy*, ed. Thomas C. Faulkner, Nicolas K. Kiessling, and Rhonda L. Blair, intro. by J. B. Bamborough, 6 vols. (Oxford, 1989–2000), 1.2.2.6 (i. 245).

[2] *Politics* (1598), sig. D6, citing Aristotle, *Ethics*, 7.1.

mystic sufferer of all human misfortunes. Jan Přeučil gave an astonishing performance, twisting his body into painful contortions and straining his voice harshly in gasps, sobs, and screams.'[1]

Přeučil called to mind the self-sacrifice of Jan Palach, who on 16 January 1969 doused himself in petrol and set himself alight in Prague's Wenceslas Square. He was the best-known example of a wave of public suicides and attempted suicides in protest against the occupation. To compare Timon with Palach is bound to raise questions as to Timon's relatively weak justification in extruding himself from human society in an act that has limited political significance; but it also points to a recognition that in both cases the grand gesture of self-isolation and agonized, angry self-destruction has a quasi-religious foundation. In Timon's case, the agony that he undergoes in the woods relates directly to the hints in the banquet scene that he enacts a Christlike Last Supper in which he offers himself as a sacrificial body on which his gathered friends feed.[2]

The Timon who is an unlikely sacrificial subject and the Timon who is gift-giver are intimately connected, as is suggested in a short poem by Ted Hughes. It begins:

> As Mary bore
> The Son so mourned
> Tortured, murdered
> And returned
>
> Timon gives all.[3]

Timon of Athens is a key early modern literary text relating to the area of cultural study known as gift theory, which takes its beginnings in Marcel Mauss's important work of 1950, *The Gift*.[4] The importance of the gift is that goods are transferred without financial transaction or any other material or economic exchange; it therefore offers a challenge to the economic determinism of Marxism. The benefit to the donor cannot be described in purely economic terms; human agency is critical. Mauss explains the

---

[1] Leiter, p. 727.

[2] See Jarold W. Ramsey, 'Timon's Imitation of Christ', *Shakespeare Studies*, 2 (1966), 162–73.

[3] '12. Knave of Diamonds', in the sequence 'A Full House', in *An Anthology of Poetry for Shakespeare*, ed. Charles Osborne (1988), p. 19.

[4] 'Essai sur le don', in *Sociologie et anthropologie* (Paris, 1950); trans. as *The Gift* by E. Cunnison (1954).

phenomenon in terms of anthropology. He studied tribal societies in the American North-west in which the gift-giving of the 'pot-latch' was an aggressively competitive orgy of excessive generosity in which recipients were placed under an obligation eventually to reciprocate. Critics of *Timon of Athens* have repeatedly referred to the potlatch. Though Timon does not bid to increase his status and conspicuously lacks any rivals against whom to compete, his display of luxury nevertheless relates to potlatching. Gift-giving places an individual within a social structure and implies the need for reciprocity, and this is where Mauss's relevance to *Timon of Athens* lies.

Mauss influenced Georges Bataille, whose darkly obsessive cultural theories are perhaps even more pertinent to *Timon of Athens*, though they have not been cited as such. In *The Accursed Share*, Bataille placed economic exchange within a larger framework that included the flow of energy in nature itself from its source in 'the remote depths of the sky, in the sun's consumption'.[1] This concept relates significantly to Timon's speech describing theft as the universal principle exemplified in the sun and moon. For Bataille, the realm of the economic reaches as far as the production of surplus but no further; the use to which a society puts that surplus is without economic determination and itself determines the character of that society. The function of wealth is to enable gift-giving. The gift-giver expresses a need to lose or destroy the surplus, and yet by this means to gain in prestige and sense of virtue. In words that might well be describing Timon, he says, 'He enriches himself with a contempt for riches'.[2] Pre-capitalist societies found a place for the gift-giver that has been lost in modern societies driven by the utilitarian urge. The position of *Timon of Athens* as an early modern text allows it to anticipate the modern in its description of a society driven by monetary laws, whilst Timon himself conforms to the munificence of the gift-giver of a pre-capitalist society in which patronage plays a central role.

For Bataille, the gift is related to sacrifice and therefore to the realm of the spiritual. This too sets it apart from economistic society. One might say, then, that Timon seeks to attain the position of the sacred subject through his sacrificial acts of gift-giving, only to

---

[1] *The Accursed Share*, Vol. 1, *Consumption* (1967, trans. 1988), quoted from *The Bataille Reader*, ed. Fred Botting and Scott Wilson (Oxford, 1997), p. 193.

[2] Bataille, p. 203.

find that the world he inhabits is economistic rather than spiritual in its foundations. His rage in the woods is then a negative version of the sacred subject, one founded on hostility to any communion with fellow humanity.

Bataille's view of the human subject is strongly influenced by the anti-determinist Nietzschean subject. Nietzsche and Mauss both also influenced George Wilson Knight's views of Timon—which indeed might assume a new dimension if related to Bataille's correlation of gift-giving and sacredness through the notion of sacrifice, and his emphasis on the imminent moment of the present as against the abnegating telos of life endured for the benefit of tomorrow. Knight grounded his unequalled admiration for *Timon of Athens* on a religious reading combined with Nietzschean romanticism. This he developed over a number of years both in his writings and as a performer. The interest was sustained over many years but was most concentrated in 1940, the year of his Toronto production and two essays on the play.[1]

Knight observes that the play is unusual in pre-modern drama for insisting that economics lies at the root of evil. However, it does not condemn any economic system, but rather the behaviour of individuals; by implication, then, the critique is Christian rather than Marxist. These propositions are both contestible: plays such as Jonson's *Volpone* and Middleton's *Chaste Maid* give strong expression to the corroding effect of money on humanity; and, though the idea of an economic system is anachronistic, *Timon of Athens* does show a society organized in such a way that economistic behaviour is unavoidable. But Knight finds his focus elsewhere, in Timon's 'resplendent personality'. His generosity is supremely benevolent, and the disillusioned Timon is 'embittered by his own degraded social consciousness'. The paradox at the heart of Knight's criticism is to be found in his suggestion that 'within each curse lies a supreme positive, each accent is barbed by truth and winged by a fierce love'.[2] This claim, at first sight implausible, can be interpreted to mean that Timon is not disillusioned simply in the sense of lacking belief in human worth, as might be said of Apemantus. Instead, he is enraged at the discrepancy between his benevolence and the world in which it takes effect. Hence he

---

[1] 'Shakespeare on the Gold Standard' and 'Isaiah in Renaissance Dress', reprinted in Knight's *Shakespearian Dimensions* (Brighton, 1984), pp. 66–71.

[2] *Dimensions*, p. 69.

condemns the world for failing to meet up with his idealizing love. If one compares the equally problematic proposition that jealousy is testimony of love, one can see the compelling strength of Knight's position, and also, as evidenced in *Othello*, its limitation.

In Knight's view of Shakespearian tragedy, *Timon of Athens* provided a more elemental and extensive example of the tragic than any other Shakespeare play. It is 'vast and Aeschylean'; 'The emotional meanings rise in rough-hewn slabs and blocks'.[1] He admired how those emotional meanings are located entirely within the experience of the tragic hero: there are 'no external Dionysian effects, no external magic or tempests'.[2] Instead, the play is organized so as to give massive expression of the heights of tragic passion, containing them firmly within the person of Timon. Other Shakespeare figures visit this area of experience only more briefly, and the external apparatus of 'Dionysian effects', 'magic or tempests' diffuses the focus on the individual. *Timon of Athens* bypasses the physical and social world, reaching towards 'the eternal and ever-present interaction in which are both God and man'.[3]

Because of this emphasis on the play's concentration on the immediate experience of Timon, Knight held strong views on the physical, bodily performance of the role. These arise from his wider endorsement of Edward Gordon Craig's view of the actor as 'übermarionette' or 'semi-divine "symbol of man"',[4] but more particularly from his understanding of Timon as the fullest physical embodiment of the tragic impulse. This Timon is a prophetic figure recalling Isaiah, looking at humanity, as it were, from the perspective of an angry god. For all its waywardness, Knight's criticism at best offers a valuable insight as to why the spectacle of rage and hate is theatrically powerful in a way that reaches beyond sheer negation. His perception that Timon embodies something like religious areas of experience has been developed by other critics, and has been intimated in stage performance too.

Though not effectual as a figure of redemption, Timon is Christ-like in a number of specific respects. His banquet in Sc. 2, in which he virtually offers himself to be consumed, has distinct echoes of the Last Supper, as does the second banquet, in which

[1] *Dimensions*, p. 71.   [2] *Shakespeare's Dramatic Challenge* (1977), p. 114.
[3] *The Wheel of Fire* (1930, rev. edn. 1949), p. 239.
[4] Knight, *Shakespearian Production* (1964), p. 223, quoting Craig, *On the Art of the Theatre* (1924).

the bread and wine of the sacrament have been, as it were, anti-miracled into stones and water. In Sc. 2 he speaks a language of communitarian love, he places his actions within a framework of significance that is beyond the comprehension of his friends, and his aspirations to end social ills through acts of loving generosity are little short of Messianic. Even though it is not knowingly self-destructive, his giving is an act of self-sacrifice in both spirit and effect. His later rage is a simple inversion of the charity that he over-indulged in the first part of the play. On the stage, the point can be emphasized by having Timon in Sc. 11 overturn the tables and chairs, like Christ's attack on the moneylenders and tradesmen in the Temple in Mark 11: 15–17.[1]

Developing the idea of sacrifice as an extreme action that transcends the ordinary exchanges of social life, Ken Jackson advances a sophisticated reading informed by Jacques Derrida's writings on gift theory.[2] For Derrida, drawing again on Mauss, the absolute gift is the epitome of the impossible, for real gift-giving always involves some form of exchange, even if the benefit to the donor is purely psychological. The pure gift without reciprocity belongs to the *tout autre* or 'utterly other', a realm alien to human activity that Derrida associates with the religious impulse. Derrida cites Matthew 6: 3–4, 'But when thou doest thine alms, let not thy left hand know what thy right hand doeth, that thine alms may be in secret; and thy father, that seeth in secret, he will reward thee openly'. This text prompts Derrida to explore the contradiction in Christianity between the religious desire to sacrifice, to give to God unconditionally, and the repressed banal expectation that God will reward the giver.[3] He also emphasizes the loneliness of the sacrificer, exemplified in Abraham, who detaches himself from humanity and human values in his willingness to submit to God. Derrida claims that 'a duty of hate is implied' (Jackson, p. 46).

This observation leads Jackson directly to Timon, whose 'misanthropy is implied in his giving . . . his attempts at "truly" giving or moving outside the economy of exchange in the first part of the

[1] As in the BBC production: see pp. 118–20.

[2] Jackson draws on Jacques Derrida, *Given Time: 1. Counterfeit Money*, trans. Peggy Kamuf (Chicago and London, 1992), and *The Gift of Death*, trans. David Willis (Chicago and London, 1995).

[3] Jackson notes that Reformation Protestantism confronted the self-interest of charity by urging of that, in Calvin's words, 'we may not trust or glory in them [good works], or ascribe salvation to them' (n. 86).

play are passionately, profoundly religious' (p. 47). When Timon declares 'there's none | Can truly say he gives if he receives' (2.10–11), Jackson sees him as attempting to assume the altruistic position that is actually impossible. Apemantus provocatively invokes the comparison with Christ in commenting 'It grieves me to see so many dip their meat in one man's blood', but the effect is to demystify: 'Timon is not Christ; men cannot give absolutely'.[1] Timon comes to understand the impossibility of the gift, and, lacking the option of being Christ, he responds by satirizing the world as governed by the universal pursuit of wealth. Timon's own view here takes us away from gift theory to Marx, and, further back towards the early modern period, Thomas Hobbes's view that human life is competitive, nasty, brutish, and short.

Male and Female

The configuration of the subject as an Abraham or a Christ is distinctively male. Defying this and other aspects of the play's male orientation, Timon has more than once been performed by a female actor as a woman, thus artificially creating a new sense in which Timon is marked out as the exception from the rest of Athens. For Kate Fenwick, who played Timon with the Red Shift theatre company in 1989, Timon was generous because submission, giving, and smiling, were her learnt forms of behaviour, and she followed them to the point of damage to herself.[2] Her withdrawal from society expressed not only hatred of society but also loathing of the self that society had constructed around her. This interpretation is arbitrary in that it rewrites a fundamental aspect of the dramatic role. However, it accords with the criticism that has recognized an element of femininity in Timon. In *Timon of Athens* as a play, female roles are notably absent, but the idea of the female in this all-male world has a disturbing and strong presence.

Timon of Athens shows a social regime in which women are aggressively excluded, or, at best, marginalized. Neither of the authors wrote another stage-play in which so few lines are spoken by female roles. This owes something, no doubt, to the early mod-

[1] Jackson, p. 50. Jackson's account of how the play eventually resolves this philosophical crux is considered below (pp. 81–2). On Timon as parodic Christ, see also Ramsey.

[2] Georgina Brown, 'Not so simple Timon', *Independent*, 8 Feb. 1989, quoted in Walton, pp. 193–5.

ern idea of Greece. Women, after all, figure little in Plutarch, and are absent from the Lucianic tradition of Timon. The Platonic symposium that underlies the play's banquet scene was a male affair. In Athens, members of the Areopagus—the play's senators—were all men. But so too were their equivalents in England, the Members of Parliament and City aldermen. Moneylenders were also almost exclusively male. And some of Middleton's city comedies, such as *Michaelmas Term*, depict a strongly homosocial world with little place for women. The exclusion of women in *Timon of Athens* grows out of the academic and literary traditions on which the play draws, and the areas of social life it depicts. What is significant, however, is the way the play deals with the very idea of exclusion and makes it an active part of the play's theatrical and poetic fabric.

Not surprisingly, there is an implicit misogyny to the all-male Athens. One way of describing *Timon of Athens* would be to say that it shows misogyny as a precondition for the wider hatred of humankind that Timon will embrace. In this world without family and without sexual love, the possibilities for forging strong emotional bonds are severely curtailed. Women make up a large part of the 'middle of humanity' that Apemantus says Timon never knew. There is a correlation between the absence of women and the quality of emotional life as restricted and dangerously unsure.

Even the women who appear in the play are not engaged in affective relationships. The ladies in the masque are showgirls whose roles are confined to dancing. Their spokesperson is a male Cupid; they themselves say nothing. The speaking women are the whores who accompany Alcibiades in Sc. 14. In the few lines they speak, their language fits their status. The fact that there are two of them—even speaking some of their lines together in surreal chorus—precludes even a suggestion of a one-to-one relationship such as exists between Witgood and the Courtesan in Middleton's *Trick to Catch the Old One*. In contrast with this example, *Timon of Athens* stages a community that is defective because it is all-male. It has no capacity to show how women are; it can show only how women are configured in such an aberrant world.

Timon's banquet in Sc. 2 starts out as an all-male affair, though some modern directors, such as Greg Doran at Stratford-upon-Avon in 1999, have made a point of introducing female attendants here and elsewhere in the play to underline the peripheral position of women. Coppélia Kahn, combining a psychoanalytic and historicist approach, has cited a passage just before the masque in which, as she draws out the implications of the imagery, the male community, and Timon in particular, seem to undergo a feminization:

TIMON . . . O, joy's e'en made away ere't can be born: mine eyes
  cannot hold out water, methinks. To forget their faults, I drink
  to you.
APEMANTUS Thou weep'st to make them drink, Timon.
SECOND LORD (*to Timon*)
  Joy had the like conception in our eyes,
  And at that instant like a babe sprung up.
APEMANTUS
  Ho, ho, I laugh to think that babe a bastard.
                              (2.100–7)

This is, Kahn notes, 'at once the most intimate moment in the play and the most hollow' (p. 50). Timon, overwhelmed with generous love to his friends, breaks into tears, which the lord obsequiously and Apemantus satirically describe in terms of childbirth. The flow of bounty has been transformed into a flow of tears, which in turn is metamorphosed into an image that identifies Timon as a mother, and falsely identifies his friends as sharing his attributes.

This exchange provides a context for the speech in which the 'forerunner' Cupid announces the masque. In this speech he says:

Hail to thee, worthy Timon, and to all that of his bounties taste!
The five best senses acknowledge thee their patron, and come
freely to gratulate thy plenteous bosom. (2.118–21)

Timon is acknowledged as the patriarchal 'patron' of the five senses, and yet also as the maternal source of all bounties. The phrase 'plenteous bosom' identifies him in the latter role. *Bosom* can refer to the nurturance of breast-milk, but in the period could also mean 'womb'. The word is therefore richly overdetermined as a signifier of the maternal.

The phrase 'plenteous bosom' falls within a network of imagery running through the play. Much of this relates to Timon. Here the key word is 'bounty' and its adjectival forms 'bountiful' and 'bounteous'. Bounty is a key attribute of Timon. At the beginning of the play he is introduced elliptically when the Poet notes how the 'Magic of bounty' has called up Timon's visitors. Timon promises his friends that they will 'share a bounteous time | In different pleasures' (1.258–9), and the First Lord picks up on the phrase by proposing to go in and 'taste Lord Timon's bounty' (1.277). This in turn is the phrase echoed in the Cupid's speech, 'of his bounties taste'. And so the word continues to thread itself through the play. It is the Cupid's speech that interprets this bounty as a female attribute, or at least an androgynous one. And it again relates to the figuration of Timon as a gender-ambivalent source of liquid fecundity or nurturance who 'pours it out' as his wealth 'flows from him'. 'In *Timon*', Kahn writes, 'otherness is not maleness as distinguished from femaleness by means of desire and the problematics of eros, but rather, identification with the mother as opposed to alienation from her', adding that both the identification and alienation are 'projected onto the entire dramatic landscape'.[1]

Timon is therefore figured as an unnatural breeder embodying both the male and female principles and bringing forth objects different from himself. In Renaissance terms he is a monster, a creature who defies nature's normal distributions and functions.[2] His replacement of the missing female element echoes the predicament of actors in the early modern all-male theatre. Timon relates to sexually ambivalent figures such as Androgyno and Castrone in Jonson's *Volpone*, and connects with a wider preoccupation seen in cross-gender role-playing by female characters such as Shakespeare's Viola or Middleton's Roaring Girl, and to the symptomatically rare cases of the man dressing as a women such as Falstaff's pantomimic disguise as the Wise Woman of Brentford. Given the absence of women on stage, gender ambiguity becomes a precondition for artistic creativity, and therefore can readily be emblematic of it.[3] Timon relates also to the androgynous masculinity of the male Jacobean courtier, not to mention King James's self-representation as 'a loving nourish-father' to the church and source of bounty to his people.[4] Actor and king both have the hermaphroditic character associated with Timon's generative bounty.

---

[1] Kahn, p. 51. See also Janet Adelman, *Suffocating Mothers* (New York and London, 1992), pp. 165–8.

[2] Compare Mark Thornton Burnett, *Constructing 'Monsters' in Shakespearean Drama and Early Modern Culture* (Basingstoke, 2002).

[3] I am grateful to Christine Buckley for these points.

[4] Kahn, pp. 43–4, citing James's *Basilikon Doron* and *True Law of Free Monarchies*. See also Curtis Perry, *The Making of Jacobean Culture* (Cambridge, 1997), pp. 115–24. Perry traces the idea to Isaiah 49: 23, 'kings shall be thy nursing fathers' (p. 250 n. 11).

He has, indeed, himself supplanted a female deity, the 'sovereign lady' Fortune, whom the Poet depicts on her mount in the play's opening passage. Lady Fortune was usually depicted with a wheel. A less common figuration was the Castle of Fortune, which in many respects brings us closer to the Poet's description: a sixteenth-century Italian woodcut shows a similar picture of clambering supplicants, the unsuccessful falling with, in the Poet's words, 'The foot above the head' (Illustration 1). The Poet recognizes Timon as one who is favoured by Fortune and who may, in his turn, be kicked off her mount. The main difference between the image in the woodcut and the Poet's account is that the woodcut shows a tiered castle whereas the Poet describes a 'hill' or 'mount', which is at once breast-like and venereal. Fortune's hill, with its connotations of the erotic female body, relates to Timon's later account of mother earth in Sc. 14. The word 'bosom', for instance, is used to describe both. Within the false exclusions of Timon's banqueting hall it looks otherwise: he seems to have displaced Lady Fortune, and to have become himself the all-dispensing and nurturing arbiter of good fortunes. Here the 'plenteous bosom' is his.

It is logical enough, then, that the masque should present another species of gender-monster. In *Troilus and Cressida* Troilus claims that 'In all Cupid's pageant there is presented no monster' (3.2.71–2), but this claim cannot be applied to the masque introduced by Cupid in *Timon of Athens*. John Knox had described the Amazons as 'monstrous women'. As female warriors they usurped a function that defined masculinity. They were supposed traditionally to have seared off one breast so that they could fight with bow and arrow more effectively whilst retaining the other breast to feed infants.[1] Thus, mirroring Timon as he is presented in the banquet scene, they combined the attributes of both male and female. The appearance of Amazons in classical and Renaissance tales often signifies a threat to the cohesion of the patriarchal worldview, representing the intrusion of what Jeanne Addison Roberts calls 'a potentially unassimilable Wild'.[2] In his 'Life of Theseus' Plutarch records that the invading Amazons placed their camp 'within the very city of Athens'.[3] This breach of the Athenian walls is represented symbolically and ceremonially in the lady masquers' entry

---

[1] Simon Shepherd, *Amazons and Warrior Women* (Brighton, 1981), pp. 14–15.

[2] *The Shakespearean Wild* (Lincoln, Nebr., 1991), p. 125.

[3] 'Life of Theseus', in *Lives*, p. 15.

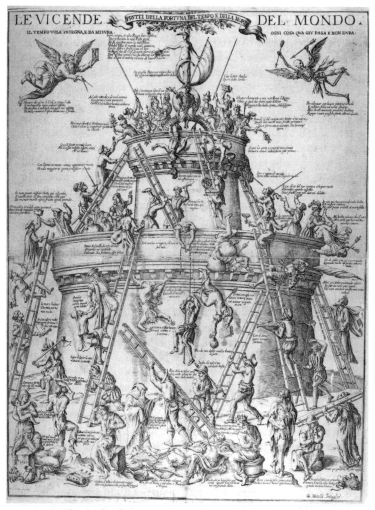

1. The Castle of Fortune. Sixteenth-century Italian woodcut.

into Timon's banqueting hall—which is to say, in theatrical terms, the space of the stage.

The potential for danger presented by the Amazons is dissipated because they are merely figures in a masque. Masques were driven by the imperative to harmonize the potential for disorder as a sign of the patron's or dedicatee's beneficence and grace. So it is in *Timon of Athens*, which is a relatively early example of Jacobean plays that represent a court masque, scaled down so that it could be realized within the more modest resources of the public stage. The very fact of court masque is an intrusion into the play, and the unusual circumstance that it is ladies who perform this particular masque-in-a-play, in contrast with the male masquers in, for example, *The Malcontent* and *The Revenger's Tragedy*, gives the intrusion its particular emphasis. One of the ways in which masques differed from plays of the public theatre was that, to the scandal of some commentators, women, specifically female courtiers, appeared on stage. Of course this would never have happened in any early performance or envisaged performance of *Timon of Athens* in the public theatre. Nevertheless, the play breaches its own decorum. Boy actors would probably have performed the role of lady courtiers performing the Amazons.

As compared with a court masque, it is striking that there is no provision for song. Singing in masques was performed by theatre professionals, and vocal silence is consistent with the role the courtiers played. Following masque convention, the emblematic pageant gives way to general dancing when the masquers take partners with members of the audience. The symbolic value of the dancing lay in its celebration of social harmony. Here the image is of reasserted heterosexual norms: '*The Lords rise from table, with much adoring of Timon; and, to show their loves, each single out an Amazon, and all dance, men with women*' (2.141.1–3). But, as we have seen, 'men with women' simplifies the issue, and indeed falsifies it. This is a play about men with men, and the masque, along with its heterosexual dancing, has little substance beyond its function as flattery.

Even the dancing diminishes the role accorded to the ladies. In a masque it would be the masquing ladies who would 'take out' partners from the audience to dance. Here the guests at Timon's table choose partners from the performing dancers '*to show their loves*', an eagerness on the part of the lords that deprives the ladies of initiative in constructing the harmony between masquers and guests. More striking is the demeaning treatment of the ladies at the end of the masque, when they are ushered out of sight as quickly as is decently possible. After complimenting the ladies, Timon immediately invites them to an 'idle banquet' off stage, so that they take no further part in the scene—or, perhaps, the whole play, unless two of them reappear as Alcibiades' whores. If the ladies are social equals, the gendering of the 'great' and 'idle' banquets is particularly misogynistic.

This treatment of the ladies would indeed be more appropriate to professional male actors in a masque, who had lower status and would have played no further part once the show was over. The 'ladies', moreover, perform in ways that are unexampled in the court masque or any species of drama in the Jacobean period: masquing female courtiers would dance, but they would never play lutes. Music, like acting, was left to the lower-status professional performers. In Renaissance illustrations, David Munrow notes, 'The lute is often found in the hands of courtesans' (*Instruments of the Middle Ages and Renaissance* (1976), p. 76). Thus if Timon treats the masquers virtually as though they were whores, their role in the masque offers some substantiation. In Middleton's *Your Five Gallants*, a boys' company comedy written perhaps shortly after *Timon of Athens*, ladies again are presented on stage playing music, but only in appearance. They are prostitutes in a brothel that passes itself off as a music school for young gentlewomen. It may be significant here that blind Cupid was the sign for a brothel. It may be significant too that even Queen Anne and her ladies had been accused of wearing apparel 'too light and courtesan-like' in the 1605 *Masque of Blackness*.[1]

The representation of the lady masquers as Amazons seems to reflect a complex and partly misogynistic reaction to female courtiers on stage in court masques, a reaction that had wider currency in Jacobean London and that here takes the form of re-enactment on the public stage. It remains artificial to ask whether the play's 'ladies' might actually be supposed to be courtesans or prostitutes rather than courtiers, though some indication could be given by their representation on stage, and two of them may (or may not) be recognizable as the whores Phrynia and Timandra in

[1] Dudley Carleton, writing to Sir Ralph Winwood, quoted in Ben Jonson, *Works*, ed. C. H. Herford and Percy and Evelyn Simpson, 11 vols. (Oxford, 1925–52), x. 448.

Sc. 14. The scene perhaps raises questions, rather than providing answers. What reality, or whose reality, we are looking at? Is Timon's a world in which there are no women apart from whores, one in which ladies cannot be seen other than as potential whores . . . ? Whatever the case, the image of the ideal community as a symposium of men is quickly reasserted by excluding them.

Thus, as Kahn has argued, in the first half of the play Timon acts as an unsustainable, temporary, and artificial male surrogate for what Shakespeare elsewhere calls 'bountiful fortune'. In the second half he acts as agent for another female force, mother earth. The ramifications are explored below (pp. 64–6). The shift is decisive, alienating Timon from the usurped role of provider and relocating that role in feminized nature.[1]

When Timon rejects humanity, the underlying misogyny of Athens finds explicit expression in the furious words he utters against womankind. Unlike his critique of gold, Timon's misogyny has no anchorings in the misfortunes that have befallen him, which arise specifically through his dealings with men. His attacks on women are apparently unmotivated onslaughts against the gender itself, and specifically against female sexuality: 'Be a whore still . . . Give them diseases . . . bring down rose-cheeked youth' (14.83–6). When Timon realizes that Alcibiades wages war on Athens he identifies a similar power to destroy in Alcibiades' army, and now he makes women the symptomatic victims: 'Strike me the counterfeit matron . . . Let not the virgin's cheek | Make soft thy trenchant sword' (14.113–16). There are other imagined victims too, but the emotional energy is most vividly and obsessively directed against women: 'for those milk-paps | That through the window-bars bore at men's eyes | Are not within the leaf of pity writ' (14.116–18). The 'leaf of pity' sounds divinely authored, but, in Timon's version of it, the exclusion of the representative woman, metonymically identified by her 'milk-paps', is of his own devising. He speaks like an angry god. His language dangerously collapses the very distinction of verbal modes: the indicative 'is', the subjunctive 'should be', and the imperative 'must be' all seem present, enabling Timon to invoke a destruction on women based on his own negative volition that they should be destruction-worthy.

The obsessive concern in this and other passages finds no origin

---

[1] For the implications in terms of the play's authorship, see pp. 149–50.

in the source materials. However, when Robert Greene's *Gwydonius* (1584) condemns verbal abuse of women, Timon is mentioned as an example: 'But ah, blasphemous beast that I am, thus recklessly to rail and rage without reason, thus currishly to exclaim against those without whom our life, though never so luckly, should seem most loathsome, thus Timon-like to condemn those heavenly creatures whose only sight is a sufficient salve against all hellish sorrows'.[1] Timon's particular status here as a negative model of misogyny within a prose romance connects ultimately with the Shakespearian romance theme of the journey from the city to the wild woods. The Greene text serves as a reminder that the feminized pastoral romance of Shakespeare's *As You Like It* is an important model in reverse for *Timon of Athens*.

Rosalind and Celia in *As You Like It* extract themselves from patriarchal authority to enjoy in Arden a control over life and action they could scarcely have dreamt of at court. Timon extracts himself from homosocial Athens only to confront the vast maternality of the earth. His limited actions confute his needs, because the earth yields gold instead of food. Faced with this universalized 'Common mother' from whom he cannot or will not separate himself, he can only rage and die.

Janet Adelman has argued strongly that Shakespeare as author is himself absorbed in the fantasy expressed through Timon, citing 'the insistence on Timon's nobility and his aggrandizing difference from others, the absence of a fully realized social world, especially of fully realized female characters, the magical appearance of gold and especially the whores as Timon requires them'.[2] It may be so; but it may equally be that the play is sceptically analytic of such a fantasy. The world Timon lives in and makes around himself strikes the present reader as being articulated in tones of both fascination and strong antipathy. The play exposes an infantilism in Timon that diminishes him. He himself is a product of a pointedly deformed society with a pointedly deformed cultural poetics.

Debt

One way of understanding *Timon of Athens*'s disturbingly strong male orientation is in the light of the usually man-to-man nature

---

[1] Ed. Carmine Di Biase (Ottawa, 2001), p. 100.   [2] Adelman, p. 174.

of debts and obligations.[1] It was men who possessed estates and had the main power to lend and give. Even marriage, as a contractual matter, was usually settled by men, and Sc. 1 pointedly shows a marriage settlement resolved between the suitor, Timon as his patron, and the intended wife's father: 'What you bestow, in him I'll counterpoise, | And make him weigh with her' says Timon, referring to money (1.149–50). The girl herself does not appear in the play, and the issue of romance is defused in an image that translates the lovers into sums of money.

As in this example, Timon is the exclusive source of wealth, but his apparently limitless reserves are an illusion. The reality is debt. In this, the play addresses anxieties about the foundations of monetary economy in a world at once increasingly mercantile and increasingly unable to conduct its transactions in hard coin.

Although Spanish bullion increased the supply of gold over the continent of Europe, the general increase in trade in the early modern period meant that the demand for gold was racing further and further ahead of the supply. Money tended to be hoarded, and so the supply of coin in circulation diminished further. The majority of transactions took place without the exchange of money. In early seventeenth-century England there were no banks. Barter was extraordinarily widespread, and so too was deferred payment. Craig Muldrew argues that it was not coinage but debt that was the mainstay of the early modern economy. It was both ubiquitous and complex. Written transactions increasingly supplemented the various forms of oral credit. Formal sealed bonds were in widespread use. Interest, legalized by the 1571 Act of Parliament that distinguished between interest and usury, was always charged. From the late sixteenth century the peerage also raised loans by the expedient of mortgaging land, default on which could lead to immediate foreclosure; Timon himself succumbs to this dangerous practice: 'His land's put to their books' (2.200). Credit created complex and interdependent relationships based on trust, without which, according to Robert South, 'there can be no correspondence maintained either between societies or particular persons'.[2] Traditionally, 'faithful' service had been a mainstay of feudal

[1] This section and the following section 'Gold' rework material in John Jowett, 'Middleton and Debt in *Timon of Athens*', in *Money and the Age of Shakespeare*, ed. Linda Woodbridge (Basingstoke, 2003), pp. 219–35.

[2] Quoted in Muldrew, p. 125.

dependency; in the early modern period, however, it was challenged by a new model based on the idea of a civil society in which service was owed to the monarchical state and was enforced by legal institutions. It was this new model that instilled an insistence on credit, honesty, and conscience as personal attributes.

Middleton is the play's primary poet of debt. The satiric scenes showing Timon's servants and the moneylenders follow through the consequences of Timon's misconstructed friendship based on parasitism. They enact pure city comedy in Middleton's most characteristic vein. The symptomatic figures are usurers and creditors. These persons, the anonymous 'friends' who have been seen at Timon's table in their functions as lords and senators, acquire a specific identity only in order to sustain the satirical thrust of each episode in which the demands of friendship are refused.

Criticism sometimes depicts Middleton as a reductive materialist, and, although in this play and elsewhere he also writes in more emotional and sentimental vein, the tendency in that direction is clearly evident in many of the scenes he contributed to *Timon of Athens*. Words such as 'friendship' and 'honour' are mercilessly reduced to code-words for mercenary relationships. As elsewhere in the usage of the period, the term 'credit' switches between being a moral attribute and being the basis for financial arrangements. Middleton performs the critical act of the satirist in producing a depiction that both claims verisimilitude and produces an alteration at the key point where the potential for the absurd can be released with what appears to be inevitability.

Middleton's longest single scene, Sc. 2, presents an orchestrated overview of the community Timon generates around him and its economic foundations. It begins with hautboys and a great banquet served in, signifying that the scene will be a display of social theatre, in the manner of King James's court (the new Banqueting Hall was probably rising at the time the play was written), or in the manner of aristocrats who were themselves imitating the style of the court. The banquet proceedings that then unfold involve the lords standing on ceremony and then being invited to sit, the skulking guest Apemantus being made welcome, a toast, a grace before eating, another toast during the eating, a masque, some ceremonious dancing, and Timon's gifts of jewels to his guests before they depart. In other words, in terms of theatre as a vehicle for social spectacle the banquet is a formal and structured social occasion that is given exceptionally full articulation—as is the case with other banquets in Middleton such as those in *No Wit/Help Like a Woman's* and *Women Beware Women*. But the function of the scene as drama, as opposed to theatre, is to puncture the proceedings with a series of implied or explicit ironic commentaries. There are similar effects in Middleton banquets elsewhere, as with Leantio's embittered asides during the banquet in *Women Beware Women* 3.2, and the Ward's ridiculous commentary on Isabella's song in the same scene at ll. 145–57.

The dialogue opens with the unfestive discussion of money where Timon refuses Ventidius' offer to return the talents that redeemed him from prison. Timon's response is that such bondage is redundant in his world of friendship. But Apemantus understands the banquet otherwise. It is not an example and image of a society of friends, but an emblem of how the guests are actually consuming their host: 'What a number of men eats Timon, and he sees 'em not' (2.39–40). The connotations of the Last Supper have been noted above. It is Middleton who constantly emphasizes the 'ceaseless *flow* of riot', 'your great *flow* of debts', the 'spilth' that the Steward says has 'set mine eyes at *flow*', and juxtaposes it with the bounded, limited human body that can be consumed only so much.

Timon's belief that he is, notwithstanding his debts, 'wealthy in my friends' who can 'command each other' refers to debts of obligation that would have been clearly understood in early modern England. Timon's acts of giving in Sc. 2 are based on verbal and written expressions of friendship that Lynne Magnusson has described as the oil in the machinery of early modern commercial transaction.[1] But Timon makes them dangerously literal. The performative utterance expressing unlimited good will is naively translated into an act, a one-way transaction of unconstrained generosity. *Timon of Athens* can be taken to imply that in the world of credit to mean what you say would be to indulge in what Shakespeare refers to as 'ridiculous excess' (*King John* 4.2.16). The Puritan critique of language insisted on transparent sincerity, but credit and debt are facilitated by language of another kind. This

---

[1] Lynne Magnusson, *Shakespeare and Social Dialogue: Dramatic Language and Elizabethan Letters* (Cambridge, 1999), pp. 114–37. Magnusson points out that the language of friendship originated in courtly exchange before it was picked up as a way of consolidating bonds of trust between merchants. See commentary to 6.55–7.

threatens the ontological foundations of economistic society itself. Transactions based on credit depend on trust, which is itself manufactured through conventionalized insincerity.

The critique of the language of commercial 'friendship' is apparent not only in Timon's insistence on over-matching words with deeds. It is re-exposed in his friends' language of moral probity as they justify denying him aid: in Lucius' self-condemnation as a 'wicked beast' for, as he says, parting with his available wealth just the other day (6.42), in Sempronius' hypocritical protests that Timon has shown 'but little love or judgement' and 'disgraced' him by not giving him the first chance to show *his* love (7.10–13), and even in the First Stranger's declaration that he would have given Timon half his wealth if (but only if) Timon had requested it out of his love for Timon (6.80–2). The comic moral outrage depends on a sense that Lucius, Sempronius, and even the First Stranger are abusing language as well as friendship.

The Stranger is the unexpected example, because the group of three Strangers seems to be on hand simply to express their disgust at Lucius' behaviour. Because they are strangers—'I never tasted Timon in my life' says one of them—they can speak without their words becoming subject to irony; or so, at least, it might appear. Their condemnation, unequivocal, clear, and simple: 'O see the monstrousness of man', 'Religion groans at it'. Perhaps these strangers to Athens anachronistically hail from Geneva, the seat of Calvinism. But, as Klein notes, the Stranger reveals a parasitic attitude not far removed from those he criticizes in subscribing to the equation of friendship and *bounties*: 'Nor came any of his bounties over me | To mark me for his friend' (6.75–6). The suspicion that the moralizer may be reserving a position of self-interest is common in Middleton.

Middleton is also the writer of the soberest criticism of Timon himself, in the voice of Flavius the Steward. Despite Nigel Bawcutt's warning that we cannot in any simple sense depict Middleton as a Puritan in the full religious and political meaning of the word,[1] there is in *Timon of Athens* a strong Calvinist critique of both a culture of debt and a culture of wasteful extravagance. Both were seen to typify the court of King James, who was notorious for giv-

---

[1] 'Was Thomas Middleton a Puritan Dramatist?', *Modern Language Review*, 94 (1999), 925–39. He contends mainly with Margot Heinemann, *Puritanism and Theatre* (Cambridge, 1980).

ing jewels and other rich presents to attractive younger men and for cultivating unreliable favourites. The play's attack on values associated with the court is underpinned by the social role of the Steward as well as the words he speaks. The character referred to just once in the dialogue as Flavius is with this single exception always identified by function as 'Steward'. Lines such as 'Plutus the god of gold | Is but his steward' (1.279) may activate an ironic pun on the King's surname Stuart, which is no more than a Scottish variant of 'Steward'. If so, attributes of James are distributed between Timon, the James-like wastrel, and the Steward, who represents the characteristics of stewardship that should properly be denoted by the royal name.

The masque of Sc. 2 also invites a reading of the play as what Albert H. Tricomi has termed 'anti-court satire'.[1] Here, underscoring the possibility of reading the scene as a guarded satire of the profligacy of King James, the play represents Timon's own imitation of the splendour of the Renaissance court. James was the local example of royal profligacy, copying the splendours of Catholic European absolutism. But, as Lisa Jardine and others have noted, virtually all courtly munificence depended on debt. The splendours of the imperial Habsburg court were paid for with money lent by the financiers of the Függer family. Patronage of the arts, Platonic glorifications of the patron, the transcendence of economic prudence in bestowing gifts, the spendours of banquet and masque, all flowed from the hidden munificence of the creditor.[2]

Timon's own brand of ostentatious display makes the recipient the same person as the creditor. The situation is neatly summarized in the simple stage property of the empty box that Timon's servant Flaminius takes to Lucullus' house in Sc. 5. What lies within the box is signified outwardly, by precedent and by social practice. It is Timon who bears the arbitrary labels. As long as Timon is 'that honourable, complete, free-hearted gentleman of Athens' (5.10–11) the container promises content. The truth, known already to the audience, lies in the opposite but equally logical possibility, that the box has been brought to be filled with talents.

---

[1] *Anti-Court Drama in England,* 1603–1642 (Charlottesville and London, 1989).
[2] Lisa Jardine, *Worldly Goods: A New History of the Renaissance* (1996), pp. 93–114.

A single talent was a huge sum, amounting to over fifty pounds of silver. If Lucullus were by some inversion of his role actually to fulfil Flaminius' request for fifty talents, he would need to supply him with in excess of a metric tonne of silver, which is, to put it mildly, more than could conveniently be carried in a portable box hidden under a cloak. The inflation continues exponentially in the following scene, where Servilius is understandably shocked to receive a request for what he thinks to be 'fifty' talents but he immediately realizes is no less than 'five hundred'. Though Lucius is prepared to pretend shock at the large but lesser sum, the arithmetical spread to five hundred truly does shock him. The real wealth is, in all this, conspicuously absent, the empty box being the emblem for the whole string of episodes.

The moneylenders characteristically speak a prose that, if inflected with personal idiolect, is also aggressively spare; the audience is assigned the position of hostile critic. It is a parsimonious language of insincerity and guarded social negotiation, a language that lies removed from communicative self-expression. The creditor scenes are satirical in part because they are linguistically reductive.

A scene that is removed from the temper of city comedy writing is Alcibiades' meeting with the senate (Sc. 10), where he mounts an impassioned defence of a soldier in his army who has killed an opponent in a brawl. If we suppose that Alcibiades invites us to make a judgement on the case for mercy, the scene is puzzling.[1] The conduct of the episode seems to assume that we will be more sympathetic to Alcibiades than the apparent facts of the matter permit. When a Senator points out that, 'You cannot make gross sins look clear' (10.38), it is hard to disagree. Alcibiades is subverting the course of justice, and there is a danger that the scene fails as satire because it makes the senators, the theoretical targets of the scene as satire, look quite reasonable.

But this scene is not an impartial trial scene. It too is about what Muldrew calls the economy of obligation, as Alcibiades' protest eventually makes clear:

> Though his right arm might purchase his own time
> And be in debt to none—yet, more to move you,
> Take my deserts to his and join 'em both.
> And for I know

[1] See pp. 71–2 below.

> Your reverend ages love security,
> I'll pawn my victories, all my honour to you
> Upon his good returns.   (10.75–81)

'Purchase', 'debt', 'security', 'pawn', 'returns'—the language is insistently that of credit and debt. Alcibiades is claiming a debt of obligation, and offering to discharge it in return for mercy towards his soldier. When he says 'Call me to your remembrances' he invokes himself and his very body as a figuration of his deeds. Within this context Alcibiades remains a more sympathetic figure, and potentially indeed, like Timon, a figure of sacrifice. The scene therefore stages a conflict between different codes of public behaviour, one based on judicial standards that are more immediately accessible to the modern reader, the other on rules of obligation that need to be understood within their historical context.

Middleton shows a society in which love, honour, and friendship did exist, in imagination at least, once upon a time; they have given way to a world which is now instead governed by policy, and by 'usury | That makes the senate ugly'. The impression is of a rapacious 'now', governed by an explosion of debt, and in revolt against an idealized communal past. This picture, drawing on the traditional view of usury as a sin, is not unique to Middleton, but it is highly characteristic of him. The past is an era of pre-economy in which a stable society is governed by reciprocal obligations; it was a time when, to quote *No Wit/Help like a Woman's*, 'Charity was landlord' and the fire in the Christmas hall gave welcome to 'forty russet yeomen' (9.79). The present is an era of usury and debt economy, in which all behaviour is driven by notional sums of money. Though social etiquette demands that the language of nobility and honour is upheld, the elite are aristocrats in name only, for even the lords and senators are usurers.

This seems appropriate to a depiction of Athens as a city republic, but as Lawrence Stone has noted, like the play's senators, London aldermen 'waxed rich on usury and forfeited mortgages'.[1] In Jacobean terms, then, the play reflects the emergence of new merchant oligarchies in the cities of England at a time when the aristocratic and gentry elites still held sway in the country.[2] In the

---

[1] *The Crisis of the Aristocracy* (Oxford, 1965), p. 542.

[2] J. A. Sharpe, *Early Modern England: A Social History* 1550–1760, 2nd edn (1997), pp. 183–90.

city, the old feudal values were being replaced by a harsher mercantile ethos. Though the play transports the audience from the city to the country, it ruthlessly excludes any suggestion of rural community with countervailing social values. Outside the city there are only wild beasts, metaphors for the city itself; outside Timon's house there is no place left for charity to be landlord. Moreover, in Athens the delicate social mechanisms that regulate the debt nexus are missing. Debts of obligation that are not written in bonds as sums of money can safely be ignored. In that respect Alcibiades suffers just the same experience as Timon when the senate rejects his claim on their favour.

Middleton's social drama is without metaphysics, though its Calvinist social sensibility and nostalgia for a lost pre-economic age play a similar role in establishing an ideal standard against which the fallen world is measured. Abstract virtue seems threatened. It seems to be in the course of becoming what Raymond Williams would call a residual ideological formation.[1] Virtue is increasingly manifested as a form of labelling, empty in itself, on social positions within the debt economy.

Gold

Karl Marx, struck more forcibly by *Timon of Athens* than any other Shakespeare play, read Timon's vitriolic attacks on the power of gold as a critique of capitalist money economy. In *Economic and Philosophical Manuscripts of 1844* Marx quotes *Timon of Athens* 14.26–45 and 382–93, and, weaving Timon's language into his own, he comments, 'Does not money, therefore, transform all my incapacities into their contrary? . . . is not money the bond of all *bonds*? Can it not dissolve and bind all ties?' He attributes to money 'The disturbing and confounding of all human and natural qualities . . . it is the general *confounding* and *confusing* of all things . . . It makes contradictions embrace'.[2] The echoes here suggestively conflate Timon's critique of gold with his curse on Athens in Sc. 12; and indeed Timon does attempt to use his gold to bring his curses into effect, intending to demonstrate its power, in Marx's words, of 'turning an *image* into *reality*'.

[1] *Marxism and Literature* (Oxford, 1977), pp. 121–7.
[2] *Collected Works*, vol. iii (1976), pp. 323–5.

Another specific mention of *Timon of Athens* occurs in the resonant passage where he depicts money in its magically double incarnation as the raw means for exchange and as a glittering commodity in its own right. Part of that passage reads:

Circulation is the great social retort into which everything is thrown, and out of which everything is recovered as crystallised money. . . . Not even the bones of the saints are able to withstand this alchemy; and still less able to withstand it are more delicate things, sacrosanct things which are outside the commercial traffic of men. Just as all the qualitative differences between commodities are effaced in money, so money on its side, a radical leveller, effaces all distinctions. But money is itself a commodity, an external object, capable of becoming the private property of any individual. Thus social power becomes a private power in the hands of a private person. . . . Modern society which, when still in its infancy, pulled Pluto by the hair of his head out of the bowels of the earth, acclaims gold, its Holy Grail, as the glittering incarnation of its inmost vital principle.[1]

The telling confusion between Plutus, god of gold, and Pluto, lord of the underworld, is to be found in Shakespeare and other early modern writers (in *Troilus and Cresida* Ulysses refers to 'every grain of Pluto's gold'). It is perhaps a characteristic mark of western civilization to conflate the precious metal with hell on account of gold's power to corrupt and its origin in the earth. This certainly pertains to *Timon*, where Timon prospers as long as 'Plutus the god of gold' remains his steward (1.279), and later in the play we are actually shown the extraction of gold from the earth as a kind of impossible actuality that returns Timon once again to arbitrary possession of 'social power'. Marx finds early modern Europe becoming aware of this power and turning from medieval contempt to admiration of gold. He correlates the lines from *Timon of Athens* with Christopher Columbus' comment in a letter written in Jamaica in 1503: 'Gold is a wonderful thing! Whoever owns it is lord of all he wants'. If in fact gold remained in short supply, that shortage could only make the infusion of gold from America into the economies of Europe all the more dramatic. To some, the fantasy of the rare substance in abundance seemed to be tantalizingly within reach of being realized, as in 1610 Jonson's *The Alchemist* would suggest.

---

[1] *Capital*, trans. Eden and Cedar Paul (1930; repr. 1974), pp. 112–13. Marx again quotes most of 14.26–45, in a note keyed to 'all distinctions'.

The word 'gold' occurs far more often in *Timon of Athens* than in any other Shakespeare play: there are thirty-six instances, distantly followed by *Comedy of Errors* at nineteen. Yet no more than three instances of this key word were evidently written by Middleton. Of these three, two fall in passages Middleton added to Shakespeare scenes, and probably reflect Middleton's accommodation to a Shakespeare theme.[1] Otherwise the word 'gold' is restricted to a Shakespeare stint that is little more than half the length of a typical Shakespeare play.

As these figures suggest, Shakespeare writes as a poet of the idealizing vision of gold. In Shakespeare's Sc. 3 a Senator protests:

> Still in motion
> Of raging waste! It cannot hold, it will not.
> If I want gold, steal but a beggar's dog
> And give it Timon, why, the dog coins gold.
> (3.3–6)

Even in this broadly satirical scene, Shakespeare emphasizes both the illusoriness and the appeal of this fantasy of literally infinite wealth. Timon enjoys a life in which boundaries and limits do not exist, and in which nature unnaturally gives forth coins as offspring: 'the dog coins gold'. The legend of Midas seems never far away. This is a life in which money transcends the very calculus on which it is based.[2] And the absence of any need to account for money leads Timon to suspend judgement on what is feigned and what is sincere in human behaviour.

In Sc. 14, after debt has exerted its prerogative, the earth turns the tables once more, mimicking the Renaissance fantasy of American gold by providing Timon with gold in unbelievable excess. But, to come down to earth, what is the origin of the gold that allows this vigorous and absurd confutation of the laws of debt? Trevor Nunn's 1990–1 Young Vic production began with a dumbshow of thieves burying loot, one of whom was shot by plainclothes policemen.[3] Nunn therefore explained that when Timon later finds gold he unearths a product of the violent society he had

---

[1] The lines attributable to Middleton are 1.279, 13.51, and 14.540. The three instances Spurgeon cites of metal as base and worthless (p. 345), 'base metal' (7.6), 'iron heart' (8.82), and 'Flinty mankind' (14.483), are all in Middleton passages.

[2] Compare Marc Shell's discussion of natural and mercantile 'generation' in *Merchant of Venice*, in *Money, Language, and Thought* (Baltimore, 1982).

[3] Peter Holland, *English Shakespeares* (Cambridge, 1997), p. 100.

attempted to leave behind. Such is unambiguously the case in Lucian's dialogue, where we are told that the treasure consists of 'coined gold'. There has been a widespread preference on stage for the hidden hoard. Phelps in 1851 had Timon discover the gold within a buried urn. In Langham's 1963 production at Stratford, Ontario, the gold remained hidden within what Wilson Knight described as 'rusty earth-soiled caskets'. As Knight pointed out, in purely theatrical terms it makes sense to have a property that is adequate to Timon's description of 'Yellow, glittering, precious gold' (14.26), something 'lovely to hold and address'.[1]

Ingots, coins, caskets, and urns all belong to the world of human culture, as will most things 'lovely to hold and address'. Yet the gold comes from the earth as though Timon had mined it. The text says nothing about robbers and buried hoards. This is not to insist that the gold should be represented as unrefined ore, but to point out that it has contradictory qualities. Doran's RST 1999 production saw Timon finding lumpy ingots with a dull gleam. This catches the ambiguity nicely. In Timon's own account, it is indeed 'yellow, glittering, precious', but these are not its only attributes: within sixteen lines it is 'damned earth', as though physically as well as morally filthy and impure. In some sense, then, Timon's gold is a product of culture. In another sense it is a natural product of the earth. Strict naturalism of presentation is not necessary, because the qualities attributed to the gold are emblematic as well as descriptive, and because the scene presents a kind of miracle so unlikely that naturally occurring ingots are scarcely less out of question than an accidentally unearthed hoard.

This ambiguity is crucial to the play's representation of nature in its relation to human activity, and perhaps ultimately even to our reading of Timon himself. After all, if nature is prodigal, Timon is more justified in being prodigal himself: fortune favours him, and the generosity of the earth is limitless even when its gifts are not wanted. On the other hand, if Timon stumbles on someone else's hoard, the total resources available to humanity have not increased; Timon recirculates wealth that has circulated before, and so paradoxically he finds himself in the very middle of economic culture at the very point when he was most sure that he had escaped it.

---

[1] Knight, *Shakespearian Production*, pp. 296–7.

The Iron Age

The Shakespearian contrast between the metaphysical ideal and what Timon sees as the nihilistic real draws on Ovid's account of humanity's fall from the Golden Age to the Bronze Age and thence to the Iron Age. This was the *locus classicus* for identifying human impiety and human violence with the extraction of metals from the earth, and therefore with humankind's denatured and violent relationship with the natural world and with itself. The Golden Age saw a Utopian society that needed no laws: 'which of itself maintained | The truth and right of everything unforced and unconstrained'. There was harmony with nature in a world with no use for trade by sea or agriculture:

> The lofty pine-tree was not hewn from mountains where it stood,
> In seeking strange and foreign lands, to rove upon the flood . . .
> The fertile earth as yet was free, untouched of spade or plough,
> And yet it yielded of itself of everythings enough;
> And men themselves, contented well with plain and simple food
> That on the earth of nature's gift without their travail stood,
> Did live by raspes, hips and haws, by cornels, plums and cherries,[1]
> By sloes and apples, nuts and pears, and loathsome bramble-berries,
> And by the acorns dropped on ground from Jove's broad tree in field.
> (*Metamorphoses*, trans. Golding, 1.109–21)

Shakespeare recalls this passage in several plays, including *Timon of Athens*, but they give little credence to prelapsarian Utopias. In both *As You Like It* and *Timon of Athens* he stresses the harshness of the natural world. For Ovid, the Golden Age, like the Eden of Genesis, was a place of perpetual summer; it was not until the Silver Age that 'icicles hung roping down' (1.136). Shakespeare's postlapsarian wild is a place of savage beasts, 'the icy fang | And churlish chiding of the winter's wind' (*As You Like It* 2.1.6–7), and frost-edged brooks. And in *The Tempest* 2.1.149–74 Gonzalo's evocation of an ideal commonwealth based, indirectly, on Ovid's Golden Age is given short shrift. One might not agree with the treatment meted out to Gonzalo by Antonio and Sebastian, but they do seem right in regarding his Utopia as merely fatuous. These examples bear witness to a sceptical fascination with the prelapsarian ideal in Shakespeare's plays.

---

[1] 'Raspes' are raspberries. 'Cornels' are the edible fruit of the Cornelian cherry (*Cornus mas*), native to southern Europe and sometimes cultivated in Britain.

If the Silver Age brought the four seasons, the Iron Age brought all that is bad in human behaviour, and it all follows from the discovery of metal: gold for wealth, iron for cultivation, mining, and warfare, and brass for the 'brazen tables' of the 'threat'ning law':

> Not only corn and other fruits, for sustenance and for store,
> Were now exacted of the earth; but eft they gan to dig,
> And in the bowels of the ground unsatiably to rig
> For riches couched and hidden deep, in places near to hell,
> The spurs and stirrers unto vice, and foes to doing well.
> Then hurtful iron came abroad, then came forth yellow gold,
> More hurtful than the iron far. Then came forth battle bold,
> That fights with both and shakes his sword in cruel bloody hand.
> Men live by ravin and by stealth. The wand'ring guest doth stand
> In danger of his host, the host in danger of his guest,
> And fathers of their son-in-laws. Yea, seldom time doth rest
> Between born brothers such accord and love as ought to be.
> The goodman seeks the goodwife's death, and his again seeks she.
> The stepdames fell their husbands' sons with poison do assail.
> To see their fathers live so long the children do bewail.
> All godliness lies under foot.

(1.154–69)

Jonathan Bate demonstrates the recurrent influence of this passage on Shakespeare's writing, accurately describing the second half of it as 'Timon-like'.[1]

In *Timon of Athens* this worst-of-the-Iron-Age picture of humanity is both contrasted and correlated with the dystopian and wintry state of Iron-Age nature. It is, however, the committed city-dweller Apemantus who points to the bleak air and the cold brook candied with ice. Timon for his part contrasts *human* nature, which he sees as beast-like and irredeemable, with his isolated habitation of the natural world of the woods. His life there offers a restricted kind of salvation. He can hope to demonstrate the theory that one can be sustained by mother earth without becoming involved in the extravagance, the abstraction from nature, and the detestable sociality of living in the city.[2]

But Timon's vision of a subsistence livelihood is compromised. At 14.416–21 he commends to the thieves a vegetarian diet based on

---

[1] *Shakespeare and Ovid* (Oxford, 1993), p. 171.

[2] One of the middles of humanity that Timon does not understand is life in a small town such as Shakespeare's Stratford-upon-Avon.

the plenitude of roots, oak-mast and hips. A seventeenth-century Scottish reader of the Folio inscribed his copy with an annotation against this passage: 'The earth everywhere furnishes herbs and water for men's refection more natural than flesh and fishes'.[1] For the Thief, the natural diet is unsustainable; he complains that 'We cannot live on grass, on berries, water, | As beasts and birds and fishes' (14.422–3). Neither the Thief nor the Scottish annotator mentions roots. This may be significant in that digging up roots with a spade lies at a stage beyond the gathering of nature's surplus. As is physically manifested in the staging of the scene, Timon digs. Using an implement characteristic of the Iron Age, he engages in the Iron-Age activity of breaking open the ground. It is this that leads to an Iron-Age outcome—which now looks less paradoxical than one might otherwise think—the discovery of gold. This discovery in turn gives Timon the power to unleash the destruction that typifies the Iron Age, in his fantasy at least:

> Go on; here's gold; go on.
> Be as a planetary plague when Jove
> Will o'er some high-viced city hang his poison
> In the sick air. Let not thy sword skip one.
> [. . .] Swear against objects.
> Put armour on thine ears and on thine eyes
> Whose proof nor yells of mothers, maids, nor babes,
> Nor sight of priests in holy vestments bleeding,
> Shall pierce a jot. There's gold to pay thy soldiers.
> Make large confusion, and, thy fury spent,
> Confounded be thyself. Speak not. Be gone.
>
> (14.108–29)

Once he is left alone, Timon's rhapsody relates his hatred for humanity to his own new position, no longer a provider for others, but a potentially starving dependant on the earth. He meditates on the 'unkindness' of earth's 'proud child, arrogant man', who, wallowing in the excess of 'liquorish draughts', lacks all 'consideration' of his debt to the earth for his being and sustenance.[2] He twice uses the phrase 'ingrateful man', transferring his sense of personal injury to injuries committed against the earth. This allows an impersonal critique of the human mode of existence that has ramifications wider than his own grievances.

---

[1] Yamada, p. 215.   [2] 14.177, 181, 195, 197.

The language is, again, Ovidian. It has strong antecedents in Shakespeare's own development of Ovid's lyricism in plays such as *A Midsummer Night's Dream*, and in other writers of the 1590s such as Spenser. The list of beasts at 14.180–5 is the most obvious example of Ovidian writing. The earth produces objects like elaborate jewels: black toad, adder blue, gilded newt. There is a strong effect of artifice: like the glittering gold itself, the gilded newt seems refined and objectified.

Shakespeare places these creatures on the borderline of the natural world in another respect too. They are associated with 'all th'abhorrèd births below crisp heaven', in other words the creatures that are monstrous, prodigious, and unnatural. The catalogue of reptiles and amphibians focuses on animals that were considered poisonous or physically abnormal. Timon therefore makes two related but incompatible statements. The first is based on an antithesis: proud humans come from the same earth as the most humble creatures. The second is based on a similitude: the perverse vices of man find a counterpart in animals of unnatural or distorted form and poisonous nature. The address to the earth therefore sees her as a general mother to all living creatures, but also, more narrowly and more provocatively, as a mother fit for the Iron Age who produces only monsters or poisonous creatures that are fit to range alongside vile humankind.

Timon's language itself inhabits unnatural extremes, ranging rapidly from the minimal to the apocalyptic. He first petitions the earth to produce 'one poor root', a small demand.[1] He next radically contradicts himself, calling on the earth to make herself sterile so that humanity may cease:

> Ensear thy fertile and conceptious womb;
> Let it no more bring out ingrateful man.
> (14.188–9)

Then suddenly he is imploring the earth neither to produce a poor root nor to ensear her womb:

> Go great with tigers, dragons, wolves, and bears;
> Teem with new monsters whom thy upward face

---

[1] For what Timon might mean by a root, see commentary note to 14.23.

Hath to the marbled mansion all above
Never presented.

(14.190–3)

On the one hand, Timon invokes universal sterility; on the other hand a new world teeming with monsters. He is torn between teleologically imagining revenge in the shape of humanity exterminated and analogically generating beast-metaphors whereby humanity is translated as though by Circe's spell. The earth responds to Timon's grandiloquent, contradictory, and impossibly harsh visions with comic bathos, providing at last a root, the basic thing he asked for in the first place. But the vacillations are not quite over, for there is a final call for sterility: 'Dry up thy marrows, vines, and plough-torn leas'.

Sudden and striking turns from one idea to another are intrinsic to the speech, and consistent with the sudden wrenches that typify Timon's enraged language elsewhere. The highly polarized quality of the writing in this speech upholds Apemantus' observation that Timon does not know 'The middle of humanity' (14.302). To extrapolate, he does not comprehend the middle ground in any area of possibility. Timon's whole character from beginning to end is built on occlusion of the in-between. The particular oscillation seen here swings between reverence towards the feminized earth and execration, between pity and his own brand of sadistic violence.

The passage also has religious resonances. Proverbially, and echoing the words of Christ, 'the desire of money is the root of all evil' (1 Timothy 6: 10). The initial stage image of Timon digging is translated from a picture of a hungry man to an emblem of the biblical text. The biblical train of thought is underlined in Timon's suggestion that the heavens are 'clear', that is to say innocent, if they grant him roots rather than gold (14.28). They have just played the sardonic trick of providing him with the root of all evil: a joke because it is based on an unexpected and quibbling fulfilment of the text, but a literally wicked joke at that. The theological dimension of the episode seems to point to the issue of God's responsibility for the presence of evil in the world. Timon is an 'idle votarist' because he gets what he does not want, which is, precisely, the means for evil. The Christian God escapes blame only because of the setting, at least nominally in classical Greece where petitions are made to multiple 'gods'.

Shakespeare would have found Timon's discovery of gold in Lucian, but Lucian's Timon proposes to continue his solitary life, now in a state of luxury. Shakespeare instead proposes an extravagant and savagely ironic reworking of the biblical warning about the evil effects of riches. Timon is the sermonizer. He speaks from the point of intersection between his misanthropy and his preoccupation with the earth as maternal body. His outbursts are too unstable to be described as a state of knowledge, but, like Lear's insights into social inequality and the partiality of law, they offer glimpses of a radical critique of humanity's abuse of the ecology. The production of wealth is not an innocent activity. The uses of wealth are not benevolent. Gold is the surplus that, as in Bataille's analysis, can be used in an orgy of warfare that destroys everything.

Mammon

Though grounded in Ovid and the Bible, the poetics of the scene belong to a wider tradition acknowledged and developed in some of the major literary texts of the period. Shakespeare was evidently aware of the allegorical account of Mammon in Spenser's *Faerie Queene*, Book II, canto vii, where he would have found Ovid and St Paul already conflated. One can be particularly confident in identifying the influence of this passage on *Timon of Athens* because the same passage influenced Shakespeare's account of the wedges of gold and heaps of pearl lying at the bottom of the sea in Clarence's dream in *Richard III* 1.4.21–33.

The biblical 'Mammon' means riches. The more literal sense of the word, 'that which is hidden', establishes just how the word configures the riches it refers to. It reminds us that precious metals as they circulate in human society are a product of excavation and extraction, and also that they are subject to hoarding. In Spenser's picture of Mammon personified, Guyon finds Mammon in a hidden place, in a glade 'Cover'd with boughes and shrubs' in a 'desert wildernesse', presiding over his vast pile of wealth. Mammon represents neither the gold in itself as it might lie buried, nor gold circulating freely as a commodity, but the point of threshold between a gold gleaming with possibility but as yet inert and the human society in which it potentially circulates. He is a kind of global banker for whom the earth itself is the bank, operating outside the everyday economy but potentially affecting it severely. In himself Mammon is as antisocial as Timon. He is presented as the very opposite of civil man, 'An uncouth, salvage, and uncivile wight' (St. 3). Mammon's anti-civil appearance indicates his malign bearing on the world in which gold circulates. When he sees Guyon, Mammon hurriedly pours the gold 'through an hole full wide, | Into the hollow earth' (St. 6), the cavity suggesting both the mine from which the gold was originally extracted and a hiding place.

This first but provisional reaction is repeated by Timon. When he hears the drum of Alcibiades he says to the gold, 'Thou'rt quick; | But yet I'll bury thee' (14.45–6). Both Mammon and Timon soon overcome this purely retentive attitude to their treasure and go on to use the gold to tempt the visitor to enhance his earthly power. Mammon offers Guyon a beguiling vision of wealth and authority, whilst Timon offers Alcibiades the power to strengthen his army so that it can march on Athens and destroy it.

The rude man cloistered in the wild woods surrounded by a mass of gold he has extracted from the earth, which he first hides from a visitor and then uses to tempt him: this is already enough to suggest that Timon is in this scene an iconographical reworking of Spenser's Mammon. Moreover, as a god of riches, Mammon is equivalent of the classical god of riches, Plutus. When in Lucian's dialogue Plutus and the other gods visit Timon in the obscure 'solitary place' where he digs as a common labourer, he accuses Timon in the days of his wealth of 'prostituting me basely to lewd and vile persons that bewitched you with praises so to get me into their fingers'. *Timon of Athens* specifically registers the figure of Plutus and correlates him with Timon. When it is said of Timon in his days of wealth: 'He pours it out. Plutus the god of gold | Is but his steward' (1.279–80), the words recall Spenser: 'I me call, | Great *Mammon*, greatest god below the skye, | That of my plenty poure out vnto all' (St. 8).

Both texts deal with the dangers of wealth, with *Timon of Athens* showing first the corruption of human relationships in a world awash with high living, and then the power of gold to unleash destruction on that same society. *The Faerie Queene*, like *Timon of Athens*, blends expositions based on Paul's 'root of all evil' lines in 1 Timothy and Ovid's account of the Iron Age. Spenser leads towards the full Shakespearian conflation in which the 'root' stands not only for food, not only for riches as a source of evil, but also to gold's own origin in the ground. In Guyon's phrase, riches are 'the roote of all disquietnesse'. As he elaborates:

> Infinite mischiefes of them do arize,
> Strife, and debate, bloudshed, and bitternesse,
> Outrageous wrong, and hellish couetize . . .
>
> (St. 12)

Guyon accuses Mammon, 'But realmes and rulers thou doest both confound' (St. 13), and he moralizes the needlessness of wealth:

> But would they [men] thinke, with how small allowaunce
> Vntroubled Nature doth her selfe suffise,
> Such superfluities they would despise,
> Which with sad cares empeach our natiue ioyes . . .
>
> (St. 15)

He continues his defence against Mammon by retracing the Ovidian fall from the original state of humanity to the age of greed and metal:

> Then gan a cursed hand the quiet wombe
> Of his great Grandmother with steele to wound,
> And the hid treasures in her sacred tombe,
> With Sacriledge to dig. Therein he found
> Fountaines of gold and silver to abound . . .
>
> (St. 17)

Mining the fountains of gold and silver is both violent and sacrilegious, and, as in *Timon of Athens*, is directed against Mother Earth. Human intrusion into the earth is given a specifically gendered and sexualized figuration. The phrase 'Common mother' by which Timon addresses the earth (14.178) means shared female antecedent, as one might speak of Eve as the common mother of humanity, and is virtually synonymous with Spenser's 'great Grandmother'. As Carolyn Merchant has demonstrated, figurations of the earth as a sentient, living being can be traced back to the Stoics, and specifically to Cicero and Seneca.[1] *OED* shows the expression 'mother earth' entering the English language in the late 1580s—Spenser's *Faerie Queene* provides one of the earliest exam-

---

[1] *The Death of Nature* (1982).

ples—but the Latin '*Terra mater*' goes back to antiquity—for example, to Pliny's *Historia naturalis* and to Ovid's *Metamorphoses*. In alchemical belief, it was not only living creatures who owed their origin to the earth. Metals themselves were supposed to grow and to transmute from base to pure within the womb-like ground, fed by mineral juices that flowed through the earth (Merchant, p. 25). Spenser's 'Fountaines of gold and silver' reflects this vitalism, with the metals as it were bleeding from ruptured veins.

Merchant traces a tradition of ethical objection to 'the extraction of the metals from the bowels of the living earth' (p. 30). She cites Pliny, who urged that 'It is what is concealed from our view, what is sunk far beneath her surface, objects, in fact, of no rapid formation, that urge us to our ruin, that send us to the very depths of hell'. Pliny asked, with rhetorical premonition, 'when will be the end of thus exhausting the earth, and to what point will avarice finally penetrate!' Georgius Agricola's *De re mettalica* of 1556 was the standard textbook on metallurgy for two centuries, and along with Ovid evidently a source for Spenser's treatment of Mammon. Agricola contrasted earth as 'a beneficent and kindly mother' who 'yields in large abundance from her bounty and brings into the light of day the herbs, vegetables, grains, and fruits, and trees' with her retentive treatment of minerals, which 'she buries far beneath in the depth of the ground'. He goes on to summarize what might be called the early anti-mining lobby's criticism of the pollution caused by mining operations. Such efforts, in this view, exemplify the extraordinary lengths to which miners go to defeat the earth's purpose of hiding her minerals. Agricola's purpose is, however, to answer these objections: recalling Ovid, he argues that without metals men would 'return to the acorns and fruits and berries of the forest'—for Agricola, clearly an undesirable development.[1]

Pre-eminent among early modern representations of miners is the descendant of Spenser's Mammon, Satan's follower Mammon in *Paradise Lost*. Alastair Fowler notes that Milton 'had a special admiration for Spenser's account of the Cave of Mammon', and the passage influenced Milton's account on Mammon in *Paradise Lost* following 1.684. In this, perhaps the best early modern poetic description of mining, Milton claims that mankind 'Rifled the bowels of their mother earth | For treasures better hid' in imitation

---

[1] Quoted from Merchant, p. 34.

of Mammon and his followers who 'digged out ribs of gold' as they started to build Pandaemonium. The line from Spenser to Milton confirms that Mammon is not only a devil but also a miner, and that mining itself is an act of violence against mother earth motivated by pride and greed. Within this tradition, Timon stands as a representative of humanity's problematic relationship with the ecology, an instance of the man who tries to escape the effects of the Iron Age only to find that he too is a digger and a miner. He is, in effect, a self-moralizing picture. The instability of his words can be understood not only in terms of his psychological make-up: he speaks as reductive and emblematic image of man as miner and abuser of earth's riches, and he speaks also as commentator on that very image.

From another point of view the scene in *Timon of Athens* reworks another digging scene, the gravediggers' scene in *Hamlet*. Here too we find the device of using the trapdoor in the stage floor to represent an opening in the earth which is also a profound opening into fundamental questions of human existence. Here too the earth yields symptomatic objects—not gold but the skulls of dead men. Each class of object becomes the focus for each play's examination of human life in relation to an Other—death in *Hamlet*, feminized nature in *Timon of Athens*. Both scenes investigate the idea of material recirculation between things buried in the earth, and living, social humanity. Both scenes meditate on topics traditional in sermons and in secular literature: the *memento mori* in *Hamlet*, and in *Timon of Athens*—as in Chaucer's 'Pardoner's Tale', where the gold is buried at the roots of a tree—the moralization on the destructiveness of riches. Both scenes are penultimate: if not literally, at least figuratively so. They stand at just one remove from the main character's final encounter with death. All this stems from the stage device itself, the rupture of surface that takes the actor's body wholly or partly below the stage, meaning into the ground, and then out again, a sequence with few parallels in the drama of the period.[1] Timon, like Hamlet, is aware that we are all in a sense merely borrowed from the earth. He strongly anticipates his own burial; he depicts the earth yielding deadly creatures and producing metal for the instruments of death.

---

[1] This is not the tragicomic motif of supposed death and later 'resurrection' as, for example, in *Winter's Tale* and *Chaste Maid*. A closer analogy is the pit in *Titus Andronicus* 2.3, which also happens to be associated with hidden gold.

The specific quality of the scene in *Timon of Athens* is that it correlates this borrowing and stealing from the earth with the idea of economic man. In Timon's mind at this stage in the play, borrowing is simply a euphemism for theft, and indeed all motion and exchange including the functions of nature are forms of robbery: he charges that even 'The sun's a thief' (14.436). This draws on the traditional theory of correspondence between the earthly and the heavenly, whilst presenting a shocking challenge to the view that the heavens are orderly and constant. In *Troilus and Cressida* Ulysses contrasts the weakly commanded Greek army with the orderliness of the heavens: 'the glorious planet Sol | In noble eminence enthroned and sphered' has a 'med'cinable eye' that 'Corrects the ill aspects of planets evil' (1.3.89–92). Timon, in contrast, finds no reproof of human disorder in the heavens. Either a lawless heaven shapes human lawlessness, or, just as disturbing, the influence flows in the reverse direction from earth to the heavens. In either case, Timon finds examples in nature that are illustrative of his thesis, so demonstrating its general truth. This is the strategy not only of the sermon writer, but also of the Renaissance paradox writer who seeks by ingenious arguments to demonstrate the truth of unlikely or even impossible propositions.[1] Timon—or rather, his vision of humanity—reinvents nature to put it on the wrong side of the human laws engraved in brass.

Timon as the Mammon-like gatekeeper regulating the flow of riches from the earth to humanity indulges in ironized forms of gift-giving, using gold as a product of corrupted nature. As in the first half of the play, giving destroys him. The excess of invective, and the excess of angry extraction from the earth, drain his will to live. The gold is taken (without the advice that goes with it), and Timon is left quite literally exhausted. Though he pays for the destruction of Athens that will not happen, he stays aloof from humanity and turns to death. So the play seals up the wounded earth with Timon's body in it, and allows the crisis of thought about the Iron Age uneasily to subside as the warriors, the lawmakers, and the merchant capitalists come back into alignment with each other and make friends.

[1] Guillaume de Saluste Du Bartas's *Divine Weeks and Works* (1605) reprints Odet de la Noue's 'Paradoxe que les adversitez sont plus necessaires que les prosperités' (paradox that adversities are more valuable than prosperities). Thomas Dekker and George Wilkins's *Jests to Make You Merry* (1607) conatains 'a paradox in praise of sergeants'.

The point at which Timon's invectives are quite startlingly modern is where he sees earth's imagined infertility as a direct consequence of humankind's misuse of her produce. The story of the vengeful god who destroys humanity for its wickedness goes back at least as far as the Book of Genesis, but in this respect too *Timon of Athens* has a modern take on the story, substituting the male and controlling figure of Jehovah with the feminine earth, generous by nature, and merely reactive when not so. This is different too from *King Lear*, where Lear calls on the instruments of the male Jove, thunder and lightning, to 'Smite flat the thick rotundity o'th' world', so that the natural storm becomes an image of God punishing the earth. It is different again from the Christian masterplans of Spenser and Milton, where the sins of the Iron Age will ultimately be punished and the virtuous will be saved. Timon's vision is without redemption, and without much evidence of masculine deity.

Shakespeare's characterization of all his tragic heroes depends on their assaulting the audience with attitudes and behaviours that oscillate violently between the empathetic and the disgusting. In the case of Timon, a harmonization of response to their various utterances is the last thing we should look for. To put the matter in theological terms, Shakespeare's characters take shape at points of intersection between grace and despair, and Timon is Shakespeare's most despairing character. It is no small grace in him that in his very despair he articulates something of value about the Iron Age.

Friends

When he imitates Mammon, becoming the uncouth solitary man who rejects human society, Timon's self-abasement contrasts with the early modern social case of the gentleman who retires from the city to his country seat. Equally, he differs from the literary type of the contemplative or melancholic man of solitude, such as Jaques in *As You Like It*.[1] And yet, like the retired country gentleman, and like Jaques in another forest, Timon paradoxically intermixes with his friends. It is this that places his discovery of gold within the Iron-Age world of economic life, and it is this that sustains him as social man, never quite a god or a beast.

---

[1] Compare Janette Dillon, *Shakespeare and the Solitary Man* (1981).

Aristotle suggests that people need each other in order to maintain civil and economic life, but also that they stay together because social life is a benefit in itself. One of the classical texts both Shakespeare and Middleton would probably have encountered at school was Cicero's *De amicitia*, 'On Friendship'.[1] Here is a source for some of the key ideas in the play. Cicero quotes the Roman tragedian Ennius as saying 'Where Fortune's fickle the true friend is found', a comment interpreted in its most sceptical meaning in the depiction of Lady Fortune in Sc. 1 and in the whole sequence of the play's events thereafter. Anticipating Timon's communitarian ethic of friendship, he writes, 'As, therefore, in friendship, those who are superior should lower themselves, so, in a measure, should they lift up their inferiors'. Timon similarly refers to one's duty to 'help the feeble up' (1.109), though he neglects the qualification 'in a measure'. On generosity to friends Cicero says, 'Now, in the first place, you must render to each friend as much as you can', but this statement is also qualified, here by an interrogation of the meaning of true friendship that would debar Timon's beneficiaries in the first half of the play.

Cicero mentions Timon of Athens, commenting that 'even such a man could not refrain from seeking some person before whom he might pour out the venom of his embittered soul'.[2] The second half of the play provides Timon with just such opportunities. His friends, whether false or true, are presented twice over. In the early scenes Timon stakes all on friendship as something of substance and plenitude, and as a source of meaning for the world he shapes around him. Yet, though affable and courteous, he remains reserved, sometimes unexpectedly silent, failing to strike convincingly resonant bonds of friendship with anyone. In the woods he becomes articulate, covering a range of highly charged issues including his relationships with his friends, but now the feelings he expresses are overwhelmingly hostile.

The following sections will review these dramatic roles and their interaction with Timon. They will be considered not simply as

[1] This work lies behind Bacon's essay of the same title in which, in the 1625 revised version, he was to cite Aristotle's *Politics*. Another text influencing the play is Montaigne's essay 'Of Friendship': see commentary to 6.71 and 14.3–6.

[2] Quotations from Cicero, *De senectute, De amicitia, De divinatione*, with English trans. by William Armistead Falkner (Cambridge, Mass., and London, 1959), pp. 175, 181, 182–3, and 195.

representations of persons, but as bearers of historical or mythical allusion (as prominently with Alcibiades), as figures that belong to literary or dramatic traditions (Apemantus), or as examples of socially or culturally significant types (Steward, Painter)—and also as key constituents of the play as dramatic action. In the background are the minor Athenian roles with their generally Latin names and their split connotations of the contemporary Renaissance ('lords' who wear hats and gowns and watch masques) and the Roman ('senators' in a city state without a monarch). The vantage point will be the core scene, Sc. 14, where in slow pageant each of the 'friends' has his fullest dialogue with Timon in the entire play.

Alcibiades, Apemantus, and the Steward are all almost as isolated from Athenian society themselves as is Timon, and they are even more isolated from each other; but each has already formed a specific if limited relationship with Timon.[1] Now Timon is presented with the evidence of actual friendship that potentially confutes his universal hatred. As these three major dialogues progress, Timon's posture towards humanity is placed under increasing pressure as he engages in effectual conversation and communication of a kind not seen earlier in the play. He faces, therefore, a temptation not to hate. His difficult resistance to that temptation provides the dramatic mainspring to the sequence. If he needs any reinforcement of his beleaguered beliefs, the whores, bandits, Poet and Painter, and senators provide it.

Alcibiades

In Plutarch's 'Life of Alcibiades', he is a young, volatile, beautiful warrior, a womanizer, and the friend and lover of Socrates. He is also a special friend of Timon, who is said to have 'kissed him very gladly' when banqueting him. Plutarch describes him as having spoken with a 'fat lisping tongue', in a way that gave him 'a certain natural pleasant grace' (p. 211). His homoerotic relationship with Socrates was well known to early modern writers; both Edmund Spenser and Christopher Marlowe refer to it.[2] The play gives only a

---

[1] As noted by Honigmann.

[2] Spenser's note on 'January', l. 59, *Shepheardes Calender*, in *Poetical Works*, ed. J. C. Smith and E. de Selincourt (1912), pp. 422–3; Marlowe, *Edward II* 1.4.391–7; as noted by Newman (see p. 27 n. 1).

sketchy impression of this figure, perhaps because the source was scarcely consulted, but perhaps also because the play was able to offer no more than hints about homosexual conduct. Alcibiades is impetuous and lustful perhaps, and his entry in Sc. 2 allows a potential opportunity for homoerotic display, but any such characteristics can only be brought out in the staging.

If Alcibiades has importance, it is signified by his 'companionship' or retinue (1.245) and the paraphernalia of war, including loud military music and, later in the play, camp followers. In the early scenes he has strikingly little to say. It is only in Sc. 10 that Alcibiades first takes a positive role in the action, now in solo confrontation with the senate. The account of the soldier and friend who has committed murder, which has no basis in the sources, has often been criticized for its lack of connection to the play. It provides the strongest instance of the embryonic nature of the Alcibiades plot-line, engaging as it does with issues of which the audience has no knowledge. Thus even when Alcibiades becomes eloquent there remains something unexplained about him. One might suspect that the play is still dealing obliquely with the topic of homoeroticism. Alcibiades is insolently passionate about his friend, extragavant in his arguments, and emotionally excessive in resolving to wage war on Athens in revenge for the senate's rejection of his plea and banishment of him. The Second Senator's account of the soldier's crime uses some ambiguous language that can be imagined to apply in an altered context to a judicial condemnation of homosexual acts: 'He's a sworn rioter; he has a sin | That often drowns him and takes his valour prisoner . . . In that beastly fury | He has been known to commit outrages' (10.66–70). These are mere clues, but they help to explain the text's lack of explanation.

Even allowing for the possibility that homoeroticism is treated allusively, it remains difficult to understand why the matter dramatized in earlier scenes should not supply the germs of the motive for Alcibiades' revolt. It has been plausibly argued that this scene, by Middleton, reflects a different perception of Alcibiades' role in the play from that seen in Shakespeare's episodes.[1] Shakespeare made Alcibiades a revenger on behalf of Timon, whereas Middleton made him a rebel against Athens for grievances of his own. According to the Shakespearian trajectory, if Alcibiades were

[1] Delius and Wright, as in p. 134 n. 1 below. See Vickers, *Co-Author*, pp. 474–7.

to have appealed to the senate it should have been on behalf of Timon himself rather than a riotous soldier who makes no appearance in the play. The senate scene has proved to be the most difficult discontinuity in the Folio text for both critics and performers.[1]

At first sight the case for conflict between authors is compromised by the dialogue in Shakespeare's Sc. 14, where Alcibiades claims to know nothing of the supposed wrongs Timon has suffered. A warrior up in arms on Timon's behalf would not need to ask 'How came the noble Timon to this change?' (14.66). Alcibiades' apparent ignorance of Timon's plight is, however, partly revoked when he says, ten lines later, 'I have heard in some sort of thy miseries'. Particular significance must therefore be attached to Holdsworth's judgement of Timon's answer to Alcibiades' question at l. 66; he describes it as 'The only occasion where I can find close links with Middleton outside the Middleton sections'.[2] If the question and answer were inserted by Middleton, they would establish some degree of consistency between this passage and the senate scene, in which Alcibiades' revolt against Athens has nothing to do with Timon, and Middleton establishes a strong but different motivation.

Sc. 10 suggests marked thematic parallels between Timon and Alcibiades. Alcibiades' rage at the senate's ingratitude is closely equivalent to the rage Timon directs against the city, including its senators, which is also provoked by ingratitude. The debts to Alcibiades, as he defines them, are moral obligations, but that is true also of Timon. The conflict between Timon's financial debts and the moral obligations of his friends is precisely the issue that has been dramatized in the scenes immediately before Sc. 10. Both characters are traumatically rejected in their petitions. Both experience extreme alienation from the city in which they had shone as eccentric luminaries. Both verbally manipulate their rejection so as to claim that it is they themselves who reject Athens. Alcibiades' words have application to Timon's resolve to hate Athens and see it destroyed: 'It comes not ill; I hate not to be banished. | It is a cause worthy my spleen and fury, | That I may strike at Athens' (10.110–12). Both leave the city to pursue campaigns of hatred against it. In Sc. 14 Shakespeare may have made Alcibiades the first

---

[1] See p. 115.

[2] See commentary. Holdsworth also notes *Love's Labour's Lost* 5.2.211–14, but the parallel is less close.

of Timon's visitors for reasons of rank, or in anticipation of his role at the end of the play, but the parallels generated by Middleton point to the same arrangement.

The event immediately before Alcibiades' arrival is Timon's discovery of gold, the 'common whore of mankind, that puts odds | Among the rout of nations' (14.43–4). When he extracts the gold to 'make thee | Do thy right nature', he seems to lack any prospect of implementing this plan to use the wealth to put odds among the rout of nations. But as soon as he says these words, the off-stage drum beats as if on cue. Timon can only admire the gold's 'quick' potency. It is part of the magical rhythm of the play itself that Timon's words should function in a kind of mystical dialogue with some ironically-minded outer force, whether we understand it to be the hand of the dramatists or a twisted version of fate.

The opportunity for a military spectacle in the warrior's entry can lead to an idealized stage picture (see below, pp. 115–17). The moment offers a vivid contrast between the purposeful soldier marching with his army to the sound of military music and the solitary, impotent curser. Yet Alcibiades' aim to reduce proud Athens to a heap (14.101) is similar to the punishments Timon expresses in purely verbal rhetoric. As the dialogue develops Alcibiades pities the fall of 'noble' and 'brave' Timon, but he himself suffers a loss of dignity as his mercenary mistresses upstage him. His confession that his soldiers are revolting for want of pay adds to a less than glorious picture.

Timon is quick to correlate warfare with the power to destroy he imagines or invests in Phrynia and Timandra: 'This fell whore of thine | Hath in her more destruction than thy sword' (61–2). Alcibiades tries to raise 'noble Timon' to a higher level of discourse, but Timon's speeches return insistently to the women. Alcibiades is '*warlike*' but compromisingly 'held with a brace of harlots'. The presence of soldiers and prostitutes offers Timon an assurance that he can project his fantasies of destruction on to Athens and make them real. But the vision of sexual and military terror lies in Timon's thoughts only. Phrynia and Timandra treat the verbal assault on them as a kind of sexual perversion on Timon's part: they will tolerate listening if he will pay, a sure token that though they hear the 'counsel' they will not respect it. Alcibiades implies a friendship that can be expressed at all only in the circumstances of this passing and accidental encounter, made both more and less possible by the events that have befallen both, enabled and delimited by the framing stage picture of the paraphernalia of war. He also accepts gold. Though he later mentions Timon's wrongs as part of his cause, his purposes seem unaltered by his meeting with Timon, and Timon's cherished vision of the razed city will not be realized.

Apemantus

Apemantus has been seen as an older man and a voice of admonition. An engraving in the 1773 text of Richard Cumberland's version pictured the text of 'There's a medlar for thee; eat it' (14.306) by showing a bearded philosopher in Greek-style robes. Byam Shaw illustrated the 1902 Chiswick edition with a drawing of Apemantus' grace in Sc. 2 in which he stands, again bearded and robed, with folded arms and a quizically stern expression.[1] These images present Apemantus as a wryly ironic philosopher whose secular sermonizing engages with Timon, but whose lessons Timon fails to learn.

The list of roles in the First Folio describes him as a 'churlish philosopher'. The phrase may owe more to a scribe such as Ralph Crane than to Shakespeare or Middleton. It might reflect early performances, if such there were, and it certainly echoes Timon's own comment at 2.26, 'thou'rt a churl'. He first enters in Sc. 2, where the entry direction spells out his conspicuous refusal of companionship: '*Then comes, dropping after all, Apemantus, discontentedly, like himself*'. Robert Weimann has noted how the apparently tautologous phrase 'like himself' sets up an implied contrast with the other friends, who for their part put on ceremonial airs and graces, as Timon chides them for doing at l. 15.[2] The staging resembles many stage productions of Hamlet's first entry, with the anti-festive character holding himself back from the general celebrations in hand. As Weimann explains, Apemantus belongs to the stage-picture yet is marginal to it; he sits at a separate table (it should perhaps be placed closer to the audience than the main one), and he addresses the audience without the others hearing him. During the masque, as he delivers a scathing critique of the

---

[1] For these two depictions, see Butler, plates IV and IX.
[2] *Author's Pen and Actor's Voice* (Cambridge, 2000), p. 209.

spectacle as an emblem of Timon's folly, his behaviour becomes more aggressively antisocial.

Apemantus' cynic philosophy here leads him into stubborn rudeness and self-isolation. As he assigns him a separate table, Timon says that he is a 'churl' and that his behaviour 'Does not become a man' (2.26–7). His view that Apemantus is of base origin is confirmed forcibly and at length later in the play (14.250–77). Samuel Johnson's note on the play in his edition agrees, and William Hazlitt refers to Apemantus' 'lurking selfishness'.[1] He is called a dog almost whenever he appears on stage. He implies his own currishness when he imagines changing places with Timon so that Timon will be 'Timon's dog' at 1.185. The Painter is soon insulting him 'You're a dog' (1.204), and a lord calls him 'unpeaceable dog' at 1.274. At 4.48 Isidore's Servant joins the fray, as at 4.82–3 does the Page. Timon's turn comes at 14.252, where he describes Apemantus as 'bred a dog'. The hint has been taken up by actors in more recent productions: in 1965 at the Royal Shakespeare Theatre, Paul Rogers played Apemantus as 'a snarling old dog who occasionally shows his rotten teeth in a grin'.[2]

As was well known in the Renaissance, the word 'cynic' literally means 'dog-like', referring to the allegedly barking, whining, or howling tone of the philosophy. In John Marston's 'A Cynic Satire', the cynic is addressed as a 'currish mad Athenian, | Thou cynic dog'.[3] Marston's *Scourge of Villainy*, in which the poem appears, is an example of the prose satires that flourished a few years before *Timon of Athens* was written, before they were banned in 1599. Middleton himself wrote *Microcynicon*, with its canine subtitle *Six Snarling Satires*. Apemantus is typical of the stage figures who emerged after the banning of prose satire, as the writers found other outlets for the venting of spleen. He harks back in particular to the abusive cynic Malevole who has a fool's sanction to rail in Marston's *The Malcontent* (1603), with the difference that Malevole turns out to be a deposed duke in disguise, whereas Apemantus turns out to be, according to Timon, of base origin. *The Malcontent* is unique amongst extant plays in that it was written for performance by a boys' company but was subsequently appropriated by the King's Men; it therefore imports the cynic mode into the

---

[1] Quoted in Bate, ed., p. 542.   [2] Review in *The Times*, 2 July 1965.
[3] In *Works*, ed. A. H. Bullen, 3 vols. (1887), iii. 344.

repertory of the adult company for which *Timon of Athens* was written.

The satirists who turned to writing drama could look back to John Lyly's *Campaspe* of 1581, where the Greek philosopher Diogenes is presented as a cynic. *Campaspe* had been performed by the Children of the Chapel Royal, one of an earlier generation of boys' companies.[1] In this play, Diogenes is identified as a cynic in the same way as Apemantus, as 'dog' (1.2.8, 2.1.8), and he turns the tables by claiming to seek 'For a man and a beast' (2.1.10). In accordance with classical accounts, Lyly's character inhabits a tub as a protest against society, rising from it to rail on his visitors from the court of Alexander. Hazlitt noted that 'The soul of Diogenes appears to have been seated on the lips of Apemantus'.[2] Diogenes was renowned as a free-thinking and fearless critic of riches and luxury. As Apemantus jokes about the absurdity of seeking an honest Athenian (1.196–8), Diogenes was depicted carrying a lantern in his pointedly vain search for an honest Athenian. Apemantus' preference for eating roots in Sc. 2 is borrowed from Diogenes, whose diet of roots is mentioned, for example, in Stephen Gosson's *Ephemerides of Philao* (1579), in a passage that clearly influenced *Timon of Athens*.[3]

By Sc. 14, however, tables appear to have turned so that the soul of Apemantus sits on Timon's lips. At least, Apemantus thinks so: 'Men report | Thou dost affect my manners, and dost use them' (199–200). If we think of Apemantus as a Diogenes figure, it is a fair criticism. An anonymous and undated work of the period called *A Dialogue between Lucian and Diogenes* presents a debate between Lucian and Diogenes as representatives of two contrasted modes of satire. It is Diogenes who, like Timon, leads a subsistence life in the wilds, where 'I need little and use not many things' and it looks as though 'I lead a beastly life'.[4] When Lucian urges making the most of what God and Nature provide, Diogenes claims that his lifestyle brings him closer to the condition of the gods than other humans. Timon has taken over Apemantus' earlier Diogenes role, along with his preference for roots. Apemantus now corresponds with the *Dialogue*'s more sociable Lucian. It is now his function to persuade Timon, in vain, to take a moderate view, and to 'mend

[1] Bullough prints passages from *Campaspe* as a 'Possible Source' (pp. 339–45).
[2] Quoted in Bate, ed., p. 541.   [3] See commentary to 2.97–8.
[4] STC 16894, p. 7.

thy feast', and he himself evidently now has better fare than roots in his picnic.

In this role, Apemantus brings out the difference between being a cynic and a hater of humanity. Lyly's Diogenes says: 'Ye term me an hater of men; no, I am a hater of your manners' (*Campaspe* 4.1.29–30). This is true of Apemantus too, and his phrase 'affect my manners' reflects his own perception of behaviour as a matter of alterable surface. He was always, after all, more at home in Timon's house than, say, Hamlet was in the court of Claudius: in Joan Rees's phrase, 'comfortably domesticated'.[1] Timon, in contrast, becomes the undomesticated self-declared hater of men, and of women, seeing humanity as utterly depraved beyond the transient realm of manners. It is a philosophy involving total commitment, whereas Apemantus can enjoy a cooler, more rational and perhaps bemused detachment, as in János Kulka's performance of the role (Illustration 6).

The actor Richard McCabe as Apemantus in Doran's 1999 production arrived in the woods with sunshades and a hamper of food, very clearly the city boy on holiday who was unused to roughing it in the wilds.[1] Apemantus' consistency lies perhaps in his function of criticizing whatever he finds, and especially of criticizing Timon. In the city he commends the root; in the woods he commends the civil life where there is 'use for gold'. His pragmatic preference for a bed at night is a trait he shares with the Fool in *King Lear*.

As a debate about ideas, the episode considers what it is that makes a misanthrope. Timon attributes it to his experience of fall from high fortune. He derides Apemantus as an upstart of base parentage, born miserable and naturally vicious, and so incapable of nobility. The satirical dog-philosopher is a fool-like attendant on the households of the great. This account falters in so far as Apemantus does not seem to be rewarded in any material way for his presence at Timon's great banquet; he even brings his own food. Timon's attempt to dignify himself stands on shaky ground here. But the episode is not so much a rational debate as a dramatic and bitterly comic exploration of friendship-denial. Whether properly anguished or self-indulgent to the point of faint humour, Timon clings on to his sense of higher grief, and finally expels Apemantus like a dog.

[1] *Shakespeare and the Story: Aspects of Creation* (1978), p. 131.
[2] On McCabe's performance, see also below, p. 114.

For his part, Apemantus, finding Timon adopting the role of a railer, responds in two ways. He exposes Timon's higher cynicism as a kind of fraud in order to pull him back from the brink. He also engages in what sociolinguists and students of authorship attribution call 'accommodation', in that his own mode of utterance becomes correspondingly similar to that of his interlocutor, a phenomenon that can be observed too in Othello's language as he responds to the corrosive presence of Iago. In his satire against the society of trees at 14.222–32 Apemantus speaks more lyrically than could have been imagined from his earlier speeches, and in his correlation of nature and social life he echoes Timon's own deliberations. As a result there is, despite the mutual insult-slinging, a consonance between the two figures. It is a consonance of opposition, with Apemantus satirizing Timon's life as a recluse and Timon railing against the baseness underlying Apemantus' hostility to society. But it is also a consonance of interchange, in which Timon turns railer and Apemantus turns lyricist.

What binds them together is their shared participation in a mode of speech aimed at differentiation. Their exchanges of insult express bare rage, but teeter between almost erotically intense reciprocation and slapstick comedy, the antagonists hurling abuse like fighting lovers or children: 'Beast!', 'Slave!', 'Toad!', 'Rogue'. This last Timon utters three times as he collapses exhausted into 'I am sick of this false world . . .' (14.376). Compared with the quarrel between Brutus and Cassius in *Julius Caesar* this is rough caricature, but the emotional rhythms and energies are not far distant.

Timon's withdrawal from dialogue with Apemantus after this exchange is strongly marked but not final. He thinks of death as though he would speak no more to any human: 'Lie where the light foam of the sea may beat | Thy gravestone daily' (14.379–80). The line echoes William Painter, whose account suggests the emphasis Timon's words have: 'By his last will he ordained himself to be interred upon the sea shore, that the waves and surges might beat and vex his dead carcass'. But this is not quite Timon's last will, or at least not his last words. The sight of the gold reanimates his hatred, and provides Apemantus with his opportunity to re-enter the dialogue. By extending the exchange to this coda Shakespeare suggests some measure of complexity in the dynamic between Timon and Apemantus. It also provides the key for the rest of the scene, by setting in opposition Timon's death-wish with Apemantus' warning that, punishingly, there will be visitors to keep him alive: 'Thou wilt be thronged to shortly' (14.395).

Thieves

There is some doubt as to the sequence of the following episodes, or at least as to Shakespeare's original design for the scene, if a stable design there was. At 14.351 Apemantus taunts Timon by observing 'Yonder comes a poet and a painter'. Yet these figures fail to appear until almost two hundred lines later. Holdsworth's diagnosis that Middleton wrote the Steward episode (ll. 458–536, ending immediately before the Poet and Painter enter) opens up the possibility that it was Middleton who changed the sequence. This turns out to be likely (see pp. 148–9).

The almost comic-operatic eruption of the *Banditti* or thieves on to the stage is perhaps all the more effective because it is unpredictable. The episode might be considered an epilogue to the visit of Alcibiades. They are his former soldiers, now revolted for lack of pay. It is ironic that by the time they arrive Timon has supplied Alcibiades with the wealth that would have kept them loyal to his cause.

The cornerstone of the episode is Timon's magnificent speech identifying theft as the unifying principle of the universe. Timon succumbs to the 'pathetic fallacy', imposing a view of the natural world to accord with feelings that have nothing immediately to do with nature's behaviour. He pictures the sun as a thief not because it intrinsically is so, but because it gives universal validity to his view of humanity. This attitude follows logically from his soliloquy about mother earth spoken immediately after Alcibiades leaves. Here too the initial substance is humanity, 'ingrateful man', but the speech develops its own poetic impetus by relating this subject to the immediate elements of Timon's solitary existence. The difference in the speech to the Thieves is that Timon has actual men to address. He speaks a sermon, as it were, on the theme of an imagined anti-Commandment, 'Thou shalt steal'. 'I'll example you with thievery', he says as he launches into his justificatory account of theft in nature. The speech ends with an anti-moral admonition and an anti-blessing, 'Steal less for this I give you | And gold confound you howsoe'er', and then 'Amen' (14.448–9). The religious connotations could not be clearer, and Timon almost wins a convert too: 'I'll believe him as an enemy, and give over my trade'. This is darkly comic business. Could there be a nugatory hint that one of the thieves might be saved as in Luke 23: 43? It is not implausible, and the idea is perhaps echoed also in the repentance of one of the murderers of Clarence in *Richard III* 1.4. Timon's own aim, however, is nothing to do with salvation. He wants the thieves to add to the military efforts of Alcibiades and the sexual efforts of his whores in wrecking Athens.

Steward

The Steward may, like Apemantus, be a representative of an older generation, as was the case with John Woodvine's solid and dignified performance in the 1999 Stratford-upon-Avon production. Despite the role's affinities with Kent in *King Lear*, it seems to have been developed mainly by Middleton. He stands between Timon and his lesser servants, who in turn stand between Timon and his creditors. He is a figure of integrity whose function within Timon's household as 'Steward' is more significant than his personal name of 'Flavius'. As noted above (p. 50), 'Steward' as a spelling variant of 'Stuart' provokes the dangerous possibility that the figure in the play represents qualities of financial prudence conspicuously lacking in King James. By a similar inversion of significance, the loyal Steward in *Timon of Athens* ironically echoes Christ's parable of the Unjust Steward.

The parable, reprinted in Appendix B, is notoriously difficult to interpret. At face value Christ seems to praise the steward's dishonesty, and simultaneously to commend and disparage the worship of Mammon: 'make you friends of the unrighteous Mammon . . . ye cannot serve God and Mammon'. The biblical steward is accused of wasting his master's goods, but redeems himself by calling in his master's debtors and telling them to reduce the repayments. It is unclear why they agree, or what effect it has; one conjectural possibility is that the steward has lent out his master's wealth at high rates of interest but with repayment in kind, and that he reduces the debts either as an act of merit or to secure their repayment. Whatever the nature of the steward's success, it restores him to the favour of his master. In *Timon of Athens* the unjust steward becomes just, the debtors become creditors, the successful ploy becomes unsuccessful, and the steward's thought 'I cannot dig' foreshadows his master's digging in the woods. Where the biblical parable leads to the well known text 'ye cannot serve God and Mammon', Timon's digging, as established already, recalls a Spenserian version of Mammon.

The inverted analogies and the New Testament background return us to a theme already introduced, the inverted analogy between Christ as God of love and Timon as self-sacrificing hater of mankind. Here, then, we pick up once more Ken Jackson's exposition (see above, pp. 35–6). For Jackson, the problems of the motivated gift and the unattainability of the gift absolute are resolved precisely in the Steward's visit to Timon in Sc. 14. Timon sees the possibility of motivated generosity in asking 'Is not thy kindness subtle, covetous . . .?' The Steward replies:

> My most honoured lord,
> For any benefit that points to me,
> Either in hope or present, I'd exchange
> For this one wish: that you had power and wealth
> To requite me by making rich yourself.
>
> (14.517–21)

This repeats the Stranger's offer to help Timon at 6.76–85, without the Stranger's qualifying and deactivating 'Had his necessity made use of me'. Nevertheless, there is no immediate prospect of the wish being fulfilled. The Steward, unlike the Stranger, actually is poor. The fantasy of the enriched Steward making himself poor so that Timon can be returned to wealth is also impossible for the reason Jackson cites, that Timon is already in possession of riches. Timon's 'Look thee, 'tis so' seems to say that the wish has come true, but it has done so without any gift-exchange at all.

Jackson takes this paradox as a token of the Derridean impossibility of the absolute gift. Yet the Steward has already acted altruistically in the scene immediately preceding Timon's appearance in the woods, where he distributes his last money to the servants under his authority, reserving only what he intends to give to Timon. This does not greatly enrich the servants because the money is so little, and the script is written so that the servants express no gratitude beyond the communal embrace shared by giver and receivers alike. The Steward describes them all as 'rich in sorrow'. It may be that this sacrificial sharing of gold is, symbolically, a prerequisite for Timon's discovery of gold. More certainly, it is a moment of altruism that strongly challenges Jackson's argument that it can be achieved only at the point where it is impossible. Here the play shows not so much a moment of contact with the religious 'utterly other' as a direct, humdrum, effectual, and symbolically potent moment of altruistic charity.

Poet and Painter

Timon's last visitors in the woods are the characters who open the play, the Poet and Painter. Their first dialogue in Sc. 1 is sophisticated, swift and vivid in sketching a society with its own discursive and poetic idiolect. Here, conversation is conditioned by an awareness of art, wealth, and power; art is conditioned by an awareness of wealth and power. Patronage is the defining contingency, colouring every utterance with the need to praise and the knowledge that insincerity is part of the condition of life. Fortune is the deity, but her clambering votarists cannot be distinguished from the anxious flatterers who 'Rain sacrificial whisperings' in Timon's ear.

The opening debate about art is therefore cryptically poised between an intellectual exchange of ideas and a vying for place at Timon's court. 'Magic of bounty' is both the artists' subject-matter and the air they breathe in their occupations. Their dialogue relates the play to Renaissance debates about artistic representation and its relation to nature, and on the merits of poetry versus painting, in the Renaissance tradition of the 'paragone'.[1] But it is constrained by the vanity of patron-seeking. Art, in their dialogue, finds no resting place between sycophancy and satire.

Their approaches to art are not identical. The Painter's work, to judge by the Poet's appreciation of it, idealizes its subject, who is presumably Timon:

> Admirable. How this grace
> Speaks his own standing! What a mental power
> This eye shoots forth! How big imagination
> Moves in this lip! To th' dumbness of the gesture
> One might interpret.

$$(1.30-4)$$

---

[1] Literally 'comparison'. See John Dixon Hunt, 'Shakespeare and the Paragone: A Reading of *Timon of Athens*', in *Images of Shakespeare*, ed. Werner Habicht, D. J. Palmer, and Roger Pringle (Newark, Del., and London, 1988), 47–63.

The Poet's approach to his own work is both wordy and nuanced. Poetry is generated autonomously; the poet defends the integrity of his 'free drift'. Warming to his theme, he immediately goes on to relate Timon to his account of Lady Fortune bestowing good fortune, with a warning that there comes a time when Fortune 'Spurns down her late belovèd'. He implies that his own work is satirical, making the standard but always troublesome apology, recently rehearsed by Jonson, that satire is levelled against humanity in general rather than particular persons.[1]

The Poet claims to be a critic of the world he sees, and up to a point the pair speak a framing introductory chorus like the Romans Demetrius and Philo in the opening scene of *Antony and Cleopatra*. But they are also seekers of patronage themselves, and so, unlike the Romans, they belong entirely to that world. Any claim they have to represent the moral of the play is accordingly compromised. The Poet has sounded the keynote of the play, as it were with personal disinterest and moral fervour; yet his claim not to have any person in mind when depicting Fortune's rejection of her favourite is clearly disingenuous, and the Poet too will present himself and his work to Timon, seeking favour from the man whose destruction he has depicted. The Poet is no Apemantus and, from the standpoint of Apemantus' gritty cynicism, he is simply a liar.

The Poet and Painter might appear mannered and amusingly camp in the opening scene, but they are, as Nuttall notes, 'not so much talking persons as walking texts, speaking pictures' (p. 16). Nuttall refers to the 'ecphrasistic' mode whereby the play emphasizes its own artificiality. But when the Poet and Painter visit Timon in the woods, stripped of their congenial social setting, they, more than any other visitors, seem to have deteriorated, or to have had their calculating self-interest most plainly exposed. This scene is committed to an emotionally engaged representation of Timon, and one might conclude that the ecphrastic mode has by this stage collapsed.

The episode offers some limited vindication of Timon's view of the Athenians. Placed as it is, it comes too late for other visitors to suggest afterwards a more encouraging picture. Timon's ironic contempt seems appropriate. After baiting the Poet and Painter he drives them away by throwing stones. He sardonically challenges

---

[1] *Poetaster*, 'Apologetic Dialogue', l. 72.

one of the artists to 'make gold of that', implicitly repeating Apemantus' earlier charge that the Poet's translations of the truth into art make him a liar. The stone-throwing disturbs Bradbrook: 'What is Shakespeare doing to himself?' (p. 27). One might be uncomfortably reminded of the poet Cinna, torn apart by a mob of plebeians in *Julius Caesar* 3.3. The Poet in *Timon of Athens* has turned out to be no admirable or even neutral representative of his craft, though it might be recalled that Shakespeare's and Middleton's art too inhabited the market place.

Four Words, Three Epitaphs

Shakespeare's tragic heroes usually die on stage and talking.[1] In contrast, Timon's withdrawal from society finds its strongest expression in his withdrawal from the stage itself. The pageant of well-willers and self-seekers in Sc. 14 might be compared with Renaissance rituals of death as a public event, but the linear construction of the scene makes any equivalent of the gathering of family and friends around the dying man impossible. Instead, it leads to his death in solitude, which, especially by early modern criteria, is another token of the beast-like quality of his existence in the woods.

Being unseen, Timon's going from the world is left an enigma. It is entirely unclear whether he commits suicide, wills himself to die, or is overcome by the privations of life in the wild. Yet as the sequence of Timon in the woods draws to a close it is clear that he aspires to die. In the wilderness as in Athens there are gold and friends; here too Athens exerts an inexorable influence over him. The verbal and emotional energy involved in hating Athens, repelling its inhabitants, thrusting or throwing gold at them, is another form of consumption, now clearly interpreted as aggression; it is literally exhausting. The only way to repay the sins of extraction from the earth is to repay what is owing to nature and return one's body to the earth.

By such postulates we may understand why Timon dies, but the text itself provides only hints: his anticipation of his death in his 'writing of my epitaph' (14.720), what might be understood as his philosophical embrace of death in his declaration that 'nothing

---

[1] Technically at least, Macbeth is an exception.

brings me all things' (14.723), and the consonance of the on-stage hole Timon digs in the earth mysteriously to find gold with the grave in which he is mysteriously buried. Timon's final speech in the play welcomes the silence of death:

> Come not to me again, but say to Athens,
> Timon hath made his everlasting mansion
> Upon the beachèd verge of the salt flood,
> Who once a day with his embossèd froth
> The turbulent surge shall cover. Thither come,
> And let my gravestone be your oracle.
> Lips, let four words go by, and language end.
> What is amiss, plague and infection mend.
> Graves only be men's works, and death their gain.
> Sun, hide thy beams. Timon hath done his reign.
>
> (14.749–58)

These would seem to be the last words Timon has to utter against Athens. The imagery of lying buried in a grave washed by the sea looks forward to Shakespeare's late plays, the sea acting as an agent of both time and immortality. Kahn (p. 55) detects the 'quasi-maternal embrace' of 'the systole and diastole of intra-uterine life'. According to the Pythagorean philosopher Apollonius of Tyana, as cited by Bacon, 'the ebbing and flowing of the sea was the respiration of the world'.[1] The concept of the world as a living creature and hence 'the world's soul' is invoked at 6.61, where it is transferred to the debased human behaviour Timon shuns.

These lines lack much of the aggressive vehemence found in his earlier onslaughts. Hostility is still there, but is modulated by quiet lyricism. The peculiar precision of the 'four words' Timon reserves before his silence has puzzled commentators. However, they may well refer to the four subjunctives directed at 'plague and infection', 'Graves', 'death', and the 'Sun'. These 'words' (in the sense 'utterances', 'maxims', or 'commands') recapitulate Timon's former anger. But the final word of each phrase compromises its negativity: 'mend', 'works', 'gain', and 'beams'. Like Lear, Timon has perhaps attained a state beyond rage and suffering. But because Timon has no Cordelia he exists in unhealed relation to the world for as long as he speaks. Before going to his grave he must

[1] Francis Bacon, *Sylva sylvarum* (1626), Century 10, 900; cited by Bradbrook, p. 23.

wish to drag the hated world to its grave. 'Sun, hide thy beams' continues the calls for universal death, but it is specifically Timon who is facing the grave.

The image of the tide suggests that Timon wishes simultaneously to be covered and uncovered, to utter thoughts that cry out from the grave like projected stones in the form of epitaphs and yet to be silent. He must have his 'four words', and he already anticipates that he will continue to speak from beyond the grave: 'let my gravestone be your oracle' (14.754). This subjunctive has no more power than the others. The thieves, Poet, Painter, and senators visited Timon in search of gold, not wisdom. Phrynia and Timandra's 'More counsel with more money, bounteous Timon' (14.167) has defined the mercenary terms on which his words find some of their recipients. Alcibiades himself uses strikingly similar words 'I'll take the gold thou giv'st me, | Not all thy counsel' (14.130–31). Even the Steward fails to observe the terms on which Timon gives him gold. After his death Timon will be remembered honourably in Athens, but the meaning of his words, his critical antagonism, will not register.

It is in this context that the epitaphs make their appearance. The words from Timon's grave, or at least a wax copy of them, are physically, materially brought into the city. Here is a dramatized image of a theme recurrent in Shakespeare's Sonnets: the capacity of verse to outlive its writer. 'Not marble nor the gilded monuments | Of princes shall outlive this powerful rhyme', claims the poet in Sonnet 55, proposing the poem itself as 'The living record of your memory'. As with Lear and Cordelia, the Sonnet proposes a bond, here uniting the poet and the young man, who is the object of praise and the figure who will be memorialized. It is the idealized goodness of fit between poet and subject that ensures the poem's permanence as a record and as a poetic monument, ensuring its resilience in the face of 'sluttish time'. The epitaphs in *Timon of Athens* are different indeed. Their subject is the author himself. There is no bond between the dead and living, and no praise. Or rather, the bond is between Timon as maker of his own memorial, writer of his own epitaphs, and Timon as the now-dead subject of the epitaphs, bound together in aversion to the world instead of praise.

The grave is characterized in the first place by its remote location in the woods. The soldier who finds it reads out the epitaph with the line 'Some beast read this. There does not live a man' (16.4). Whilst clearly this proclaims the inhumanity of 'man', it also happens to remind us that few people are likely to stumble on this obscure memorial and read it. By taking a wax impression, the soldier is able to reproduce the text, and his copy can be alienated from the monument and from the body of Timon, to become a physically mobile text that can be brought into the city as a dislocated and disembodied reminder of Timon.

His voice, moreover, is fragmented. In effect, there are no fewer than three epitaphs. It is tempting to agree with commentators who have detected some accidental redundancy. In the Soldier scene, the Soldier reads an epitaph then tells the audience 'What's on this tomb | I cannot read'.[1] In the final scene the apparently single epitaph runs together two epitaphs in the source material. The first two lines derive from an epitaph written, according to Plutarch, by Timon himself. Plutarch attributes the second pair to the poet Callimachus. Shakespeare's conflation of the two produces an awkward contradiction: first the reader is urged to 'Seek not my name', but then is told 'Here lie I, Timon'.

From another point of view, the contradiction acts as a reminder that there are two separate utterances here, even if in the play they are both attributed to Timon himself. To a sophisticated reader familiar with North's Plutarch, the inconsistency might draw attention to the play's basis in another text; and this reader might note also that Timon has taken over the voice of Callimachus. If the play's Poet was silenced by means of stone missiles, this poet is silenced through intertextual appropriation. From this perspective, the epitaphs do not simply originate with the character Timon but emerge from a textual transmission from shadowy origins in writings before Plutarch to North's English translation to *Timon of Athens* that preserves the words in question as quoted inscription at every stage. This is one of the few moments at which the play so to speak hails its source, and here the effect might be to make the play itself a memorial to Timon.

But the play's story has not quite ended, and what remains is a more immediate placement of Timon within history, the political history that Alcibiades is making. It is, of course, Alcibiades who reads out Timon's epitaph (17.71–4). It speaks of him as someone

[1] See commentary to 16.3–4.

absent and potentially irrelevant. As a text, it belongs to its on-
stage readers, who can make what they will of it to suit their occasions. Timon calls for plague and utters curses in the epitaphs, but
Alcibiades arbitrarily, if not perversely, takes them as a reminder of
'faults forgiven' (17.80). The speciousness is so swift that we cannot tell from Alcibiades' phrasing whether the faults are those of
Timon or those Timon himself suffered. In either case, the phrase
'faults forgiven' is brought into immediate relation with Alcibiades'
political agenda, and so prompts the play to conclude: 'Bring me
into your city'. The epitaph's 'stay not here thy gait' is therefore
applied—misapplied—to 'here' before the walls of Athens, and to
the 'here' that will become the final cleared stage.

   The ending would be more consolidated and conventional if the
epitaph were to move Alcibiades towards mercy, but it has no such
effect: he relents well before the epitaph arrives. This has often been
perceived as a fault in the script, as is evidenced by the history of
altered endings discussed below (pp. 117–18). But the play's avoid-
ance of a more romantic closure seems consistent with its overall
experimentalism, and also with the uneasy tone of the final lines:

> And I will use the olive with my sword,
> Make war breed peace, make peace stint war, make each
> Prescribe to other as each other's leech.

$$(17.83–5)$$

The golden-age fruit of the olive is co-opted to join with the iron-
age weapon of war. Blood is reciprocally exchanged from body to
body, just as the image of the ebb and flow of the tide over Timon's
grave contrives to suggest an endless weeping that is miraculously
without any expense. The uneasy kind of flowing within a sealed
double body that is implied in the image of acting as each other's
leech escapes the dangers of profligacy and debt. It achieves a
stable economy at the expense of becoming revoltingly surreal, so
leaving our feelings towards it unsettled and perhaps hostile. The
soft glutinosity of the olive and leech abating the edge of war
emblematically reasserts a civic ideology that has been placed
under severe strain. Timon, the absolute of Utopian and anti-
Utopian thought, is kept out, and his residual voice contained.
There will be no Apocalypse; neither will there be the establishment of the heavenly city. Alcibiades allows personal sentiment as
much scope as is compatible with decorum, and no more. This is

still, inevitably, an Iron Age ruled by money, law, and the sword.

'The Man-hater' and After

The play that has been described in the previous sections is the play printed in 1623, which has had a sporadic but intriguing history of performance over the past two centuries. Its potential for realization on the early modern stage has already been considered. Whether it was ever staged before the Restoration we do not know. Thomas Shadwell's adaptation *Timon of Athens: Or, The Man-hater* appeared on stage in about 1674.[1] Shadwell claims on the title-page that Shakespeare's work is now 'Made into a Play'. The boast is notorious for the dismissive comment it seems to imply on the original, but it may have meant no more than that he made the play fit for the altered conditions of the stage of his day.

Women, previously excluded from the public stage, now assumed a prominent role, so there was an urgent need for Shadwell to introduce new female roles. The adaptation includes a romantic plot concerning the two women in Timon's life, figures entirely absent from the Folio text. In the early scenes Timon has lost interest in his own former love Evandra, who remains sadly loyal to him, and has become infatuated with Melissa, the former fiancée of Alcibiades. She is equivalent to Callimela in the academic comedy *Timon* (see p. 21). When Timon falls on hard times, Melissa deserts him, but Evandra follows him to the woods. Taking on some of the Steward's function, and some of his lines, she can now be seen even by Timon to be the female exemplification of true love and friendship. After Timon dies, so too does she.

As this new plot exemplifies perfectly, the presence of women on the Restoration stage led to modulations in the genres of plays. Tragedies became more romantically heroic, and the changes to *Timon of Athens* accordingly shift the play away from nihilistic disgust and towards a more affirmative sense of tragedy. There was space, nevertheless, for comedy, and the adaptation was generously provided with music, including a semi-opera that replaced the masque (see pp. 111–12).

---

[1] John David Edmunds, 'Thomas Shadwell's *Timon of Athens*' (Ph.D. dissertation, University of Birmingham, 1968), pp. 270–1. Edmunds provides a detailed account of the adaptation. *The Manhater* was first published in 1678.

2. The first banquet (Sc. 2): Larry Yando as Timon offers a toast. Directed by Michael Bogdanov, Chicago Shakespeare Theater, 1997.

3. The second banquet (Sc.11): (a) Larry Yando as Timon gives thanks to the gods. Directed by Michael Bogdanov, Chicago Shakespeare Theater, 1997.

(b) Paul Scofield sprinkles water. Directed by John Schlesinger. Royal Shakespeare Theatre, 1965.

4. 'Let me look back upon thee. O thou wall | That girdles in those wolves' (12.1–2). Engraving in J. and J. Boydell, *Graphic Illustrations* (1805), plate 78.

5. 'Hold up, you sluts, | Your aprons mountant': Timon throws gold into the whores' aprons, Alcibiades looking on (14.135–6). Engraving in J. and J. Boydell, *Collection of Prints* (1803), vol. 2, plate 32.

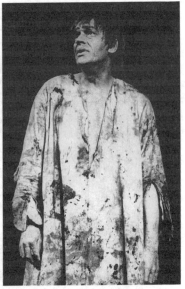

6. János Kulka as Apemantus looks down on György Cserhalmi as Timon (Sc. 14). Directed by Sándor Zsótér. Radnóti Színház, Budapest, 2000–1.

7. Paul Scofield as Timon (Sc. 14). Directed by John Schlesinger. Royal Shakespeare Theatre, 1965.

8. Michael Pennington as Timon (Sc. 14). Royal Shakespeare Company, 1999.

Shadwell initiated a stage tradition that outlived his adaptation of presenting Alcibiades in a heroic light as the opponent of tyranny who restores democracy. The figure is fleshed out partly by taking details of his life from Plutarch, partly by making him a recognizable analogue of the Duke of Buckingham, who was Shadwell's dedicatee in the 1678 edition.[1] By means such as these, Shadwell made his play responsive to the political climate of the moment, not only in terms of personalities but also in terms of the political philosophy expounded by another of Buckingham's clients, Thomas Hobbes. Shadwell postpones the meeting between Timon and Alcibiades in the woods, allowing a more immediate connection between this episode and the warrior's arrival at Athens, which in turn allows a closer integration of the two plots. The deaths of Timon and Evandra take place on stage, and the action then moves directly to show Alcibiades establishing justice and liberty in Athens. Thus the disquieting anti-heroism of the Folio text is gone, replaced with a far less equivocal resolution of the political plot.

Shadwell's adaptation was successful for over sixty years, and was staged more often than *A Midsummer Night's Dream* or *Henry V*. It played most years of the early eighteenth century, an achievement that the Shakespeare–Middleton play is unlikely to match. It was most regularly performed at Drury Lane, with sporadic competition from other companies.[2] The last Drury Lane production was in 1741. After a Covent Garden production in 1745, it slumped into obscurity, and performance of the play in any version became an unusual event.

When in 1761 the Smock Alley Theatre, Dublin revived the play for the first time since 1741, it was based, for the first time, on the Folio text. A new version by 'James Love' (a pseudonym of the actor and writer James Dance) appeared at the Richmond Theatre in 1767. It too restored much of Shakespeare,[3] though not without sentimentalization, and it also took on Rowe's act structure. Melissa was abandoned as a role, and in a reduced version of the

---

[1] Gunnar Sorelius, 'Shadwell Deviating into Sense: *Timon of Athens* and the Duke of Buckingham', *Studia Neophilologica*, 36 (1964), 132–44.

[2] For details, see Appendix D, and C. Beecher Hogan, *Shakespeare in the Theatre*, 1701–1800, 2 vols. (Oxford, 1952–7), i. 437–47.

[3] This part of the discussion uses the words 'Shakespeare' and 'Shakespearian' without reference to Middleton, reflecting the play as then perceived.

Evandra plot Timon finally urges Evandra to live before he departs to die off stage.[1] In 1771 another adaptation, by Richard Cumberland, was staged by David Garrick at Drury Lane.[2] The text adheres to the language of the Shakespearian original where the plots coincide, but the reduction of Apemantus' role, the removal of Sempronius, the cutting of some of Timon's misanthropic speeches, and the introduction of a daughter of Timon called Evanthe ensured that this was a softer-edged play. Timon died on stage in the presence of his daughter, in an ending that was gentler than *Lear* too, but echoed Nahum Tate's adaptation in which Cordelia lives (Soellner, p. 6).

John Bell's acting edition of 1773, based on Shakespeare's text, probably anticipated a London revival that was not realized on stage. The fashion for radical adaptation was on the wane. A year earlier George Steevens had signalled a change in attitudes with his comment that 'the coarse daubing of Shadwell' disfigures *Timon of Athens*.[3] Yet another adaptation for Drury Lane, composed by Thomas Hull in 1786, evidently reverted to something closer to Shadwell than the versions of Cumberland or Bell, and is said to have been 'coldly received' (Edmunds, p. 280).

The Folio text was finally though imperfectly restored to the London stage in 1816 in Edmund Kean's performance of George Lamb's version. Lamb claimed to confine his omissions to lines that had become offensive as a result of 'the refinement of manners' since Shakespeare's time. These were mainly passages of a sexual nature, though the Poet and Painter episode in Sc. 14 was deleted, and the dialogue between Timon and Apemantus in the same scene was curtailed.[4] These alterations are no more radical than those imposed on many subsequent performances. Shadwell's 'coarse daubing' was seen no more. Unfortunately the Shakespeare play, now invariably favoured over Shadwell, was itself not seen often. Samuel Phelps's 1851 production at Sadlers Wells was the only other London production in the nineteenth century. Against the grain, it was an outstanding success.[5]

The first production of *Timon of Athens* outside Britain and

---

[1] The 1768 second edition of the text has been reprinted in facsimile in the Cornmarket series (1969).

[2] Also reprinted in the Cornmarket series (1969).

[3] Quoted in Vickers, *Critical Heritage*, vi. 191.

[4] Gary Jay Williams, p. 163. On this production, see also pp. 115–16 below.

[5] See also pp. 116–17 below.

Ireland took place remarkably early, in Prague in 1778. Other early productions in non-Anglophone Europe were in Mannheim (1789), Budapest (1852), and Stockholm (1866). The later strong performance tradition in Germany and Eastern Europe should be seen in the light of German admirers of *Timon of Athens* such as Friedrich Schiller, Karl Marx, Gerhart Hauptmann, and Bertolt Brecht. The first radio broadcast was in German in 1930, with Karl Kraus adapting the text and reading Timon. North America first saw the play in 1839, in a New York production with Nathaniel Harrington Bannister as Timon. In the twentieth century productions gradually increased in number and diversified, as with other Shakespeare plays. A full production was first seen on television in the BBC Shakespeare series in 1981. But *Timon of Athens* remains far less regularly performed than most other Shakespeare plays. It has proved possible to list major productions in Appendix D of this edition. This should be consulted alongside the remaining sections of this introduction dealing with stage history.

The relevance of *Timon of Athens* to modern audiences has repeatedly been affirmed. On the other hand, *Timon of Athens* has been regarded as a seriously flawed drama, and hence a high-risk play to put on stage. In some cases, such as at the Old Vic in 1956, the Stratford, Ontario, Shakespeare Festival in 1963, and the BBC television and video version, it has been performed more or less out of necessity, as part of a project to stage all Shakespeare's plays, though at least the latter two productions made a great virtue of this necessity, establishing themselves as landmarks in the modern history of the play's performance. Some productions, such as that in London, Ontario, in 1983, were box-office failures despite their conviction and quality in artistic terms. The challenge of performing the play is therefore sometimes declined; when taken up, it has not always led to success. But audiences have acclaimed the play too. Michael Langham's 1991 production at Stratford, Ontario, attracted the fullest houses of the season, and was taken to Broadway two years later. Doran's production challenged the assumption that *Timon of Athens* belonged to a group of Shakespeare plays that were too risky from the box-office point of view to stage at the main house of the Royal Shakespeare Theatre in Stratford-upon-Avon. The play's liabilities can be turned to assets. Its unfamiliarity as compared with school-text plays such as *Romeo and Juliet* can be liberating. For directors, actors, and audiences alike, the drama is excitingly discovered rather than present-ed yet once more. Indeed, *Timon of Athens*'s reputation as a prob-lematic text can converge with its urgency and experimentalism. The play invites a positive approach to making cuts, transpositions, and reconstructions, in the spirit of discovering, or inventing, the idea behind the text, on the premiss that the text itself delivers the idea with only intermittent clarity.

Despite its topical relevance to the time in which it was written, *Timon of Athens* is rarely performed in Jacobean period costume. One example is the BBC production of 1981 (see pp. 118–20). Some modern productions such as the Old Vic in 1956 have favoured sug-gestions of an Athenian setting, and the 1936 Pasadena produc-tion was presented in a season of Graeco–Roman plays. On the whole, though, there has been little attempt to create a convincing and solidly historicized image of ancient Athens. The play has appealed as a timeless myth, or as a work that can be related direct-ly to the social, political, and philosophical issues familiar to the audience.

Modern Worlds: Britain

The 1921–2 Old Vic production harked back to the romantic tradi-tion through its choice of incidental music. It began ostentatiously with Beethoven's 'Coriolan' as overture. A march by Peter Cornelius and Felix Mendelssohn's 'War March of the Priests' were used probably to accompany Alcibiades' arrival at Timon's cave and his approach to Athens. If the music suggests an unpromis-ingly latterday Victorian affair, by the standards of its time it was modern. That meant a return to staging in the non-scenic style of the Elizabethan theatre, in the spirit of William Poel and Harley Granville-Barker. Only in the decades since the end of the Second World War has *Timon of Athens* been acclaimed for its exceptional relevance to the day and staged accordingly.

It was perhaps not until the 1940s that the play was presented in modern dress: first at Yale Repertory Theatre in 1940, and seven years later in Willard Stoker's production at the Birmingham Repertory Theatre, with John Phillips as Timon. The latter was the first major post-war production. It was staged a year after A. S. Collins had published an article significantly proclaiming *Timon of*

Athens's experimental modernity.[1] The proprietor Barry Jackson, who prepared the text for this production, wrote of the play's Athens that 'it has a good deal in common with contemporary Birmingham'.[2] The set for the first half placed the action in a commercial city much like Birmingham itself, with the blackout curtains of night bombing raids. The second half evoked the detritus of war still evident in the bombsites littering the English urban landscape of 1947. The 'woods' were transformed into wrecked city location beside a bomb crater, an early instance of treating the passage as ironic urban pastoral.

In the following decades *Timon of Athens*'s unremitting harshness of vision made it recognizable as one of the most audacious and unorthodox plays in the Shakespeare canon. In 1959 the play was identified as an outstanding example of the Shakespeare who addressed modern sensibilities in Jan Kott's influential *Shakespeare contemporain*.[3] For the philosopher Walter Kaufmann, writing in the same period, Timon's loneliness and the play's sense of futility was symptomatic of an existential view of life.[4] Once the notional location changes to the woods, the play becomes a theatre of words, a theatre in which, quite simply, nothing happens. The corrosive stasis of the scene, the stage-picture of the ragged, more or less static, and sometimes half-buried man, his rejection of companionship and community: all these have reminded directors and performers of the Theatre of the Absurd. This may not be accidental. Samuel Beckett knew Shakespeare well, and *King Lear* is a recognized antecedent of his *Endgame*. Beckett may have responded to *Timon of Athens* much as his contemporary Eugène Ionesco responded to *Richard II*: 'All men die in solitude; all values are degraded in a state of misery: that is what Shakespeare tells me'.[5]

On the levelled, placeless space of the stage Timon is presented as a figure who remains static while his visitors wash to and fro. This

---

[1] A. S. Collins, '*Timon of Athens*: A Reconsideration', *Review of English Studies*, 22 (1946), 96–108.

[2] Quoted in J. C. Trewin, *The Birmingham Repertory Theatre, 1913–1963* (1963), p. 142.

[3] Paris, 1959; translated into English as *Shakespeare our Contemporary* (1965).

[4] *From Shakespeare to Existentialism* (New York, 1960), p. 28. Also in this period, Vladimir Nabokov took Timon's principle of universal theft as a model for his editor–narrator's appropriation of the work of a recently killed poet, in *Pale Fire* (1962).

[5] Quoted in Martin Esslin, *Theatre of the Absurd* (1962, repr. 1966), p. 305.

minimalism, this rejection of plot, is perhaps the play's most daring and radical manoeuvre. The earth's crucial provision of gold when Timon implores it for roots is an ironic reversal designed to surprise the audience by suggesting that the earth is, after all, or at least might be, sentient and responsive. The theatrical device can be compared with the leaves that appear on the tree in the second half of *Waiting for Godot*, and the reappearance of Estragon's lost boots. The soliloquies in *Timon of Athens* express a need to signify one's existence in relationship to an Other, the entity Beckett calls Godot. They speak of the actual impossibility of existence without relationship, and specifically of the desire to be heard by some partly anthropomorphized being even when the utterance is misanthropic. Their typical verbal forms are those of the subjunctive, as in prayer to God, 'Let it be so', and the frustrated imperative of speech directed at those that cannot hear. It is destined not to fall out as Timon prays unless by accident. A subjectivity expressed in exertion of the will of this kind can only produce self-abnegation, and that is perhaps the desire it expresses.

John Schlesinger's production in 1965, absorbing influences from both Beckett and Brecht, responded to the challenge. Ralph Koltai's sets revealed in the first half a mix of 'garish splendour and peeling dissipation'. An impression of modern life was interjected by way of details such as setting Sc. 6 in a massage parlour. Once Paul Scofield as Timon reached the 'woods' he presented a shattered and ragged figure (Illustration 7), playing against a set that had become 'a bare desert, a wasteland'. It was guarded by a single tree, a property that by this date was immediately recognizable as an index of the 'Godot-like' world invoked by the staging.[1] The affinities between the play's second half and *Waiting for Godot* were now firmly established. A tree is not required by the text, though once it is placed on stage it signifies a minimal version of the woods of Athens, perhaps ravaged by war or industry, and the property gains in its Beckettian resonance when Timon directs the Painter and the Poet to hang themselves on the fig-tree in his yard. It might even be inferred that Timon will, like Judas Iscariot, eventually meet his death by hanging himself from the tree. Vladimir and Estragon in *Waiting for Godot* comparably debate the practicalities of committing suicide in this way. The simple device of the tree

[1] Leiter, p. 726.

therefore carries immediate resonances of a philosophically Absurd vagabond life agonizingly played out in an indeterminate hinterland.

In 1971 the RSC daringly planned a production in masks. With the director Cifford Williams ill and the company overstretched, circumstances dictated that the project was abandoned. The programme suggests an emphasis on the surreal.[1] The actors were to have worn white masks over their forehead, eyes, and nose.[2]

Nine years later, the play had retreated to Stratford's studio theatre, The Other Place. The production was again stylized, though less intrusively. Roger Warren describes a restrained Japanese style reminiscent of the Noh play; there was 'no riotous excess', and Timon was a 'sweet-natured, smilingly courteous host'. In the second half, in contrast, the stylization was replaced with 'a kind of realism with a very intrusive sound-track of waves and howling beasts'.[3] The result did not convince this reviewer, but the principle involved in distinguishing between the artifice of Athens and the world of nature responds directly to the play's division of experience.

As the century drew towards a close, directors found in the play a critique of Thatcherite materialism. In 1988–9 a student production in the Drama Department at Bristol University showed a world of financial speculation, mortgage debt, credit cards, and VDU technology. The set of scaffolding and newspaper readily fragmented to suggest an urban wilderness, with Timon's cave a large metal rubbish drum. In 1990 Trevor Nunn showed a world shadowed by paramilitary assassins, a dirty derelict (Apemantus), and a tramp (the Fool). The influence of Beckett is evident in the recurrent motif of the destitute, and the RSC production of 1999 once again invoked Beckett. The director Greg Doran took risks by maximizing the length of time Michael Pennington as Timon spent relatively immobilized in the downstage hole (see Illustration 8). At the back of the stage hung a dark disc backlit in orange light: an allusion, perhaps, to the solar eclipse of 1999, but also reminiscent of the sun and moon whose rise and fall punctuate the action of

---

[1] Walton, p. 134.

[2] As evidenced by rehearsal photographs in the Shakespeare Centre archives, Stratford-upon-Avon.

[3] 'Shakespeare in Performance, 1980', *Shakespeare Survey* 34 (1981), pp. 149–60; p. 153.

Godot.[1] Apemantus looked particularly out of place in a second-half set that again portrayed the 'woods' as a place of uncomfortably blazing heat.

Stephen Oliver's full-scale opera of 1991, a valedictory summation of the composer and theatre musician's work, was performed a year before his death. He had written the pastiche early modern music for the BBC video of *Timon of Athens* issued ten years earlier. The operatic form enabled the production to develop the emotional range of Shakespeare's work. Oliver wrote the singer's parts in a semi-recitative style accompanied by a startlingly rich orchestral score. The near-absence of contralto and soprano voices added to the stringent muscular melancholy of the vocals, the male voices establishing a fractured community of experience within their more limited pitch range.[2]

Modern Worlds: Europe

The landmark production in mainland Europe was staged by Peter Brook in 1974 at the Bouffes-du-Nord, Paris. Gary Jay Williams describes the theatre as remaining 'as it stood after a fire a quarter of a century ago—the cavernous shell of a once red-and-gilt Victorian theatre, pocked and fire-scorched, with a gaping, curtainless proscenium that exposed a deep cavity where the stage had been'.[3] This intercultural production made the theatre building as a relic of imperial days signify in itself.[4] The audience sat around and defined the shape of a semicircular acting area in the former orchestra. There was little separation between actors and audience. Apemantus was played by the African actor Malik Bagayogo, who suggested a Third World prophet denouncing western decadence.[5] One reviewer described the production as 'a living emblem of the West brutally awakened from its paradisial consumer's dreams by the oil crisis'.[6] Jean-Claude Carrière's French script was stripped of much

---

[1] And possibly alluded to Richard Rhodes's study of the making of the hydrogen bomb called *Dark Sun* (1995).

[2] For further details, see Murray Biggs, 'Adapting *Timon of Athens*', *Shakespeare Bulletin*, 10 (1992), 5–10.

[3] Gary Jay Williams, p. 183.

[4] Dennis Kennedy, *Looking at Shakespeare* (Cambridge, 1993), pp. 279–82.

[5] Kennedy, p. 279.

[6] Pierre Schneider, *New York Times*, 3 Dec. 1974, quoted in David Williams, ed., *Peter Brook: A Theatrical Casebook* (1982), pp. 246–7.

of the imagery and rhetorical power of the English text. The actors' performances were physical and sometimes acrobatic. Their every-day clothes were visible beneath their costumes, which were based on a variety of cultures and time-periods. Cultural diversity was evident too in the range of spoken accents and idioms. The produc-tion drew on the company's experience of theatre in Africa and elsewhere for its techniques of story-telling, creating 'an intimate and luminous event',[1] and seeking, in the words of the actor Malik Bowens, to replace 'scenographical hardware' with 'a human décor'.[2]

The play has lent itself to political allegory in a number of eastern European productions. Jaroslav Gillar's 1969 Prague production at the time of the Soviet occupation of Czechoslovakia emphasized the betrayal of friendship, adding a couplet at the end of Act 3 highlighting the production's relevance to the times:

> Those that have power to hurt and smother
> Will heap one injury upon another.[3]

The corruption of Athens was shown 'by perverse sexuality and transvestism . . . a slippery, decadent society where appearances are deceptive and everything is subject to betrayal'. Alcibiades' whores, constantly present, formed 'a silent chorus of perversion and venality; they fondled each other lasciviously and offered themselves in any combination'.[4] This outcry against the hidden decadence of Stalinist regimes contrasts with productions reflect-ing other aspects of the Warsaw Pact era, such as that staged in Budapest in the same year. The production combined Brechtian alienation effects, including elements of circus, with a passionate denunciation of emergent capitalism that harked back to Marx's comments (see pp. 53–4). The 1976 production in Szolnok, Hungary, showed a 1930s society of 'stock-exchange profiteers, Nazi-figures in prospect, decadence, despair, bitter struggle to live, and refined selfishness'.[5] Only the suffering Timon, played by George Constantin, remained human, gentle and kind, even when refusing to help the Athenians.

---

[1] Williams, p. 248.   [2] Quoted in Kennedy, p. 282.
[3] Leiter, p. 726.   [4] Leiter, pp. 726–7.
[5] Ileana Berlogea, 'Shakespeare in Romania', *Shakespeare Quarterly*, 30 (1979), 281–5.

Less direct political meanings were suggested in Frank Patrick Steckel's 1990 postmodern production in Bochum, Germany. Dieter Hacker's set was described as 'a gold-bronze autumn-coloured square rake', his costumes luminous and heavily pleated, and the actors' heads buried in 'hugely oversize headmasks, grotesquely distended, alienated creations, yet each also, unaccountably, indicative of its wearer'.[1] The exception was Apemantus, whose head was 'stuck in a black box'. Wilhelm Hortmann offers a provocative explanation for the effectiveness of such an approach: 'The play often fails to convince on stage because the vividly articulated facial and bodily expression of the unmasked actor is at variance with the crude, woodcut psychology of this Everyman-like parable . . . The masks were the perfect medium to illustrate this.' Hortmann describes Timon in these terms: 'Resignation, martyred thoughts about the fallen nature of Man, the ravages of bitterness and self-hatred—these were expressed in the mask, just as [Peter] Roggisch's delivery, tone and gesture were guided by the sorrow over an irredeemable world'.[2] The production proved to be both intellectually stimulating and deep in its emotional impression.

A ruined church at Kiscelli, Budapest, in 1992 provided a self-referential performance space in the mode of Brook's Bouffes-du-Nord theatre. The production, staged shortly after the overthrow of communism, sought to avoid ostentatious political overtones. Nevertheless, it presented Alcibiades in the final scene in severe military uniform, a warning against the dangers of counter-coup and the return of an authoritarian regime.

Director Imre Csiszár's interpretation of Alcibiades ran against the traditional and problematic view of him as upholder of democracy, a view that was evident again in Walter Pagliaro's 1995 distinctly post-Cold War production in Florence. This was given a contemporary setting in Silvio Berlusconi's 'telefascist' Italy, suggesting to one commentator 'a desire to re-suture Italian consciousness in its left-wing humanist past'.[3] Alcibiades' attack on the senators' involvement in usury indicted the fiscal policies of Berlusconi. As in the Szolnok production, the critique of Athenian

[1] Wilhelm Hortmann, *Shakespeare on the German Stage: The Twentieth Century* (Cambridge, 1998), pp. 319–20.

[2] Hortmann, p. 321.

[3] William Van Watson, review in *Theatre Journal*, 48 (1996), 98–9.

society was sustained by Massimo Venturiello's portrayal of Timon as a sympathetic figure. In conflict with the text, he was not prone to excess.

Another experimental production was staged at the Radnóti Színház in Budapest in 2000–1. Actors were presented as isolated and uncommunicating objects. In its effect the production was dreamlike, inexplicable, and sometimes disconcerting. The action began in the theatre foyer, where a crammed audience, in some discomfort, saw an unusually sceptical Timon handing over money to Ventidius so that he could purchase his fiancée from the Old Athenian her father. The production was shot through with post-Brechtian alienation effects. Actors partly modernized the standard Hungarian translation, delivering the play with attention to the language but without rhetoric. Money was the fixation of unhappy men, with the exception of Apemantus, whose philosophy allowed him to stand serenely aloof. The wilderness was represented by dusty bales of shredded paper. Gold extracted from the bales was a glittering marmalade that stuck to the hands.[1]

Modern Worlds: North America

Despite the relative preference for period costume productions of Shakespeare in North America, *Timon* has a strong record of modernization. Michael Langham's important 1963 production in Stratford, Ontario, came two years before Schlesinger's comparable staging in Stratford-upon-Avon. It found in F. Scott Fitzgerald's *The Great Gatsby* a twentieth-century equivalent of the Renaissance patronage on display in the early part of the play.[2] The production modulated between its Twenties period flavour and references to contemporary life by featuring incidental music by Duke Ellington. The *Timon of Athens* suite, one of several Ellington wrote for Shakespeare plays, comprises 'Impulsive Giving', 'Ocean', 'Angry', 'Gold', 'Regal Formal', 'Skilipop', 'Smoldering', 'Gossippippi', 'Counter Theme', 'Alcibiades', 'Gossip', 'Banquet', and 'Revolutionary'. These titles provide a suggestive indication as to how the matter of *Timon of Athens* melded with the rhythms and

---

[1] Information from http://www.lap.szinhaz.hu/html/2001jun/forgach.shtml and http://www.lap.scinhaz.hu. See Illustration 6.

[2] *The Great Gatsby* was quoted also in the 1965 Stratford-upon-Avon programme.

modern sociality of jazz. The feel-good and nostalgically evocative Ellington score was adapted for Langham's 1991 revival of the play, and again found a prominent role in the Stratford-upon-Avon production of 1999.

In the 1963 production, this society of nouveau-riche decadence was flanked by Apemantus as a journalist and Alcibiades as a guerilla fighter. Cutting across the jazz-age evocations were allusions to the sexual scandal of the Profumo affair rocking Britain in the same year as the production. The Cupid who introduces the masque pointedly resembled the sophisticated go-between Dr Stephen Ward, who introduced the cabinet minister John Profumo to prostitutes. Thus the theatre of visual display was tempered by the theatre of satire, and Langham successfully retrieved the satirical thrust of the original play. In the woods, the Theatre of the Absurd was a clear point of reference. The figure of Timon half-buried in the ground was 'suggestive of Beckett's *Happy Days*, or Albee's *The Sandbox*'.[1] In *Happy Days* the opening stage direction describes Winnie '*Embedded up to above her waist in exact centre of mound*'. The stage image is visually emblematic of the human condition as the play describes it.

When Jerry Turner directed the play for the Oregon Shakespeare Festival in 1978, the first part took place in a modern living room inhabited by figures in white suits. The presence of Arab sheikhs and a Texan oil magnate identified the setting as post-Oil Crisis America. The production was staged a year after Carlos Fuentes's novel *The Hydra's Head* told of a shadowy figure called Timon at the centre of a story of international espionage and intrigue over oil resources. The affluent society was transformed in the second part by means of a revolve which turned to show a wooden shack at the back of the house.

Robin Phillips's 1983 staging at London, Ontario, set the play in an earlier and more restrained Edwardian society. The second part was played before 'panels vibrating with an orange heat'.[2] Men with 'white hats and umbrellas and clothed in shantung suits' formed 'a striking image of fake civilization in the wilderness'.[3] The incongruity of transplanting the city-bound Athenians to Timon's savage place of abode made its own point.

---

[1] Leiter, p. 724.   [2] Leiter, p. 731.
[3] Ralph Berry, quoted in Leiter, p. 731.

In 1997 Michael Bogdanov at the Chicago Shakespeare Theater was granted the freedom to translate the play into modern times that he had been denied when he had been the prospective director of the BBC production. Larry Yando as Timon, dressed in a white suit, was a slick, unlikable charmer in early scenes (Illustration 2), and presided over a clinically minimal mock banquet (Illustration 3a). David G. Brailow, reviewing the production, noted that 'because he is at the start a knowing member of a fundamentally shallow, inhumane society with which we are all too familiar, his misanthropy acquires a ferocious authority we cannot ignore'.[1] Ralph Koltai, who had previously worked on the set for Schlesinger's RSC production, now showed a 1980s world of metallic design and electronic accessories. It transformed after the interval into a junkyard of garbage in which Timon's cave was represented by the shell of a burnt-out car. The satire was 'aimed at our own technological, ruthlessly acquisitive, morally vacuous world'.[2] The scenes showing Timon's creditors refusing financial aid reflected seedy aspects of contemporary life. Lucullus entered from a hot bath and fondled a woman in a pink robe, and Lucius was drinking at a bar with two prostitutes; Sempronius was at the stock exchange.

At the Shakespeare Theatre, Washington, DC, in 2000 Michael Kahn again updated the play to a materialist 1980s in which Timon falls from successful businessman to destitute vagrant. For Philip Goodwin, who played the lead role, *Timon of Athens* was 'a Washington story'.[3] The high fashion of the glass and steel set transformed into a landfill. According to the designer Walt Spangler, 'It's as if a bomb goes off in his immaculate world, and leaves him [Timon] in this desolate, burnt-out landscape, where he must re-evaluate his life and times'.[4] This deliberate reference to the bombing of the World Trade Center in 1993 ominously prefigured al-Qaeda's devastating attack on the Twin Towers in 2001.

Timon of Athens indeed points uneasily to re-evaluation of life and times. The history of modern performance has manifested its

---

[1] David G. Brailow, review in *Shakespeare Bulletin*, 15.3 (1997), 22–4 (p. 24).

[2] Brailow, p. 23.

[3] Quoted by Roberto Aguirre-Sacasa, 'Poor Little Rich Boy', Shakespeare Theatre website, at http://www.Shakespearedc.org/pastprod/timonasi.html.

[4] Quoted by Aguirre-Sacasa, 'Houses of Steel, Hearts of Glass', Shakespeare Theatre website.

pertinence to a society preoccupied with the consumption and display of material goods, a society that sees itself as shallow in the forms of human relationship it offers, as abusive towards the ecology, and as alienated from spiritual values and a sense of harmonious existence in the world. Wealth is enjoyed with disregard for its foundations. Crisis and catastrophe are close at hand.

Timon: Approaches to the Role

As with other Shakespeare plays such as *Macbeth* and *Coriolanus*, the play's power is to take the audience into emotionally engaged but critical understanding of a figure who occupies an extreme and solitary position within the spectrum of human experience. Timon's remorseless excess of generosity followed by his aggressive antihumanitarianism is the play's distinctive form of passion. The role is strenuous, and not only on account of the extravagantly sustained emotions represented in Sc. 14 and elsewhere. Performers can scarcely avoid the contrast between Timon of Athens and Timon of the woods, the civil if enigmatic host and the raging misanthrope. To some extent, the origins of this contrast lie deep in the pattern of collaboration and in differences between the source materials on which the dramatists worked. Yet Timon is not unique among Shakespeare roles in demanding a different quality of performance at the beginning from that at the end; Richard III is another example. All Shakespeare's major roles involve the performance of different moods and different forms of social existence, and a number of them change, or as it is commonly said 'grow', from one state to another during the course of the play. Timon belongs to an even smaller group where the character inhabits a universe of experience later in the play so different that it risks becoming incommensurate with his earlier world. If the design of a production highlights the emblematic contrast between the worlds of Athens and the woods, the modern actor will need to decide whether to find a Stanislavskian line of psychic and emotional development to drive the role across the divide, or to accept a less psychologically realistic portrayal of a figure who changes from sociable beneficence to antisocial hatred because that is simply the given structure of the story as a myth or parable.

It is hard to find an interpretative centre to the role that does not lean either to the Timon of Athens or the Timon of the woods. The eighteenth century, while neglecting to stage the original text, developed a perspective on its principal role that would influence later performances. As Rolf Soellner comments, the century's penchant for moralizing the play 'avoided facing the full pessimism' (p. 7). Just before the turn of the century, in 1699, James Drake mentioned *King Lear*, *Timon of Athens*, and *Macbeth* as remarkable for the extent to which they are 'moral and instructive'.[1] For Johnson, Timon was a symptomatic or illustrative figure. In the general note on the play in his edition, he wrote, 'The catastrophe affords a very powerful warning against that ostentatious liberality, which scatters bounty, but confers no benefits, and buys flattery, but not friendship'. That is not an effective formula for realizing the Aristotelian tragic qualities of pity and fear, nor the Aristotelian antisocial traits of beast and god. William Richardson's important essay of 1783 refused to take Timon's dangerously excessive generosity at face value: 'Real goodness is not ostentatious'.[2] His ostentation is the cause of his conversion to misanthropy. Richardson admired the play for purposefully demonstrating its thesis, but he did not admire Timon. Further afield, in Russia, Catherine the Great worked on an adaptation that was evidently designed to commend financial prudence to her nobility.[3] Moralized readings such as these are classical in temper. Timon is regarded with detachment, as an example rather than as an empathetically suffering human. The focus is placed on the city.

The original text was restored to the theatre at the time when Romanticism as a literary movement was at its height. Edmund Kean's biographer describes how, with his mercurial intensity as an actor, he was able to show 'the bitter sceptic, but not the easy, lordly, and magnificent Timon'.[4] That expectation of lordly magnificence is new in recorded comment on the play. A Timon was now becoming apparent who was different from the figure described by Johnson and Richardson, a man of passion who was too big-hearted for the world in which he lived. William Hazlitt and Friedrich Schiller both admired Timon as a figure whose disgust with the world articulated a romantic truth. In 1817 Hazlitt referred to Timon's 'lofty spirit of self-denial, and bitter scorn of the

---

[1] Quoted in Vickers, *Critical Heritage*, ii. 95.

[2] Quoted in Vickers, *Critical Heritage*, vi. 361.

[3] Zdeněk Stříbrný, *Shakespeare and Eastern Europe* (Oxford, 2000), pp. 31–3.

[4] B. W. Procter [Barry Cornwall], *The Life of Edmund Kean*, 2 vols. (1835), ii. 164.

world, which raise him higher in our esteem than the dazzling gloss of prosperity could do'.[1] Schiller was inspired to attempt his own tragedy of misanthropy, *Der Menschenfeind*, but left it incomplete.[2] The Victorians idealized Timon and Alcibiades as victims of greed and corruption who responded with magnificence to the oppression they suffered. This Byronic view was realized in Samuel Phelps's productions of the 1850s. Phelps was dignified, and bore himself with an easy manner in the early scenes. His performance was effective in showing a gradual transition, through the 'fierce indignation of a sensitive man terribly shocked' to a figure given over to bitterness and isolation.[3] According to Henry Morley in 1866, Phelps had treated Timon as an aristocratic misanthrope, and 'as an ideal, as the central figure in a mystery'.[4]

The twentieth century found a place for both the 'classical' and 'romantic' readings. The director Tyrone Guthrie's programme note for his 1952 Old Vic production explained that 'Timon is not a hero in whose sufferings we are supposed to share with pity and with terror. He is the spoilt Darling of Fortune, whom Fortune suddenly spurns . . . He is peevish, hysterical; he adopts the cynicism of *Apemantus* not from intellectual or moral conviction but as a kind of compensatory gesture against society'. Guthrie's approach to the role, beneath its overlay of Freudian psychology, is not far removed from Samuel Johnson's and William Richardson's. When Paul Scofield came to the role at Stratford-upon-Avon in 1965, the year after he performed Lear in Peter Brook's acclaimed touring production of *King Lear*, he modified the reserved existential anguish he had perfected in that role with a more expressive psychological verisimilitude.[5] In the programme note, the director John Schlesinger, like Guthrie, described the role with resort to Freudian terminology: 'But can a man who goes so suddenly to such neurotic excesses of human loathing be simply a noble creature crushed by misfortune and ingratitude? . . . Timon's generosity is to me suspect. The only way I can make sense of the extreme plunge into morbid hatred is to suppose that the open-handedness

---

[1] Quoted in Bate, p. 542.   [2] Soellner, p. 8.

[3] Shirley S. Allen, *Samuel Phelps and Sadler's Wells Theatre* (Middletown, Conn., 1971), p. 178.

[4] Henry Morley, *Journal of an English Playgoer from 1851–1866* (1866), p. 132; quoted in Gary Jay Williams, p. 170.

[5] Leiter, p. 725.

of the first act is mainly a fantasy life which Timon subconsciously uses to suppress his real nature, his isolation and inability to make any genuine human contact.' The failure to engage with reality in Schlesinger's Timon might owe something to Schlesinger's recent direction of a film about another fantasist, *Billy Liar*.

In his 1963 production Langham had similarly seen Timon as 'a spendthrift playboy and something of a fool'. Guthrie, Schlesinger, and Langham therefore shared a sceptical view of Timon that contrasts radically with Phelps's earlier romanticism. It seems appropriate enough that the twentieth century should have rejected a vision based on the difference in social class between a lordly Timon and a rapaciously mercantile Athens. But by 1991 Langham had converted to the opposite view that he was 'a man who is possessed with a passionate vision, and who is learning how to live it, and wished to share it with all who are living at the same time as he is'.[1] For Langham, the classical view had yielded to the romantic, though he writes in terms of the communitarian rather than aristocratic ideal.

The role involves absolute vehemence of expression, and is, of course, written predominantly in verse. The risk of descending into repetitious rant is all too evident; in 1816 Leigh Hunt noted that Timon's curses should be 'not loud but deep'.[2] Loudness has sometimes been avoided at the cost of understatement. Ernest Milton's 1935 performance at the Westminster Theatre was too lightweight for James Agate, who declared 'Timon must be drawn to heroic size'.[3] Philip Hope-Wallace scathingly described Ralph Richardson in the second part of the 1956–7 Old Vic production as 'like a Richard Strauss opera, for baritone bore on property rock; light thickened and distant harpings and sea birds gave a gentlemanly, elegiac close'. At The Other Place in 1980, Richard Pasco played Timon in an emotionally restrained production with Japanese stylization. Three years later, in London, Ontario, William Hutt took on the lead role in another production in which the savagery of the verse was held in check. Lines were described as having been

---

[1] Noted by Ray Conlogue, 'A Terrific Timon at Stratford', *Globe and Mail*, 17 June 1991.

[2] From *The Examiner*, 4 Nov. 1816; quoted in *Shakespeare in the Theatre: An Anthology of Criticism*, ed. Stanley Wells (Oxford, 1997), pp. 46–50 (p. 48). Hunt alludes to *Macbeth* 5.3.29.

[3] Quoted by Gary Jay Williams, pp. 174–5.

delivered in a 'peculiar robotic hesitation', or 'almost sotto voce, as if attitudes and insinuations were all that counted'.[1]

But the avoidance of rant does not necessarily lead to a reserved performance. 'What matters is the music threaded uncannily through the gale', J. C. Trewin noted,[2] and actors and critics have repeatedly referred to the musicality of the role. Whether psychologically flawed or, in the Steward's words, his 'worst sin is he does too much good' (13.39), Timon is, from the beginning, an isolated and vulnerable figure. In 1965, in a performance that seems to question Schlesinger's approach to the role quoted above, Paul Scofield highlighted 'the inconsolable broken phrasing, the unresolved cadences, the sweetness of his top register'; his verse-speaking suggested 'a man struggling to lift a heavy weight'.[3] Richard Pasco, the RSC Timon of 1980–2, is an actor noted for beautiful verse-speaking. Musicality was strongly in evidence in Michael Pennington's performance at the RSC in 1999. When he spoke 'his hate may grow | To the whole race of mankind, high and low' at 12.39–40, his voice rose to a high-pitched wail on the word 'high' before sinking to a despairing baritone on 'low'. His intonations sometimes opened towards an almost enraptured state of mind, suggesting that anger and hatred could become attenuated into a quasi-religious lyrical agony.

Staging the Masque

Jerzy Grotowski has drawn a distinction between 'rich theatre' and 'poor theatre'. Poor theatre generates rich signification out of limited resources—resources such as the human body and voice. Rich theatre is committed to spectacle rather than meaning. 'The notion of theatre as a synthesis of disparate creative disciplines— literature, sculpture, painting, architecture, lighting, acting': for Grotowski this is 'Rich Theatre', which is, he sardonically adds, 'rich in flaws'.[4] Grotowski's description can be applied to the banquet of *Timon of Athens*, with the important proviso that the play treats such theatre satirically. Poetry, painting, music, dancing: these are the arts that in *Timon of Athens* parallel Grotowski's

---

[1] Gina Mallet, quoted in Leiter, p. 730; Conlogue, 'Terrific Timon'.

[2] *Shakespeare on the English Stage* 1900–1964 (1964), p. 31.

[3] Review in *The Times*, 2 July 1965.

[4] *Towards a Poor Theatre* (1969), p. 19.

catalogue—or, in the words of Frank Benson, commenting on the high points of his 1892 production, 'Banquets, dancing girls, flutes, wine, colour, and form'.[1]

By the time Benson wrote, the form of the court masque had long been abandoned. In accordance with the Restoration taste for drama blended with elements of Italian and French opera, Thomas Shadwell introduced a short opera to replace the masque in Sc. 2. This swelled the performance time of the banquet scene, and heightened the contrast between the scenes in Athens and the scenes in the woods. Shadwell's opera, opening in pastoral vein with shepherds, nymphs, and '*A Symphony of Pipes imitating the chirping of Birds*', presented a rather weakly relevant dialogue between Cupid and Bacchus, with choruses. The original score was composed by Louis Grabu, the French composer and violinist who settled in England in 1665 to become Master of Music to Charles II, and wrote music for plays by John Dryden, the Earl of Rochester, and others. There is also extant entr'acte music composed probably by James Paisible, which is likely to belong to an early Shadwell performance.[2]

Henry Purcell's later reworking, commissioned for a revival of 1694, accepted the first part of Shadwell's text of the masque, and introduced a new second part in which Bacchus' condemnation of love would have held immediate relevance to the hollow relationship between Timon and Shadwell's new role of Melissa. Purcell wrote a trumpet overture to the play and an anguished chromatic curtain tune that was probably played at the beginning of Act 4, when Timon leaves Athens. The opera was now integrated more firmly with the new elements of romantic tragedy.

The significance of these changes lies not simply in the fact that they shifted the episode from outmoded court masque to modish semi-opera. In the Folio text there is a dialectic between sleazily lavish entertainment and caustic satire. In Shadwell both the sleaze and the satire have gone. The scathing choric commentary of Apemantus disappeared in the musical Restoration versions of the masque. Lavish entertainment of the play's audience had

[1] Stanley T. Williams, 'Some Versions of *Timon of Athens* on the Stage', *Modern Philology*, 18 (1920), 269–85 p. 277.

[2] Gooch and Thatcher, p. 1675.

become the end in view, and operatic music the principal means by which it was delivered.[1]

The masque offers an opportunity for a production to impose its style and adapt the play to the tastes of the day, no matter what they might be. By the time of Richard Cumberland's adaptation, staged by David Garrick at Drury Lane in 1771, opera was no longer appropriate to a stage play, and the singing was replaced with dance. Timon ushered in a troupe of Lydians, who performed a 'grand dance' to martial music in honour of Alcibiades, part of the strong theatrical tradition of idealizing Alcibiades. There was still no sniping from Apemantus.

George Lamb's 1816 production, featuring Edmund Kean as Timon, was based on the Folio text, but introduced a new mytho-logical narrative for the masque, now realized as a ballet. The ballet master Oscar Byrne devised a piece which figured Hercules instead of the Cupid. He himself played the role of Hercules, danc-ing in mock-heroic combat with no less than twenty Amazons. The playbill made a special point of advertising '*In Act I. A GRAND BANQUET*, AND AN INCIDENTAL BALLET'. This spectacle was performed 'with appropriate Splendour, new Scenery, Dresses, and Decorations'. The banquet scene was made impressively lavish; the prompt book calls for the scene and its properties to be ornamented 'as much as possible'.

Charles Calvert's production at the Princes Theatre, Manches-ter, followed the example of Lamb. The playbill gave prominence to Rita Sangalli's performance in the Grand Dance of the Amazons, to the extent that Calvert was suspected of exploiting the appeal of the female dancers in order to raise interest in an otherwise unpop-ular play.[2] In 1904 J. H. Leigh produced 'a lovely ballet and a Cupid who might have strayed out of Offenbach's *Belle Hélène*'.[3] The opportunity for musical display of the female body has rarely been rejected. The modern theatre has achieved this by finding alternatives to the opera and ballet of earlier productions. In pro-ductions such as Langham's in 1963 and Bogdanov's in 1997 the masque was realized as a strip-show. Langham's juxtaposition of

[1] The Habsburg Emperor Leopold I wrote an opera *Timone Misantropo*, performed in 1696, but according to Gooch and Thatcher this is probably based on Lucian rather than Shakespeare.

[2] Richard Foulkes, *The Calverts* (1992), p. 64.

[3] *Times* review, quoted by Gary Jay Williams, p. 172.

politics and brothel seems appropriate. Trevor Nunn similarly sought to convey upper-class decadence: 'The floor show is more sophisticated than a striptease, but is based on the same principle, as the women divest 18th century ball-gowns to reveal contemporary sleaze beneath—and eventually dance with the wealthy men.'[1]

But if the play constructs the other to Timon's world as the female, it thereby presents the possibility that the other can be reinterpreted along different lines. When *Timon of Athens* first played in New York in 1839 the production engaged Master Diamond, who was described as 'the most distinguished of the "negro dancers"'.[2] Perhaps for the first time the masque in this production highlighted the play's main action as not so much all-male as all-white. In Langham's second production, of 1991, the masque imitated the 'banana skirt' dance of the black erotic entertainer Josephine Baker. Thus race as well as gender can be the basis for highlighting the cultural insularity of Timon and his friends.

The highlighting of difference was reversed in Doran's version, where the dancers, like their on-stage audience, were now male. Overt homoeroticism offered a new way of presenting the masque as exotic spectacle. Evidently making irreverent allusion to the Sadler's Wells and Piccadilly Theatre production of *Swan Lake* in which the swans were played by male dancers, Doran's Cupidesque 'Amazons' were played by men wearing thongs and little black masks and large white feather wings. They descended from aloft to the accompaniment of Ellington's music, firing flirtatious arrows from silly bows at Timon's guests, then taking partners in an all-male dance.

In this production Richard McCabe's Apemantus spoke his satirical commentary into a microphone, climbing to the balcony to detach himself from the dancing revellers. He was partly a preacher in the mould of Rhonnie Washington's black Baptist in San Francisco's Thick Description Company production of 1993, a staging in which the actor's African-American identity set up a different line of demarcation from the established line between lords and ladies. Washington gave 'ringing pulpit rhythm' to lines such

---

[1] Quoted from Nunn's notes on the 1990 production in the Young Vic archives.
[2] Joseph Norton Ireland, *Records of the New York Stage from 1750 to 1860*, 2 vols. (New York, 1966), ii. 288.

as 'Rich men sin and I eat root'.[1] McCabe, in contrast, merged his intonation of the speech as sermon with the rhythms of blues music as he took to playing a keyboard. With his leather jacket and sunshades, he became a participant even as he was a critic. The elements of satire and irony, conspicuously missing from most of the extravagant little operas and ballets, were here vigorously present, if a little softened by the indulgent exuberance of a spectacle. Apemantus' separateness was compromised by his involvement in the music.

From Apemantus to the Baptist preacher or the Blues Brothers is a long but logical step. In contrast, to lose Apemantus' commentary entirely, as in many earlier productions, is to lose a theatre art of split focus, and to collapse the episode into a moment of entertainment: absolute entertainment, mere entertainment. The modern resources of cabaret and Brechtian drama have restored to performance of the scene much that vanished in the interim. The visual theatre of the episode draws on conventions of seeing and interpreting that are lost to us, but if enactment can no longer make the episode signify fully, the episode will always provide a moment in which the nature of the visual art will be deeply revealing of the complexion of the theatre of the era. It will sometimes also provide a moment in which vivid spectacle co-exists with hostile analysis.

Staging the Alcibiades Plot

The play's subplot involving Alcibiades has often been thought to offer the most conspicuous example of its failure to consolidate its own narrative and theatrical structure, and this perception has led to some complex and assertive handling. At issue here are the relationship between two plots, the nature of Alcibiades as a dramatic role, and the question of how a production reaches a satisfactory closure.

In his notes in John Bell's 1773–4 performance edition of Shakespeare, written at the very time that the tide was turning away from Shadwell's version, Francis Gentleman wrote some negative comments on *Timon of Athens* that turned out to be prescient in identifying deficiencies that performers would seek to address once

---

[1] Steven Winn, *San Francisco Chronicle*, 13 Jan. 1993.

the Shakespeare play was established on stage. Gentleman found the Alcibiades plot 'episodical' and irrelevant. Everything that follows after Timon's 'languid departure' he considered 'so detached from the main plot, except Timon of Athens's epitaph, that cutting every line out would rather serve than maim the piece'.[1] Gentleman's two complaints regarding the Alcibiades plot and the play's ending relate to each other, for the more clearly the subplot is articulated, the more straightforwardly convincing the ending will seem to be.

The difficulty many readers have felt about the lack of preparation for Alcibiades' appearance before the senate has been addressed in a number of ways. Shadwell filled out the dialogue at the beginning of the senate scene to provide a firmer sense of context. In the 1990–1 Young Vic production, Alcibiades explained his friend's crime to Timon in a few lines of added dialogue in Sc. 4. Michael Benthall at the Old Vic in 1956–7 had clarified the situation by bringing the soldier on stage as a chained prisoner, a device echoed in Doran's 1999 production, in which there was a tableau at the end of the scene showing the soldier being hanged. Earlier in the performance Doran introduced a violent homoerotic mime sequence in which one of the male dancers in the masque flirted with Alcibiades' soldier but rejected him when he made a pass at him at the end of Sc. 2; the disgruntled soldier later stabbed the dancer and killed him.

The history of adaptations, performances, and criticism shows a strong tendency to idealize Alcibiades in ways that the text does not in itself allow. Stage tradition has made much of the entry direction '*Enter Alcibiades with [soldiers playing] drum and fife, in warlike manner; and Phrynia and Timandra*'. Timon's isolation is punctured by a military procession to music, the two whores adding an element of scurrilous flamboyance (see Illustration 5). This is one of the play's defining moments of spectacle. Phrynia and Timandra notwithstanding, it provides opportunities to present an idealized picture of Alcibiades as representative of military glory. Such a picture contributes to a romantic heightening of Timon too. Though he based his script on the Folio version, George Lamb continued Shadwell's heroic view of Alcibiades as revenger of Timon's death and reformer of Athens. This was in 1816, the

---

[1] Quoted in Vickers, *Critical Heritage*, vi. 30 and 96.

year after the British defeat of Napoleon at the Battle of Waterloo. From Leigh Hunt's description, it is clear that Lamb's production made a stunning spectacle of Alcibiades' arrival in the woods:

First, you heard a sprightly quick march playing in the distance; Kean started, listened, and leaned in a fixed and angry manner on his spade, with frowning eyes, and lips full of the truest feeling, compressed but not too much so; he seemed as if resolved not to be deceived, even by the charm of a thing inanimate; the audience were silent; the march threw forth its gallant note nearer and nearer; the Athenian standards appear, then the soldiers come treading on the scene with that air of confident progress which is produced by the accompaniment of music; and at last, while the squalid misanthrope still maintains his posture and keeps his back to the strangers, in steps the young and splendid Alcibiades, in the flush of victorious expectation. It is the encounter of hope with despair.[1]

The whores Phrynia and Timandra, too demeaning for this warrior, were excluded.

At the end of the play in Lamb's version, Alcibiades singles out Timon's chief false friends Lucius and Lucullus for punishments that reflect their harshness to Timon. They are stripped of their wealth and banished from Athens.[2] This is another way in which Alcibiades emerges as a better leader: a fair dispenser of measured justice rather than a commander who imposes artibrary death by decimation.

Samuel Phelps's spectacular, splendid, and highly successful production of 1851 also made much of Alcibiades' visit to Timon and altered the play's ending. The scenes in the woods were staged in a spirit of full Romanticism. The prompt book describes the set for Sc. 14 as 'A Woody Dell with a high raking platform . . . Cave . . . set flush'. Timon was discovered 'on bank in a mean dress, with a spade'. In stark contrast, Alcibiades and his army entered marching magisterially down the platform on to the stage, a crucial moment in Phelps's ennoblement of the role. His drastic reshaping of the final scene, like Lamb's, sought to give the closing sequence a stronger plot-line and in particular to create new links between Alcibiades and the dead Timon. When the Soldier tells Alcibiades of Timon's death, he replies 'Conduct me to the spot, that we may be assured'; then, as the prompt book directs, '*Music. Troops face about, Mark time / Diorama moved on, and closes them in, they descend,*

---

[1] In Wells, *Shakespeare in the Theatre*, p. 48. [2] Gary Jay Williams, p. 163.

and Woody opening in Diorama Shows them on their march, again Closed in, and Diorama worked entirely off R2E, Showing Timon's Tomb, Sunlight Sea Shore backing, with rolling waters'. The diorama, a continuous painted cloth, was wound across the stage to show the change of location as the troops marched from Athens to the tomb. It thus enabled a return to the woods, which was another way of addressing the difficulty Shadwell had perceived in the Folio's anticlimactic ending (see p. 93). Alcibiades' impressive march brings the closing action from Athens to the evocatively lit seashore where Timon lies buried, so turning the final focus back to Timon. There is no need for the Soldier who takes an impression of the epitaph, for now Alcibiades can read the real thing directly *in situ*. His final speech continues to 'on faults forgiven' (l. 80), after which he orders 'Let our drums strike' and, to slow music, the soldiers '*lower their arms in grief*'. This romantically solemn seashore-*Hamlet* close is a far cry from the play's insistence on an inconclusive peace in an Athens where Timon is no more.

There have been several imitations of and variants on Phelps's altered ending. Frederick Warde introduced one of them in 1910. To quote Gary Jay Williams's account, 'At the end of the play, the "senators, citizens, women and children of Athens" have come out to Timon's cave to beg his assistance against Alcibiades when Alcibiades and his army enter. The captain demands that the Athenians kneel and promise to restore Timon to honour and wealth. A soldier seeking Timon finds him dead in his cave, and his body is borne off with a long procession of Athenians behind.'[1] Even the Folio-faithful Robert Atkins at the Old Vic in 1921–2 introduced a final tableau in which soldiers and senators salute Timon's grave.

The view that something needs to be done to tighten up the play's conclusion remains widespread. Schlesinger was amongst those who shortened the final scene. Timon's potentially bathetic off-stage death challenges expectations, and has sometimes been altered to make the event visible to the audience. This treatment ultimately goes back to Shadwell's adaptation, by way of productions such as Charles Calvert's, who in Manchester in 1871 had Timon die in the arms of his servants.

In 1989 the Red Shift company staged two endings, one after the other. The first, and the more romantic, showed Timon gently

---

[1] Gary Jay Williams, p. 173.

sinking into a sea of black silks held by actors, each printed with a gold emblem of one of the senses. The second, more political, presented an altered transposition of the mock banquet, in which Timon was silently murdered by assassins. A year later at the Young Vic, David Suchet as Timon shot himself with a pistol abandoned by the thieves. In Stephen Oliver's opera at the London Coliseum in 1991 Timon killed himself, as in the Young Vic production, but with the critical difference that now Timon had to obtain help from Alcibiades. His was an act of friendship in a world where friendship was otherwise exposed as hollow and absent, and as such was the only effectual thing that could be done for Timon. Even Doran's textually conservative 1999 production sought a coherence in the ending in the spirit of Atkins and the Victorian adapters that the text does not encourage. Alcibiades directed an onslaught against Athens from a gangway hung over the main stage. After the dry ice cleared and Alcibiades established order, the Athenians on the main stage departed, leaving Alcibiades above, the Steward centre stage, and Apemantus downstage by the proscenium wall. So the ending resolved into a silent triptych of Timon's friends, widely separate, each, as the audience might imagine, remembering Timon in his own way.

'Timon of Athens' on Television

The BBC television production issued on video deserves special consideration both for its merits and for its rare representation of how the play can be adapted for the screen. It is, moreover, a resource available to many readers of this edition who may never see the play on stage. Carefully directed by Jonathan Miller, it takes advantage of the camera close-up to present a studied and softly spoken production. Plain monumental architecture with gaps and archways defines Timon's house and Athens. The woods are realized as an underlit pebble beach backed by the concrete of sea defences.

The director originally designated to work on *Timon of Athens* was Michael Bogdanov, who planned a modern-dress production. In the event, he was replaced by Miller, who was prepared to use period costume in line with the conservatism of the BBC series.[1]

---

[1] Susan Willis, *The BBC Shakespeare Plays* (Chapel Hill, 1991), p. 26. For the script, comment by Jonathan Miller, and illustrations, see the accompanying edition (1981).

The Athenian men wear smart black doublets with white ruffs, and the general uniformity of appearance in the early scenes is emphasized by trim beards. Miller used the severe formality of the costume as a point of contrast with Timon's ragged near-nakedness in the later scenes. Jonathan Pryce played a Timon whose benevolence was tinged with edgy anxiety from the outset. At his banquet in Sc. 2, he wears similar apparel to his friends; in appearance he is first amongst equals. The buttoned-up doublet and ruff gives way to open doublet and shirt as he becomes aware of his financial straits, and so to a loin-cloth and a blistered body-stocking of a shirt on the beach.

Miller chose the satirists John Fortune and John Bird to play the Poet and Painter. Despite Fortune's acquisition of a beard, they perform their roles with mannerisms recognizable from their performance style in satirical television programmes. In Miller's production they echo the complacent hypocrisy of modern forms of patronage as acted out in their own performances in these shows. Apemantus, played by Norman Rodway, is an older and wiser man than Timon. He shows wry concern, but finally, in the second part of the play, admits wry defeat, faced with a Timon who has learnt his lessons from Apemantus all too well.

Miller interprets the masque as a display of both the Amazons and the five senses, but resolves the potential overload of information by splitting the entertainment into two sections. This allows him to dwell at length on the banquet scene as a typification of Timon's life in Athens. The first episode shows adolescent girls dressed in white representing the five senses with emblematic objects, which are presented to Timon as gifts. This dumbshow is accompanied by Cupid singing a musical setting of his speech 'Hail to thee, worthy Timon'. Women then enter dressed as rather feminine Amazons in pale yellow dresses loosely based on Inigo Jones's Penthesilea.

The production observes the common practice of cutting episodes such as the Fool and Page in Sc. 4, the dialogue of the Strangers in Sc. 6, the short Sc. 15 showing the senators as they hear the news of Timon and Alcibiades, and Sc. 16 showing the Soldier discovering his tomb. More innovative and interesting is the cut at the turning-point of the play where Timon leaves Athens. The end of Sc. 11 and the first three lines of Sc. 12 are deleted, with the result that the rest of Timon's soliloquy in Sc. 12 is played as a continuation of the mock banquet scene. As he delivers the soliloquy, Timon smashes pots and overturns furniture, giving 'Take thou that too' at 12.34 an immediate explanation. In the following scene, the Servant's 'Such a house broke' at 13.5 is true literally: the debris is all around. This arrangement has the advantage of providing an immediate context for Timon's anger. It avoids the scene of transition, and simplifies the location sequence from Timon's house to outside the walls, back to Timon's house, and so to the woods. Thus it sharpened the division of the play into two halves.

The contrast is also sustained by the sudden elimination of colour as the scene shifts to the pebbled beach. In the darkness, Timon's head is backlit by a film-noirish light suggestive of a stark dawn, the 'blessed breeding sun' of Timon's soliloquy. Colour seeps in reluctantly as the light fills out. From this point on, Timon never stands up. His visitors encroach on his subhuman space by sitting or kneeling by him, their heads joining his in the frame of the camera shot. As they approach and leave, their footsteps crunch harshly on the pebbles.

Near-naked and no longer attaining the upright posture of *Homo sapiens*, Timon degenerates physically as the scene continues. His cave is a concrete box build into the sea wall; he crawls in and out of it like an animal. He is dying by the time the senators visit. The camera looks down on to his head on the stones; the face on the screen is upside-down. The last shot of him shows a close-up hand clawing at pebbles, as though to cover him in the cave where he will die.

Text

It is to foundational questions of text that this introduction now turns. As has been seen in the preceding critical discussion, much flows from the identification of Middleton as a collaborator, and some further critical implications of studying this play as a collaboration between Shakespeare and Middleton will be explored below. The play as it appears in the First Folio was evidently printed from a manuscript in the hands of the two dramatists. The printing itself involved some rare circumstances that probably point back to the collaborative nature of the printer's copy.

The printer William Jaggard's compositor who is customarily

80

THE LIFE OF TYMON
OF ATHENS.

Actus Primus. Scœna Prima.

Enter Poet, Painter, Ieweller, Merchant, and Mercer, at seuerall doores.

Poet.

Ood day Sir.

Pain. I am glad y'are well.

Poet. I haue not seene you long, how goes the World?

Pain. It weares sir, as it growes.

Poet. I that's well knowne:
But what particular Rarity? What strange,
Which manifold record not matches: see
Magicke of Bounty, all these spirits thy power
Hath conur'd to attend. I know the Merchant.

Pain. I know them both: th'others a Ieweller.

Mer. O 'tis a worthy Lord.

Iew. Nay that's most fixt.

Mer. A most incomparable man, breath'd as it were,
To an vntyreable and continuate goodnesse:
He passes.

Iew. I haue a Iewell heere.

Mer. O pray let's see't. For the Lord *Timon*, sir?

Iewel. If he will touch the estimate. But for that——

Poet. When we for recompence haue prais'd the vild,
It staines the glory in that happy Verse,
Which aptly sings the good.

Mer. 'Tis a good forme.

Iewel. And rich: heere is a Water looke ye.

Pain. You are rapt sir, in some worke, some Dedication to the great Lord.

Poet. A thing slipt idlely from me.
Our Poesie is as a Gowne, which vses
From whence 'tis nourisht: the fire i'th'Flint
Shewes not, till it be strooke: our gentle flame
Prouokes it selfe, and like the currant flyes
Each bound it chafes. What haue you there?

Pain. A Picture sir: when comes your Booke forth?

Poet. Vpon the heeles of my presentment sir.
Let's see your peece.

Pain. 'Tis a good Peece.

Poet. So 'tis, this comes off well, and excellent.

Pain. Indifferent.

Poet. Admirable: How this grace
Speakes his owne standing: what a mentall power
This eye shootes forth? How bigge imagination
Moues in this Lip, to th'dumbnesse of the gesture,

One might interpret.

Pain. It is a pretty mocking of the life:
Heere is a touch: Is't good?

Poet. I will say of it,
It Tutors Nature, Artificiall strife
Liues in these touches, liuelier then life.

Enter certaine Senators.

Pain. How this Lord is followed.

Poet. The Senators of Athens, happy men.

Pain. Looke moe.

Po. You see this confluence, this great flood of visitors,
I haue in this rough worke, shap'd out a man
Whom this beneath world doth embrace and hugge
With amplest entertainment: My free drift
Halts not particularly, but moue it selfe
In a wide Sea of wax, no leuell'd malice
Infects one comma in the course I hold,
But flies an Eagle flight, bold, and forth on,
Leauing no Tract behinde.

Pain. How shall I vnderstand you?

Poet. I will vnboult to you.
You see how all Conditions, how all Mindes,
As well of glib and slipp'ry Creatures, as
Of Graue and austere qualitie, tender downe
Their seruices to Lord *Timon*: his large Fortune,
Vpon his good and gracious Nature hanging,
Subdues and properties to his loue and tendance
All sorts of hearts; yea, from the glasse-fac'd Flatterer
To *Apemantus*, that few things loues better
Then to abhorre himselfe; euen hee drops downe
The knee before him, and returnes in peace
Most rich in *Timons* nod.

Pain. I saw them speake together.

Poet. Sir, I haue vpon a high and pleasant hill
Feign'd Fortune to be thron'd,
The Base o'th'Mount
Is rank'd with all deserts, all kinde of Natures
That labour on the bosome of this Sphere,
To propagate their states: among'st them all,
Whose eyes are on this Soueraigne Lady fixt,
One do I personate of Lord *Timons* frame,
Whom Fortune with her Iuory hand wafts to her,
Whose present grace, to present slaues and seruants
Translates his Riuals.

Pain. 'Tis conceyu'd, to scope
This Throne, this Fortune, and this Hill me thinkes

Wit

identified as Compositor B spent part of the summer of 1623 setting *Timon of Athens* in type. The text appeared later that year as part of the Folio edition of William Shakespeare's *Comedies, Histories, and Tragedies* (F). *Timon of Athens* was duly entered in the Stationers' Register alongside a number of other previously unpublished titles on 8 November 1623. This entry secured the right to publish the plays in question, and less than four weeks later, on 4 December, came the first recorded purchase of the Folio.[1]

The following account of the complex bibliographical details of the printing of *Timon of Athens* makes reference to key terms whose meaning should be explained at the outset. The Folio is built up in *quires* or gatherings each consisting of three paper sheets folded together. These make up a booklet of six leaves or twelve pages; each regular page presents the text in two columns. The term '*forme*' refers to the assembled type that is put under the press during printing, and hence to one side of the printed sheet that is produced by this operation; it is the latter sense that is of most concern here. It is usual practice in the Folio for the first three leaves to have *signatures*. These appear at the foot of the *recto* (the right-hand page when the book lies opened). They consist of one to three letters identifying the quire followed by a number showing the leaf in the case of the second or third leaf in the quire; for instance, K, K2, and K3. Readers have to count on to identify the fourth, fifth, and sixth leaves. The unsigned pages overleaf from the recto are referred to as the *verso*, abbreviated with superscript 'v'. Hence one refers to the page that appears overleaf from K2 and opposite K3 as K2^v. The three sections of the Folio have separate sequences of page numbers. It is usual to refer to Folio pages by signature instead of page number, and, as will be seen, *Timon of Athens* offers a case in point of the page numbers being inaccurate.

The play occupies most of quire Gg, beginning on Gg1^v, and all of quire hh. The signatures are part of the evidence for extraordinary developments during the printing of the Folio. *Timon of Athens* is printed immediately after *Romeo and Juliet*. The final pages of *Romeo* and the first pages of *Timon of Athens* have duplicate or near-duplicate signatures on the alternate recto pages, as follows:

---

[1] Peter W. M. Blayney, *The First Folio of Shakespeare* (Washington, DC, 1991), p. 25.

Romeo	p. 73	gg
	p. 75	gg2
	p. 79	Gg
Timon	p. 81	gg2

The following leaf has the signature 'gg3'. After three unsigned leaves, a new quire hh begins; it has the regular signatures hh, hh2, and hh3 and is a regular quire of six leaves. At the end of *Timon of Athens* the sixth and final leaf of quire hh displays on the recto a list of 'THE ACTORS NAMES.' (actually listing the roles, not their performers).[1] The following verso leaf is blank. Opposite it is the first page of *Julius Caesar*, which is the first page of the new quire kk.

What is immediately striking about this sequence is that there are two extra leaves added to quire gg and there is a gap in the signatures between hh and kk which does not correspond to any disruption of the text. The gap amounts to a single missing quire, ii (for 'i' and 'j' were treated as a single letter). Moreover, there is a comparable breakdown in the page numbering at the end of quire hh. The final page of text is numbered 98; the leaf with the list of roles and the blank leaf are unnumbered, and then the page sequence for *Julius Caesar* resumes at 109. To judge by the page numbering, there are apparently eight pages missing. This figure is not altered by two anomalies in the page numbering. Pages 77 and 78 are missing, but the page numbers 81 and 82 appear twice, on the four pages of the leaves already mentioned as signed gg2 and gg3. These errors cancel each other out. The eight pages, or four leaves, missing from the pagination add up to less than a full quire, but the numbers are exactly made up by the two extra leaves at the beginning of gg: four leaves missing from the pagination plus two paginated leaves added to the signatures make up a total that corresponds with the six leaves of the missing quire. The page numbering therefore confirms what the signatures tell us.

It is clear from Charlton Hinman's bibliographical analysis of F, based largely on the recurrence of distinctive type that had been set, printed, and returned to the compositors' type-trays, that *Julius Caesar* was printed well before the compositors completed work on *Romeo* and turned to *Timon of Athens*. The number of leaves allocated to *Timon of Athens* had been determined well before work

---

[1] See p. 168 for a transcript.

began on the play, and the page number and signature of the first page of *Caesar* could not be altered. The original plan for the Folio allowed extra space sufficient to hold the best part of half a typical Shakespeare play. *Timon of Athens* proved to be considerably too short to fill the allocated leaves, even after one of them was given over to the list of roles followed by a blank leaf.

The situation in 'gg' turns out to be complex. As we have seen, the page before the first page of *Timon of Athens* is signed 'Gg'. This signature identifies the page as the first page of a new quire, but the same seems to be true also of 'gg' two leaves earlier. Examination of the way in which the sheets of paper are folded into quires reveals that gg and gg2 in fact make up a single-leaf quire. The 'Gg' on the final page of *Romeo* indicates the beginning of a new regular six-leaf quire, and it is for this reason that it is distinguished from the two preceding leaves gg and gg2 by the use of a capital G. The pages in *Timon of Athens* signed gg2 and gg3 should therefore more accurately be referred to as Gg2 and Gg3, so that the initial capital 'G' can differentiate them, and the quire in which they appear, from the preceding two-leaf quire gg. This is the convention that bibliographers adopt: what is referred to as Gg2 is the page in *Timon of Athens* signed gg2.

To summarize, where one would expect three regular quires of six sheets, signed gg, hh, and ii, one actually finds an anomalous one-leaf quire (gg), two six-leaf quires (Gg and hh), and no quire ii at all.

This account has so far been based on the majority of copies of F, and represents the final arrangement of the volume. However, in one surviving copy of F (Folger Shakespeare Library, copy 71) the text of the final page of *Romeo* appears in an earlier setting; it has been cancelled by crossing the text out with a single stroke of the pen. Whereas the reset page that appears at the end of *Romeo* and immediately before *Timon of Athens* in other copies of F is signed Gg (i.e. Gg1), this cancelled page is signed gg3. It continues the original quire gg. However, it does not form part of the text of *Romeo* as printed in this copy of F. The leaf in question appears at the beginning of an anomalous section of the Folio between the Histories and the Tragedies that presents the text of *Trolius and Cressida* in the same bibliographically isolated position as in all other copies of F. So it is that the verso of the leaf contains, not the first page of *Timon of Athens*, but the first page of *Troilus*. This crucial piece of evidence shows that work began on printing *Troilus* on the assumption that it would appear immediately after *Romeo*. *Troilus* was then pulled out of this position, and *Timon of Athens* was brought in as a substitute. As a measure that turned out to be merely interim, a few pages of *Troilus* as designed to appear in its original position were reused in its new position, and the final page of *Romeo* got caught up in this relocation. The details of *Troilus* need concern us no further, but there were clear consequences for *Timon of Athens*. It happens that *Timon of Athens* is a much shorter play than *Troilus*. The relocated *Romeo* page is the key to understanding the peculiarities in the quire-structure, signatures, and pagination within and around our play.

Hinman explained the sequence of events in previously unmatched detail.[1] The original scheme for the printing of *Troilus* after *Romeo* can be seen in Fig. 3, Stage 1. The inexperienced Compositor E evidently began work on the quire identified as *gg. (The asterisk here denotes the quire as planned and partly executed before cancellation.) As was standard practice in the composing of F, Compositor E began work on this quire in the middle, setting *gg3^v-4, which contained early parts of *Troilus*, and from here he moved outwards towards the beginning and end of the quire. Half of his work therefore entailed moving backwards through the first half of the quire towards the beginning of *Troilus* and the end of *Romeo*.

However, after he had composed four pages of *Troilus* (*gg3^v-4, *gg4^v, and *gg5) and the end of *Romeo* (*gg3 and *gg2^v), his work was curtailed (Fig. 3, Stage 2). *Troilus* was for the time being given up as a lost cause, evidently for reasons of copyright. The end of *Romeo* at this stage was partly unprinted (*gg1, 1^v, and 2) and was partly printed on pages paired up on the same sheet with pages of *Troilus* (*gg2^v, paired with *gg5, and *gg3, paired with *gg4^v). One forme of one sheet was given over entirely to *Troilus* (*gg3^v-4); the other forme of the same sheet contained *gg3, the final page of *Romeo*.

As a provisional measure ensuring that *Romeo* could if necessary be separated from *Troilus*, Compositor E now established four of the five final pages of *Romeo* as a bibliographically separate unit. He set

---

[1] *The Printing and Proof-Reading of the First Folio of Shakespeare*, 2 vols. (Oxford, 1963), ii. 231–85.

1. *Original Plan* The plan was to print three regular quires with in a regular sequence containing the end of *Romeo* and the beginning of *Troilus*:

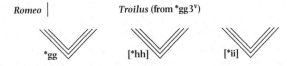

2. *Initial Printing* The beginning of *Troilus* and the last two pages of *Romeo* were printed according to the original plan. The compositor worked from the middle of the quire outwards, as usual. In the following diagram, 'rv' indicates a leaf printed on both verso and recto pages. 2v and 5r are conjugate printed pages on the inner forme of the sheet. The outer forme of this sheet remained unprinted.

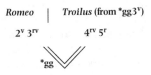

3. *Interim Arrangement* Before the printing of the quire was completed, work was stopped, and the printed pages of *Troilus* and the last page of *Romeo* were set aside. The type of the penultimate page of *Romeo*, *gg2ᵛ, was still assembled from the initial printing, so it was reused, now as part of a one-leaf quire containing the end of *Romeo* except for the last page.

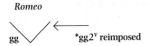

4. *Final Arrangement* The one-leaf quire was followed by two new quires containing the last page of *Romeo*, now reset, with the whole of *Timon*:

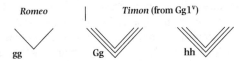

5. *Troilus and Cressida* *Troilus* was eventually inserted before the Tragedies section. The first three pages of the original printing were used, with the last page of *Romeo* in place but crossed out on the recto of the first page of *Troilus*. This arrangement is seen in a single extant copy. The first page was then reset, with a newly printed Prologue on the recto of the leaf.

Figure 3: The Replacement of Troilus and Cressida *with* Timon of Athens

what would otherwise have been the opening four pages of the abandoned quire *gg as the single, four-page sheet of leaves gg1 and 2, containing all but the final page of the end of *Romeo*. Of the pages in this new sheet, gg1, gg1ᵛ, and gg2 had not previously been printed. The type of *gg2ᵛ was still locked up after its printing alongside *gg5, and so could be reused, now matched with the new and earlier page from *Romeo*, gg1 (Fig. 3, Stage 3).

Things were left in this state for several weeks while work proceeded on the remaining parts of the Tragedies section. When only three other plays to appear in the Tragedies section remained completely unprinted, it was decided to fill the gap so far reserved for *Troilus* by printing *Timon of Athens* instead. The play may conceivably have been brought forward from an anticipated position later in the Folio, but it is strongly to be suspected that there was no original intention to publish it. This has a bearing on the question of the play's authorship. *Timon of Athens* might have been seen in the same group as the other plays excluded from the Folio that involved Shakespeare (see p. 144). It should be remembered that the Folio editors were not rigorous on this issue, for some of the plays printed in the volume also contain more than one hand. But co-authorship is the only consistent ground that can be identified on which plays were excluded.

If so, the temporary exclusion of *Troilus* for completely different reasons was decisively fortunate for our play. There is no other surviving early text. The later Folios reprint their predecessors, and have no independent authority. Without the Folio text, *Timon of Athens* would simply have disappeared without trace. The case would have been even worse than with the known but lost Shakespeare–Fletcher collaboration *Cardenio*: as there is no record of performance, allusion, or documentation of any kind, we would not even have heard of this play.

The play's unscheduled inclusion in the Folio explains the major peculiarities of the text noted above. Quire ii was not needed because *Timon of Athens* is considerably shorter than *Troilus*. The lack of correlation between the quires, with their signatures, and the continuous page numbering of the Tragedies section based on the inclusion of the quire ii caused the difficulties with the page numbering. Even with the elimination of quire ii, *Timon* was too short for the space allocation of two full quires. It is one consequence of this surplus of space that a page of the potentially unused leaf at the end of the play could take the list of 'THE ACTORS NAMES'. It was straightforward to integrate the end of *Romeo*, though this required some extra work. The final page of *Romeo*, previously set as *gg3 on a sheet otherwise containing three pages of *Troilus*, was now reset as the first page of the new quire Gg, with *Timon of Athens* beginning on the verso of the same leaf (Fig. 3, Stage 4; for the opening page of *Timon of Athens*, see Illustration 9).

Compositor B, who was responsible for more of the Folio text than any other single compositor, set most but probably not all of *Timon of Athens*. Bibliographical study has suggested that another workman was engaged on at least one page, Gg3, which prints 2.10–129. A. S. Cairncross suggested that the inexperienced Compositor E set this page, and intermittently contributed to the work on other pages in the same quire.[1] Some of his evidence, particularly that based on irregular spellings, was subsequently dismissed by Trevor Howard-Hill. On a narrower but more secure basis of evidence, primarily the tendency on Gg3 not to insert a space after a comma in unjustified type-lines, Howard-Hill argued that Compositor B set all but this one page.[2] This is consistent with the fact that this is the only page set from the type held in Case x, where the rest of the play is set from Compositor B's usual Case y.[3] Compositor E is the only workman who has been suggested as the alternative to B, but Howard-Hill cautions that yet another compositor might have set the page instead.

Work proceeded on quire Gg in the usual order, beginning with the middle pair of pages and working backwards and forwards towards the outer pair of pages. Work on hh was slightly irregular in sequence. Compositor B set the formes of the outer sheet in alternation with the formes of the inner sheet, instead of after the middle sheet.[4] Meanwhile, as Compositor B was still working on quire hh of *Timon*, Compositor E set formes ss3^v:4 and

---

[1] 'Compositors E and F of the Shakespeare First Folio', *Papers of the Bibliographical Society of America*, 66 (1972), 369–406.

[2] 'A Reassessment of Compositors B and E in the First Folio Tragedies' (typescript, 1977); private communication.

[3] In quires qq and rr, printed immediately before *Timon of Athens*, and quire ss, printed during and immediately after, Case x is used only by Compositor E, and Compositor E made no use of Case y.

[4] Hinman conjectures that the blank page hh6^v in the outer forme provided an opportunity for Compositor B to complete the forme quickly and turn for a while to another book (ii. 288–9).

ss2^v: 5.[1] These are 'intercalary' formes made up of pages separate from the main sequence of printing, here pages of *Lear* and *Othello*.

The sequence of work on the Folio during the printing of *Timon of Athens* can be summarized as follows, with all work attributable to Compositor B except the pages set by Compositor E, here marked '[E]':

Gg3^v: 4	
Gg3[E?]: 4^v	
Gg2^v: 5	
Gg2: 5^v	
Gg1^v: 6	Gg1^v is the first page of *Timon*
Gg1: 6^v	Gg1 is the reset page of *Romeo*
hh3^v: 4	
hh1: [6^v blank]	Out of regular sequence (as seen in Gg)
hh3: 4^v	
hh1^v: 6	Out of regular sequence; hh6 lists 'THE ACTORS NAMES'
ss3^v[E]: 4[E]	The first pages of *Othello*
hh2^v: 5	
hh2: 5^v	hh5^v is the last page of *Timon*
ss2^v[E]: 5[E]	The penultimate page of *Lear* and the fourth page of *Othello*.

It was only later that *Troilus* was inserted separately before the Tragedies, making some use of the leaves already printed (Fig. 3, Stage 5).

The change of compositor for the setting of Gg3 needs to be taken into account when assessing the evidence for the hand of a second author, not least because this page contains the larger part of a scene attributed to Middleton, Sc. 2. The authorial markers identified by author attribution studies (see pp. 137–41) are strongly represented in this page, but they are by no means confined to this Folio page, and some of them are in any case most unlikely to have been affected by a compositor. If the compositor of this page was indeed Compositor E, one would expect from his work elsewhere that he would treat his copy more conservatively than

---

[1] The formula ss3^v: 4 designates two pages that make up a forme. Figure 3 gives an indication of how these pages match up in the folded booklet that makes up the quire.

Compositor B, so if anything Gg3 is likely to be distinctive because it more fully reflects features of the copy rather than because the compositor introduced his preferences.

The tendency of Compositor E (or another compositor) to regularize less thoroughly than Compositor B can explain one oddity. A cluster of three instances of 'there' as a spelling for *their* at 2.41, 45, and 96 is without example in the Folio, other instances being isolated and rare.[1] Some explanation seems called for. Though 'there' for *their* is found occasionally in his holograph manuscripts, Middleton's preferred spelling was 'theire'. As the Folio compositors never set the usual Middletonian form 'theire' for either word, the possibility arises that the cluster results from the combination of Middleton's 'theire' in the copy and misregularization by a compositor who played little or no part in setting the rest of *Timon of Athens*.

The indications are, therefore, that the change of compositor for the setting of Gg3 makes very little difference indeed to the argument surrounding the play's authorship, but it may have had the isolated effect of allowing a Middleton spelling to cause an unparalleled cluster of unusual spellings in the printed text.

Notwithstanding the introduction of the list of dramatic roles as a space-filler, the text barely stretched to fill the required length. Compositor B tried to improve matters. He used generous spacing, in quire hh especially, to ensure that hh5^v, the play's last page, was left with a respectable quantity of type (about half a page). He went further. A passage of stichomythic single lines at 14.358–65, for example, is split into false part-lines, wasting an extra type-line in each case. The widespread confusion between verse and prose, though probably in large measure intrinsic to the text as a result of Middleton's mixing of prose and verse in single speeches, may have been compounded by the compositor's willingness to break to a new type-line.

One technique of space-consumption not available to the compositors was manipulation of the setting of act–scene breaks. After a promisory '*Actus Primus. Scoena Prima.*' at the head of the play, a feature this text shares with other undivided plays in the Folio, there are no further indications of act or scene number. The

---

[1] Two examples are *Coriolanus* TLN 1823 (Compositor B) and *Hamlet* TLN 3467 (Compositor E). 'TLN' is the through line number in the Norton Facsimile, ed. Charlton Hinman (New York, 1968).

absence of act divisions is consistent with the performance practices of the King's Men before 1608–9 (see pp. 4–5).

To judge by the various loose ends and inconsistencies, the copy for *Timon of Athens* seems to have been an authorial rough draft. Many such features are to be found within the sections of both Shakespeare and Middleton, and need no reference to a second dramatist in order to explain them. There is inconsistency as to how the roles of Timon's high-ranking friends are identified collectively: the 'Lords' of Sc. 1 and Sc. 2 are presumably more or less the same group as the 'Senators' of later scenes.[1] The numbering of lords and senators is based on their order of speaking in the scene, which can produce inconsistency between scenes.[2] Other textual problems arising from confusion, uncertainty, or illegibility in the manuscript, though they are not remarkable individually, are more common than in most Folio plays. The stage directions need regularization, though, as William B. Long has demonstrated, inconsistencies could remain in a company playbook.[3] The confusion in the stage directions for the masque in Sc. 2 (see collation and commentary to 2.109–26) are of another order, and suggest that the manuscript was here distinctly pre-theatrical. The persistent indications of pre-theatricality in *Timon of Athens*, together with the absence of evidence for the manuscript's use in the theatre, encourage no other conclusion than that the Folio copy stands at a significant distance from stage performance. Perhaps the most compelling argument in support of this view stems from the unfinished quality of the text, especially as regards the anomalies that arise from co-authorship. These are discussed below (pp. 147–8).

The headnote to *Timon of Athens* in Edward Capell's 1780 commentary on Shakespeare claimed that 'The multitude of its corruptions in old copies . . . distinguish the play before us from almost any in Shakespeare'.[4] The theory that the compositors were working from a rough draft of a collaborative play makes many of these features comprehensible. For the most part they are not 'corruptions', in that there would not have been any uncorrupted

---

[1] For details, see notes to 11.0.2 and 11.1.

[2] See commentary to 15.1 and 13.

[3] 'Stage Directions: A Misinterpreted Factor in Determining Texual Provenance', *TEXT*, 2 (1985), 121–38.

[4] Quoted in Vickers, *Critical Heritage*, vi. 243.

antecedent to the printer's manuscript. An inelegant though more accurate term would be 'pre-completions'. Whether the script was ever brought to a state that would have made it more readily playable must remain a matter of speculation. The question that can be more fully addressed, left hanging from the opening pages of this introduction, concerns the authorship issue and the pattern of collaboration.

A Divided Play

The fact that *Timon of Athens* was published in the Shakespeare First Folio of 1623 is strong testimony to Shakespeare's hand, but not to his exclusive authorship. The Folio does not include any play that was not at least partly written by Shakespeare, but the book says nothing about Shakespeare as a collaborator, and in this respect its presentation of Shakespeare as author is misleading. As has been recognized with increasing clarity over the past few years, a number of plays in the volume almost certainly contain the writing of other dramatists. These include *1 Henry VI*, *Henry VIII*, and probably *Titus Andronicus*, as well as two plays that were probably adapted after Shakespeare's death by Middleton, *Measure for Measure* and *Macbeth*.[1] The presence of *Timon of Athens* in the Folio does not therefore establish that Shakespeare alone wrote the play. As has been seen, bibliographical considerations make it quite probable that the Folio editors orginally rejected the play. If *Timon of Athens* had been earmarked for exclusion, collaborative authorship was almost certainly the reason.

Timon of Athens was identified in the nineteenth century as a flawed text that needed some form of special explanation: typically, either that it was abandoned by Shakespeare or that it was produced by more than one hand.[2] Hermann Ulrici's study of 1839 laid the foundations of the theory that the play was left unfinished. He

---

[1] See especially: Gary Taylor, 'Shakespeare and Others: The Authorship of *Henry the Sixth Part One*', *Medieval and Renaissance Drama in England*, 7 (1995), 145–205; MacD. P. Jackson, 'Stage Directions and Speech Headings in Act 1 of *Titus Andronicus* Q (1594): Shakespeare or Peele?', *Studies in Bibliography*, 49 (1996), 134–48; Gary Taylor and John Jowett, *Shakespeare Reshaped, 1606–1623* (Oxford, 1993) (on *Measure for Measure*); *Textual Companion*, pp. 128–9 (on *Macbeth*); and Vickers, *Co-Author* (on *Titus*, *Pericles*, and *Henry VIII*).

[2] For full discussion of the history of debate on the play's authorship (but without direct reference to Holdsworth), see Vickers, *Co-Author*, pp. 244–90.

observed that 'The thoughts are frequently huddled and packed
together without order or connection; the turns are striking and
sudden, while the abruptness and obscurity of the language are
extreme'. On grounds such as these he judged that 'the piece may
have wanted the author's last finishing touch', inferring from this
in turn that Shakespeare's work on 'this wonderful drama' was
suspended either by his supposed retirement to Stratford or his
death.[1] In the same period, Charles Knight in his pictorial edition
first proposed that Shakespeare revised an inferior play by another
dramatist. He initiated a tradition of trying to separate off various
episodes for qualities such as 'languid, wearisome want of action'
in order to retrieve the muscle and bone of the play as Shakespeare
contributed to it.[2]

Writing in the early decades of the twentieth century, E. K.
Chambers agreed with Ulrici as to the characteristics of the writing
and the explanation for it. Though he found 'much fine Shakespearean poetry', the longer speeches 'contain Shakespearean
ideas, sometimes inchoate, and scattered Shakespearean phrases.
But they are not constructed as articulated paragraphs at all.'
Moreover, 'the structure of *Timon* as a whole is incoherent'.[3]
Chambers goes so far as to suggest that Shakespeare 'dealt with it
under conditions of mental and perhaps physical stress, which led
to a breakdown'. If Chambers had been making a *bête noire* of disintegration, his own alternative turned out to be itself an example
of suppositious scholarship. In 1934 C. J. Sisson devastatingly
attacked what he called the 'mythical sorrows' of Shakespeare:
the postulate that *Timon of Athens* and other plays result from a
psychological crisis in Shakespeare's life.[4] In the case of *Timon of*

[1] *Ueber Shakspeare's dramatische Kunst* (Halle, 1839), trans. by Alexander J. W.
Morrison as *Shakespeare's Dramatic Art* (1846), pp. 238–9.

[2] Quotation from Frederick Gard Fleay, *Shakespeare Manual* (1878), p. 204.

[3] *William Shakespeare*, i. 481. Chambers had advocated the theory that the play
was unfinished rather than of joint authorship as early as 1908, in his Introduction
to the Red Letter edition of Shakespeare, as noted by Francelia Butler, *The Strange
Critical Fortunes of Shakespeare's 'Timon of Athens'* (Ames, Iowa, 1966), p. 46. He
influentially formulated his opposition to co-authorship theories in 'The Disintegration of Shakespeare', British Academy Shakespeare Lecture, 1924, repr. in *Aspects
of Shakespeare* (Oxford, 1933), pp. 23–48. On *Timon of Athens*, see also Una Ellis-
Fermor, '*Timon of Athens*: An Unfinished Play', *Review of English Studies*, 18 (1942),
270–83.

[4] 'The Mythical Sorrows of Shakespeare', British Academy Shakespeare Lecture,
1934; repr. in *Studies in Shakespeare*, ed. Peter Alexander (1964), pp. 9–32.

Athens, the theory of the psychologically fractured author, which had served as a mainstay against theories of collaboration, proved itself to be the house built on sand.

As Brian Vickers has pointed out (*Co-Author*, p. 170), Chambers had been able to make easy capital of the sheer diversity of 'disintegrationist' theories about *Timon of Athens*. This is conspicuous when Chambers writes: 'Thus a draft or fragmentary play by Shakespeare is held to have been rehandled by Heywood (Verplanck), Tourneur (Fleay in 1874), Wilkins (Fleay in 1886), Chapman and perhaps Field (Parrott), Middleton ([William] Wells). And again Shakespeare is held to have rehandled the work of Wilkins (Delius), Chapman (Robertson), Day and Middleton (Sykes).'[1] The insistent listing undermines the reader's confidence in any of the studies it includes. As will be seen, it now looks as though there is a certain amount of valid scholarship buried in this catalogue.

Despite the variety of theories that Chambers summarizes, notably absent is the possibility that Shakespeare worked laterally alongside another dramatist. If the task of scripting was distributed between two dramatists, the two authorial sections could scarcely avoid creating inconsistencies, and the presence of a second style could produce at least some of the 'unusual' quality of writing noted by Chambers.[2] This, moreover, places *Timon of Athens* within an extraordinarily commonplace technique for the production of scripts in the early modern theatre, where perhaps up to half of all plays were co-authored. The early attribution studies were more willing to think of Shakespeare as a reviser, the role suggested by the hostile description of Shakespeare as an 'Aesop's crow beautified with our feathers' in *Greene's Groatsworth*

---

[1] *William Shakespeare*, i. 482. The studies Chambers cites are: *The Illustrated Shakespeare*, ed. Gulian C. Verplanck, 3 vols. (New York, 1847); Frederick Gard Fleay, 'On the Authorship of *Timon of Athens*', *New Shakspere Society Transactions*, 1 (1874), pp. 130–51; Fleay, *A Chronicle History of the Life and Work of William Shakespeare, Player, Poet, and Playmaker* (1886); Thomas Marc Parrott, *The Problem of 'Timon of Athens'* (1923); William Wells, '*Timon of Athens*', in *Notes and Queries*, 112 (1920), 226–9; N. Delius, 'Ueber Shakespeare's *Timon of Athens*', *Shakespeare Jahrbuch*, 2 (1867), 335–61; J. M. Robertson, *Shakespeare and Chapman* (1917); H. Dugdale Sykes, *Sidelights on Elizabethan Drama* (Oxford, 1924). See also Ernest Hunter Wright, *The Authorship of 'Timon of Athens'* (New York, 1910). Sykes's suggestion that John Day contributed is revived without amplification in the Riverside Shakespeare, 2nd edn. (Boston and New York, 1997), p. 1523.

[2] However, the writing within individual speeches shows little evidence of collaboration.

of Wit (1592). They could imagine him as a writer whose works were subject to adaptation by others, as was already recognized to be the case with *Macbeth*, and as was known to have become commonplace in the Restoration period. The thought that Shakespeare might have engaged in the perfectly normal process of sharing the original writing with another dramatist eluded the critics whom Chambers cited.

Chambers's dismissal of 'disintegration' was of vital significance in upholding the mid-twentieth-century assessment of Shakespeare as a stylistically diverse writer who stood apart from and above his contemporaries. But its effect on the reception of *Timon of Athens* was deleterious. At worst, deprived of the possibility of disintegrated authorship, the play was left the ruined product of a disintegrated mind. The editors who prepared the most influential editions of the second half of the century remained troubled by the text but denied that its features related to collaboration. The Arden editor of 1959, H. J. Oliver, sought to dismiss the potential textual effects of collaboration by positing that the text was in part copied by the scribe Ralph Crane, who imposed his own traits. Though he seems to have prepared the printer's copy for several other Folio plays, the case for Crane's involvement in *Timon of Athens* does not withstand scrutiny.[1] This theory put forward to undercut the case for divided authorship must be rejected as purely wishful.

If the mid twentieth-century rejection of Shakespeare as a collaborator stemmed from a view of Shakespeare as a writer who stood aloof from the everyday practices of commercial playmaking, the late twentieth-century reluctance to identify Shakespeare as a collaborator had almost the opposite foundation. By then, critics were suspicious of the notion of authorship itself. Although collaboration could be celebrated as a factor that diminished the authorial authority of the early modern dramatist, there was some reluctance to divide texts into author-based segments. Paradoxically, Shakespeare remained visible as a non-collaborating dramatist by default. As will be seen, however, the techniques for discriminating between authors as stylistically distinct as Middleton and Shakespeare were steadily improving, to the extent that by the end of the century the presence of Middleton's hand in *Timon of Athens*

---

[1] T. H. Howard-Hill, 'Ralph Crane's Parentheses', *Notes and Queries*, 210 (1965), 334–40, p. 339; David Lake, *The Canon of Thomas Middleton's Plays* (Cambridge, 1975), p. 284; Jackson, *Studies in Attribution*, pp. 55–6.

had been demonstrated clearly enough to convince almost anyone who examined the evidence.

Middleton's Hand

It was William Wells who in 1920 first explicitly suggested that Middleton had a hand in *Timon of Athens*. But Frederick Gard Fleay could be said to have anticipated him by almost half a century, because he advanced his claim for Cyril Tourneur on the basis of metrical similarities between the un-Shakespearian portion and a play now identified as by Middleton:

The ratio of rhyme to blank verse, the irregularities of length (lines with four accents and initial monosyllabic feet), number of double endings &c., agree with only one play of all those I have analyzed (over 200), viz., *the Revenger's Tragedy*.[1]

Fleay's scholarship is often chaotically hit and miss.[2] However, reviewed in the light of more recent work, his findings in this case are cogent, not least because they are based on quantifiable factors. The far stronger preference for rhyming couplets—proportionally eight times as many as in the Shakespearian passages—the greater tolerance of irregular verse-lines, and the frequency of feminine endings, are all confirmed features of this section of *Timon of Athens* that also characterize Middleton's writing elsewhere.

The more recent studies focus in the first place on linguistic features that discriminate between one writer and another. It is a valid criticism in principle that presuppositions about the nature of the collaborative process might influence the outcome of such studies. But attribution study proves sufficiently flexible to postulate different authorial situations within a single text such as *Timon of Athens*: for instance that one scene is attributable to one dramatist, another scene is of mixed authorship, another was supplemented at the beginning or end by the second dramatist. It is able also to distinguish between a complex and nuanced collaborative pattern such as this and a relatively crude division of material such as in *Pericles*, where it emerges simply that the other dramatist wrote the first section.

Timon of Athens is a reasonably straightforward text to investi-

---

[1] 'Authorship', pp. 137–8.

[2] As is painfully exemplified in his later deferral to Delius in accepting that the second hand might after all be that of Wilkins.

gate, because the compositors, as far as can be ascertained, worked directly from an authorial draft that had been neither transcribed nor altered by theatre personnel, and because the text was mostly set in type by Compositor B, a compositor whose habits and preferences are well understood. Unless one resorts to unsubstantiated conjecture, any shift in linguistic usages that does not correspond with the change of compositors for one page (sig. Gg3) can therefore be attributed with a reasonable degree of confidence to a change in the authorial complexion of the text.

The modern reappraisal leading to the successful identification of Middleton as a collaborator in *Timon of Athens* began in the work of David Lake and MacD. P. Jackson, and was given its fullest expression in R. V. Holdsworth's study devoted entirely to presenting the evidence for Middleton's hand in this play.[1] Unlike the earlier phase of 'disintegration', it is characterized by convergence, as regards both the identity of the collaborator and the attribution of particular scenes and passages to him. Lake established a series of Middletonian colloquialisms and contractions in his proposed Middleton section of *Timon of Athens*; Holdsworth was to add to the catalogue. Jackson noted that the spellings 'O' and 'Oh' resisted compositorial alteration in this text as elsewhere in F, and provided evidence of two authorial sections. The Middletonian section tolerated either spelling, with a preference for 'Oh', whereas in the Shakespeare section the spelling was uniformly 'O'. The spelling 'Oh' is therefore a marker of Middleton's presence (see Appendix C).

Holdsworth made up a broad compilation of features that distinguish the two sections. Building on Lake, he noted, for example, that the contractions 'I'm', 'I'd', 'I've', 'on't', 'ne'er', and 'e'en' are much more common in Middleton than in Shakespeare: the overall rates per 20,000 words are 13 in Shakespeare's works and 93 in Middleton's. He showed that closely similar rates apply to the two sections of *Timon of Athens*: 13 in the 'Shakespeare' section, as against 98 in the 'Middleton' section. The 'Middleton' section is entirely exceptional for Shakespeare and fully in accord with Middleton. Similar results were obtained from other contractions favoured by Middleton, whether examined individually or in groups: 'ha'' (for 'has'), ''has' (for 'he has'), ''tas (for 'it has'), and

[1] Jackson has privately confirmed that his original reservations regarding his ascription of parts of the play to Middleton have been largely removed by Holdsworth's work.

''had' (for 'he had); forms ending in '-'t' such as 'is't'; ''em' (for 'them'); 'they're' and 'she's'; ''bove', ''mongst', 'yonder's' (see Appendix C). In every case Middleton's preference is for the contraction and the 'Middleton' section of *Timon of Athens* follows this preference. In contrast, Shakespeare but not Middleton uses the variant 'moe' for 'more' (1.41, 3.7, 4.107, 14.380, 14.433).[1] Similar considerations apply to the choices between 'has' and 'hath', or 'does' and 'doth' (see Appendix C). Middleton overwhelmingly prefers the more modern forms 'has' and 'does', whereas Shakespeare favours 'hath' and 'doth'. As can be seen in Appendix C, the two sections reflect these preferences. The marked fluctuation between Shakespearian norms and non-Shakespearian norms absolutely demands some form of explanation, and the presence of Middleton's hand supplies it. The strength of Holdsworth's work rests on four qualities: the volume of evidence, the transparency of his methods, the frequent correspondence not only in the preference itself but in the preference ratio between the two authorial sections and the two authors' other works, and the emphatic consistency of results from different tests.

Holdsworth and others supplement these findings by identifying other Middleton characteristics in the 'Middleton' scenes. There are, for example, variations in spelling that reflect the authorial division.[2] Shakespeare correctly spells 'Apemantus', where Middleton has 'Apermantus'.[3] Shakespeare again more correctly spells 'Ventidius' or 'Ventiddius', where Middleton has 'Ventigius' or 'Ventidgius'.[4] The names of the lords Lucius, Lucullus, and Sempronius are confined to Middleton's writing,[5] whereas the servant

---

[1] But the first is in a passage also showing signs of Middleton's hand.

[2] A possible example is the spelling 'deny'de', found six times in Middleton scenes, but nowhere else in the play, and elsewhere only three times in F. *Timon*: TLN 993, 995, 1043, 1082, 1083, 1356 (6.14, 6.16, 6.63, 7.7, 7.8, 10.93). Elsewhere: *Antony and Cleopatra* TLN 3483, *Hamlet* TLN 1006, *Henry VIII* TLN 436.

[3] Sc. 1 (Shakespeare, with minor additions by Middleton): 'Apemantus' 11, 'Apermantus' 2. Sc. 2 (Middleton): 'Apermantus' 18. Sc. 4 (mixed): 'Apementus' 5, 'Apermantus' 1. Sc. 14 (Shakespeare): 'Apemantus' 5. These figures include speech-prefix '*Aper.*' but not potentially ambiguous '*Ape.*' The instances of 'Apermantus' in Sc. 1 (1.179, 183) are in a passage attributable to Middleton (see commentary notes to 1.180 and 1.181). The example in Sc. 4 (4.72) is close to other Middleton markers (see commentary notes to 4.73–4 and 4.75).

[4] Sc. 1 (Shakespeare, with minor additions by Middleton): 'Ventidius'. Sc. 2 (Middleton): 'Ventigius'. Sc. 4 (mixed): 'Ventiddius' (4.214, 216). Sc. 7 (Middleton): 'Ventidgius'.

[5] They are present or mentioned in Scs. 2, 4, 5, 6, 7, 8, and 9. For the Middletonian passage in the collaborative Sc. 4, see commentary to 4.119–227.

called Lucilius is found only in a Shakespeare scene. The intermixture of verse and prose, as in Apemantus' speech at 2.38–50, can be disconcerting to readers trained on Shakespeare, and has sometimes been attributed to textual corruption, but reflects instead a recognized trait of Middleton's writing. A discrepancy between small and large numbers of talents is similarly explained in authorial terms, with Shakespeare nominating the smaller numbers. The explosion from Shakespeare's more modest sums of five or three talents in Sc. 1 to fifty talents at 4.187, to 1,000 talents at 4.193, suggests an intervention from Middleton in Sc. 4, whereas the sober five talents at 4.223 might indicate Shakespeare in control again.[1] The larger numbers continue in Middleton's Sc. 5 and Sc. 6.

The stage directions, Holdsworth noted, show several idioms and formulae that are unShakespearian, well exampled in Middleton, and for the most part more compatible with Middleton than any other dramatist. The formula '[person/people] *meeting* [person/people]', as found at 8.0.1 and 10.0.1, is not found in Shakespeare and is fairly rare except in Middleton, in whose plays it is found at least thirteen times.[2] '*In a rage*' in the stage direction at 8.77.1 uses a word, 'rage', again found nowhere in the stage directions of Shakespeare plays; the formula has both close and exact parallels in those of Middleton's plays.[3] Similarly exampled in Middleton's stage directions but not Shakespeare's are the phrases in the opening direction for Sc. 2, '*loud music*',[4] the relative pronoun construction in '*which Timon redeemed from prison*', '*after all*', and '*discontentedly*'.[5] The Folio directions equivalent to those in the edited text at 2.117 and 2.126 read '*Enter the Maskers of Amazons, with Lutes in their hands, dauncing and playing*' and '*Enter Cupid with*

---

[1] See commentary to 4.118–230.

[2] By my own count as follows: *Changeling, Five Gallants, Game at Chess* (Trinity MS) (2), *Hengist* (2), *Michaelmas* (2), *No Wit, Fair Quarrel* (2), *Puritan, Revenger's, Trick.*

[3] Holdsworth notes two examples of the exact phrase 'in a rage' in Middleton stage directions. Dessen and Thomson record just one other example after *c.*1590, in Thomas Heywood's *Escapes of Jupiter*. Middleton also has two examples of the analogous 'in a fury'.

[4] To the example in *No Wit* we can now add another in a play more recently added to the Middleton canon, *Bloody Banquet*, at 3.3.19.1. The un-Shakespearian stage-direction phrase is to be found in a number of non-Middleton plays too.

[5] Dessen and Thomson note one stage-direction instance of the adverb, in *Lady's Tragedy*, and one non-Middleton instance. The root adjective is also Middletonian but not found in stage directions of Shakespeare's plays.

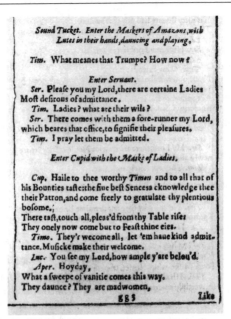

Sound Tucket. *Enter the Maskers of Amazons, with Lutes in their hands, dauncing and playing.*

Tim. What meanes that Trumpe? How now?

Enter Seruant.

Ser. Pleafe you my Lord, there are certaine Ladies Moft defirous of admittance.

Tim. Ladies? what are their wils?

Ser. There comes with them a fore-runner my Lord, which beares that office, to fignifie their pleafures.

Tim. I pray let them be admitted.

Enter Cupid with the Maske of Ladies.

Cup. Haile to thee worthy *Timon* and to all that of his Bounties tafte: the fiue beft Senecsa cknowledge thee their Patron, and come freely to gratulate thy plentious bofome.;

There taft, touch all, pleas'd from thy Table rifes They onely now come but to Feaft thine eies.

Timo. They'r wecome all, let 'em haue kind admittance. Muficke make their welcome.

Luc. You fee my Lord, how ample y'are belou'd.

Aper. Hoyday,

What a fweepe of vanitie comes this way.

They daunce? They are madwomen,

gg3   Like

10. The foot of column b, signature gg3, in the 1623 First Folio.

the Maske of Ladies' (see Illustration 10); these share a number of distinctive traits with a stage direction in Middleton's *The Nice Valour* at 2.1.147: '*Enter . . . Cupid*', '*women masquers*', '*dance*', and '*singing and playing*'.

To this evidence, Holdsworth adds a large catalogue of parallels of diction, phrasing, collocated words, and concepts that are distinctive to Middleton.[1] They occur in works written both before and after *Timon of Athens*, and it would be impossible to dismiss them as one dramatist's borrowings from the other: one would have to assume, absurdly, both that Shakespeare was heavily influenced by a wide range of Middleton works written before *Timon of Athens* in this play but not his other plays, *and* that Middleton was uniquely influenced by this play in a wide range of his later works; moreover, one would have to explain why this bizarre two-way influence operates only in certain parts of the play, and why these

[1] Some of them had been noted by earlier commentators such as William Wells and H. Dugdale Sykes.

same parts show other Middleton characteristics. Many of Holdsworth's examples are cited in the commentary to this edition, which adds a number of others to the catalogue. In some cases the word or phrase in question is unexampled in the works of any early modern dramatist other than Middleton, therefore supporting his authorship absolutely, and not only in comparison with Shakespeare. In other cases what counts is, more modestly, the cumulation of un-Shakespearian material that is well exampled in Middleton.

Holdsworth also examines distinctive words and phrases that recur from scene to scene. Sometimes they cross the authorial divide, whether by coincidence or as a reflection of one writer's awareness of the other, but the overall tendency is for the repetitions to be contained within the two sections. This evidence too therefore offers some support for mixed authorship.

Independent verification at least of the presence of a second hand has been offered by Gary Taylor. His study of 'function words' (common and frequently occurring words) shows that the frequency of four of them ('by', 'so', 'the', and 'to') in the Middleton scenes deviates markedly from the rate found in Shakespeare's works. The test suggests that 'Shakespeare is more likely to have written *Tamburlaine* than to have written those scenes of *Timon*'.[1]

The co-authorship studies have been endorsed, with a note of caution, in Jonathan Hope's sociolinguistic study.[2] He tests the extent to which the auxilliary verb 'do' is 'regulated'—in other words, used as a marker of certain sentence types such as questions and affirmations, as is the practice in modern English. A differentiation between the authorial sections can be seen. It places the Middleton section outside Shakespeare's usage but close to Middleton's, and the linguistically more old-fashioned and less regulated Shakespeare section outside Middleton's usage but within Shakespeare's. This shows 'broad support' for the division as proposed by Lake. A test of the distribution of relative pronouns again supports the overall hypothesis of Middleton's presence, though less clearly; it suggests to Hope that some of Lake's 'Middleton' passages may instead have been written or transcribed by Shakespeare, or that Middleton was 'accommodating' to Shakespeare's

---

[1] *Textual Companion*, p. 86.
[2] *The Authorship of Shakespeare's Plays*, pp. 100–4. (See p. 6 n. 3.)

style.[1] Hope does not suggest any specific passages in Lake's Middleton section that might correspond better with Shakespeare's usage.[2]

On the basis of a complex stylometric study, M. W. A. Smith also agrees that the play is collaborative, adding some substance for the differentiation between the Shakespearian section and the rest, though he is more sceptical than Holdsworth as to the nature and extent of Middleton's role.[3] His investigation produces different and indeed conflicting indications as he moves from test to test. For example, in a test on the Middletonian section based on the first word of speeches, Middleton is the favoured author in five out of six comparisons, whereas the same test applied to words that are not first in speeches variously posits George Chapman, Thomas Dekker, Thomas Heywood, Shakespeare, Middleton, and John Webster as the most favoured author; a collocation test produces essentially the same mixed results.[4] His hypothesis, based on a literal reading of these conflicting indications, is that 'a number of dramatists collaborated to try to rescue the play before its final abandonment, and the task of creating a fair copy from the ensuing indecipherable foul papers of the part Shakespeare had left least complete fell to Middleton'. Despite the *sui generis* model of *Sir Thomas More* for a complex authorial genesis of this kind, the hypothesis seems intrinsically unlikely; the discussion of date above has drawn attention to difficulties in supposing that Middleton worked on the play significantly later than Shakespeare as seems to be the case with the revisions of *Sir Thomas More*; Middleton is not known otherwise to have worked with Chapman or Heywood; the other collaborators are left without any specific passages capable of being plausibly attributable to them; and the emphati-

---

[1] It is also possible that the numbers in the Middleton passages as low as 13 (for 'which') and 6 (for the absence of a relative pronoun) are too low for the discrepancy between the percentages in the Middleton passages (21 per cent and 10 per cent respectively) and Middleton's work elsewhere (17 per cent and 18 per cent respectively) to be conclusively significant.

[2] It happens that Lake assigns all of Sc. 11 to Middleton where Jackson and Holdsworth more plausibly find the middle section of the scene to be Shakespearian; but this passage would not significantly affect Hope's findings.

[3] 'The Authorship of *Timon of Athens*', *Text*, 5 (1991), 19–240.

[4] Figs. 7a, 8a, and 9a; pp. 228–30. Smith's Middletonian section is based on the summary of Holdsworth's attributions in the one-page introduction to the Oxford Shakespeare *Complete Works*.

ćally Middletonian poetics and ideation in the non-Shakespeare sections remain inadequately explained.

A simpler interpretation of Smith's study would be that the 'Middleton' section also contains work by a third hand. But it is very difficult to identify subsections that are stylistically un-Middletonian. Anyone looking for traces of the hand of a writer such as Chapman might begin with Sc. 4, which is the least securely divided between Shakespeare and Middleton.[1] Even this scene contains highly positive indications of both the established collaborators (though in an irregular pattern). There remains limited scope for attributing even a section of it to a third hand.

It is, indeed, the consistency of Holdsworth's findings over a broad range of individually significant tests that makes his findings compelling. They keep reaffirming the same distribution of authorship of scenes in a way that is impossible to reconcile with any explanation other than a split between Middleton and Shakespeare. They also accord, as it happens, with more frail and subjective considerations such as literary judgement and common sense. Middleton the ironic satirist who shows social relationships built on foundations of greed and self-interest is a familiar figure, and that is precisely what we find in his contribution to *Timon of Athens*. His theatre is most characteristic when it deals with the objective and material world of the city, and is always at a remove from the world of nature. Shakespeare takes characters out of the city and into the metamorphosizing natural world, as he does in plays as different as *Midsummer Night's Dream* and *King Lear*.

Holdsworth's doctoral study has not at the time of writing been published in book form. *Timon of Athens* has, however, been presented as a collaboration with Middleton in the Oxford *Complete*

---

[1] I am not aware of linguistic evidence that would significantly support Chapman's involvement. Vocabulary that falls outside both Shakespeare's and Middleton's usage includes: 'untirable' (1.11), 'confluence' (1.42), 'unpeaceable' (1.272), 'detention' (4.38), 'unagreeable' (4.40), 'indisposition' (4.124), 'unaptness' (4.125), 'sermon' (verb; 4.166), 'backwardly' (7.18), 'recoverable' (8.15), 'repugnancy' (10.45), and 'decimation' (17.31); perhaps also 'dialogue' (verb; 4.50; see commentary). Shakespeare's habit of word-formation with prefixes should be taken into account. 'Confluence' is fairly common, and is exampled in the works of Thomas Heywood, Marston, Jonson, and Chapman. 'Sermon' as a transitive verb is otherwise unknown in the early modern period. The occurrences of the other words in works of dramatists working for the public theatre in the early 1600s are restricted to Chapman's one instance of 'detention' and Jonson's one instance of 'indisposition' (neither in a play).

Works of Shakespeare, and will be presented similarly in the Oxford *Collected Works* of Thomas Middleton. The 2001 New Cambridge Shakespeare editor Karl Klein briefly dismisses the case presented in the Oxford Shakespeare in comments that have little substance.[1] In the present edition I have regarded the part-attribution to Middleton as sufficiently convincing for it to be accepted as a firm basic premiss.

Shakespeare and Middleton

Timon of Athens can be located within normal practices of play writing as they operated in the period and as they involved Shakespeare elsewhere. He probably shared in the authorship of *1 Henry VI*, *Titus Andronicus*, *Edward III*, and the revision of *Sir Thomas More*, all written before *Timon of Athens*. Of his later plays, *Pericles*, *All is True* (*Henry VIII*), *Two Noble Kinsmen*, and the lost play *Cardenio* all have a second author.

When *Timon of Athens* was written, Shakespeare was probably a more experienced collaborator than Middleton. But Middleton too collaborated in many plays. He was the obvious choice of dramatist to contribute scenes in a mode that was relatively unfamiliar to Shakespeare, the mode of satirical city comedy. He is also one of the few major dramatists known to have been working for the King's Men in this period. In 1606 Middleton was no novice, but an experienced dramatist at the height of his creativity.

Collaboration is only visible at the points where it fails to produce a harmonious meshing of the playwrights' contributions. The marks of collaboration are easily translated as the marks of failure. In contrast, where the play succeeds in meshing across the authorial divide the effect is to render collaboration invisible and so, in the case of *Timon of Athens*, to encourage those who would deny the presence of any hand other than Shakespeare's. This double bind, always prejudicial against co-authorship, is not inevitable. The model of a human relationship such as that between collaborators can be useful in picturing the nature of the text as a collaborative product in a more constructive way. The idea of friendship is extra-

[1] He claims, for instance, that the Oxford editors place little significance on linguistic evidence. The *Complete Works*, like the present edition, leans heavily on the work of Holdsworth, whose primary investigations are, precisely, of linguistic traits. See Vickers, *Co-Author*, pp. 288–90.

ordinarily prevalent in both authorial stints (most especially Middleton's), and Jeffrey Masten, referring to *The Two Noble Kinsmen*, is right in noting the significance of such a theme within a collaborative work.[1] Collaboration is a process whose finer convolutions can and must be expected to elude secure interpretation. The 'and' in the authorial identifier 'Shakespeare and Middleton' signifies both division and joining. It is well established that dramatists will tend to converge in their writing practices when they collaborate. It can also be seen in well-fashioned collaborations such as Shakespeare and Fletcher's *Two Noble Kinsmen* or Middleton and Rowley's *The Changeling* that key ideas and images travel between authorial stints.

It is clear that the linguistic, stylistic, and ideational texture of Middleton differs markedly from Shakespeare, and there are significant differences of staging technique too. Part of readers' difficulties with *Timon of Athens* arise from the unexpected and unfamiliar authorial idiolect of Middleton, or from the play's character as a dialogue between different authorial voices. This edition seeks to turn the obstacle into a source of re-engagement with the play on different terms, to make up the contextual deficit, and so to turn the disconcertingly un-Shakespearian into the relishably Middletonian.

It is sometimes pointed out that audiences, whether early modern or modern, do not respond to fluctuations in authorship when seeing a play on stage. But the interpretative concerns of an audience, if and when they can be known, offer a partial and restricted view of the range of critical and contextual responses that a play can elicit, being a response to a performance at a moment in time rather than to the basis for that performance in the text. Moreover, effects that might not register consciously can still contribute strongly to the play's impact. From the vantage of a collaborative play text, standing, as it always does, in between inscription and performance, and in between the past and our present, the context of collaboration should never vanish entirely, in the sense that the assumption of solo authorship by Shakespeare never vanishes from discussion of a play such as *Hamlet*. And in the light of collaboration this play, *Timon of Athens*, looks not only different, but better. Questions of coherence are reframed. The play can be

---

[1] *Textual Intercourse* (Cambridge, 1977).

granted a particular licence to ebb and flow, and the cause of some of its disjunctions becomes self-evident.

In scenes of mixed authorship it is usually clear that Shakespeare supplied the core and Middleton added passages to it. MacD. P. Jackson suggests that Shakespeare might have similarly added to Middleton scenes. This accords with Hope's impression that Shakespeare may possibly have some kind of presence in some of the Middleton episodes. The combined authority of these scholars must be treated with respect, but there is little particular evidence to support their suggestions. The hints in the incidence of contractions that Middleton may have transcribed parts of Sc. 14 (see Appendix C) again support the view that Shakespeare took the initiating role. Shakespeare as senior dramatist, as theatre company sharer, as the writer with an ongoing interest in North's Plutarch, would presumably have made the first decision about working on the play, perhaps in conjunction with other members of the company, perhaps already in consultation with Middleton. He would perhaps have put together a 'plot' sketching out the order of scenes in the usual way with dramatists of the period seeking company approval. Scenes of Middleton's immediate authorship therefore might have a Shakespearian element in their plotting. So much is suggested by the Shakespearian plot elements in Middleton's Sc. 10 : not only its Plutarchian source and its anticipation of the exile and intended revenge of Coriolanus, but also its resemblance to a short passage in *Richard III* (2.1.96–102) where Stanley unsuccessfully pleads for mercy for his servant who 'slew today a riotous gentleman'.[1]

There are no positive indications that Shakespeare was involved by the end, though we cannot rule out the possibility that he worked further on the play in a transcript of the Folio copy. For his part, Middleton supplied two major sequences, Sc. 2 and Scs. 5–10, and added passages of various length to Shakespeare scenes. Several of these, in Sc. 4, Sc. 13, and Sc. 14, develop the role of Timon's Steward. Middleton's expansion of Sc. 11 connects the mock banquet to his scenes showing Timon's false friends denying him help. Sc. 1 has a few short passages evidently in Middleton's hand that affect the staging and connect the scene to his own Sc. 2.

---

[1] Bullough, p. 237. In *Timon of Athens*, however, it is the condemned man who is the riotous gentleman.

There are some hints that Middleton added at least a brief touch to Sc. 17.

In general Middleton focuses on secondary characters. Alcibiades is one example; others include the Steward, Timon's servants, and his creditors. The lack of relationship between secondary characters can be regarded as a purposeful aspect of the play's design, but it is also an effect of the compartmentalization of authorial responsibility. These apparently conflicting explanations start to blur once one begins to dwell on the positive possibilities of play structure that emerge from a collaborative writing technique.

Of course, the collaboration is more successful in some places than other. Sc. 4 and Sc. 13 emerge as having fundamentally mixed authorship.[1] In Sc. 13 Middleton fuses his own writing and Shakespeare's into a scene of pungent focus. It is otherwise in Sc. 4, a conspicuous example of an episode with textual loose ends that arise from disconnections within the collaborative process.

The scene introduces two roles, the Fool and the Page, who serve no purpose but to provide some theatrically relevant but rather humourless comedy and who appear nowhere else in the play. The Page has letters to deliver to Timon and Alcibiades, but the play makes no reference to them being delivered and read. There is also a major failure to follow through another plot-line anticipated in Sc. 4. At 4.214–25 Timon attaches considerable weight to his hopes for financial relief from Ventidius (the spelling in this passage, 'Ventiddius', is probably Shakespeare's). Whereas Timon's lower-ranking servants petition the other creditors, Timon sends his Steward, the manager of his household, to Ventidius. Recollecting events in Shakespeare's Sc. 1, he reminds the Steward of Ventidius' special obligation to Timon for redeeming him from prison, and informs him and us that Ventidius has become wealthy since his father's death. It is Ventidius who will disprove 'That Timon's fortunes 'mong his friends can sink'. Though the scene between the Steward and Ventidius is more strongly anticipated than any of the episodes that actually follow, this scene does not materialize. Ventidius is mentioned again at 7.3–8 as among the friends who

---

[1] Oliver's argument for single authorship on the basis of parallel passages within the play cites 4.165–6, 11.28–31, and 14.260–7 as leading examples. As the first two passages turn out to be in collaborative scenes, all three passages could be by Shakespeare.

have failed to aid Timon, and thereafter disappears from the play or blends into the anonymous lords and senators.

The difficulties just reviewed concern a failure to follow through situations begun or anticipated in Sc. 4. The following series of scenes is in Middleton's hand. This time there is an absent antecedent rather than an absent sequel. In Sc. 10, Alcibiades unexpectedly appears before the senate defending a soldier who has committed manslaughter. There is no preparation for this scene, and no other reference to the crime that Alcibiades excuses. It may be that this deficiency, like those already mentioned, relates to the writing of Sc. 4. Near the beginning of the earlier scene Timon enters from hunting with 'My Alcibiades', but Alcibiades is silent and plays no further part in the scene. Conceivably a planned episode was unwritten, cancelled, or lost.

Another pattern of co-authorship is evident in Sc. 14, which is largely in Shakespeare's hand but elicited a more complicated response from Middleton than any other part of the play. As well as adding the major episode of the Steward's visit to Timon, he probably supplied a few very short and isolated passages elsewhere in the scene,[1] and transcribed parts of Shakespeare's draft of Sc. 14.[2] There are indications that he also changed the position of the Poet and Painter episode. The Poet and Painter enter almost two hundred lines after Apemantus says 'Yonder comes a poet and a painter' (l. 350). The usual explanation is couched in terms of the text's origination in a rough draft of Shakespeare's sole authorship. But Samuel Johnson noted the alternative possibility that 'some scenes are transposed'. As the scene's reviser, Middleton might have been responsible.

This theory leaves a difficulty to resolve, which is that the Painter knows that 'He likewise enriched poor straggling soldiers with great quantity' and that ' 'Tis said he gave unto his steward a mighty sum' (14.543–4). These lines presuppose that the Poet and Painter episode is placed after the passages with the Thieves and the Steward, as in F. But the lines may have been added by Middleton as part of his reorganization of the text. The statement about the Steward refers to an episode that he wrote. The speech contains diction that is evidently Middletonian, and the errors for the

[1] See the scene headnote in the commentary.

[2] As is evidenced by the higher frequency of Middleton linguistic forms than is typical elsewhere in Shakespeare scenes: see Appendix C.

names Phrynia and Timandra in the same speech could reflect Middleton's misrecollection of names elsewhere supplied by Shakespeare.[1] Middleton, indeed, appears to have added several touches to this episode.

The most plausible sequence is that Shakespeare originally planned to follow the Apemantus episode with those of the Poet and Painter, and then the senators; he later added the potentially free-floating Thieves episode, introducing roles that appear nowhere else in the play; finally Middleton added the Steward episode and made adjustments to establish the sequence as printed in the Folio.

Allowance must be made for another possibility that might affect any part of the text: that Middleton read all or parts of Shakespeare's draft and responded to it in his own writing. That too is part of the business of collaboration.[2] The strongest indication that Middleton did so relates to a particular line in Sc. 14, and so presents another aspect of his engagement with that scene. The phrase 'plenteous bosom' occurs at 2.120–1 (Middleton; referring flatteringly to Timon's generosity) and again at 14.187 (Shakespeare; referring to the fecundity of the earth). Moralized references to finding or eating roots occur at 2.71 and 130–1 (Middleton), and also 14.23, 28, 186, and 192 (Shakespeare). What is noteworthy here is that a single line at 14.187, 'From forth thy plenteous bosom, one poor root', is a meeting point for both sets of images shared between authors.[3] In other words, a strong authorial crossover probably results from Middleton's response to a single line by Shakespeare.

Both the general frame of thought and the specific phrasing are clearly Shakespearian, as can be seen by comparing a passage in *Measure for Measure*:

> As those that feed grow full, as blossoming time
> That from the seedness the bare fallow brings
> To teeming foison, even so her plenteous womb
> Expresseth his full tilth and husbandry.

$$(1.4.40–3)$$

---

[1] See commentary to 14.540–3.

[2] For details, see John Jowett, 'The Pattern of Collaboration in *Timon of Athens*', in *Words That Count*, ed. Brian Boyd (Cranbury, N.J., forthcoming in 2004).

[3] This single line is the minimal extent of Shakespeare writing that, by the present revised reading of Oliver's evidence (see previous note), has convincing parallels in Middleton's writing.

Juliet's pregnancy is described in language of fertile growth of crops to harvest; her 'plenteous womb' is equated with the plenitude of the earth itself. The passage in *Timon of Athens* is 'natural' to its place in Sc. 14 in more than one way: Timon speaks of nature in proximity to nature, and his desire for 'one poor root' is entirely literal. This contrasts immediately with the reference to 'plenteous bosom' in Sc. 2. Here, in the banquet scene, the plain gifts of nature have been transformed into high artifice and sensual gratifications. There is a translation from the imagery of nature rooted in Shakespearian idiom and idea to Middletonian artifice. This runs counter to the sequence of scenes, and therefore suggests that Middleton wrote Sc. 2, or at least parts of it, after Shakespeare wrote a draft of Sc. 14.

The thematic and theatrical cohesion of Middleton's creditor scenes is self-evident. His contribution to the mock-banquet scene was decisive for establishing the plot through-line from the creditor scenes to the woods of Athens, and the scene showing Alcibiades' banishment did much the same for the second plot, albeit at the expense of making Alcibiades' motive for revolt against Athens disconcertingly underexplained. One-shot treatments though these scenes are, they bind the play together into what is, apart from the lacunae already mentioned, a strongly formed structure. Middleton's most substantial scene was the first banquet of Sc. 2, which is foundational. It presents the state from which Timon falls, it sounds the theme that is ironically varied in the mock banquet, and it articulates the vision of Athenian community that is unravelled and inverted in Sc. 14. Middleton's smaller additions also have an integrating effect on the play as a whole, and they also nudge it towards a more Middletonian aesthetic. They introduce a more crowded but alienated staging in the opening scene, a mixture of homoerotic banter, tragicomic sentiment, and rhyming moralization in Sc. 4, some sardonic lines in the Poet and Painter episode of Sc. 14, and an expansion of the morally anchoring role of the Steward sustained over several scenes.

It has been described earlier in this introduction how Middleton develops a stance towards money that can be summarized in the word 'debt', where Shakespeare's stance can be summarized in the word 'gold'. What remains is to consider the influence of co-authorship on the play's central role, and on our reading of the play in so far as it depends on the role most strongly developed by Middleton, the Steward.

Timon himself is divided between being the object of satire himself and the source of satire against Athens. This too relates to the division of authorship. One must be careful not to drive the authorial contributions into simplified moulds: the characterization grows out of and beyond the dynamic of collaboration. Nevertheless, this central and vital ambiguity of the role has some basis here.

The Timon Shakespeare primarily depicted is quietly benevolent in the first scene. He undertakes common forms of philanthropy: he redeems a debtor from prison and provides one of his servants with a dowry. These acts are consistent with noble liberality, as described by way of personification in the list of speakers in the morality play *Liberality and Prodigality* as 'chief steward to Virtue'.

In contrast, then, the Timon of Middleton's Sc. 2 is a prodigal who parts with vast wealth needlessly; his gifts are without utility but have what Bataille calls 'the radiance of glory'.[1] Middleton strongly satirizes Timon; he is presented in the spirit of what Bradbrook identifies as the 'new bitter comedy' of plays such as *A Mad World, My Masters* (p. 16). Middleton's scenes also satirize the world of Athens; they recognize the Utopian aspect of Timon's generosity, and find a lovingness of spirit in him that survives in attenuated form in his final meeting with the Steward.

Shakespeare's Timon comes into his own in Sc. 14, where he develops a resentful and highly vocal anger against humanity that goes far beyond any measured response to real injuries suffered. To force the contrast slightly: in Middleton, both satire and sentiment are forms of moralization; in Shakespeare, it is the pitch of emotion that counts. As in Montaigne's description of the figure, 'Timon wished all evil might light on us; he was passionate in desiring our ruin'.[2] Describing Timon's Shakespearian apostrophes to gold at 14.26–45 and 382–93, Bradbrook remarks, 'This rôle touches the very frontiers of the articulate, the borders of what can be known of the state of dereliction, where conflicts are revealed so deep and elemental, so painful and relatively inaccessible, that only through

---

[1] Bataille, pp. 200–1. The distinction between liberality and prodigality is made, without reference to authorship, by Bradbrook, p. 5, citing W. K. Jordan, *Philanthropy in England, 1480–1660* (1959). See also commentary note to 2.161.

[2] Montaigne, 'Of Democritus and Heraclitus', in *Essays*, i. 345.

the most lightly established form can they be projected in words' (p. 20). These 'Middletonian' and 'Shakespearian' narratives interweave and complement each other, and cannot be isolated in uncontaminated authorial sections. Nevertheless, the collaborative authorship has a strong bearing on critical and theatrical responses to the role of Timon.

The expansions to the role of the Steward lean towards the sentimental rather than the cynical. In contrast with any of Middleton's other contributions to the play, we are here presented with three separate episodes that develop a distinctive plot-line. Middleton's additions made the Steward a far more important and engaged figure in the second half of the play. Middleton added some at least of the Steward's self-justification to Timon in Sc. 4. He also supplied the soliloquy in Sc. 13 that consolidates the audience's impression of the Steward's personal feelings for Timon and that sets up his visit to Timon in the woods: 'I'll follow and enquire him out. / . . . / Whilst I have gold I'll be his steward still' (13.49–51).

That final added episode provides one of the most moving moments in the play. It decisively alters the plot of the Steward. It also establishes a firm standpoint from which Timon's attitude to life can be dissociated from the viewpoint of the play as a whole. And it adds an otherwise missing recognition of human worth to the range of responses to humanity that Timon himself articulates in the woods. Here too, critical interpretation of the entire play is at stake.

Nevertheless, its demands on our attention can also be summarized in a series of questions that go beyond the issue of collaboration. Is satire a valid mode of expression? What is the nature of an all-male community? What is the nature of obligation, how is it constructed and interpreted? What is it to love unconditionally, indiscriminately, and without understanding? Can hatred be pitied or even admired? Is there altruism? Is generosity noble or stupidly self-indulgent? Does the existence of surplus generate a need for destruction and loss? Is it madness to see human behaviour as driven by money? Is there a place beyond the economistic and over-consuming community? The play deals with all these questions eloquently and with sophistication.

Timon himself is treated not only as a case of generosity, loss, and misanthropy, but as the example of the extreme itself, with all the disgust and wonder that it may provoke. His hatred, as an absolute anti-gift, is perhaps a variation on the Derridean impossible. We can have as much as we choose of *Timon of Athens* as a significant moral fable, but it is perhaps at the point where moralization is left with little more to say that the play is most distinctively, and yet unusually, Shakespearian.

EDITORIAL PROCEDURES

Text and Collation

THE text, based on the 1623 First Folio, has been modernized in spelling and punctuation.[1] Some indication as to what the standard editorial processes involve can be gained by comparing Illustration 10 with the edited text at 2.109.1–129. The layout has been brought within the format for the Oxford series, with the first verse-line of a speech printed on the type-line below the speech-prefix but prose beginning on the same line as the prefix. Spellings such as 'plentious' and 'daunce' have been brought into line with modern forms; long 's' has been reproduced as the normal modern letter-form, as has the 'u' for modern 'v' in 'fiue' (five). The abbreviation 'y'are' has been translated into its modern equivalent 'you're'. The italicization of the name '*Timon*' has been removed, as has the capitalization in common nouns such as 'Trumpe', 'Lord', 'Bounties', and 'Patron'. Speech-prefixes have been expanded from contracted forms and set in capitals. The Middleton spelling '*Aper.*' for Apemantus has been normalized to the more usual spelling without 'r'. The mis-spacing in 'Sencesa cknowledge' has been corrected, and the missing 'l' in 'wecome' has been inserted.

These are all routine changes. Others are more specific to difficulties in this particular passage. The stage directions require unusually heavy alteration. '*Sound Tucket.*' has been detached from the long direction in which it appears in F, and the editorial clarification '⌈*within*⌉' added. The rest of this direction has been conflated with the part of the later entry that calls for the '*Maske of Ladies*', on the basis that '*Enter the Maskers of Amazons*' and '*Enter . . . the Maske of Ladies*' are two separate directions for the same event, and the whole is deferred until after Timon says 'Let 'em have kind admittance'. The entry for the Servant has been brought forward slightly so that he is already on stage when Timon addresses him 'How now?' The remnant of the entry for the Cupid has been retained in the same position as in F, but the wording has been adjusted to reflect that this is an actor in a role in the masque;

---

[1] There are few variant readings in F to take into account, and no example of a press correction that affects the edited text. For details, see Hinman, ii. 297–8.

hence '*Enter one as Cupid*'. None of these interventions is in itself unusual, except for the conflation of the two entrances for the masquers. The peculiar concentration of alterations in this passage arises, presumably, from complexities in a manuscript that had not been adjusted to meet the needs of the stage.

The lineation in F has also been adjusted. The Servant's first speech at ll. 112–13 is set as verse in F; however, as it is too irregular for verse even in Middleton's hand, it has been emended to prose, as is the case with his next speech at ll. 115–16.

In the edition as a whole, emendations and a number of rejected emendations made by other editors are recorded in the collation line between text and commentary, as in the following example, where this edition follows Johnson's reading and rejects both F and the alternative emendation made by Pope:

21 oozes] JOHNSON; vses F; issues POPE

Modernizations of spelling and punctuation are recorded where the form is ambiguous or there is other significant doubt as to how the form should be modernized. Modernizations are recorded, without attribution to an editor, in the form:

1 you're] F (y'are)

7 So, fitly!] F ($\sim_\wedge \sim$?)

In the second example the swung dash $\sim$ signals that the word is the same, and so that the punctuation is the element that is being recorded. The caret $_\wedge$ signifies that there is no punctuation in that position.

Stage directions and speech-prefixes have been brought into accordance with the requirements for stage action. All 'aside' stage directions and directions indicating to whom a speech is addressed are editorial. In line with the procedures for the Oxford Shakespeare series, 'broken' brackets are introduced where editorial alterations or additions to the Folio's stage directions are contentious. Editorial changes to all stage directions except 'aside' and directional 'to . . .' directions are recorded in the collation. The abbreviation '*subs*.', for 'substantively', indicates that the named editor stipulated the stage action concerned, or something close to it, but used different wording.

One category of emendation not recorded in the collation is the alteration of line-breaks in verse and of verse–prose distinctions, which are recorded in Appendix A.

In the text, little attempt has been made to establish a consistent correlation across scenes between the named Lucius, Lucullus, Sempronius and Ventidius and the anonymous 'Friends', Lords, and Senators (but see commentary note to 11.0.2), or to correlate these anonymous figures. However, contradictory stage directions and speech-prefixes within a scene have been regularized (see commentary note to 11.1).

Commentary

In addition to its other functions, the commentary provides a generous sampling of Middleton parallels. These are designed to illuminate the focus and register of the language as well as to demonstrate its consonance with Middleton. It has been considered unnecessary to cite Shakespeare parallels entirely to the same extent, as the context is more familiar. Unless otherwise stated, when Middleton is cited there is no equal parallel in Shakespeare. Many of the Middleton citations have evidential value in showing that the passage has more in common with Middleton than Shakespeare, but it is beyond the scope of the commentary either to evaluate each parallel in this respect or to offer an exhaustive record of such evidence.

Abbreviations and References

Quotations from early texts are presented with modern spelling and punctuation unless the quotation is made for its documentary significance. References to other Shakespeare works are from the Oxford Shakespeare. References to *King Lear* are from *The History of King Lear* in that edition, as the version thought to be closer in date to *Timon of Athens*. References to Middleton are from the Oxford Middleton as that edition stood in the late stages of preparation in 2002–3. In the list of Middleton Works Cited, dates are dates of composition, as given in the Oxford Middleton chronology.

EDITIONS OF SHAKESPEARE

| F, F1 | *Comedies, Histories, and Tragedies* (1623) |
| F2 | *Comedies, Histories, and Tragedies* (1632) |

F3	*Comedies, Histories, and Tragedies* (1663–4)
F4	*Comedies, Histories, and Tragedies* (1685)
Alexander	Peter Alexander, *Works* (1951)
Bevington	David Bevington, *Complete Works* (Glenview, 1973)
Cambridge	W. G. Clark and W. A. Wright, *Works*, 9 vols. (Cambridge, 1863–6)
Capell	Edward Capell, *Comedies, Histories, and Tragedies*, 10 vols. (1767–8)
Charney	Maurice Charney, *Timon of Athens* (New York, 1965)
Collier	John Payne Collier, *Plays*, 8 vols. (1842–4)
Collier 1853	John Payne Collier, *Plays* (1853)
Delius	Nicolaus Delius, *Werke*, 7 vols. (Elberfeld, 1854–61)
Dyce	Alexander Dyce, *Works*, 6 vols. (1857)
Dyce 1864–7	Alexander Dyce, *Works*, 2nd edn, 9 vols. (1864–7)
Hanmer	Thomas Hanmer, *Works*, 6 vols. (Oxford, 1743–4)
Hibbard	G. R. Hibbard, *Timon of Athens* (Harmondsworth, 1970)
Hinman	Charlton Hinman, *Timon of Athens*, in *Complete Works*, gen. ed. Alfred Harbage (Baltimore, 1969)
Hudson	H. N. Hudson, *Works*, 11 vols. (1851–6)
Johnson	Samuel Johnson, *Plays*, 8 vols. (1765)
Klein	Karl Klein, *Timon of Athens*, Cambridge 3 (Cambridge, 2001)
Knight	Charles Knight, *Comedies, Histories, Tragedies, & Poems*, 55 parts [1838–43]
Malone	Edmond Malone, *Plays and Poems*, 10 vols. (1790)
Maxwell	J. C. Maxwell, *Timon of Athens*, Cambridge 2 (Cambridge, 1957)
Oliver	H. J. Oliver, *Timon of Athens* (1959)
Oxford Shakespeare	William Shakespeare and Thomas Middleton, *The Life of Timon of Athens*, ed. John Jowett, in William Shakespeare, *Complete Works*, gen. eds. Stanley Wells and Gary Taylor (Oxford, 1986)
Pope	Alexander Pope, *Works*, 6 vols. (1723–5)
Pope 1728	Alexander Pope, *Works*, 2nd edn, 10 vols. (1728)
Rann	Joseph Rann, *Dramatic Works*, 6 vols. (Oxford, 1786–94)
Rowe	Nicholas Rowe, *Works*, 6 vols. (1709)
Rowe 1714	Nicholas Rowe, *Works*, 3rd edn, 8 vols. (1714)
Singer	Samuel W. Singer, *Dramatic Works*, 2nd edn, 10 vols. (1856)

Sisson	Charles J. Sisson, *Complete Works* (1954)
Staunton	Howard Staunton, *Plays*, 3 vols. (1858–60)
Steevens	George Steevens and Samuel Johnson, *Plays*, 10 vols. (1773)
Steevens 1778	George Steevens and Samuel Johnson, *Plays*, 10 vols. (1778)
Steevens–Reed	George Steevens and Isaac Reed, *Plays*, 2nd edn, 15 vols. (1793)
Theobald	Lewis Theobald, *Works*, 8 vols. (1733)
Warburton	William Warburton, *Works*, 8 vols. (1747)
White	Richard Grant White, *Works*, 12 vols. (Boston, 1857–66)

MIDDLETON WORKS CITED

Oxford Middleton	William Shakespeare and Thomas Middleton, *The Life of Timon of Athens*, ed. John Jowett, in Thomas Middleton, *Collected Works*, gen. eds. Gary Taylor and John Lavagnino (Oxford, forthcoming; proofs prepared before publication of the present edition)

Ant and Nightingale: The Ant and the Nightingale (1604)

Black Book, The (1604)

Bloody Banquet, The (1608–9; with Thomas Dekker)

Changeling, The (1622; with William Rowley)

Chaste Maid: A Chaste Maid in Cheapside (1613)

Civitatis Amor (1616)

Dissemblers: More Dissemblers Besides Women (1614)

Fair Quarrel, A (1616; with William Rowley)

Five Gallants: Your Five Gallants (1607)

Game at Chess, A (1624)

Ghost of Lucrece, The (1600)

Hengist: Hengist, King of Kent (or *The Mayor of Queenborough*; 1620)

1 Honest Whore, The (or *The Patient Man and the Honest Whore*; 1604; with Thomas Dekker)

Honourable Entertainments, The (1620–1)

Lady's: The Lady's Tragedy (or *The Second Maiden's Tragedy*, or *The Maiden's Tragedy*; 1611)

Mad World: A Mad World, My Masters (1605)

Meeting of Gallants: The Meeting of Gallants at an Ordinary (1604)

Michaelmas: Michaelmas Term (1604)

Microcynicon (1599)

News from Gravesend (1603)

Nice Valour, The (1622)

No Wit: No Wit/Help like a Woman's (1611)

Old Law, The (1618–19; with William Rowley; revised by Philip Massinger?)

Owl's Almanac (1618)

Peacemaker, The (1618)

Penniless Parliament, The (1601)

Phoenix, The (1603–4)

Plato's Cap (1604)

Puritan Widow, The (1606)

Quiet Life: Anything for a Quiet Life (1621; with John Webster)

Revenger's: The Revenger's Tragedy (1606)

Roaring Girl, The (1611; with Thomas Dekker)

Solomon Paraphrased: The Wisdom of Solomon Paraphrased (1597)

Tennis: The World Tossed at Tennis (1620; with William Rowley)

Trick: A Trick to Catch the Old One (1605)

Triumphs of Integrity, The (1623)

Triumphs of Truth, The (1613)

Two Gates: The Two Gates of Salvation (1609)

Weapons: Wit at Several Weapons (1613; with William Rowley)

Widow, The (1615–16)

Witch, The (1616)

Women Beware: Women Beware Women (1621)

Yorkshire Tragedy, A (1605)

OTHER WORKS CITED

Abbott	E. A. Abbott, *A Shakespearian Grammar* (1869)
Arrowsmith	W. R. Arrowsmith, 'A Few Supplemental Notes on Some Passages in Middleton's Plays', *Notes and Queries*, 2nd Series, 1 (1856), 85–6
Bate	Jonathan Bate (ed.), *The Romantics on Shakespeare* (1992)
Becket	Andrew Becket, *Shakespeare's Himself Again*, 2 vols. (1815)
Blake	N. F. Blake, *A Grammar of Shakespeare's Language* (Basingstoke and New York, 2002)

Blayney	Peter W. M. Blayney, *The First Folio of Shakespeare* (Washington, DC, 1991)
Bloody Murders	*Two most Unnaturall and Bloodie Murthers* (1605), repr. in A. C. Cawley and Barry Gaines (eds.), *A Yorkshire Tragedy* (Manchester, 1986)
Bradbrook	M. C. Bradbrook, *The Tragical Pageant of 'Timon of Athens'* (Cambridge, 1966)
Bullough	Geoffrey Bullough (ed.), *Narrative and Dramatic Sources of Shakespeare*, 8 vols. (London and New York, 1957–75), vol. vi
Butler	Francelina Butler, *The Strange Critical Fortunes of Shakespeare's 'Timon of Athens'* (Ames, Iowa, 1966)
Collier MS	Manuscript emendations in John Payne Collier's copy of F2, probably by Collier
Crystal	David and Ben Crystal, *Shakespeare's Words: A Glossary and Language Companion* (2002)
Dent	R. W. Dent, *Shakespeare's Proverbial Language* (Berkeley and London, 1981)
Dessen and Thomson	Alan C. Dessen and Leslie Thomson, *A Dictionary of Stage Directions in English Drama, 1580–1642* (Cambridge, 1999)
Gooch and Thatcher	Bryan N. S. Gooch and David Thatcher, *A Shakespeare Music Catalogue*, 5 vols. (Oxford, 1991)
Gosson	Stephen Gosson (trans.), *Ephemerides of Philao* (1579)
Hinman	Charlton Hinman, *The Printing and Proof-Reading of the First Folio of Shakespeare*, 2 vols. (Oxford, 1963)
Holdsworth	R. V. Holdsworth, 'Middleton and Shakespeare' (unpublished Ph.D. dissertation, University of Manchester, 1982)
Holdsworth, 'Biblical Allusions'	R. V. Holdsworth, 'Biblical Allusions in *Timon of Athens* and Thomas Middleton', *Notes and Queries*, 235 (1990), 188–92
Honigmann	E. A. J. Honigmann, '*Timon of Athens*', *Shakespeare Quarterly*, 12 (1961), 3–20
Hulme	Hilda M. Hulme, *Explorations in Shakespeare's Language* (1962)

Jackson, Ken	Ken Jackson, 'Derrida, the Gift, and God in *Timon of Athens*', *Shakespeare Quarterly*, 52 (2001), 34–66
Jonson, *Poetaster*	Ben Jonson, *Poetaster*, ed. Tom Cain (Manchester, 1995)
Jonson, *Sejanus*	Ben Jonson, *Sejanus His Fall*, ed. Philip J. Ayers (Manchester, 1990)
Jonson, *Volpone*	Ben Jonson, *Volpone*, ed. Brian Parker (Manchester, 1983)
Kahn	Coppélia Kahn, '"Magic of Bounty": *Timon of Athens*, Jacobean Patronage, and Maternal Power', *Shakespeare Quarterly*, 38 (1987), 34–57
Kinnear	B. G. Kinnear, *Cruces Shakespearianae* (1883)
Kyd	Thomas Kyd, *The Spanish Tragedy*, ed. Philip Edwards (1959)
Leiter	Samuel L. Leiter (ed.), *Shakespeare Around the Globe* (New York, Westport, Conn., and London, 1986)
Literature Online	Online subscription database of literary texts at *http://lion.chadwyck.co.uk*
Lyly	John Lyly, *'Campaspe' and 'Sappho and Phao'*, ed. G. K. Hunter and David Bevington (Manchester, 1991)
Magnusson	Lynne Magnusson, *Shakespeare and Social Dialogue* (Cambridge, 1999)
Marlowe	Christopher Marlowe, *'Doctor Faustus' and Other Plays*, ed. David Bevington and Eric Rasmussen (Oxford, 1995)
Milton, *Paradise Lost*	John Milton, *Paradise Lost*, ed. Alastair Fowler (1968)
Montaigne	Michel Eyquem de Montaigne, *Essays*, trans. John Florio (1603; repr. in 3 vols., Oxford, 1910)
Muldrew	Craig Muldrew, *The Economy of Obligation* (Basingstoke, 1998)
Nuttall	A. D. Nuttall, *Timon of Athens* (Hemel Hempstead, 1989)
OED	*The Oxford English Dictionary*, online edition
Onions	C. T. Onions, *A Shakespeare Glossary*, rev. Robert D. Eagleson (Oxford, 1986)

Plutarch	Plutarch, *Lives of the Noble Grecians and Romans Compared Together*, trans. Thomas North (1579)
Shadwell	Thomas Shadwell, *The History of Timon the Man-Hater* (1678)
Sisson	C. J. Sisson, *New Readings in Shakespeare* (Cambridge, 1956)
Soellner	Rolf Soellner, *'Timon of Athens': Shakespeare's Pessimistic Tragedy* (Columbus, 1979)
Spenser	Edmund Spenser, *The Faerie Queene*, ed. J. C. Smith, 2 vols. (1909)
Spurgeon	Caroline Spurgeon, *Shakespeare's Imagery and What It Tells Us* (Cambridge, 1935)
Stone, *Crisis*	Lawrence Stone, *The Crisis of the Aristocracy, 1558–1641* (Oxford, 1965)
Textual Companion	Stanley Wells and Gary Taylor, with John Jowett and William Montgomery, *William Shakespeare: A Textual Companion* (Oxford, 1987)
Tilley	Morris Palmer Tilley, *A Dictionary of the Proverbs in England in the Sixteenth and Seventeenth Centuries* (Ann Arbor, 1950)
Timon [comedy]	*Timon*, ed. J. C. Bulman and J. M. Nosworthy, Malone Society Reprints (Oxford, 1980, for 1978)
Vickers, *Co-Author*	Brian Vickers, *Shakespeare, Co-Author: A Historical Study of Five Collaborative Plays* (Oxford, 2002)
Vickers, *Critical Heritage*	Brian Vickers (ed.), *Shakespeare: The Critical Heritage*, 6 vols. (1974–81)
Walker	W. S. Walker, *A Critical Examination of the Text of Shakespeare*, ed. W. N. Lettsom, 3 vols. (1860)
Walton	N. B. Walton, 'Waiting for Timon' (unpublished Ph.D. dissertation, University of Birmingham, 2001)
Webster	John Webster, *The Duchess of Malfi*, in *Works*, vol. i, ed. David Gunby, David Carnegie, and Antony Hammond (Cambridge, 1995)
Williams, Gary Jay	'Stage History, 1816–1978', in Soellner, pp. 161–85
Williams, Gordon	*A Dictionary of Sexual Language and Imagery in Shakespearean and Stuart Literature*, 3 vols. (1994)

Wright   George T. Wright, *Shakespeare's Metrical Art* (Berkeley and London, 1988)

Yamada   Akihiro Yamada (ed.), *The First Folio of Shakespeare: A Transcript of Contemporary Marginalia* (Tokyo, 1998)

The Life of Timon of Athens

THE PERSONS OF THE PLAY

TIMON of Athens

ALCIBIADES, an Athenian captain
APEMANTUS, a churlish philosopher
LORDS and SENATORS of Athens
VENTIDIUS, one of Timon's false friends

Flavius, Timon's STEWARD
FLAMINIUS, one of Timon's servants
SERVILIUS, another
Other SERVANTS of Timon
A FOOL
A PAGE

A POET
A PAINTER
A JEWELLER
A MERCHANT
A Mercer
LUCILIUS, one of Timon's servants
An OLD Athenian MAN

LUCULLUS ⎱
LUCIUS   ⎰ two flattering lords
LUCULLUS' SERVANT
SEMPRONIUS, another flattering lord
Three STRANGERS, the second called Hostilius

CAPHIS, servant to a usuring Senator
ISIDORE'S SERVANT
Two of VARRO'S SERVANTS ⎫
TITUS   ⎬ servants to usurers
HORTENSIUS   ⎪
PHILOTAS   ⎭

One dressed as CUPID in the masque
LADIES dressed as Amazons in the masque
PHRYNIA ⎱ whores with Alcibiades
TIMANDRA ⎰

The Banditti, THIEVES
A SOLDIER of Alcibiades' army

Other attendants and soldiers

The above arrangement is editorial. The Folio prints the following list on a separate page at the end of the play:

THE
ACTORS
NAMES.

TYMON *of Athens.*
Lucius, And
Lucullus, two Flattering Lords.
Appemantus, a Churlish Philosopher.
Sempronius another flattering Lord.
Alcibiades, an Athenian Captaine.
Poet.
Painter.
Jeweller.
Merchant.
Certaine Senatours.
Certaine Maskers.
Certaine Theeues.

Flaminius, one of Tymons Seruants.
Seruilius, another.
Caphis.
Varro.
Philo. ⎱ *Seuerall Seruants to*
Titus. ⎰ *Vsurers.*
Lucius.
Hortensis
Ventigius. one of Tymons false Friends.
Cupid.
Sempronius.
With diuers other Seruants,
And Attendants.

168

The Life of Timon of Athens

Sc. 1 *Enter Poet ⌈at one door⌉, Painter, carrying a picture,*
⌈at another door⌉; ⌈followed by⌉ Jeweller, Merchant,
and Mercer, at several doors

POET

Good day, sir.

PAINTER   I am glad you're well.

POET

I have not seen you long. How goes the world?

Title THE LIFE OF TYMON OF ATHENS. F (*head-title*); *Timon of Athens.* F (*Catalogue and running-title*)

    Sc. 1] OXFORD MIDDLETON; *Actus Primus. Scaena Prima.* F. F *is subsequently without act or scene divisions.*   0.1–2 *at one door . . . at another door*] OXFORD SHAKESPEARE; *not in* F   0.2 *followed by*] OXFORD SHAKESPEARE; *not in* F   0.3 *and Mercer*] F; *not in* JOHNSON; *and divers others* CAPELL   1 you're] F (y'are)

Sc. 1 (1.1) Shakespeare wrote most of the scene. Middleton evidently added the Mercer at l. 0.3, ll. 275–85, and perhaps also the senators at ll. 38.1–42. Hibbard considers that the writing becomes less assured, thinner, and more uneven at l. 179: not itself evidence for another hand, but Middleton might have adjusted the text at ll. 179–83 (see notes). See also notes to ll. 9–10, 42, 49–50, and 255–6.

    After '*Actus Primus: Scaena Prima.*' here, *F* is undivided. For editorial act and scene divisions, see Introduction, pp. 9–11.

0.1 *Poet . . . Painter* Reminders, perhaps, that the play itself is a representation—and depends on previous renditions of the story. It may be no coincidence that one of the sources is by William *Painter*. The Painter is identifiable because carrying a picture; portraiture flourished in the early Jacobean period, especially in the form of miniatures. The Poet might wear a crown of laurel and is carrying a manuscript.

0.2–3 *followed . . . doors* Clients converging on Timon start up two separate conversations: Poet and Painter, Merchant and Jeweller. The Jeweller, Merchant, and Mercer may not enter until l. 5.

0.3 *Mercer* a dealer in silks, velvets, etc. He might be denoted on stage by carrying cloths or garments, and/or an account book: 'the mercer's book' was proverbial for the debts of his customers. Mercers were favourably placed to act as creditors (Stone, *Crisis*, p. 532). Some editors remove the Mercer as an accidental duplication of the Merchant, or a 'false start' (Hibbard); but Middleton probably introduced him. In Shakespeare *mercer* occurs only at *Measure* 4.3.10, in a passage identified as a Middleton addition (see *Collected Works*); he has sued for debt. In *Michaelmas Term* one mercer might provide a large loan (2.1.85), another is called 'Master Profit' (2.3.152). The Mercer visually introduces the theme of consumption and debt. He adds to the bustle of gathering clients ('all these spirits', l. 6). Compare the passage over the stage of the senators at ll. 38.1–42, another possible Middleton addition.

    several different. In stage directions of the period, usually denotes just two doors (Dessen and Thomson), as can be managed here if the entrances are staggered.

2 **long** for a long time

    How goes the world? Proverbial (Dent W884.1); equivalent to 'how are things with you?' or 'what's the news with you?'

PAINTER

It wears, sir, as it grows.

POET   Ay, that's well known.
But what particular rarity, what strange,
Which manifold record not matches?—See,   5
Magic of bounty, all these spirits thy power
Hath conjured to attend.

⌈*Merchant and Jeweller meet. Mercer passes over the
stage, and exits*⌉

                                   I know the merchant.

PAINTER I know them both. Th'other's a jeweller.

MERCHANT (*to Jeweller*)

O, 'tis a worthy lord!

JEWELLER   Nay, that's most fixed.

MERCHANT

A most incomparable man, breathed, as it were,   10
To an untirable and continuate goodness.
He passes.

---

7 *Merchant . . . exits*] OXFORD SHAKESPEARE; *not in* F

---

3 **It . . . grows** The Painter answers as
though the Poet had asked about the state
of the world in general. So the exchange
of greetings slips into conversation. For
the idea, compare *Lear* 20.129–30: 'O
ruined piece of nature! This great world |
Shall so wear out to naught.'
  wears wears away, wears out
  grows grows older
4 **what strange** what that is strange
5 **record** Applies to both memory and
recorded history. Stressed on the second
syllable.
6 **Magic of bounty** The Poet's sight of the
other visitors answers his own question:
the power of patronage is such that the
supernatural is happening here and now.
'Magic of bounty' is in effect an apostrophe to Timon. Conjuration could involve
music, which therefore might be played
by unseen musicians within, the clients
seeming to appear in response to it. Compare Ariel's music that draws Ferdinand
to the stage in *The Tempest* after 1.2.376.
  bounty liberality in giving, munificence;
goodness, excellence, high estate. *Bounty*
and its cognates are key words in the play,

occurring 18 times out of 77 in all Shakespeare, mostly in the Middleton section.
Exceptionally common in Middleton's
works.
6 **spirits** (a) supernatural beings, (b) people
7 **conjured to attend** Applies to (a) magical
conjuration of spirits and (b) the magnet-
ism of patronage. Bradbrook notes that
'*Good* spirits were not conjured into a
circle' (p. 7).
9 **'tis** he is
  fixed certain, securely established. A
sense found in Middleton: 'He kills my
hopes of woman that doubts her. | FIRST
LORD No more, my lord, 'tis fixed' (*Dissemblers* 1.2.68–9).
10 **incomparable** Middletonian as a description of a person.
  breathed accustomed through exercise
  as it were A 'discourse marker' colouring
the Merchant's speech (Blake 8.3.3); perhaps an affectation.
11 **untirable** A rare word, not elsewhere in
Shakespeare.
  continuate continual. Elsewhere, in a
different sense, in *Othello* 3.4.175.
12 **passes** surpasses, excels

JEWELLER   I have a jewel here.

MERCHANT

O, pray, let's see't. For the Lord Timon, sir?

JEWELLER

If he will touch the estimate. But for that—

POET ⌐*reciting to himself*⌐

'When we for recompense have praised the vile,   15
It stains the glory in that happy verse
Which aptly sings the good.'

MERCHANT (*looking at the jewel*) 'Tis a good form.

JEWELLER

And rich. Here is a water, look ye.

PAINTER (*to Poet*)

You are rapt, sir, in some work, some dedication
To the great lord.

POET   A thing slipped idly from me.   20
Our poesy is as a gum which oozes
From whence 'tis nourished. The fire i'th' flint
Shows not till it be struck; our gentle flame

---

15 *reciting to himself*] HANMER (*conj.* Warburton); *not in* F   17 *looking at the jewel*] POPE; *not in*
F   21 gum] POPE; Gowne F   oozes] JOHNSON; vses F; issues POPE

12–14 **I have . . . estimate** The Jeweller's presentation to Timon might satirize James I's well-known fondness for spending large sums of money on jewels.

13 **Timon** Commonly anglicized to rhyme with 'Simon', though perhaps more correct to rhyme with 'demon', or as 'Teemown'.

14 **touch the estimate** meet the expected price. *Estimate* is Shakespearian.

15–17 **When . . . good** These lines seem to be a recitation of verses the Poet has composed; see ll. 19–20. Or an aside is just possible.

15 **we** i.e. poets

16 **happy** fortunate in its subject; felicitous

18 **form** (a) shape, (b) kind, quality
   Here is a water i.e. what a fine water is here! *Water* is transparency, lustre. *OED*'s earliest instance of this sense (*sb.* 20a). Found also in *Pericles* at 12.99, again collocated with *rich* (12.100). The suggestion of fluidity contrasts with *form* and anticipates the Poet's description of his work as liquid-like in ll. 20–5.

19–20 **dedication | To the great lord** Professional writers, including Shakespeare and Middleton, dedicated poems in the hope of securing patronage.

21–5 **Our . . . chafes** Poets, the Poet claims, are not subject to external and spasmodic stimulations (such as a patron's favour); their verse flows slowly, spontaneously, at any time.

21 **gum which oozes** The emendations adopted here are accepted by most editors. Hulme defends F's 'Gowne, which vses' (*Explorations*, pp. 81–2), comparing proverbial 'The gown is his that wears it and the world his that enjoys it' (Dent G387). This explanation is 'strained' (Dent), and 'uses from' is almost impossible. The line might result from misreading of, for instance, 'Gomme, which ouses' ('ouse' was an acceptable spelling of *use* until at least the 16th century).

22 **nourished** nurtured, nursed

22–3 **The . . . struck** Varies the proverb 'In the coldest flint there is hot fire' (Dent F371).

Provokes itself, and like the current flies
Each bound it chafes. What have you there?   25

PAINTER

A picture, sir. When comes your book forth?

POET

Upon the heels of my presentment, sir.

Let's see your piece.

PAINTER (*showing the picture*) 'Tis a good piece.

POET

So 'tis. This comes off well and excellent.

PAINTER

Indifferent.

POET   Admirable. How this grace   30
Speaks his own standing! What a mental power
This eye shoots forth! How big imagination
Moves in this lip! To th' dumbness of the gesture
One might interpret.

---

25 chafes] THEOBALD; chases F   28 *showing the picture*] He examines the painting (*after* 'your piece') BEVINGTON; *not in* F

24 **Provokes itself** i.e. stimulates or kindles itself without needing friction against something else

24–5 **like . . . chafes** The image is now of a river whose current bends away from a bank as it were to avoid friction and turbulence.

24 **flies** rushes away from

25 **bound** bank
chafes Theobald's emendation sustains the idea that poetic creativity avoids stimulation through contact with the outside world. The 'long s' at the beginning and in the middle of a word in Jacobean handwriting resembled 'f'.

27 **Upon the heels of** immediately after
my presentment i.e. my presentation of the book in manuscript to its dedicatee, Timon, as a step towards publication in print; or perhaps the Poet's being presented to Timon for patronage. *OED*'s earliest example of this sense (*sb.* 3).

29 **This** The Poet indicates a detail of the picture (or perhaps the picture as a whole).
comes off turns out, works

30 **Indifferent** Expresses false modesty.

30–1 **How . . . standing** how well the grace of this painted figure conveys the

subject's eminence. The reference to graceful execution suggests a mannered awareness of style, as suggested too by 'Artificial strife | Lives in these touches' (ll. 37–8).

32 **How big** how greatly; what a large **imagination** i.e. the painted subject's power to form ideas and concepts

33 **Moves in** i.e. is expressed by the apparent movement of

33–4 **To . . . interpret** It was a commonplace that 'Painting is a dumb poesy, and a poesy is a speaking picture' (attrib. Simonides, in Coignet, *Politic Discourse*, trans. E. Hoby (1586), in G. G. Smith, ed., *Elizabethan Critical Essays* (1904), i. 342). Malone saw a reference to puppet shows, the 'interpreter' being the speaker of the puppets' words. Compare also the 'excellent dumb discourse' of the spirits in *The Tempest* 3.3.39, and the 'speech in their dumbness, language in their very gesture' in *Winter's Tale* 5.2.13–14. The example from *The Tempest* clearly alludes to the interpretation of gesture in accounts of encounters with New World peoples. But interpretation of allegorical or representative figures was widespread in Renaissance painting, literature, and theatrical dumbshows.

PAINTER

It is a pretty mocking of the life.   35

Here is a touch; is't good?

POET   I will say of it,

It tutors nature. Artificial strife

Lives in these touches livelier than life.

    Enter certain Senators

PAINTER How this lord is followed!

POET

The senators of Athens, happy men!   40

PAINTER Look, more.

    ⌈*The Senators pass over the stage, and exeunt*⌉

POET

You see this confluence, this great flood of visitors.

41 more] F (moe)   41.1 *The . . . exeunt*] CAPELL (*by adding 'and pass over' to the entry at l. 37.1*);
not in F

35 **pretty** neatly contrived, artful
    mocking imitation (in an approving
    sense); counterfeit
36 **touch** neat brushstroke; fine, natural, or
    lifelike detail. In *OED* the earliest example
    of the sense '. . . a stroke or dash of
    colour in a picture, etc. . . .' (*sb.* 10a).
37 **tutors nature** instructs nature as to how it
    should be. Conflates two claims for poetry
    in Philip Sidney's *Defence of Poetry*: that it
    makes 'things better than nature bringeth
    forth' and has the ability 'to teach and
    delight' (*Miscellaneous Prose*, ed. K.
    Duncan-Jones and J. Van Doren (1973),
    78.25 and 80.2).
    Artificial strife i.e. art's skilful attempt to
    outdo nature. Presumably refers to the
    result or manifestation of 'Artificial strife'
    in the more-than-lifelike picture. But the
    phrasing suggests, more extremely, that
    the artifice *per se* has life. The idea recurs
    in Shakespeare; for instance, 'A thousand
    lamentable objects there, | In scorn of
    nature, art gave lifeless life' (*Rape of
    Lucrece* 1373–4).
38 **livelier** Both 'more lifelike' and 'more full
    of vitality'.
38.1 *Senators* The term applied to members
    of the Athenian Council, as sometimes in
    North's Plutarch. It might call for classi-
    cal robes, perhaps in contrast with
    Jacobean costume for the tradesmen and
    artisans, as with the mix of aristocrats in
    Roman attire and others in Elizabethan
    dress in Henry Peacham's sketch of *Titus*

Andronicus (ed. Eugene M. Waith (Oxford,
1984), p. 21). In the English context,
could imply Members of Parliament, or,
as in Middleton's civic works, aldermen of
the City of London, where they are typically described as 'grave' or 'honourable'.
The words *senators* and *aldermen* both etymologically indicate elders or old men.
39 **How this lord is followed** Compare 'behold
    | How pomp is followed' (*Antony and
    Cleopatra* 5.2.146–7), and 'That lord has
    been much followed' (*Mad World* 2.1.16).
    Significantly, the lord in *Mad World* is
    called Lord Owemuch, indicating that he,
    like Timon, has been over-bounteous to
    his followers. The *Mad World* passage con-
    nects with the 'Mercer': see note to l. 0.3.
    this lord i.e. Timon
    followed sought after
40 **happy men** The senators are prosperous
    in themselves, or fortunate in following
    Timon. Theobald emended 'men' to
    'man', making the comment reflect on
    Timon's fortune. This appeals in that the
    single 'happy man' can more readily be
    the favourite of fortune. But it is fitting
    that Timon is the standard by which
    the good fortune even of the great is
    measured.
42 **this confluence . . . of visitors** *Confluence*,
    though well established, is nowhere else
    in Shakespeare or Middleton. It may echo
    Jonson's *Sejanus* (publ. 1605): 'The multi-
    tude of suits, the confluence | Of suitors'
    (3.605–6). The staging of *Timon's*

(*Showing his poem*) I have in this rough work shaped out
　　a man
Whom this beneath world doth embrace and hug
With amplest entertainment. My free drift   45
Halts not particularly, but moves itself
In a wide sea of wax—no levelled malice
Infects one comma in the course I hold—
But flies an eagle flight, bold and forth on,
Leaving no tract behind.   50

43 *Showing his poem*] BEVINGTON (*subs.*); *not in* F

opening scene is similar to that of *Sejanus*.
this great flood Perhaps glances at the Del-
uge (Genesis 6–9). This would relate the-
matically to Timon's later desire to
destroy mankind. The biblical perspective
is sustained in 'beneath world' (l. 44). In
Bloody Murders, the source for *Yorkshire
Tragedy*, ll. 123–4, the same phrase
occurs, referring to the effect that visitors
such as Timon's will have on their hosts:
'restrain *this great flood* of your expense,
before your house be utterly overthrown'
(Holdsworth, unpublished notes). This
strongly suggests Middleton's hand in ll.
38.1–42. *Literature Online* identifies no
other instance of 'this great flood' in literature of the period of any genre, and only
one other occurrence of 'great flood of'.

44 **beneath world** lower, earthly world (mortal and changeable, as distinct from the
heavens), as with the earth and air below
the moon's 'orb' at 14.2. *OED*'s only
example of *beneath* used adjectivally. For
this function of adverbs, see Blake
3.3.3.1(f).

45 **entertainment** welcome, favourable treatment. The word's possible sexual meaning relates to 'embrace and hug'.

45–50 **My . . . behind** Sisson (p.   167)
helpfully identified 'no . . . hold' as a
parenthesis. The two 'but' clauses are
equivalent to each other. The speech perhaps demonstrates the syntax of 'free
drift'.

45–8 **My . . . hold** Echoes the Jonsonian
defence of satire in which the writer aims
'To spare the persons, and to speak the
vices' (*Poetaster*, 'Apologetic Dialogue', l.
72). The Poet's interpretation of his own
writing (beginning at l. 52) shows that it
does, nonetheless, apply in particular to
Timon.

45 **free drift** Suggests the lack of external
constraint (compare ll. 21–5), and anticipates the image of moving at sea.
46 **particularly** to mark out specific
individuals
47 **of wax** growing, becoming more potent.
As of the unstoppable 'wax' of an incoming tide, and correlating with the 'great
flood' of visitors. Probably also refers to
the practice of writing on tablets of wax.
In the final scene a *wax* impression of
Timon's epitaph is 'brought away' from
Timon's grave by 'the very hem o'th' *sea*'
(17.67–9; see Nuttall, pp. 9–11). Some
commentators find an allusion to Icarus,
who was wearing wings attached with
wax when he disastrously flew too near
the sun; this makes little immediate sense
in the context. 'Wax' is often emended
'tax', i.e. censure, in defence of which
Hibbard compares *As You Like It* 2.7.70–2
and 85–7.
levelled aimed at particular targets. The
writer's quill is implicitly like a quilled
arrow. The latent idea of the feather leads
to the image of the eagle at l. 49.
48 **Infects** affects; taints; infests
comma (a) i.e. the punctuation mark, as
the slightest pause in a sentence (almost
as though the comma were itself the
infection, potentially disrupting the
'flight, bold and forth on'), (b) phrase. For
(a), compare *Hamlet* 5.2. 42–3, 'As peace
should . . . stand a comma 'tween their
amities'.
49–50 **But . . . behind** Evidently suggested by
Wisdom of Solomon 5: 10–11: 'as a bird
that flieth through in the air . . . whereas
afterward no token of her way can be
found' (Shaheen, p. 672). The passage is
closer to Middleton's *Solomon Paraphrased*
5.97–108, where the bird is an eagle. The
eagle proverbially flies alone (Dent E7).

PAINTER How shall I understand you?

POET I will unbolt to you.

> You see how all conditions, how all minds,
> As well of glib and slipp'ry creatures as
> Of grave and austere quality, tender down   55
> Their services to Lord Timon. His large fortune
> Upon his good and gracious nature hanging
> Subdues and properties to his love and tendance
> All sorts of hearts; yea, from the glass-faced flatterer
> To Apemantus, that few things loves better   60
> Than to abhor himself—even he drops down
> The knee before him, and returns in peace,
> Most rich in Timon's nod.

PAINTER   I saw them speak together.

POET

> Sir, I have upon a high and pleasant hill
> Feigned Fortune to be throned. The base o'th' mount   65

---

56 services] F; service POPE

---

49 **flies** The subject is the Poet's course, or 'free drift'.

50 **tract** trace, trail. The sense is as in the parallel in *Solomon Paraphrased*: 'The eye can never see | What course she takes, or where she means to be'. Perhaps also glances at polemical or satirical pamphlets.

51 **How . . . you** how will I be able to (or 'how should I') interpret your poem

52 **unbolt** *OED*'s one example of the figurative sense 'explain'.

53 **conditions** (a) social ranks, (b) temperaments

54 **glib and slipp'ry creatures** Compare *Lear* 1.216–17, 'that glib and oily art | To speak and purpose not'.
glib smooth, suave, oily (Crystal)

55 **quality** (a) rank, nobility; (b) character

56–7 **His . . . hanging** Timon's 'fortune' is pictured as a garment, his 'good and gracious nature' being the body that wears it. Because Timon's fortune is bestowed on such a good person, he attracts 'All sorts of hearts' as friends. But l. 57, 'Upon . . . hanging', easily becomes parenthetic, in which case it is Timon's fortune that attracts his friends.

56 **large fortune** great good fortune, illustriousness (hinting also at 'ample wealth')

58 **Subdues** makes subservient

properties appropriates. *OED*'s early examples of the verb *property* are all from Shakespeare. The present line provides the only example of *v.* 2 from before 1833.
his love and tendance loving and attending him

59 **glass-faced** mirror-faced (in that it reflects his patron's moods and opinions). A proverbial image for a flatterer (Dent G132.1). Compare the 'flatt'ring glass, | Like to my followers in prosperity', *Richard II* 4.1.269–70.

60–3 **Apemantus . . . nod** Inconsistent with Apemantus' behaviour in Sc. 2, perhaps because of a switch of author.

60 **Apemantus** See note to l. 179, and Introduction, pp. 74–9.

62 **returns** goes back home

63 **Most . . . nod** (a) most gratified by Timon acknowledging him, (b) most enriched by Timon's assent to a petition or approval of a gift

64–5 **I . . . throned** Fortune was usually depicted with a wheel, but see Illustration 1, which matches the Poet's description well (and see Introduction, p. 40). In the morality play *Liberality and Prodigality* performed at Court *c.*1601, Prodigality scales the wall of Fortune's house, only for him to fall down with a halter round his neck: ed. W. W. Greg, Malone Society

---

Is ranked with all deserts, all kind of natures
That labour on the bosom of this sphere
To propagate their states. Amongst them all
Whose eyes are on this sovereign lady fixed
One do I personate of Lord Timon's frame,   70
Whom Fortune with her ivory hand wafts to her,
Whose present grace to present slaves and servants
Translates his rivals.
PAINTER   'Tis conceived to scope.
This throne, this Fortune, and this hill, methinks,
With one man beckoned from the rest below,   75
Bowing his head against the steepy mount
To climb his happiness, would be well expressed
In our condition.

Reprints (Oxford, 1913), ll. 898–907. In contrast with a wheel, a hill allows post-Machiavellian human agency, or the appearance of it: people *labour* to climb. Fortune, however, is in control (l. 71). The extended image thus recollects the Poet's picture of patronage as 'magic of bounty' (l. 6). The account of Fortune has been taken as 'the moral of Shakespeare's play' (K. Muir, 'In Defence of Timon's Poet', *Essays in Criticism*, 3 (1953), p. 121), or as 'deliberately trite' (R. C. Elliott, *The Power of Satire* (1960), p. 150).

65 **Feigned** represented, fabled. There is no need for deception to be indicated, though Fortune is herself portrayed as a deceiver.

66 **ranked . . . deserts** lined with ranks of people of every kind of merit

67 **the . . . sphere** A line of dense connotation. Perhaps implies the *mount* of Fortune as a hemisphere, *bosom* suggesting its swell or the hollow below it. *This sphere* is also (as more usually explained) the earth as a globe. *Bosom* can mean 'womb'; compare the hill with 'concave womb' in 'Lover's Complaint' l. 1. This feeds into an erotic undercurrent: 'base o'th' mount . . . labour [exert themselves sexually] . . . bosom . . . propagate'; compare 'conceived to scope', l. 73, and 'Bowing . . . happiness', ll. 76–7. all relate to Fortune as a mistress. Kahn further finds a suggestion of 'a baby with its head on its mother's breast' (p. 37), of which there is some hint in the relative size of the *bosom* as breast; this complicates the psychoanalytic resonance. For

bosom in relation to mother earth, see 14.187. This connection might imply a comparison between striving for wealth and working on the land to *propagate* a crop.

68 **propagate** increase
states possessions, fortunes

69 **this sovereign lady** i.e. Fortune, often pictured with the attributes of a goddess and/or a whore

70–1 **One . . . her** This suggests, in contrast with Timon's title of 'Lord' and the vast landed wealth he possessed, that he is a parvenu.

70 **frame** Both 'disposition' and 'bodily build'.

71 **ivory** Proverbially white (Dent I109). Perhaps Fortune's other hand that 'Spurns down her late belovèd' (l. 86) is of ebony. Or perhaps *ivory* simply denotes her statuesque appearance.

72 **Whose** i.e. Fortune's
present grace graciousness (i.e. favour, generosity) of the present moment. *Grace* has theological connotations that relate Fortune to God.

72–3 **to . . . rivals** immediately transforms his rivals into his slaves and servants

73 **to scope** to the purpose, aptly (literally 'to the mark, on target'). *OED*'s only instance.

77 **his happiness** to his good fortune
expressed exemplified, displayed

78 **our condition** the circumstances we find around us; the human condition. Or possibly 'our attributes' (*OED*, *condition*, *sb.* 13), in which case the Painter refers to his art (with *expressed* in the usual sense).

POET   Nay, sir, but hear me on.
All those which were his fellows but of late,
Some better than his value, on the moment   80
Follow his strides, his lobbies fill with tendance,
Rain sacrificial whisperings in his ear,
Make sacred even his stirrup, and through him
Drink the free air—

PAINTER   Ay, marry, what of these?

POET

When Fortune in her shift and change of mood   85
Spurns down her late belovèd, all his dependants,
Which laboured after him to the mountain's top
Even on their knees and hands, let him flit down,
Not one accompanying his declining foot.

PAINTER 'Tis common.   90
A thousand moral paintings I can show
That shall demonstrate these quick blows of Fortune's
More pregnantly than words. Yet you do well
To show Lord Timon that mean eyes have seen

---

88 hands] F2; hand F1   flit] This edition; sit F; slip ROWE; sink DELIUS *conj.*; fall SISSON

---

80 **his value** him in merit; him in status
    on the moment instantly
81–4 **his lobbies . . . air** These lines seem to
    have a sexual resonance.
81 **tendance** attendance
82 **Rain . . . ear** One might *pour words* in an
    ear, or *pour sacrificial* wine or oil. *Rain*
    invokes the patter of whispered speech
    soliciting personal favour.
    sacrificial *OED*'s earliest instance of the
    word. It suggests both worship of a god
    and self-sacrificing offers aimed at curry-
    ing favour.
83 **stirrup** Held by followers when the rider
    mounts his horse. The image might sug-
    gest it is reverentially kissed.
83–4 **through . . . air** breathe his exhalations
    (or his flatulence), make themselves
    depend on him even for the air they
    breathe. Air was proverbially free.
84 **marry** indeed
88 **flit** shift, pass. Perhaps glancing at *OED v.*
    5c 'Of a horseman: to lose his seat and fall
    to the ground' (compare the image of the
    stirrup at l. 83). Editors usually emend F's
    unconvincing 'sit' to 'slip' or 'fall', but

'flit' is a more distinctive reading that
relates to a specific strand in the imagery,
and it assumes a slightly easier error in
'sit'. Shakespeare elsewhere adopts the
related form *fleet*.
89 **declining** falling, sinking
    foot As the part of the body others have
    followed upwards. It may be implied he is
    falling head first, as in emblems represen-
    tations of Fortune's victims; see Illustra-
    tion 1 and George Wither, *Emblems*
    (1635), Book 1, Emblem 6.
91–3 **A . . . words** The relative merits of
    painting and poetry were often debated
    (see Introduction, p. 82).
91 **moral** allegorical
92 **demonstrate** Stressed on the second
    syllable.
    quick (a) vigorous, sharp; (b) lively (so
    needing life-like representation). Corre-
    lates with *pregnantly* in 1.93 through the
    shared idea 'with child'.
93 **pregnantly** cogently (and see previous
    note)
94 **mean eyes** (a) the eyes of the lowly, (b)
    malicious eyes

The foot above the head.   95

> *Trumpets sound. Enter Lord Timon ⌈wearing a rich*
> *jewel⌉, addressing himself courteously to every suitor;*
> *with a Messenger from Ventidius, Lucilius, and other*
> *servants*

TIMON (*to Messenger*) Imprisoned is he, say you?

MESSENGER

Ay, my good lord. Five talents is his debt,
His means most short, his creditors most strait.
Your honourable letter he desires
To those have shut him up, which failing,   100
Periods his comfort.

TIMON   Noble Ventidius! Well,
I am not of that feather to shake off
My friend when he must need me. I do know him
A gentleman that well deserves a help,
Which he shall have. I'll pay the debt and free him.   105

MESSENGER   Your lordship ever binds him.

TIMON

Commend me to him. I will send his ransom;

95.1–2 *wearing a rich jewel*] OXFORD SHAKESPEARE; *not in* F   95.3–4 *with . . . servants*] CAM-
BRIDGE (*subs.*); *not in* F

---

95 **the foot . . . head** i.e. the foot of the fortunate of Fortune's hill advanced above the
vulnerable aspirant's head; or Fortune's
own foot set to spurn him down. As at l.
89 there is probably also a suggestion of
tumbling head first. Compare also the
proverb 'Do not make the foot the head'
(Dent F562).

95.1 *Trumpets sound* Trumpets signal the
arrival of an important person, usually a
prince, and therefore are ostentatious
here. The wording is typically Shakespearian (Dessen and Thomson).
Enter Lord Timon In a Jacobean theatre
with three stage doors, the side doors
might have been used by the clients,
reserving the central door for Timon's
entry (Klein).

95.2 *addressing . . . suitor* This probably
indicates silent gestures of conversation
as Timon and the suitors enter.

97 **Five talents** A considerable sum: a talent
in the Greek and biblical world could be
over 25 kilos or 56 lb. of silver, and was
reckoned in the early 17th century to be
worth between £100 and £180. See note

to 2.6–7, and Introduction, p. 51. Neither
Shakespeare nor Middleton elsewhere
refers to this unit of money. It is found
in Lucian's *Dialogue* and in Plutarch.
Compare the unique 'Sickles' or 'shekels'
of 'the tested gold' at *Measure* 2.2.153.

98 **strait** exacting

100 **have** who have

100–1 **which . . . comfort** if which fails, his
hopes end (or 'the failure of which would
end his hopes')

102–3 **I . . . me** Glances at the proverbs
'Swallows, like false friends, fly away
upon the approach of winter' (Dent
S1026) and 'Birds of a feather will fly
together' (B393). Compare 11.28–31.

102 **feather** Literally 'plumage'; i.e.
disposition.

103 **must need me** has no option but to seek
help from me

106 **ever binds him** makes him obliged for
ever. To 'free' Ventidius from prison is to
'bind' him with bonds of obligation.

107 **his ransom** i.e. the sum he needs
for him to be released from debtors'
prison

And, being enfranchised, bid him come to me.
'Tis not enough to help the feeble up,
But to support him after. Fare you well.   110
MESSENGER All happiness to your honour.   *Exit*
    Enter an Old Athenian

OLD MAN
Lord Timon, hear me speak.
TIMON   Freely, good father.
OLD MAN
Thou hast a servant named Lucilius.
TIMON I have so. What of him?
OLD MAN
Most noble Timon, call the man before thee.   115
TIMON
Attends he here or no? Lucilius!
LUCILIUS Here at your lordship's service.
OLD MAN
This fellow here, Lord Timon, this, thy creature,
By night frequents my house. I am a man
That from my first have been inclined to thrift,   120
And my estate deserves an heir more raised
Than one which holds a trencher.
TIMON   Well, what further?
OLD MAN
One only daughter have I, no kin else
On whom I may confer what I have got.
The maid is fair, o'th' youngest for a bride,   125
And I have bred her at my dearest cost
In qualities of the best. This man of thine

108 enfranchised] POPE; enfranchized (= -èd) F   118 this,] F (this‸)

108 **being enfranchised** when he is set free
109–10 'Tis . . . **after** Perhaps recalls the
    Good Samaritan, who in Christ's parable
    rescued the injured man and also 'made
    provision for him' by paying his expenses
    at an inn (Luke 10: 34).
110 **But** i.e. but it is also necessary (compare
    Abbott 125, and Blake 6.3.4, 'Ellipsis
    through parallelism')
111.1 *Athenian* Suggests a specifically
    ancient Greek costume.
112 **father** (respectful form of address to an
    older man)
118 **this,** I follow Blake (6.3.2.1) in under-

standing an elliptic 'this fellow here, who
is merely thy creature' rather than
the more usual and weaker double
determiner.
    creature dependent, hanger-on
121 **more raised** of higher standing
122 **one . . . trencher** i.e. a domestic servant.
    A *trencher* was a wooden plate.
124 **got** acquired
125 **o'th' . . . bride** at the youngest age to
    marry
126 **bred** brought up, educated
127 **qualities** accomplishments

Attempts her love. I prithee, noble lord,
Join with me to forbid him her resort.
Myself have spoke in vain.   130

TIMON The man is honest.

OLD MAN Therefore he will be, Timon.
His honesty rewards him in itself;
It must not bear my daughter.

TIMON Does she love him?   135

OLD MAN She is young and apt.
Our own precedent passions do instruct us
What levity's in youth.

TIMON (*to Lucilius*)   Love you the maid?

LUCILIUS
Ay, my good lord, and she accepts of it.

OLD MAN
If in her marriage my consent be missing,   140
I call the gods to witness, I will choose
Mine heir from forth the beggars of the world,
And dispossess her all.

TIMON   How shall she be endowed
If she be mated with an equal husband?

OLD MAN
Three talents on the present; in future, all.   145

TIMON
This gentleman of mine hath served me long.
To build his fortune I will strain a little,
For 'tis a bond in men. Give him thy daughter.

---

128 **Attempts** tries to attain (*OED*'s only example of this sense before Samuel Johnson); tempts

129 **her resort** access to her

131 **honest** honourable

132 **will be** i.e. will be honest

133 **His . . . itself** Based on the proverb 'Virtue is its own reward' (Dent V81).

134 **bear** carry away with it, take as its prize

136 **apt** easily impressed, sexually aware

137 **precedent** earlier (stressed on the second syllable)

138 **levity** frivolity, inconstancy

140 **If . . . missing** Paternal consent was crucial in a period when marriages were often arranged by parents.

142 **forth** out of, among

143 **all** entirely. Alternatively, as *OED* sug-

gests, *dispossess* might take a double object (*v.* 1d), with *her all* as 'her of everything she has', but the usage is otherwise unexampled.

143 **How . . . endowed** what dowry will she have

146 **gentleman** 'A man of gentle birth attached to the household of the sovereign or other person of high rank' (*OED sb.* 2). The term still contrasts with 'one which holds a trencher' (l. 122).

147 **To . . . little** Timon may show awareness that his finances are limited. More likely, he expresses wry self-deprecation, implying that really it is no effort for him to be generous. Compare ll.171–2.

148 **bond** obligation. A loaded word: legal bonds will later be Timon's undoing. Here

What you bestow, in him I'll counterpoise,
And make him weigh with her.

OLD MAN   Most noble lord,　　150
Pawn me to this your honour, she is his.

TIMON
My hand to thee; mine honour on my promise.

LUCILIUS
Humbly I thank your lordship. Never may
That state or fortune fall into my keeping
Which is not owed to you.　　*Exit with Old Man*　155

POET (*presenting a poem to Timon*)
Vouchsafe my labour, and long live your lordship!

TIMON
I thank you. You shall hear from me anon.
Go not away. (*To Painter*) What have you there, my
　　friend?

PAINTER
A piece of painting, which I do beseech
Your lordship to accept.

TIMON   Painting is welcome.　　160
The painting is almost the natural man;
For since dishonour traffics with man's nature,
He is but outside; these pencilled figures are
Even such as they give out. I like your work,

155　*with Old Man*] THEOBALD (*subs.*); *not in* F　156　*presenting a poem to Timon*] CAPELL (*subs.*)

as elsewhere, only Timon seems to be bound.

150　**with** equally with
151　**Pawn . . . honour** if you will pledge your honour to me that you will do this (Abbott 186)
154　**state** i.e. wealth
155　**owed to you** acknowledged as owing to your generosity (or 'due to you as a debt')
156　**Vouchsafe** deign to accept
160　**Painting is welcome** The mannered expression perhaps suggests a personification: the painting of the man is as welcome as if it were 'the natural man' himself.
161–3　**The . . . outside** A difficult passage. With humans, artifice more or less is human nature, for ever since dishonour had dealings with humanity (or *because* it

has), it has made outward appearance the defining characteristic of human nature. Thus the artifice of painting befits the artifice of humanity. The 17th-century annotator of the Meisei copy of the Folio glossed, 'lively pictures represent men of this age really because they are but outsides' (Yamada, p. 207). The strained conceit of Timon's language is not exactly itself 'natural', perhaps a sign of his difficulty in distinguishing between appearance and reality.
162　**traffics** has dealings (specifically, improper ones). Associates *dishonour* with commerce.
163　**but** merely; entirely
　　outside external appearance
　　pencilled painted with brush-strokes
164　**Even . . . out** just what they appear to be

And you shall find I like it. Wait attendance   165
Till you hear further from me.

PAINTER   The gods preserve ye!

TIMON

Well fare you, gentleman. Give me your hand.
We must needs dine together. (*To Jeweller*) Sir, your jewel
Hath suffered under praise.

JEWELLER   What, my lord, dispraise?

TIMON

A mere satiety of commendations.   170
If I should pay you for't as 'tis extolled
It would unclew me quite.

JEWELLER   My lord, 'tis rated
As those which sell would give; but you well know
Things of like value differing in the owners
Are prizèd by their masters. Believe't, dear lord,   175
You mend the jewel by the wearing it.

TIMON Well mocked.

MERCHANT

No, my good lord, he speaks the common tongue
Which all men speak with him.

          Enter Apemantus

---

169 suffered] POPE; suffered (= -èd) F   179 *Enter Apemantus*] POPE; *after l.* 177 *in* F   179 *Apemantus*] F (*Apermantus*). *Likewise at l.* 183, *and similarly catchword to l.* 184 (*Aper.*).

165 **find I like it** Oblique for 'be well paid for it'.

Wait attendance remain in attendance

168 **must needs** really must

169 **Hath . . . praise** i.e. cannot hope to match the high praise it has been given. The Jeweller understands *under-praise*, 'verbal depreciation'.

170 **mere** utter, absolute

171–2 **If . . . quite** Timon probably jokes self-deprecatorily, assuming his wealth is really too vast to be exhausted. By dramatic irony, then, his extravagant spending will indeed 'unclew me quite'.

172 **unclew** unwind, undo; ruin (Crystal). Refers to unwinding a ball of wool. *OED*'s earliest example of the word.

172–3 **rated . . . give** i.e. for sale at the trade price

174 **like** equal, similar

175 **prizèd by their masters** valued by others

on the basis of who owns them. Or 'differently valued by different owners'.

176 **mend** increase the value of

177 **Well mocked** well acted, counterfeited (as a sales pitch). Timon's praise of the performance may be reinforced by him paying the Jeweller, which would suggest that he knowingly pays too much for the jewel.

179 *Apemantus* He is a cynic philosopher on the model of Diogenes (see Introduction, pp. 74–7). His appearance might be dishevelled; Diogenes was often depicted with a torn cloak. 'Apemantus' perhaps means 'feeling no pain' (Bradbrook, p. 22), which suggests part of the contrast between him and Timon explored in their exchange in Sc. 14. Pronounced as four syllables. F's spelling '*Apermantus*' here and at l. 183 (at the foot of a page, Gg2) is elsewhere associated with Middleton. Middleton may have added a few lines

TIMON   Look who comes here.
   Will you be chid?   180
JEWELLER We'll bear, with your lordship.
MERCHANT He'll spare none.
TIMON
   Good morrow to thee, gentle Apemantus.
APEMANTUS
   Till I be gentle, stay thou for thy good morrow—
   When thou art Timon's dog, and these knaves honest.   185
TIMON
   Why dost thou call them knaves? Thou know'st them
      not.
APEMANTUS Are they not Athenians?
TIMON Yes.
APEMANTUS Then I repent not.
JEWELLER You know me, Apemantus?   190
APEMANTUS
   Thou know'st I do. I called thee by thy name.
TIMON Thou art proud, Apemantus!
APEMANTUS Of nothing so much as that I am not like Timon.
TIMON Whither art going?   195
APEMANTUS To knock out an honest Athenian's brains.
TIMON That's a deed thou'lt die for.

197 thou'lt] F (thou't)

(see following notes), or perhaps just
a stage direction whose spelling was
copied by the compositor a few lines
later.

180 **Will you be chid** do you want to be
   scolded. Compare *Women Beware* 1.2.212,
   'I shall be chid for't'.
181 **bear** put up with it. For the unusual
   intransitive, compare *Lady's* 4.2.36, 'I'm
   ashamed of my provision, but a friend will
   bear.'
   with along with
183 **gentle** Might be spoken with uncritical
   open-heartedness or knowing irony.
184–5 **Till . . . honest** Plays on *gentle* as
   'softly mannered' and 'noble in rank'.
   The latter sets up a role reversal: Apemantus will become the aristocrat, Timon
   will occupy Apemantus' role as 'Timon's
   dog' (see note to l. 203). *Knaves* meaning
   'base-born men' picks up on the idea of

social rank, but is turned to mean
'scoundrels'.
184 **stay . . . morrow** i.e. you will have to
   wait for a polite greeting. Perhaps suggesting that it will always be tomorrow,
   never today.
187–9 **Are . . . not** Nuttall describes Apem-
   anatus' logic here and in the following
   exchanges as 'at once Euclidian and wild-
   ly irrational': here a syllogism on the false
   premiss that all Athenians are knaves (pp.
   22–3).
191 **thy name** i.e. *knave*
197 **thou'lt** F's odd form 'thou't' occurs four
   times in *Timon*, never associated with
   Middleton. Elsewhere in F there is a single
   instance (*Coriolanus*, TLN 749). There are
   only two instances in Middleton. One of
   the few plays to use the word repeatedly
   is Dekker's *Satiromastix* (1601), where it
   characterizes the speech of the swagger-
   ing old soldier Tucca.

APEMANTUS Right, if doing nothing be death by th' law.

TIMON How lik'st thou this picture, Apemantus?

APEMANTUS The best, for the innocence.   200

TIMON

Wrought he not well that painted it?

APEMANTUS He wrought better that made the painter, and
yet he's but a filthy piece of work.

PAINTER You're a dog.

APEMANTUS Thy mother's of my generation. What's she, if   205
I be a dog?

TIMON Wilt dine with me, Apemantus?

APEMANTUS No, I eat not lords.

TIMON An thou shouldst, thou'dst anger ladies.

APEMANTUS O, they eat lords. So they come by great bellies.   210

TIMON

That's a lascivious apprehension.

APEMANTUS

So thou apprehend'st it, take it for thy labour.

TIMON

How dost thou like this jewel, Apemantus?

APEMANTUS Not so well as plain dealing, which will not cost
a man a doit.   215

204 You're] F (Y'are)   212 So₄] F3; ~, FI   214 cost] F3; cast FI

198 **doing nothing** (because there are no
   honest Athenians)
200 **for the** on account of its
   innocence (a) artlessness, guilelessness
   (perhaps because Apemantus can see
   obvious faults in the person painted that
   the Painter has failed to conceal), or
   (b) harmlessness (of the painted figure,
   in contrast with the represented person)
202 **He** i.e. God
203 **filthy** Again Apemantus' word at 2.149.
204 **dog** See Introduction, p. 75. Here and
   elsewhere an allusion to Apemantus'
   brand of philosophy, as *cynic* is derived
   from the Greek for 'dog'. Also a general
   insult. At 14.251 Timon's 'bred a dog'
   links Apemantus' cynicism with his lowly
   origins.
205 **generation** breed, species (punning on
   'age-group')
207 **Wilt** wilt thou (Blake 3.3.2.1(f))
208 **eat not lords** i.e. do not consume the
   wealth that makes lords. Or Apemantus
   takes *dine with* to mean 'dine on', as in

Measure 4.3.149, 'dine and sup with
water and bran'. Compare 2.40–1.
209 **An thou shouldst** if you did
210 **eat lords** Quibbles on spending all their
   wealth and sexually 'devouring' them,
   the latter leading to the *great bellies* of
   pregnancy.
211 **apprehension** idea, way of thinking
   about it. Plays on the physical sexual act it
   refers to, with *apprehend* as 'lay hold of'.
212 **So . . . it** as you understand it that way
   take . . . labour keep it as reward for your
   effort
214–15 **Not . . . doit** From the proverbs
   'Plain dealing is a jewel, but they that use
   it die beggars' (Dent P382) and 'Not
   worth a doit' (Dent D430).
214 **cost** By FI's 'cast', 'plain dealing' is a person who refuses to throw a coin to a beggar,
   which makes little sense in context. The
   jewel and plain dealing must somehow
   contrast, as by F3's emendation 'cost': the
   jewel is expensive, plain dealing is free.
215 **doit** (a coin of very small value)

TIMON

What dost thou think 'tis worth?

APEMANTUS　　　　　　　　　　　Not worth my thinking.—

How now, poet?

POET　How now, philosopher?

APEMANTUS　Thou liest.

POET　Art not one?　　　　　　　　　　　　　　　　　　220

APEMANTUS　Yes.

POET　Then I lie not.

APEMANTUS　Art not a poet?

POET　Yes.

APEMANTUS　Then thou liest. Look in thy last work, where　225
thou hast feigned him a worthy fellow.

POET　That's not feigned, he is so.

APEMANTUS　Yes, he is worthy of thee, and to pay thee for
thy labour. He that loves to be flattered is worthy o'th'
flatterer. Heavens, that I were a lord!　　　　　230

TIMON　What wouldst do then, Apemantus?

APEMANTUS　E'en as Apemantus does now: hate a lord with
my heart.

TIMON　What, thyself?

APEMANTUS　Ay.　　　　　　　　　　　　　　　　　　235

TIMON　Wherefore?

APEMANTUS　That I had no angry wit but to be a lord.—Art
not thou a merchant?

MERCHANT　Ay, Apemantus.

APEMANTUS

Traffic confound thee, if the gods will not!　　　240

---

219 APEMANTUS] *Ape.* F (*some copies*); *pe.* F (*others*)　226 feigned] F2; fegin'd FI　235 Ay] F
(I)　237 angry wit but] OXFORD MIDDLETON (*conj.* Holdsworth); angry wit F; augury but
OXFORD SHAKESPEARE

---

219 APEMANTUS See collation. The missing
'A' in some copies of F evidently results
from the type being pulled out of place by
the ink-ball.

223–5 Art … liest　From　the　proverb
'Painters and poets have leave to lie' (Dent
P28).

226 him i.e. Timon

231 wouldst wouldst thou

232–3 E'en … heart This is the only line in a
passage attributed to Shakespeare that
contains two forms favoured by Middleton, *e'en* and *does*.

237 angry wit wit in my anger. See collation.
Alternatively 'angry wit' can be emended
'augury but', as in Oxford Shakespeare.
However, F is based on the proverb 'He
has wit at will that with angry heart can
hold him still' (Dent W553).

240 Traffic business, trade
confound ruin, destroy. An important
word in the play. It and *confounding* occur
eleven times, over twice as often as in any
other play by Shakespeare or Middleton,
always in Shakespeare sections.

MERCHANT If traffic do it, the gods do it.

APEMANTUS

Traffic's thy god, and thy god confound thee!

Trumpet sounds. Enter a Messenger

TIMON What trumpet's that?

MESSENGER

'Tis Alcibiades, and some twenty horse

All of companionship.   245

TIMON

Pray entertain them. Give them guide to us.

Exit one or more attendants

You must needs dine with me.—Go not you hence

Till I have thanked you. (*To Painter*) When dinner's done

Show me this piece. (*To all*) I am joyful of your sights.

Enter Alcibiades with his horsemen. ⌈*They greet Timon*⌉

Most welcome, sir!   250

APEMANTUS (*aside*) So, so, there.

Achës contract and starve your supple joints!

That there should be small love amongst these sweet

    knaves,

246.1 *Exit one or more attendants*] CAPELL (*subs.*); *not in* F   249.1 *his horsemen*] OXFORD SHAKE-SPEARE (*following* Capell, '*his Company*'); *the rest* F   249.1 *They greet Timon*] OXFORD MIDDLETON; *not in* F   251–2 so, there. | Achës] CAPELL; so; their‸ Aches F   253 amongst] F (amongest); 'mongst CAPELL

241 **If . . . it** Probably refers to natural disasters such as shipwreck. Perhaps implies the corollary, that trade flourishes through blessing of the gods.

242.1 **Enter a Messenger** The opening scene demands a large number of actors, and so this Messenger might be played by the same actor as the one who entered with Timon after l. 95.

244 **Alcibiades** Though often pronounced 'al-sib-*ay*-a-deez', more accurately Anglicized 'al-kib-*ay*-a-deez' or 'al-kib-*ya*-deez'. Metre favours the four-syllable pronunciation here and at 14.704 (but compare l. 705) and 738.
horse horsemen

245 **of companionship** in one party

246 **entertain** receive, welcome

247 **You . . . me** Perhaps addressed to the Jeweller.

247–8 **Go . . . you** Perhaps addressed to the Poet.

248 **thanked** i.e. rewarded

249 **of your sights** to see you

249.1 **Enter . . . Timon** In the Jacobean theatre there would not have been twenty horsemen, as mentioned at l. 243 (nor horses). The staging of Alcibiades' arrival and greeting may be informed by Plutarch, who described 'a bold and insolent youth whom he [Timon] would greatly feast and make much of, and kissed him very gladly'. Apemantus' speech suggests (also) a lot of bowing and cringing.
his horsemen Emended from F's vague '*the rest*'.

251 **So, so, there** just look at that. F's 'their' is an acceptable spelling of *there*, but F's punctuation and prose setting wrongly confirm the possessive 'their aches' (see collation).

252 **Achës** Disyllabic form of *aches*; referring to rheumatism, arthritis, etc.
starve paralyse, disable, wither

253 **amongst** F's spelling 'amongest' is unique in the Folio. The spelling occurs also in 'The Argument' to *Rape of Lucrece*.

And all this courtesy! The strain of man's bred out
Into baboon and monkey.   255
ALCIBIADES (*to Timon*)

Sir, you have saved my longing, and I feed
Most hungrily on your sight.
TIMON   Right welcome, sir!
Ere we depart, we'll share a bounteous time
In different pleasures. Pray you, let us in.

> *Exeunt all but Apemantus*

> *Enter two Lords*

FIRST LORD

What time o' day is't, Apemantus?   260
APEMANTUS

Time to be honest.
FIRST LORD   That time serves still.
APEMANTUS

The most accursèd thou, that still omitt'st it.
SECOND LORD

Thou art going to Lord Timon's feast?
APEMANTUS

Ay, to see meat fill knaves, and wine heat fools.
SECOND LORD Fare thee well, fare thee well.   265

---

257 hungrily] F (hungerly)   258 depart] F2; depatt FI   259.1 *all but Apemantus*] ROWE
(*subs.*); *not in* F   261 FIRST LORD] F (1). *Similarly formatted as a numeral without a name for both
Lords in this passage, except l. 260,* '1. Lord.'   262 most] F; more HANMER

Compositor B might have inserted 'e' to
help justify; 'amongest' is the last word in
a line. Examples in verse of the period
suggest the 'e' is without metrical value.
Capell's metrical emendation ''mongst'
might be right.

254 **bred out** dissipated through over-
breeding, degenerated
256 **saved my longing** gratified my desire to
be with you. Varies proverbial 'to lose
one's longing' (Dent L422.1). Though
Dent rejects Oliver's claim that the phrase
is affectedly effeminate, it has an erotic
coloration. It is found in several writers of
the early 17th century, most notably Jonson, and occurs in Middleton's *Five Gallants* at 2.1.320 as 'to save her longing'.
Neither it nor 'to lose one's longing' is in
Shakespeare.
256–7 **feed . . . sight** The idea that Timon's
flatterers metaphorically devour him runs

through the play, especially in Middleton
sections. For feeding on sight compare
Solomon Paraphrased: 'feeding my fancies
with her sight' (7.137), and 'They see her
sight, yet what doth sight procure? | Like
Tantalus they feed, and yet they starve'
(14.160–1). Shakespeare refers to the
reverse idea: 'the object that did feed her
sight' in *Venus and Adonis* at l. 822.
Hungrily is not in Middleton, whereas
both the word and its present spelling
'hungerly' are in Shakespeare.
257 **your sight** the sight of you
258 **depart** part company
259 **different** various. Compare 14.258.
261 **That time serves still** it is always the right
time for that
262 **that still** that always
264 **to . . . fools** Based on proverbial 'To be
both fool and knave' (Dent F506.1).
meat food

187

APEMANTUS

   Thou art a fool to bid me farewell twice.

SECOND LORD Why, Apemantus?

APEMANTUS Shouldst have kept one to thyself, for I mean to
   give thee none.

FIRST LORD Hang thyself!   270

APEMANTUS No, I will do nothing at thy bidding. Make thy
   requests to thy friend.

SECOND LORD Away, unpeaceable dog, or I'll spurn thee
   hence.

APEMANTUS I will fly, like a dog, the heels o'th' ass.   *Exit*   275

FIRST LORD

   He's opposite to humanity. Come, shall we in,
   And taste Lord Timon's bounty? He outgoes
   The very heart of kindness.

SECOND LORD

   He pours it out. Plutus the god of gold
   Is but his steward; no meed but he repays   280
   Sevenfold above itself; no gift to him
   But breeds the giver a return exceeding
   All use of quittance.

---

275 *Exit*] HANMER (*subs.*); *not in* F   276 Come] F2; Comes F1   277 taste] F2; raste F1

---

273 **unpeaceable** quarrelsome (rare; not elsewhere in Shakespeare or Middleton)
   spurn kick

275 **heels** hooves

276–86 FIRST . . . **company** From verbal parallels, Holdsworth suggests this was wholly or partly added by Middleton, anticipating Sc. 2. Middleton's addition probably begins after 'He's opposite to humanity', which anticipates 11.103–4 (Shakespeare?) and 14.302 (Shakespeare; but see note). In contrast, 'Taste Lord Timon's bounty' (l. 277) may be Middleton (see note).

276 **opposite to** (a) antagonistic to, (b) the opposite of

277 **taste Lord Timon's bounty** Echoed at 2.118–19, and developed further at 2.133–35. Contributes to the running theme that Timon's wealth, and ultimately his person, are consumed by his friends. *Bounty* and *tasted* are collocated at *Roaring Girl* 2.1.83–5. Though not generally Shakespearian, the image recurs in

a Shakespeare episode at 14.592 (see note). See also 6.74–5 (Middleton). The expression 'to taste someone's bounty' was fairly common in the period, but it remains striking to find four examples in one play.
   outgoes surpasses

278 **heart** essence

279 **pours it out** i.e. is unrestrainedly generous. In Lucian, the destitute Timon admits to having 'poured out my riches'. And see following note.
   Plutus Personification of wealth, or 'lord of riches' (*Game at Chess* 5.3.216–17). In classical and Renaissance art represented as a naked boy, often holding a cornucopia. There are no suggestions of a boy here, but the cornucopia relates to 'He pours it out'.

280 **steward** See note to 2.0.2.
   meed gift. *OED*'s only example of this sense (*sb.* 1e).

283 **All use of quittance** repayment with full interest

FIRST LORD   The noblest mind he carries
That ever governed man.
SECOND LORD
Long may he live in fortunes! Shall we in?   285
FIRST LORD I'll keep you company.   *Exeunt*

Sc. 2   *Hautboys playing loud music. A great banquet served*
in, ⌈the Steward and Servants attending⌉; and then
enter Lord Timon, Alcibiades, the States, the Athenian
Lords, amongst them Lucius, Ventidius which Timon
redeemed from prison. Then comes, dropping after all,
Apemantus, discontentedly, like himself
VENTIDIUS Most honoured Timon,

286 FIRST LORD] CAPELL; *not in* F
2.0.2 *the Steward and Servants attending*] CAPELL (*subs.*); *not in* F   0.3 *Alcibiades*] CAPELL; *not*
in F   0.4 *amongst them Lucius*] ROWE (*subs.*); *not in* F   0.4 *Ventidius*] F (*Ventigius*). *Similarly in*
speech heading for l. 1 (*Ventig.*), *in dialogue at l.* 9, *and in* 'THE ACTORS NAMES'   1 honoured] POPE;
honoured (= -èd) F

Sc. 2 (1.2) A banquet scene may have been
suggested by Plato's *Symposium* (not
available in English, but known, for
instance, to Sidney and Chapman, to
whom Ficino's *Commentary* was familiar;
see note to ll. 115–19), in which the banquet is unexpectedly interrupted by the
arrival of Alcibiades, drunk. He is accompanied by a flute-girl, perhaps alteredly
reflected in the lady masquers. The theme
of *Symposium* is homosocial love, its cul-
minating argument 'how through the
slavish trance of sensual charm we may
pass with ever wakening and widening
powers to the best and freest activity of
our faculties, the contemplation of invisible, eternal verity' (W. R. M. Lamb, in
'*Lysis*', '*Symposium*', '*Gorgias*', ed. Lamb
(Cambridge, Mass., 1934), p. 77). *Timon*'s
masque invoking the five senses, in contrast, suggests enslavement to sensual
charm. Another possible classical influence is the absurdly extravagant banquet
of the parvenu Trimalchio in the *Satyri-*
con of Petronius.
The entire scene is attributed to Middleton.
The writing evidently follows that of Sc. 1
in that (a) there are anticipations of a feast
in the Shakespearian parts of Sc. 1 as well
as the Middletonian close, and, more particularly, (b) Sc. 2 continues the account
of '*Ventidius which Timon redeemed from*
prison' (2.0.4–5).

0.1 *Hautboys* wooden wind instruments,
also called shawms, similar to the oboe.
The arrestingly high-pitched sound was
used for ceremonial music in the theatre
and at events such as banquets.
A great banquet i.e. a full banquet, as distinct from a light dessert (as was more
usual on stage; the 'idle banquet' of
l. 151). A loaded table (and a small table
for Apemantus?—see l. 30) and chairs
need bringing on stage. The music provides the opportunity; the dialogue after
l. 228 provides an opportunity to clear
them. Banqueting was central to the
social life of the aristocracy, and particularly the court of James I, who enjoyed
banquets 'not only for food, but for the
elevation of spirits that come with wine
and good company' (David Harris Will-
son, *King James VI and I* (1956), p. 191).

0.2 *the Steward* A steward was an official
in charge of a household, including its
expenditure. 'Steward' happened to be
a spelling of King James's family name,
'Stuart' (see Introduction, pp. 49–50),
because the family was descended from
stewards of a previous line of kings. The
Steward is on stage by l. 154, but is not
specifically given an entry in F. If he
supervises the 'great banquet', his presence connects with 1.280 and prepares
ironically for his later role as failed regula-
tor of Timon's accounts.

It hath pleased the gods to remember
My father's age, and call him to long peace.
He is gone happy, and has left me rich.
Then, as in grateful virtue I am bound   5
To your free heart, I do return those talents,
Doubled with thanks and service, from whose help
I derived liberty.

TIMON   O, by no means,
Honest Ventidius. You mistake my love.
I gave it freely ever, and there's none   10
Can truly say he gives if he receives.
If our betters play at that game, we must not dare
To imitate them. Faults that are rich are fair.

0.3 **States** persons of rank, senators. It is not clear how (if at all) they might differ in appearance from the Athenian lords.

0.4–5 **which . . . prison** As Sc. 1 was evidently written by Shakespeare and Sc. 2 by Middleton, this phrase, which has no utility in the theatre, is probably Middleton's note to himself about the plot. The expression 'redeemed from prison' recurs in dialogue about Ventidius at 7.4, in another Middleton scene. *Redeemed* occurs in a description of stage action in *Civitatis Amor* l. 394, 'which were likewise redeemed', and in a stage direction in *No Wit* 8.0.2, referring to a person released from captivity.

0.5 *dropping after all* sulkily following everyone else. *Dropping* implies mood ('sulky'), physical manner ('drooping'), and position ('holding back, dragging his heels'). Compare *News from Gravesend* l. 173, 'for their pains clapped only on the shoulder and sent away dropping'.
discontentedly Found nowhere in Shakespeare, but in a Middleton stage direction (*Lady's* 4.2.0.1).

0.6 **like himself** i.e. lacking the ceremonial airs and graces of the other guests.

2 **remember** Stressed on the first and third syllables.

3 **long peace** death

4 **is gone** has died
happy (a) prosperous, (b) blessed, content

6 **free** generous (with wordplay on 'bound', l. 5, and 'liberty', l. 8)

6–7 **I . . . service** Has overtones of the parable of the talents, Matthew 25: 20, etc.: 'Master, thou delivered'st unto me five

talents; behold, I have gained with them other five talents'.

7 **Doubled . . . service** Either the thanks and service effectively double the amount returned (as debts could be repaid with 'service'), or they are added to a doubled sum of money.
service Both 'respect, homage' and an undertaking to put himself and his resources at Timon's disposal.

8 **derived** gained (as at 8.68). Compare *Trick* 4.1.44–5, 'From thousands of our wealthy, undone widows | One may derive some wit'. Stressed on the first syllable.

9 **mistake** With slight wordplay: you mis*take* what I *gave*.

10 **gave it freely ever** i.e. always gave the effects of my love without obligation. Perhaps with a suggestion of 'gave it freely and for ever'. As a comment on the speaker, *freely* is also 'with free will' and 'generously'. In context, the phrase might have a theological resonance of God's freely given grace (e.g. Romans 3: 24).

10–11 **and . . . receives** Echoes Luke 6: 34, 'if ye lend to them of whom ye hope to receive, what thank shall ye have?', and Acts 20: 35, 'It is a blessed thing to give, rather than to receive'. In the comedy *Timon*, a friend begs for money by urging that 'it is better to give than receive'—attributing the saying to Plato (l. 2579).

11 **receives** i.e. gets something in return

12–13 **If . . . them** 'Our betters' are perhaps the moneylending senators. The rejected excuse occurs (with dramatic irony) in *Revenger's* 2.1.147–8, 'And by what rule should we square out our lives, | But by

VENTIDIUS A noble spirit!

⌈*The Lords are standing with ceremony*⌉

TIMON

Nay, my lords, ceremony was but devised at first   15
To set a gloss on faint deeds, hollow welcomes,
Recanting goodness, sorry ere 'tis shown;
But where there is true friendship, there needs none.
Pray sit. More welcome are ye to my fortunes
Than my fortunes to me.   20

⌈*They sit*⌉

FIRST LORD

My lord, we always have confessed it.

APEMANTUS

Ho, ho, confessed it? Hanged it, have you not?

TIMON

O, Apemantus! You are welcome.

APEMANTUS   No,

You shall not make me welcome.

I come to have thee thrust me out of doors.   25

TIMON

Fie, thou'rt a churl. Ye've got a humour there
Does not become a man; 'tis much to blame.
They say, my lords, *Ira furor brevis est*,

14.1 *The . . . ceremony*] JOHNSON (*subs.*); *not in* F   20.1 *They sit*] ROWE; *not in* F   22 APEMAN-
TUS] F (*Aper.*). *Likewise throughout scene.* Hanged] F2; Handg'd F1   23 Apemantus] F
(*Apermantus*). *Likewise throughout rest of scene.*   26 thou'rt] F (th'art) Ye've] F (ye'haue)
27 to] F (too)

our betters' actions?', and elsewhere in
Middleton. Middleton elsewhere associates playing a game with taking risks with
one's soul; for instance, 'I have played
away my soul at one short game' (*Lady's*
2.2.2).
  dare | To imitate 'run the risk of imitat-
ing, defy heaven by imitating' (Hibbard)
13 Faults . . . fair From the proverb 'Rich
men have no faults' (Dent M579).
Holdsworth compares *Phoenix* 8.340,
'Wealth keeps their faults unknown'. The
passage has other echoes in the present
one.

15 ceremony formal displays of deference
16 faint spiritless, reluctant, indistinct

18 there needs none i.e. there is no need for
ceremony
21 confessed acknowledged. But Apemantus
alludes to the proverb 'Confess and be
hanged' (Dent C587), where the sense is
'admit guilt'.
26 churl bad-mannered peasant
humour disposition, 'warped attitude of
mind' (Hibbard)
27 much to blame F's 'much too blame' is a
mixed construction: both 'very blameworthy' and 'far too blameworthy'.
28 Ira . . . est Latin for 'anger is a short madness'; from Horace, *Epistles*, 1.2.62;
proverbial in English (Dent A246). Middleton refers to 'one angry minute' (*Fair
Quarrel* 1.1.156).

But yon man is ever angry.
Go, let him have a table by himself,   30
For he does neither affect company
Nor is he fit for't, indeed.

APEMANTUS

Let me stay at thine apperil, Timon.
I come to observe, I give thee warning on't.

TIMON I take no heed of thee; thou'rt an Athenian,   35
therefore welcome. I myself would have no power:
prithee, let my meat make thee silent.

APEMANTUS I scorn thy meat. 'Twould choke me, for I
should ne'er flatter thee. O you gods, what a number of
men eats Timon, and he sees 'em not! It grieves me to see   40
so many dip their meat in one man's blood; and all the
madness is, he cheers them up, too.
I wonder men dare trust themselves with men.

29 yon] F (yond)   ever] ROWE; verie F   35 thou'rt] F (Th'art)   41 their] F (there)   42 too]
F; to't HIBBARD (*conj.* Warburton)

29 **ever** The Latin quotation about the bre-
vity of anger is contradicted by Apemantus being *always* angry. 'Verie' angry, as
in F, does not supply the contrast.

31 **affect** Stressed on the first syllable (as
occasionally elsewhere in Middleton: see
Five Gallants 2.1.138).

33 **apperil** peril, risk. *OED*'s earliest instances
are *Michaelmas* 1.2.215, 'at her own
apperil', and the present passage
(Holdsworth).

34 **observe** watch and make critical
comments
on't of it

36 **would** wish to

37 **meat** Applies to food generally, not just
flesh, though the parallel between 'I
myself' and 'my meat' leads to Apemantus' comments on the theme of Timon
being eaten by his friends.

38–9 **I scorn . . . thee** Capell compares the
saying 'grudged meat chokes the person
that eats of it' (*Notes and Various Readings
to Shakespeare*, 3 vols. (1783)). Middleton's
Leantio in *Women Beware*, like Apemantus, acts as a sulking commentator on a
banquet, and 'eats his meat with grudg-
ing' (4.1.115).

39 **thee.** This is one point at which Apemantus might sit at 'a table by himself' (l. 30),
as in Klein's edition, but there may be theatrical advantage in keeping him on his

feet so that he can address the audience
more directly here and in his following
speech.

39–52 **O . . . throats** This and Apemantus'
following speeches are ignored by the
others. They are probably spoken without
them hearing; alternatively they might
listen to his harangues with resigned
toleration.

41 **dip . . . blood** Parodically reminiscent
of Christ's Last Supper: 'He that dippeth
his hand with me in the dish, he shall
betray me' (Matthew 26: 23). Middleton
quoted this line in *Two Gates* xvi.II, with
the marginal note 'Betraying whom I
vouchsafe to come to my table'. There
might be an underlying pun between the
host who entertains guests and the *host*
(sacrificial victim) consumed in the Lord's
Supper. In *Timon*, '*Eating* is the figure for
relationship': R. Berry, *Shakespearean
Structures* (1981), p. 102.

41 **their** Here and at ll. 45 and 96, F has the
unusual spelling 'there'. See Introduction, p. 130.

41–2 **all the madness** the maddest thing of
all

42 **cheers them up** encourages them. Compare *Widow* 2.1.207, 'I'll seek him out and
cheer him up against her'.
too Warburton's conjecture 'to't' is
plausible.

Methinks they should invite them without knives:
Good for their meat, and safer for their lives.   45
There's much example for't. The fellow that sits next
him, now parts bread with him, pledges the breath of
him in a divided draught, is the readiest man to kill him.
'T'as been proved. If I were a huge man, I should fear to
drink at meals,   50
Lest they should spy my windpipe's dangerous notes.
Great men should drink with harness on their throats.

TIMON
My lord, in heart; and let the health go round.

SECOND LORD
Let it flow this way, my good lord.

APEMANTUS 'Flow this way'? A brave fellow; he keeps his   55
tides well. Those healths will make thee and thy state look
ill, Timon.
Here's that which is too weak to be a sinner:
Honest water, which ne'er left man i'th' mire.
This and my food are equals; there's no odds.   60

---

45 their meat] F (there meate)

44–5 **knives . . . lives** The couplet strengthens the effect of the shift to prose at l. 46.

44 **without knives** Guests usually brought their own knives to eat with.

45 **Good for their meat** In that less meat would be consumed, and so the meat would be 'safer'.

46–52 **The . . . throats** Merges the 'example' of Judas Iscariot's betrayal of Christ after the Last Supper (see note to l. 41) with the proverbial treachery 'To smile in one's face and cut one's throat' (Dent F16).

47–8 **pledges the breath of him** drinks with a toast to his life

48 **divided** shared out; i.e. passed from guest to guest (earliest instance of *OED*'s sense 4). Also implies that the pledge might be duplicitous.

49 **huge** eminent, high-ranking

51 **dangerous** i.e. vulnerable
notes (a) musical sounds (quibbling on *windpipe* as a musical intrument), vibrations; (b) distinguishing marks. *Women Beware* 4.2.72 similarly puns on *strange notes* as 'unexpected sounds' and 're-markable and unusual events'.

52 **harness** armour

53–61 **My lord . . . gods** Another highly Middletonian passage (Holdsworth). In *Michaelmas* 3.1.217 Lethe bids for a drink by saying 'Let it flow this way' (Sykes).

53 **My . . . round** Either Timon responds to a guest pledging a toast to him, or he himself pledges.
in heart in good spirits, in fellowship (a toast). Compare the First Lord's unctuous use of 'our hearts' at l. 82.

55 **brave** fine, admirable (ironic)

55–6 **keeps his tides well** is sure not to miss his opportunity. *Tides* is both 'times, occasions' and the sea's *flow*. 'The tides of gold and silver | Ebb and flow in a minute' (*Widow* 3.1.113–14).

56–7 **Those . . . ill** Proverbially, 'To drink healths is to drink sickness' (Tilley H292).

59 **left man i'th' mire** Proverbial (Dent M989). For the contrast between clear water and mire, and the association of mire with *tides*, wine, and sin, compare *Solomon Paraphrased* 4.121–6: 'The swine delights to wallow in the mire, | The giddy drunkard in excess of wine . . . Mischief is mire, and may infect that spring | Which every flow and ebb of vice doth bring'.

60 **no odds** nothing to choose between them

Feasts are too proud to give thanks to the gods.
>   *Apemantus' grace*
> Immortal gods, I crave no pelf.
> I pray for no man but myself.
> Grant I may never prove so fond
> To trust man on his oath or bond,   65
> Or a harlot for her weeping,
> Or a dog that seems a-sleeping,
> Or a keeper with my freedom,
> Or my friends if I should need 'em.
> Amen. So fall to't.   70
> Rich men sin, and I eat root.
Much good dich thy good heart, Apemantus.
>   ⌈*He eats*⌉
TIMON Captain Alcibiades, your heart's in the field now.
ALCIBIADES My heart is ever at your service, my lord.
TIMON You had rather be at a breakfast of enemies than a   75
dinner of friends.

72.1 *He eats*] JOHNSON (*subs.*); *not in* F

---

61 **proud** (a) arrogant, (b) lavish
62 **pelf** wealth, possessions. Perhaps specifically 'plunder', giving wordplay on *pray* in l. 63 as *prey*. Compare *Ant and Nightingale* l. 270, 'True spirits are not covetous in pelf', rhymed with 'thyself', and *Passionate Pilgrim* 14.12.
64 **fond** foolish
65 **To** as to
66 **Or . . . weeping** From the proverb 'Trust not a woman when she weeps' (Dent W638).
68 **keeper** prison guard
70 **fall to't** start eating
71 **I eat root** An opportunity for comic business; in the 1999 RSC production Richard McCabe produced a large carrot from his pocket.
72 **Much . . . heart** A well-wishing invitation to eat and enjoy, or 'proface'. Variants on the expression are used by Middleton and Shakespeare with 'do't' or 'do it' for 'dich'. Henry Butts ended his *Diet's Dry Dinner* (1599) with a metrical grace followed by 'Proface. *Mytchgoodditchye*' (sig. P6ᵛ).

dich Accounted in *OED* as obsolete and rare, 'A corrupt or erroneous word, having apparently the sense *do it*'. But it is apparently dialectal rather than corrupt, so the line might be delivered with a mock rural accent. *OED*'s other example ('So mich God dich you with your sustenanceless sauce', 1630) is another ironic 'proface' (see previous note); so too is 'Much good dich ye, much good dich ye' in Thomas D'Urfey's *The Bath* (1701), 5.1.
'Dich' is also a standard form of *ditch*, meaning 'protect' (as with earthworks) or 'scour' (as of cleaning a ditch or sewer, suggesting that the earthy 'root' is a purgative; see note to 14.166). *Ditch* harks back to 'i'th' mire' (l. 59). Apemantus' pun allows Timon to play the good host by using one guest's words wittily to initiate a conversation with another guest: the *ditching* that improves Apemantus' *heart* suggests a field, and so Timon puts Alcibiades' *heart* in the *field* of battle.
74 **at your service** Quibbles on the military sense.
75–6 **of enemies . . . of friends** i.e. upon enemies . . . with friends. Alcibiades in his reply plays on the ambiguity.

ALCIBIADES So they were bleeding new, my lord, there's no
meat like 'em. I could wish my best friend at such a feast.
APEMANTUS Would all those flatterers were thine enemies
then, that then thou mightst kill 'em and bid me to 'em.   80
FIRST LORD (*to Timon*) Might we but have that happiness, my
lord, that you would once use our hearts whereby we
might express some part of our zeals, we should think
ourselves for ever perfect.
TIMON O, no doubt, my good friends, but the gods   85
themselves have provided that I shall have much help
from you. How had you been my friends else? Why have
you that charitable title from thousands, did not you
chiefly belong to my heart? I have told more of you to
myself than you can with modesty speak in your own   90
behalf; and thus far I confirm you. 'O you gods,' think I,
'what need we have any friends if we should ne'er have
need of 'em? They were the most needless creatures
living, should we ne'er have use for 'em, and would most

80 then thou] F; thou POPE 1728   88 thousands, did] ~? Did F

77 **So** provided that
  bleeding new bleeding freshly from
  killing. Also in *Nice Valour* 2.1.156. Later
  proverbial (Dent B448.1), but this is pre-
  dated only by one example in *Literature
  Online* (in Gascoigne).
80 **to** set to, eat
81–4 **Might . . . perfect** Conveys unctuous
  sentiment rather than expressing any
  meaning. Might suggest theoretical willingness to arrange a show expressing love
  for Timon, such as the masque that is
  about to be performed (compare l. 126);
  but if Timon has commissioned the
  masque, the offer is in real terms empty.
82 **use our hearts whereby** make use of our
  love in such a way that. *Use* perhaps
  alludes to usury, i.e. an offer of a loan on
  interest, hinting that affection comes at a
  cost. The phrase, and the diction of the
  speech as a whole and Timon's response,
  reflect and satirize the language of friendship as in transactions between merchants (Magnusson, pp. 134–5). The
  expression of friendship also takes on
  ironized religious resonances. The *heart*
  was regarded as the dwelling-place of
  Christ, *zeal* suggests fervent religious dedication. See next note.

84 **for ever perfect** eternally happy. *Perfect*
  alludes to spiritual perfection, as repeatedly in *Dissemblers*, sometimes in verbal
  contexts resembling this one: 'You have
  put my zeal into a way, my lord, | I shall
  not be at peace till I make perfect'
  (1.2.43–4); 'There's a work too | That for
  blood's sake I labour to make perfect, |
  And it comes on with joy' (1.2.76–8). See
  also *Game at Chess* 1.1.68–71.
85–7 **O . . . from you** By harsh dramatic
  irony anticipates Timon's later unmet
  need for help from his 'friends'.
87–8 **Why . . . thousands** why have you,
  from among thousands of people, that
  charitable title
88 **charitable** loving
89 **told more of you** (a) related more about
  you, (b) reckoned you up to be more
  valuable
91 **I confirm you** Given the religious association surrounding this (supposed) community or communion of friends, there may
  be an allusion to the church ceremony of
  confirmation. In this service, it is the
  responsibility of the persons being confirmed to ratify their faith.
92 **what** for what, why (Abbott 253)
93 **needless** unneeded

resemble sweet instruments hung up in cases, that keeps   95
their sounds to themselves.' Why, I have often wished
myself poorer, that I might come nearer to you. We are
born to do benefits; and what better or properer can we
call our own than the riches of our friends? O, what a
precious comfort 'tis to have so many like brothers   100
commanding one another's fortunes! O, joy's e'en made
away ere't can be born: mine eyes cannot hold out water,
methinks. To forget their faults, I drink to you.

He drinks, weeping

APEMANTUS Thou weep'st to make them drink, Timon.

---

96 their] F (there)   101 O, joy's∧ e'en] Oh∧ ioyes, e'ne F   103 methinks. To . . . faults,] ROWE;
∼: to . . . ∼. F. *Colon looks like a full stop in in some copies.*   103.1 *He drinks, weeping*] BEVINGTON
(*subs.*); *not in* F

95–6 **sweet . . . themselves** One of several
Middleton images of unused capacities
compared with musical instruments
hung on the walls in their cases; see *Roaring Girl* 4.1.87–9 and *Dissemblers* 1.3.22–5
(Holdsworth).

97 **nearer** closer in situation and social
standing, and so more closely tied

97–8 **We . . . benefits** Relates to the proverb
'We are not born for ourselves' (Dent
B141), but this passage supplies the earliest cited example. Gosson's *Ephemerides*
has the marginal note 'Man born to do
good' (sig. E2), in a passage debating the
pros and cons of liberality in courtiers; a
page earlier Gosson notes that 'neither
may that rightly be termed a benefit
which at any time is returned again'. He
later mentions Diogenes' diet of roots (see
note to 2.131) and Alcibiades (sig. E8ᵛ),
attacks flatterers, and uses the phrase 'a
pitched field' (sig. F2ᵛ; compare 2.225). It
seems that this passage is a localized
source. Another antecedent is Seneca,
'On Anger', II.13.1, in *Essays*, 'we are
born to do right'. See also *Fair Quarrel*
3.2.32–5: 'We are not born | For our-
selves only—self-love is a sin— | But in
our loving donatives to others | Man's
virtue best consists' (scene attributed to
Rowley).

98 **benefits** favours, good deeds
properer more fittingly. But the word is
also associated with *property*, that which
'we call our own'. 'What . . . properer . . .
than' occurs twice in Middleton with
properer as 'more fitting'. In Shakespeare,
properer means 'handsomer'.

99 **the riches of our friends** Ironically
poised between 'the riches that are our
friends' and 'the riches belonging to our
friends'.

99–102 **O, what . . . born** The thought,
imagery, and diction have numerous
Middleton parallels; for example 'Our joy
breaks at our eyes' (*Hengist* 15.57). 'Precious comfort' appears twice in his works.

99–101 **O, what . . . fortunes** Influenced by
Psalms 133: 1: 'Behold how good and
joyful a thing it is, brethren, to dwell
together in unity', and Deuteronomy 15:
8 (quoted in *Two Gates* 4.I), 'Thou shalt
open thy hand unto thy poor brother, and
shalt lend him sufficient for his need
which he hath'.

100 **like** Either the preposition (in the manner of) or adjective (like-minded).

101–2 **e'en made away ere't** killed before it
even. Tearful joy turns into (or at least
looks like) sorrow.

102 **mine . . . water** In modern idiom, 'I
can't keep tears out of my eyes'.

103 **To . . . you** Compares verbally with *Measure* 1.2.37–8 (in a passage attributed to
Middleton), 'learn to begin thy health,
but whilst I live forget to drink after thee'.
Timon proposes drinking as a diversion
from the *faults* of weeping, and plays on
the idea of excessive drink causing loss of
memory.

104 **Thou . . . Timon** Apemantus com-
presses Timon's words to mock their
absurdity, producing an epigram on
sacrifice.
to in order to

SECOND LORD (*to Timon*)

  Joy had the like conception in our eyes,   105

  And at that instant like a babe sprung up.

APEMANTUS

  Ho, ho, I laugh to think that babe a bastard.

THIRD LORD (*to Timon*)

  I promise you, my lord, you moved me much.

APEMANTUS Much!

    Sound tucket within

TIMON What means that trump?   110

    Enter Servant

  How now?

SERVANT Please you, my lord, there are certain ladies most
desirous of admittance.

TIMON Ladies? What are their wills?

SERVANT There comes with them a forerunner, my lord,   115
which bears that office to signify their pleasures.

TIMON I pray let them be admitted.

    Enter one as Cupid

109.1, 117.1, 126.1–2 *Sound tucket within, Enter one as Cupid, Enter . . . playing*] CAPELL (*subs.*). F
supplies two directions: (a) at l. 109.1: '*Sound Tucket. Enter the Maskers of Amazons, with Lutes
in their hands, dauncing and playing.*'; *(b) at l.* 117.1: '*Enter Cupid with the Maske of Ladies.*'
110.1 *Enter Servant*] DYCE 1857; *after* 'How now?', *l.* 111, *in* F   117.1 *one as*] OXFORD SHAKE-
SPEARE; *not in* F

105–6 **Joy . . . up** The diction reworks Luke
1: 44, 'The babe sprang in my belly for joy'.
Sprung up here means both 'broke out'
(comparing a tear to a spring of water)
and 'grew, shot up' (so as to be fully 'like a
babe' immediately after conception). Perhaps alternatively alludes to the proverb
'To look babies in another's eyes' (Dent
B8), meaning to see small images of oneself in them; i.e. the joy in our eyes
is a reflection of the joy in yours. The
conceited imagery resembles that in the
poetry of John Donne, here as a token of
insincerity.

107 **that babe a bastard** i.e. the Lord's
asserted joy is not genuine

108 **promise** assure

109.1, 117.1 *Sound tucket, Enter one as
Cupid* Both F's directions (see collation)
begin with information appropriate to the
moment: '*Sound Tucket*.', '*Enter Cupid*'.
They then add an early anticipation of the
masque (see Illustration 10). This information goes into the editorial direction

at ll. 126.1–2. Both stage directions are
strongly Middletonian (Holdsworth).

109.1 **tucket** flourish of trumpets. This marks
the beginning of the masque, which is
presented to entertain the guests and
compliment the host (but Timon appears
to have arranged it himself: see note to l.
146).

110 **trump** trumpet sound

112 **Please** if it please

113 **desirous of admittance** Mention of
women triggers an undercurrent of possible sexual innuendo (as, with *admittance*, in *Lady's* 4.1.121). *Wills* (l. 114) and
pleasures (l. 116) are in the same vein.

115 **forerunner** herald. As in 'angels are the
footmen and forerunners, bringing news
that the king is upon coming' (*Two Gates*,
Preface 175–6).

116 **that office** (of *forerunner*)
signify their pleasures announce what
they desire to do

117.1 **one as Cupid** A role, like the Amazons,
for a boy actor. Traditionally pictured as

CUPID Hail to thee, worthy Timon, and to all that of his
  bounties taste! The five best senses acknowledge thee
  their patron, and come freely to gratulate thy plenteous   120
  bosom.
  There taste, touch, all, pleased from thy table rise.
  They only now come but to feast thine eyes.

---

122 There] F; Th'ear THEOBALD (*conj.* Warburton); There th'ear *conj.* This edition (Buckley)
all] F; smell THEOBALD (*conj.* Warburton); smell, all STEEVENS–REED

blind, naked, winged, and with bow and
arrow. In Jonson's masque *Love Freed
from Ignorance and Folly* (1611) the effect
of nakedness was achieved with flesh-
coloured satin. Cupid stood for the
destructive powers of love as well as sensual pleasure (R. Fulton, 'Timon, Cupid,
and the Amazons', *Shakespeare Studies*, 9
(1976), 283–99). There are Cupids in
masques in *Dissemblers*, *Nice Valour*, and
Women Beware.

118–21 **Hail . . . bosom** Editors sometimes
set this passage as verse (see Appendix A).
It has verse rhythms, but no arrangement
produces regular metre in all lines without verbal emendation (see note to 'all', l.
122). Intermixing of prose and rhymed
verse in a single speech (see ll. 122–3) is
un-Shakespearian but common enough
in Middleton.

119–23 **The . . . eyes** On the staging, see pp.
12–13. The lines evoke a banquet of the
senses, which was related to Plato's
Symposium (see headnote to scene). A
more immediate model is Chapman's phi-
losophized erotic narrative poem 'Ovid's
Banquet of Sense' (1595), in which 'Ovid
sophistically defends the banquet of the
senses (which is implicitly opposed to the
Platonic, or Ficinian, scheme) for its own
sake' (Buxton, *Elizabethan Taste*, p. 302).

119 **best senses** Ficino stipulated a hierarchy
from spiritual to earthly of sight, hearing,
smell, taste, touch, admitting only sight
and hearing as pertaining to divine love
(Commentary on Plato's 'Symposium',
ed. S. R. Jayne (1994), p. 130). Unhierar-
chical 'best senses' may ironically suggest
spiritual attributes; in *Two Gates* xvii.I
Middleton refers to 'your best eye, your
soul'.

120 **gratulate** (a) gratify, (b) greet, (c) con-
gratulate. The verb was often used in

ceremonial contexts, as here.

120 **plenteous** bountiful. The phrase 'plenteous bosom' recurs at 14.187 (Shakespeare), referring to the earth; see also
'plenteous wounds', 10.64, and note. See
Introduction, pp. 38–9. and 149–50

122 **There** 'Plenteous bosom' refers to
Timon's generosity in producing the
banquet on his table. 'There' is therefore
acceptable in fusing the 'bosom' as the
source and the 'table' on which the effects
are displayed: the banqueting table is an
emblem of the plenteous bosom. 'There'
might, however, be a minor error for
'Th'ear'. 'Ere' was an acceptable spelling
of *ear* until the 16th century at least, and
spaces and apostrophes were not always
indicated after 'th' for *the*, making 'There'
a possible way of writing 'Th'ear'.

all As Warburton noted in support of
emending to 'Th'ear, taste, touch, smell', a
passage evidently adapted from these lines
in Philip Massinger's *Duke of Milan* (1621)
1.3.3–5 provides both 'Th'ear' and 'smell':
'All that may be had | To please the eye, the
ear, taste, touch, or smell | Are carefully
provided'. *Duke of Milan*, entered in the
Stationers' Register on 20 January 1623,
was written before the publication of F;
but, as regular dramatist for the King's
Men, Massinger may have had opportunity to read *Timon* in manuscript. The influence seems likely, but the wording is
not exact enough to bear reliable witness to
the manuscript reading. Double emendation seems implausible, not least as 'smell'
would not easily be corrupted to 'all'.
Steevens–Reed introduced the alternative
'smell, all'. This perhaps assumes an easier
error, but to the double error it adds a further difficulty with the metre, which then
needs emending by taking each 'Th'ear' to
the end of the previous line.

123 **only now come but** come now solely

TIMON

They're welcome all. Let 'em have kind admittance.
Music make their welcome!   125

LUCIUS

You see, my lord, how ample you're beloved.

*Enter the masque of Ladies as Amazons, with lutes in
their hands, dancing and playing*

APEMANTUS Hoyday!

What a sweep of vanity comes this way!
They dance? They are madwomen.
Like madness is the glory of this life   130

---

124 welcome] F2; wecome F1   126 LUCIUS] F (*Luc.*); *I. L.* CAPELL   you're] F (y'are)

124–6 **They're . . . beloved** The diction and
staging compare with *Game at Chess*
5.1.20–25, where music is played as part
of a ceremonious entertainment, the
White Knight acknowledges his welcome
by saying 'How amply you endear us',
and the Black Knight says 'Hark, to
enlarge your welcome, from all parts | Is
heard sweet sounding airs'.

126 LUCIUS F's speech-prefix '*Luc.*' could
apply to Lucius or Lucullus. As it is anomalous in this scene, it is usually emended
to the First Lord. The anticipation of a
specific role is worth preserving, though
Lucius (or Lucullus) here is likely to be
one of the three lords who speak other
lines in this scene.

ample you're F has 'ample y'are'. 'Y'are'
as a spelling of *you're* is also at 1.1,
14.610, and 14.611. The use of adjectival
forms as adverbs was common (Abbott 1;
Blake 5.1.3.1). Here it prevents 'you' from
eliding in both directions, as in (to modify
F's spellings) 'amplie y'are'.

126.1–2 *Enter . . . playing* For the basis
of this direction in F, see Illustration 9,
commentary to ll. 107.1–113.1, and following notes.

126.1 *masque of Ladies* There is a similar
masque of '*six women Masquers*' led by a
Cupid in *Nice Valour*, after 2.1.147.

Amazons Women in *Timon* are confined
to the roles of Amazons and the whores
of Sc. 14 (see Introduction, pp. 40–5
and note to l. 152). For the costume, see
p. 12.

126.1–2 *with . . . playing* The wording
seems to leave little scope for some Amazons to dance whilst others play. In con-

trast, the dancing with the lords is to the
music only of hautboys. The ladies presumably put their lutes down before the
dancing of '*men with women*'.

126.2 *playing* Bradbrook (pp. 32–3) identifies the music as a piece headed 'The
Amazonians' Masque' in British Library
MS Add. 10444, written for lutes and
hautboys, but her suggestion has not
been generally endorsed.

127–41 **Hoyday . . . sun** Apemantus offers
this satirical commentary during the
dance. This Middletonian technique is
seen again in the Ward's derogatory
comments on Isabella's song while
she is singing in *Women Beware* 3.2.
145–57.

127 **Hoyday** A Middletonian exclamation of
astonishment.

128–30 **What . . . life** Soellner compares
Agrippa (see Introduction, p. 22 n.), who
describes dancing as 'the fondest thing of
all other, and little differing from madness, which, except it were tempered with
the sound of instruments, and, as it is
said, if vanity did not commend vanity,
there should be no sight more ridiculous,
no more out of order, than dancing' (fol.
30).

128 **sweep** stately dancing motion; swish of
dresses. The suggestion of a dance 'with
a magnificent or impressive air' (*OED*,
sweep, sb. 2) sits oddly alongside the call
for the Amazons to dance while playing
lutes, which would be more appropriate
to a light, frivolous, or even lascivious
dancing.

130 **Like madness** just such a madness

As this pomp shows to a little oil and root.
We make ourselves fools to disport ourselves,
And spend our flatteries to drink those men
Upon whose age we void it up again
With poisonous spite and envy.   135
Who lives that's not depravèd or depraves?
Who dies that bears not one spurn to their graves
Of their friends' gift?
I should fear those that dance before me now
Would one day stamp upon me. 'T'as been done.   140
Men shut their doors against a setting sun.

> *The Lords rise from table, with much adoring of Timon;*
> *and, to show their loves, each single out an Amazon,*
> *and all dance, men with women, a lofty strain or two to*
> *the hautboys; and cease*

131 **As . . . to** as can be seen by comparing this pomp with

   a little oil and root i.e. a subsistence vegetarian diet. Apemantus might gesture to a root he has been eating, and *this pomp* can refer to the banquet as well as the masque. Diogenes lived on a diet of roots, as noted by Gosson in *Ephemerides*, sig. E6ᵛ (see note to ll. 97–8). Oil, used as a salad dressing, was also regarded as an opposite or antidote to poison, as in *Changeling* 1.1.121, 'One oil, the enemy of poison'; compare l. 135.

132 **to disport** in the process of amusing

133–5 **And . . . envy** See note to 1.276–86. Holdsworth adduces various other Middleton parallels.

133 **spend** (a) utter, (b) part freely with, (c) consume, exhaust

   drink (a) drink the health of, (b) consume

134 **Upon whose age** upon whom when they are old

   void vomit

135 **With . . . envy** Suggests that the vomit contains bile, a bodily excess of which was thought to cause a choleric temperament.

   envy hatred

136 **depravèd** Both 'vilified, slandered' and 'perverted'.

137 **spurn** painful insult, rejection

138 **gift** giving

139–40 **I . . . upon me** In *Revenger's*, the revengers stamp on the Duke after stab-

bing him, as likewise do the murderers of Coriolanus in Shakespeare's play.

141 **Men . . . sun** From the proverb, 'Men more worship the rising than the setting sun' (Dent S979). The saying here ironizes the following stage action where the lords '*rise*' and move away from the table to dance: the gesture of adoration visually dramatizes the setting of Timon by elevating the lords relative to him. Apemantus' comment therefore anticipates the participation of men, but responds to the spectacle of women.

   against Suggests (a) hostile *exclusion*, (b) *anticipation* of the temperature falling outside.

141.1–3 **The . . . dance** This corresponds to the moment, late in the Jonsonian court masque, when the masquers would join with members of the audience to transform the theatrical spectacle into a dance.

141.1 **adoring of** reverential gesture towards

141.2 **to show their loves** i.e. to express their devotion to Timon (or to identify which ladies are their actual or intended mistresses?)

141.3 **strain** tune

   or two This permissive phrase calls for the dancing to be extended if possible.

141.4 **hautboys** Suitable for a more formal, ceremonial dancing than the music provided by the Amazons' lutes. See note to l. 0.1.

TIMON

You have done our pleasures much grace, fair ladies,
Set a fair fashion on our entertainment,
Which was not half so beautiful and kind.
You have added worth unto't and lustre,   145
And entertained me with mine own device.
I am to thank you for't.

FIRST LADY

My lord, you take us even at the best.

APEMANTUS Faith; for the worst is filthy, and would not
hold taking, I doubt me.   150

TIMON

Ladies, there is an idle banquet attends you,
Please you to dispose yourselves.

---

148 LADY] STEEVENS 1778 (*conj.* Johnson); *Lord* F   151 attends] F; 'tends OXFORD SHAKESPEARE

142 **pleasures** Both 'pleasurable sensations' (with reference particularly to the masquers' presentation of the five senses) and the banquet itself as an indulgence of the senses (compare following line).

143 **Set . . . on** 'lent glamour to' (Oliver). *Set* and *fashion* have connotations of (a) workmanship (as in *setting* a jewel in a finely *fashion*ed ornament), (b) stylish dress and presentation.

144 **was not** would not otherwise have been
kind agreeable; courteous; gracious; loving. Also 'natural, as it ought to be': the women restore the gender balance to an otherwise unnaturally male world.

146 **And . . . device** An ambiguous phrase. Most probably suggests that Timon commissioned the entertainment and proposed at least its theme, as *device* most immediately suggests 'theatrical contrivance'. But 'idea', 'emblem', and 'impresa' are other possible meanings. If they apply, the ladies and/or lords might have based the masque on an image or idea particularly associated with Timon, and Timon might be recognizing that the masque was an effective emblematic representation of him. Klein glosses 'faculty of devising', whilst denying that Timon would be capable of the hypocrisy of designing the masque. For the phrasing, compare *Michaelmas* 4.3.45, 'I entertain both thee and thy device' (Holdsworth). For the commissioning and planning of masques, see Marston, *The Malcontent*, 5.3.47–67, where the duke

Mendoza suggests a mythological framework for the entertainment he commissions but leaves the decision to the performers, and Middleton, *No Wit*, Sc. 7, where the scholar Beveril is given responsibility for designing the entertainment.

147 **am to** must (Blake 7.1.3.2(a)); ought to, want to, and will

148 LADY F's error '*Lord*' probably arose because the manuscript had only the abbreviation 'L'. Compare note to 4.70.
take . . . best value us as highly as is possible

149 **Faith** indeed, just so
the worst is i.e. by the worst reckoning the ladies are (or 'the worst part of them is')
filthy (a) sexually disgusting; infected with venereal disease; (b) disgustingly mercenary (compare the common expression 'filthy lucre' or, in Middleton, 'fat and filthy gain' (*Tennis* l. 805)).

150 **taking** (a) taking in sexual intercourse (as by innuendo in *Mad World* 3.2.112–13); (b) financial valuation
doubt me very much suspect

151 **idle banquet** slight meal of a dessert (usually of sweetmeats, fruit, and wine); in contrast with the 'great banquet' on stage. Such a dessert banquet might be offered to guests after an entertainment, but here it is offered only to the entertainers, getting the women immediately off stage.

152 **Please . . . you selves** if you wouldn't mind taking your places (or, less patronizingly, 'please do . . .')

ALL LADIES Most thankfully, my lord.

Exeunt ⌐Cupid and⌐ Ladies

TIMON Flavius.

STEWARD My lord.   155

TIMON The little casket bring me hither.

STEWARD Yes, my lord. (*Aside*) More jewels yet?

There is no crossing him in's humour,

Else I should tell him well, i' faith I should.

When all's spent, he'd be crossed then, an he could.   160

'Tis pity bounty had not eyes behind,

That man might ne'er be wretched for his mind.   *Exit*

FIRST LORD Where be our men?

SERVANT Here, my lord, in readiness.

SECOND LORD Our horses.   ⌐*Exit one or more Servants*⌐   165

Enter Flavius the Steward with the casket

TIMON O my friends,

I have one word to say to you. Look you, my good lord,

I must entreat you honour me so much

153.1 ⌐*Cupid and*⌐ *Ladies*] CAPELL; *not in* F 155 STEWARD] *Fla<vius>*. F. *Similarly in the rest of the episode.* 165 *Exit one or more Servants*] *Exit Servant* OXFORD SHAKESPEARE; *not in* F
165.1 *Enter . . . casket*] CAMBRIDGE (*subs.*); *Enter Flauius* F (*after l.* 175)

---

154 **Flavius** The personal name is an abandoned first thought. It appears in the text here, and also as 'Fla.' in the Steward's five speech-prefixes in this scene, and in the stage direction equivalent to l. 166 after l. 175. It subsequently vanishes. See note to Varro etc., at 3.1.

158 **crossing** thwarting, challenging
    humour perverse disposition, mood

159 **well** i.e. plainly, bluntly

160 **crossed** crossed off the list of debtors (quibbling on the sense in l. 158). Or 'prevented from being as he is' (with the sense basically as at l. 158).
    an if only

161 **bounty . . . behind** 'To have an eye behind' was proverbial for wariness (Dent E236). In *Triumphs of Truth* ll. 506–9 the eye of judgement is what distinguishes *bounty* from prodigality: 'bounty must be led by judgement; and hence is artfully derived the only difference between prodigality and bounty: the one deals her gifts with open eyes, the other blindfold'. A Renaissance woodcut of Prodigality shows a blindfolded figure pouring liquid

from an upturned cornucopia (see Clifford Davidson, '*Timon of Athens*: The Iconography of False Friendship', *Huntington Library Quarterly*, 43 (1980), 181–200, p. 183). Compare note on Plutus at 1.278.

162 **for his mind** as a result of his wilfulness (or of his disposition to be generous)

163 **Where be our men?** The preparations to depart with attendants are triggered by the Steward's exit to fetch gifts. The gift-giving seems to be a well-recognized ritual, and the guests are over-eager for it. For ll. 163–5, compare *Five Gallants* 2.4.1–3: 'PRIMERO Where be your liveries? | FIRST COURTESAN They attend without. | PRIMERO Go, call the coach.'

165.1 **Enter . . . casket** F's 'Enter Flavius.' after l. 175 comes too late for him to deliver the casket holding the jewels that Timon has in the meantime distributed. A second exit and re-entry is possible, but there is dramatic purpose in having the Steward silently and reluctantly witness the giving of jewels, perhaps holding the casket himself.

As to advance this jewel. Accept it and wear it,
Kind my lord.   170

FIRST LORD

I am so far already in your gifts.

ALL LORDS So are we all.

> *Timon gives them jewels.*
> *Enter a Servant*

SERVANT My lord, there are certain nobles of the senate
newly alighted and come to visit you.

TIMON They are fairly welcome.   ⌈*Exit Servant*⌉   175

STEWARD I beseech your honour, vouchsafe me a word; it
does concern you near.

TIMON Near? Why then, another time I'll hear thee. I
prithee, let's be provided to show them entertainment.

STEWARD I scarce know how.   180

> *Enter another Servant*

SECOND SERVANT

May it please your honour, Lord Lucius
Out of his free love hath presented to you
Four milk-white horses trapped in silver.

TIMON

I shall accept them fairly. Let the presents
Be worthily entertained.   ⌈*Exit Servant*⌉

> *Enter a Third Servant*

How now, what news?   185

THIRD SERVANT Please you, my lord, that honourable
gentleman Lord Lucullus entreats your company

---

169 Accept it] F1; Accept F2   172.1 *Timon gives them jewels*] OXFORD SHAKESPEARE; *not in* F; *He offers a jewel* BEVINGTON (*after l.* 170)   175, 185, 191 *Exit Servant*] HINMAN; *not in* F   181 SECOND] ROWE; *not in* F

169 **advance** (a) wear prominently; and so (b) increase the value of
170 **Kind my** my kind. For the inversion, see Abbott 13.
171 **in your gifts** obliged to you for gifts received
 gifts. Perhaps the other lords interrupt.
173–4 **My . . . you** Seems to suggest that Timon's entertainments follow directly one from another.
174 **alighted** i.e. arrived
175 **fairly** kindly
176–8 **I . . . thee** Perhaps echoes Caesar's rejection of the Soothsayer's warnings: 'What touches us ourself shall be last served' (*Julius Caesar* 3.1.8).
177 **near** closely
180 **I scarce know how** Perhaps spoken aside.
182 **free** (a) bountiful, (b) unconstrained
183 **trapped in silver** with silver trappings
184 **fairly** in style; in full recognition of their worth
185 **worthily entertained** received with the honour they deserve
186–9 **Please . . . greyhounds** Hunting was a favourite pastime of King James, to the extent that he was accused of neglecting affairs of state.

tomorrow to hunt with him, and has sent your honour
two brace of greyhounds.

TIMON

    I'll hunt with him, and let them be received   190
    Not without fair reward.   ⌈*Exit Servant*⌉

STEWARD (*aside*)   What will this come to?

    He commands us to provide, and give great gifts,
    And all out of an empty coffer;
    Nor will he know his purse, or yield me this:
    To show him what a beggar his heart is,   195
    Being of no power to make his wishes good.
    His promises fly so beyond his state
    That what he speaks is all in debt, he owes
    For every word. He is so kind that he now
    Pays interest for't. His land's put to their books.   200
    Well, would I were gently put out of office
    Before I were forced out.
    Happier is he that has no friend to feed
    Than such that do e'en enemies exceed.
    I bleed inwardly for my lord.   *Exit*

TIMON (*to the Lords*)   You do yourselves   205

    Much wrong, you bate too much of your own merits.
    (*To Second Lord*) Here, my lord, a trifle of our love.

SECOND LORD

    With more than common thanks I will receive it.

THIRD LORD O, he's the very soul of bounty!

TIMON (*to First Lord*) And now I remember, my lord, you   210
    gave good words the other day of a bay courser I rode on.
    'Tis yours, because you liked it.

---

188 has] F (ha's)

191 **fair** generous (presumably not merely 'equitable')

194 **know his purse** take account of his finances
    yield grant

196 **make his wishes good** put his wishes into effect

197 **His . . . state** The image is of a bird flying beyond the limits of its owner's estate.

200 **for't** i.e. on his kindness
    put to their books entered in their books,

mortgaged to them. Used in the same sense in *Ant and Nightingale* ll. 352–6.

204 **such** i.e. such friends

206 **bate . . . of** diminish, lessen in value

207 **trifle** small token

211 **gave good words** spoke well. The idiom invokes gift-giving: the Lord *gave* good words about the horse, in return for which Timon gives it to him.
    bay courser reddish-brown racehorse or stallion. As in *Phoenix* 8.58; not in Shakespeare.

FIRST LORD

O I beseech you pardon me, my lord, in that.

TIMON

You may take my word, my lord, I know no man   215
Can justly praise but what he does affect.
I weigh my friend's affection with mine own,
I'll tell you true. I'll call to you.

ALL LORDS   O, none so welcome.

TIMON

I take all and your several visitations
So kind to heart, 'tis not enough to give.   220
Methinks I could deal kingdoms to my friends,
And ne'er be weary. Alcibiades,
Thou art a soldier, therefore seldom rich.
⌈*Giving a present*⌉ It comes in charity to thee, for all thy
    living
Is 'mongst the dead, and all the lands thou hast
Lie in a pitched field.   225

ALCIBIADES   Ay, defiled land, my lord.

FIRST LORD We are so virtuously bound—

---

216 friend's] F (Friends). Alternatively *friends'*.   217 I'll tell] F; I tell HANMER   223 *Giving a present*] OXFORD SHAKESPEARE; *not in* F

213 **O . . . that** Probably asks to be excused of accepting the gift. Or could be asking pardon for accidentally requesting it.
215 **but . . . affect** anything except that which he likes
216 **affection** desires, liking
   with i.e. as having just as much importance as
217 **I'll tell** Possibly an error influenced by the other 'I'll' in the line, as Middleton elsewhere has 'I tell you true'.
   call to call on, visit
218 **all . . . visitations** your visits collectively and individually
219 **kind** kindlily. *OED*'s earliest example of the adverbial use (*a.* 10).
   'tis not Probably 'there is not', i.e. 'I don't have'.
220–1 **Methinks . . . weary** Compare *Hengist* 2.4.156–7: 'methinks I could do things past man | I am so renewed in vigour'. 'Methinks I could' is not in Shakespeare; there are four instances in Middleton.
223–5 **It . . . lord** Thick in Middletonian idiom, including the pun on *living* as

'means for living' and 'life' (*No Wit* 3.224–6). In *Phoenix* 8.246–7, 'all our chief living, my lord, is by fools and knaves'. 'A pitched field' occurs in *Black Book* l. 388 (Holdsworth).
225 **pitched field** battlefield with armies drawn up in formation to fight (as in *Black Book* ll. 466–7). See following note.
   defiled land A very self-deprecatory joke, alluding to the dung-heaps where human excrement was *pitched*. Quibbles by taking *pitched* as 'covered with pitch', alluding to Ecclesiasticus 13: 1, 'He that toucheth pitch shall be defiled with it' (quoted at *Black Book* ll. 3–4, 'all those that . . . can touch pitch and yet never defile themselves'). The pun is compounded by *file* in the sense of soldiers in rows.
226 **virtuously bound** bound by your virtue; powerfully bound. *OED* supports the latter, citing this as the only example of the sense, but both are relevant. Compare 'I bind you by the virtue of this chain' (*Mad World* 4.3.24–50).

205

TIMON And so am I to you.

SECOND LORD So infinitely endeared—

TIMON All to you. Lights, more lights!   230

FIRST LORD

    The best of happiness, honour, and fortunes

    Keep with you, Lord Timon.

TIMON Ready for his friends.

          Exeunt Lords and all but Timon and Apemantus

APEMANTUS What a coil's here,

    Serving of becks and jutting-out of bums!   235

    I doubt whether their legs be worth the sums

    That are given for 'em. Friendship's full of dregs.

    Methinks false hearts should never have sound legs.

    Thus honest fools lay out their wealth on curtseys.

TIMON

    Now, Apemantus, if thou wert not sullen   240

    I would be good to thee.

APEMANTUS No, I'll nothing; for if I should be bribed too,

    there would be none left to rail upon thee, and then thou

    wouldst sin the faster. Thou giv'st so long, Timon, I fear

232.1 *and all but Timon and Apemantus*] CAPELL (*subs.*); *not in* F

228 **So infinitely endeared** Compare 6.29, *so much endeared*. Also 'I am *so endeared* to thee' (*Chaste Maid* 5.4.75) and 'how *amply* you *endear* us' (*Game at Chess* 5.1.00).

    endeared bound by affection or 'by obligation of gratitude' (*OED*, citing this line as the earliest example). A passage in *Honourable Entertainments* suggests (ironized) religious connotations: 'That . . . you may be green in *virtues*, and grow strong | In works of grace, which souls to heaven *endears*' (8.193). With a suggestion also of 'enhanced in value', i.e. made rich.

229 **All to you** all the obligation is mine to you

    Lights, more lights Needed to illuminate the lords' way out of Timon's house. If brought on stage they would add an element of spectacle to the lords' exit and would emphasize their social status. Such staging would be conventionalized, as the play was probably written for performance in daylight at the open-air Globe Theatre.

232 **Ready for his friends** i.e. if Timon's fortunes stay with him, they will be at the service of his friends

233 **coil** commotion

234 **Serving** delivering

    becks nods and bows

    bums Nowhere plural in Shakespeare, but three instances in Middleton.

235 **legs** bendings of the knee, bows. Similarly at l. 237. The contrast with 'bums' and 'hearts' establishes a pun on the limbs.

237 **false . . . legs** The punning implication is that sexually unfaithful people get the brittle and wasted bones caused by syphilis. Compare the hollow bones caused by 'impiety' in *Measure* 1.2.53–5 (a passage attributed to Middleton).

238 **on** on the basis of; in return for; to purchase

    curtseys low bows; shows of courtesy

240 **good** i.e. generous

241 **I'll** I'll have

242 **rail upon** abuse, insult, harangue

243 **sin the faster** Compare *Revenger's* 4.3.18: 'Or else they'll sin faster than we'll repent'.

me thou wilt give away thyself in paper shortly. What
needs these feasts, pomps, and vainglories?   245

TIMON Nay, an you begin to rail on society once, I am
sworn not to give regard to you. Farewell, and come with
better music.   *Exit*

APEMANTUS So. Thou wilt not hear me now, thou shalt not
then. I'll lock thy heaven from thee.   250
O, that men's ears should be
To counsel deaf, but not to flattery!   *Exit*

Sc. 3   *Enter a Senator with bonds*

SENATOR

And late five thousand. To Varro and to Isidore
He owes nine thousand, besides my former sum,

3.0.1 with bonds] CAPELL (*subs.*); *not in* F

244 **thyself** i.e. (a) your entire possessions,
or (b) your corporeal self (as your last
possession)
241 **paper** i.e. bonds
244–5 **What needs** what need is there for
246 **an . . . once** if ever . . .
  on against
  society social gatherings, company; the
  social elite
247–8 **come with better music** Based on
proverbs 'To change one's note' (Dent
N248) and 'To sing another song' (S637).
'Better music' is used figuratively in *Mad
World* 2.4.64. *Music* is often metaphorical
for conduct or a state of affairs in Middleton (Holdsworth).
247 **come** i.e. come next time
249 **So. Thou** Follows F's 'So: Thou'. Alternatively *So thou*, 'If you . . .'.
249–50 **thou shalt not then** i.e. I won't give
you another opportunity
250 **heaven** i.e. salvation, happiness (as
might be obtained through heeding
advice)
Sc. 3 **(2.1)** The plot proper begins here, with
the collapse of Timon's creditworthiness,
and the location evidently moves from
Timon's house to that of a creditor.
In contrast with later scenes showing
Timon's creditors, this one is evidently by
Shakespeare. One might link the scene's
relatively sympathetic portrayal of the
Senator with Shakespeare's own activ-
ities as a moneylender.
0.1 **Enter a Senator** The Senator might walk
on to the main stage with papers in his

hands. But, as Capell first noted, the scene
is likely to open as 'a discovery of the
Senator, sitting at a table, with papers
about him', staged by drawing back a curtain in front of the 'discovery' space at the
rear of the stage. He might rise and come
forward, perhaps addressing the audience
directly. *Five Gallants* opens with the Presenter evidently drawing back a curtain
to discover the pawnbroker Frip reading
his accounts. If Apemantus draws back
the curtain as he leaves, he too acts as a
'presenter', showing the audience the
truth that Timon cannot see.
1 **late** recently
  five thousand At 8.31 the unit is 'crowns',
  which with hindsight might be understood here.
  Varro . . . Isidore The creditors are
  named, presumably with irony, after
  ancient illustrious figures (compare Lac-
  tantio in *Dissemblers*, whose name is
  based on the early Christian father Lac-
  tantius). *Varro* alludes to Marcus Teren-
  tius Varro (116–*c*.21 BC), a Roman writer
  who helped to codify the Seven Liberal
  Arts, named in Plutarch's 'Life of Marcus
  Antonius' and known into medieval times
  as an authority on the history of the
  Roman people. Shakespeare represents
  Varro in *Julius Caesar*. *Isidore* is named
  after Isidorus Hispalensis, Spanish saint,
  Church Father, and philosopher (AD
  c.560–636), an established authority on
  the Christian faith.

Which makes it five-and-twenty. Still in motion
Of raging waste! It cannot hold, it will not.
If I want gold, steal but a beggar's dog   5
And give it Timon, why, the dog coins gold.
If I would sell my horse and buy twenty more
Better than he, why, give my horse to Timon—
Ask nothing, give it him—it foals me straight
And able horses. No porter at his gate,   10
But rather one that smiles and still invites
All that pass by. It cannot hold. No reason
Can sound his state in safety. Caphis ho!
Caphis, I say!
    Enter Caphis
CAPHIS   Here, sir. What is your pleasure?
SENATOR
Get on your cloak and haste you to Lord Timon.   15
Importune him for my moneys. Be not ceased
With slight denial, nor then silenced when
'Commend me to your master', and the cap
Plays in the right hand, thus; but tell him

---

7 more] F (moe)

3–4 **Still . . . waste** A metaphor of violent natural destruction—'always in a rush of furious devastation'—or of a stormy sea (compare ll. 12–13). More literally, *raging* is 'rash, riotous, extravagant'; *waste* is 'lavish expenditure'.

7–10 **If . . . horses** A hint that Alcibiades with his 'twenty horse' (1.243) has benefited in this way? Compare also 14.509.

9 **foals me** Ironically, the Senator's hypothetical horse, once he has given it to Timon, *foals* or 'breeds' new horses precisely *for him* ('me'), by stimulating Timon to give him horses. The construction resembles the 'ethic dative', where *me* would simply emphasize *foals*: in normal circumstances the horse that has been given away does not foal for the person who has relinquished it.
    straight (a) at once (qualifying *foals me*), (b) upright (qualifying *horses*)

10 **able** strong, vigorous, powerful
    porter The Senator retentively sees the porter's function as to keep strangers out.

11 **still** constantly

13 **sound . . . safety** measure his financial condition reliably and without risk; i.e. rely on him financially. *Sound* is literally 'test the depth of water with a plummet'. Timon's *state* is both shallow and in flux, creating danger of shipwreck. Alternatively (as Johnson read) if Timon's state is sounded, *it* will be found unsafe.
    Caphis Along with Lucullus, this name is taken from Plutarch's 'Life of Sulla'. Sulla sent his friend Caphis to the Amphictyons (council of deputies of Greek states) to request them to remit their wealth.

14 **pleasure** wish

16 **moneys** Elsewhere in Shakespeare the plural is used by the Welsh parson Evans in *Merry Wives* 1.1.46, and repeatedly (as Maxwell points out) by the Jew Shylock in *Merchant of Venice* 1.3.107–39. But Shylock is parodying Antonio's language.
    ceased stopped, appeased

17 **slight** 'off-hand' (Hibbard)

19 **thus** i.e. with shows of courtesy. Perhaps also with hints of impatience for the visitor to leave so that the cap can be put back on.

My uses cry to me, I must serve my turn   20
Out of mine own, his days and times are past,
And my reliances on his fracted dates
Have smit my credit. I love and honour him,
But must not break my back to heal his finger.
Immediate are my needs, and my relief   25
Must not be tossed and turned to me in words,
But find supply immediate. Get you gone.
Put on a most importunate aspect,
A visage of demand; for I do fear
When every feather sticks in his own wing   30
Lord Timon will be left a naked gull,
Which flashes now a phoenix. Get you gone.
CAPHIS I go, sir.

20 **uses** needs (also hinting at 'opportunities for usury'?)

21 **mine own** my own money

21–3 **his . . . credit** Compare Sonnet 18, l. 4: 'And summer's lease hath all too short a date'.

21 **days and times** Might refer to specific dates written in bonds, and/or to the duration of Timon's creditworthiness.

22 **reliances** *OED*'s earliest instance of the word. The plural accords with *Have*, but is extrametrical. It is possible that Shakespeare wrote 'And my reliance on his fracted dates | Have smit my credit', with the plural *dates* influencing the verb. If so, *reliances* would be a compositor's miscorrection.

22 **fracted** broken

23 **smit** smitten: delivered a blow to; attacked as by a disease
credit reputation; creditworthiness

25 **my relief** i.e. the demand for relief

26 **tossed and turned** bounced back and returned (as with a ball in tennis)

27 **supply** a grant of cash. The word occurs more frequently in *Timon* than in any other play by Shakespeare or Middleton. At 4.188 the noun is one of the earliest instances in *OED* of any sense denoting provision of a sum of money; it is the earliest illustration of *sb.* 8, 'A quantity or amount *of* something supplied or pro-

vided'. In the present line the absolute use of *OED sb.* 9, 'provision of funds', first recorded 1611, is closer. As a term for Parliament's subsidies to the King, *supply* is first recorded with reference to the grant of about £250,000 in 1606 (*sb.* 10).

28 **aspect** appearance. Stressed on the second syllable.

29 **visage** 'face', expression. An actorly term.

30–1 **When . . . gull** Proverbial (Dent B375), and in contrast with Aesop's crow that adorned itself with stolen feathers. Shakespeare was accused of being 'an upstart crow beautified with our feathers' in *Greene's Groatsworth of Wit* (1592).

30 **his** its

31 **gull** unfledged bird. Quibbles on the sense 'credulous fool'.

32 **Which** who
flashes now a phoenix *Flashes* suggests a fiery plumage, as befits a mythical bird associated with the sun. It is *OED*'s earliest example of *flash, v.* 13, 'To make a flash or display'. The phoenix, said to burn to ashes and emerge reborn as a new bird, was taken to emblematize the crucifixion and resurrection of Christ. This is relevant to suggestions elsewhere that Timon is a Christ-like sacrificial figure— or a 'naked gull' who fails to be such a figure.

SENATOR

'I go, sir'? (*Giving him bonds*) Take the bonds along with
    you,

And have the dates in. Come.

CAPHIS   I will, sir.

SENATOR   Go.   35

Exeunt ⌐severally⌐

Sc. 4   *Enter Steward, with many bills in his hand*

STEWARD

No care, no stop; so senseless of expense

That he will neither know how to maintain it

---

34 'I go sir'] F (I go sir? *without quotation marks*); Ay, go sir POPE; *not in* DYCE 1857   *Giving him bonds*] SISSON (*subs.*); *not in* F   35 in. Come] F; in compt THEOBALD   35.1 *severally*] OXFORD SHAKESPEARE; *not in* F

4.3 account] F (*accompt*)

---

34 **'I go, sir'** Perhaps a sarcastically impatient repetition. See collation.

35 **have the dates in** Evidently refers to a note of the 'fracted' schedule of repayments that will be annotated into the bond. The penalties for default after the expiry date could be severe; compare the threat of forfeiture at 4.31. Theobald's emendation would anticipate 'Takes no account' at 4.3. But it seems unnecessary, and 'Come' suggests the Senator's 'fussy and agitated' state of mind (Sisson, p. 169).

Sc. 4 (2.2) The scene is of inextricably mixed authorship. Middleton's hand is most evident in ll. 1–9, 45–84 (grace) (a very mixed passage), 134 (I)–143, 154 (when)–158 (flow), 171 (Secure)–193 (me), and 226–7. See notes to ll. 1–118 and 119–227.

   The scene moves on from the single creditor of Sc. 3 to the many, and shows Timon confronting his financial ruin. It seems to takes place mainly in the entrance hall of Timon's house (presumably imagined as a country mansion surrounded by a deer park), where servants and others awaiting Timon assemble, and through which the hunting party passes on its way in to dinner. But the episode with the Fool and Page is unlocalized and specifically not at Timon's house: see ll. 84–5. This suggests the fragmentary nature of the scene. The Fool and Page episode has thematic relevance to the play; but dramatically and in terms of plot it is not well integrated. It is often cut

in the theatre. Nothing comes of the letters the Page is carrying to Alcibiades and Timon (ll. 75–80).

1–118 STEWARD . . . anon. Middleton's presence is suggested by the contractions and grammatical preferences; see Appendix C. See also notes to ll. 1–5, 6, 9.1, 53–4, 55, 67, 73–4, 75, and 94. Shakespeare probably supplied some material for the Fool and Page episode; see notes to ll. 36, 40, 44.1, 50, 57–8, 65, 69, 106, and 110.

1–5 **No . . . continue** One of several accounts of Timon's profligate spending reminiscent of Calverley in *Bloody Murders* (1605), the source of Middleton's *Yorkshire*: 'he continued his expense in such exceeding riot that he was forced to mortgage his lands, run in great debts, entangle his friends for being bound for him, and in short time so weakened his estate that, having not wherewithal to carry that port which before he did, he grew into a discontent'. The equivalent passage in *Yorkshire Tragedy* begins: 'What will become of us? All will away, | My husband never ceases in expense' (2.1–2).

1 **care** (a) oversight, responsibility, (b) anxiety, grief. A key word in relation to the Steward's office and character, repeated at l. 4.

stop Perhaps specifically (a) 'a pause for consideration before acting' (*OED sb.* 2 6c; last example 1561); possibly also (b) weir, river dam (8a).

senseless without feeling or consciousness

expense expenditure

Nor cease his flow of riot, takes no account
How things go from him, nor resumes no care
Of what is to continue. Never mind   5
Was to be so unwise to be so kind.
What shall be done? He will not hear till feel.
I must be round with him, now he comes from hunting.
Fie, fie, fie, fie!

Enter Caphis, ⌈*meeting Servants of*⌉ *Isidore and Varro*

CAPHIS
Good even, Varro. What, you come for money?   10
VARRO'S SERVANT Is't not your business too?
CAPHIS
It is; and yours too, Isidore?
ISIDORE'S SERVANT   It is so.
CAPHIS
Would we were all discharged.
VARRO'S SERVANT   I fear it.
CAPHIS   Here comes the lord.

Enter Timon and his train, amongst them Alcibiades,
⌈*as from hunting*⌉

4 resumes] ROWE; resume F   9.1 *meeting*] OXFORD SHAKESPEARE (*subs.*); *not in* F   *Servants of*]
JOHNSON; *in* F, *identified in stage direction and speech-prefixes by their masters' names.*   13.1
amongst them Alcibiades] CAPELL (*subs.*); *not in* F   13.2 *as from hunting*] COLLIER MS; *not in* F

3 **riot** wild revelling
  takes no account (a) 'pays no attention to'
  (b) 'doesn't calculate the financial cost of'.
4 **resumes** assumes
  no any. *Nor* was often followed by another
  negative (Blake 6.2.1.7). Here perhaps for
  emphasis.
5 **is to continue** OED suggests either 'is to
  happen as a result', or 'is to be left afterwards' (*v.* 15), both unparalleled senses.
  Perhaps instead the active verb stands for
  the passive: 'has to be continued', referring to the continuing need for future
  income (Abbott 359; compare 'what's to
  do' for 'what's to be done').
5–6 **Never mind | Was to be** never was there
  a determination to be; never was there a
  mind that was
6 **to be so kind** in order to be so kind; in
  being so kind. 'So kind' is rhymed with
  'mind' in *No Wit* 7.201–2. There are other
  instances of 'be so kind' in Middleton, but
  none in Shakespeare. 'To be so kind' occurs in *Women Beware* at 3.1.22 (Holdsworth), one of three other examples in

pre-1642 drama (*Literature Online*).
8 **I . . . hunting** A sound of horns within (as
  in prompt books such as Phelps's of 1851)
  would enable the Steward to anticipate
  Timon's arrival.
  round blunt, plain-spoken, severe
9 **Fie . . . fie!** At this point the Steward
  becomes a silent observer for a while.
9.1 *Servants of* In F the servants are confus-
  ingly identified by their masters' names
  alone. They are addressed so too, as in
  'Varro' at *l.* 10. It is confirmed that this is
  Varro's servant at *l.* 28. The trait is shared
  with Sc. 8, which is in Middleton's hand.
10 **Good even** Could mean 'good afternoon',
  but it should be late morning (see note to
  'dinner', l. 14).
13 **we were all discharged** the debts were all
  settled with us (perhaps also 'we were all
  relieved of this duty')
  fear it i.e. suspect otherwise
13.2 *as from hunting* The party might enter
  to further sounds of horns, wearing hunting costumes, and carrying weapons or
  killed game. See note to 2.186–9.

TIMON

So soon as dinner's done we'll forth again,
My Alcibiades.

⌈*Caphis meets Timon*⌉
With me? What is your will?   15

CAPHIS

My lord, here is a note of certain dues.

TIMON Dues? Whence are you?

CAPHIS Of Athens here, my lord.

TIMON Go to my steward.

CAPHIS

Please it your lordship, he hath put me off,   20
To the succession of new days, this month.
My master is awaked by great occasion
To call upon his own, and humbly prays you
That with your other noble parts you'll suit
In giving him his right.

TIMON   Mine honest friend,   25
I prithee but repair to me next morning.

CAPHIS

Nay, good my lord.

TIMON   Contain thyself, good friend.

VARRO'S SERVANT

One Varro's servant, my good lord.

ISIDORE'S SERVANT (*to Timon*)

From Isidore. He humbly prays your speedy payment.

CAPHIS (*to Timon*)

If you did know, my lord, my master's wants—   30

VARRO'S SERVANT (*to Timon*)

'Twas due on forfeiture, my lord, six weeks and past.

ISIDORE'S SERVANT (*to Timon*)

Your steward puts me off, my lord, and I
Am sent expressly to your lordship.

15 *Caphis meets Timon*] OXFORD SHAKESPEARE; *not in* F

14 **dinner** Eaten at midday.
 forth again (to hunting)
15 **What is your will** what do you want
20 **put me off** got rid of me by using evasions
21 **To . . . days** day after day
23 **call upon his own** i.e. call in the money
 he is owed; take control of his assets.
 Perhaps suggests an image of exercising

authority over the members of his household as a metaphor for this.
24 **with . . . suit** you'll act in accordance with your other noble qualities
26 **repair** return
31 **on forfeiture** Some of Timon's property has been pledged as security.

TIMON   Give me breath.—
    I do beseech you, good my lords, keep on.
    I'll wait upon you instantly.
                        Exeunt Alcibiades and Timon's train
                        (*To Steward*) Come hither. Pray you,   35
    How goes the world, that I am thus encountered
    With clamorous demands of broken bonds
    And the detention of long-since-due debts,
    Against my honour?
STEWARD (*to Servants*)   Please you, gentlemen,
    The time is unagreeable to this business;   40
    Your importunacy cease till after dinner,
    That I may make his lordship understand
    Wherefore you are not paid.
TIMON (*to Servants*)   Do so, my friends.
    (*To Steward*) See them well entertained.   *Exit*
STEWARD (*to Servants*)   Pray draw near.
                                                    Exit

---

35 *Exeunt Alcibiades and Timon's train*] ROWE (*subs.*); *not in* F   37 broken] HANMER; debt,
broken F; date-broken STEEVENS   44 entertained. *Exit*] POPE; entertain'd. F

---

33 **Give me breath** i.e. give me breathing
    space, back off. With the three
    imperatives of ll. 33–5 Timon moves the
    scene from a claustrophobic and
    embarrass-ingly public huddle of
    creditors' servants to a private dialogue
    with the Steward.
34 **good my lords** my good lords
    keep on carry on, go on ahead
35 **wait upon you instantly** be with you (at
    your service) in a moment
36 **How goes the world** to what state have
    things come. Compare 1.2.
    thus encountered Shakespearian (*Hamlet*
    1.2.199); also in Chapman (*Conspiracy of
    Biron*, 4.1.158).
37 **of** about
    broken F precedes with 'debt,' which is
    redundant to the metre. More important,
    it adds little to the sense and causes
    a duplication in the following line.
    Theodore B. Leinwand suggests a
    distinction between 'debt-broken bonds',
    which are financial, and 'debts | Against
    my honour', referring to broken pledges
    (*Theatre, Finance, and Society in Early*

Modern England (1999), p. 33). But how
can debts break the bonds that have
constituted them, and how can 'debts |
Against my honour' be detained? Some
editors emend 'date-broken'; compare
'fracted dates', 3.22. More plausibly, as
Maxwell sug-gested, there was an
undeleted false
start in the manuscript. This would be
abandoned as the next line was thought
out. The cancelled phrase might have
been simply 'debt(s) detained'.
38 **detention** withholding, failure to pay. A
    rare word, not elsewhere in Shakespeare
    or Middleton, but once in Chapman
    (*Odyssey*, published 1616, in *Homer*, ed.
    A. Nicoll, 2 vols. (1956), vol. 2, 15.90).
39 **Against** contrary to; at the expense of
40 **unagreeable** uncongenial, unsuitable.
    Another rare word, not elsewhere in
    Shakespeare or Middleton, but Shake-
    speare often coined words with the
    prefix 'un-'. Similarly with 'unaptness',
    l. 126.
44 **entertained** treated
    draw near follow me

Enter Apemantus and Fool

CAPHIS Stay, stay, here comes the Fool with Apemantus.   45
  Let's ha' some sport with 'em.

VARRO'S SERVANT Hang him, he'll abuse us.

ISIDORE'S SERVANT A plague upon him, dog!

VARRO'S SERVANT How dost, Fool?

APEMANTUS Dost dialogue with thy shadow?   50

VARRO'S SERVANT I speak not to thee.

APEMANTUS No, 'tis to thyself. (*To Fool*) Come away.

ISIDORE'S SERVANT ⌈*to Varro's Servant*⌉ There's the fool hangs
  on your back already.

APEMANTUS No, thou stand'st single: thou'rt not on him yet.   55

CAPHIS (*to Isidore's Servant*) Where's the fool now?

APEMANTUS He last asked the question. Poor rogues' and
  usurers' men, bawds between gold and want.

55 thou'rt] F (th'art)

44.1 *Enter Apemantus and Fool* Johnson
suspected a lost passage would have introduced the Fool and Page as employed by
Phrynia, Timandra or another courtesan.
It may never have been written. In either
case, the text's lack of clarity can be associated with the authorial patchwork of
this scene.
  Apemantus The spelling in this scene is
'Apemantus', elsewhere Shakespeare's
preference; but Middletonian 'Apermantus' appears at l. 72.
46 **ha'** Contraction of 'have'.
48 **dog** See note to 1.203.
50 **dialogue** *OED*'s one earlier instance of the
verb is from 'Lover's Complaint', l. 132
(but the attribution of this poem to Shakespeare is in doubt). Not in Middleton.
53–5 **There's . . . yet** Isidore's Servant tries to
get ahead of Apemantus' game, only to
fall prey to it.
53–4 **the fool hangs on your back** the name
'fool' is attached to you (Varro's Servant);
you wear the fool's costume. Alternatively, the line is addressed to Apemantus,
with the same sense punning on the
Fool's position behind him, ready to follow him (compare 'a fool behind a knave',
etc., in *Changeling* 1.2.184–9, in a scene
attributed to Rowley); there may be comic
business with the positioning of bodies. In
either case, 'hangs on your back' has a
homosexual overtone, especially in Apemantus' reply. Compare 'turn your back

to any man living', *Mad World* 3.1.194–5.
55 **thou . . . yet** i.e. it is not true that the fool
hangs on the back of Varro's Servant (or
Apemantus himself), because Isidore's
Servant is the one true fool, and stands
separate from everyone. *Stand'st* quibbles
on 'have an erection', suggesting that
Varro's Servant's homosexual arousal is
unsatiated. *Stand'st single* is Middletonian
('Let the knave stand single', *Phoenix*
10.100), as is *on him yet* (*Puritan Widow*
2.1.75).
56 **Where's the fool now?** Perhaps
imitates Marston's *What You Will* (1601;
printed 1607), ed. A. H. Bullen (1887),
5.1.129–30, where the identical phrase
similarly turns the tables.
57 **He** he who
57–8 **Poor . . . want** Usury was often pictured as an unnatural form of sexual procreation: it increased the usurer's wealth,
the coins 'breeding' new coins (as in 3.6;
and compare Feste's comment on a single
coin, 'Would not a pair of these have
bred, sir?', *Twelfth Night* 3.1.48). Compare also Pompey's 'two usuries', one of
them prostitution, in *Measure* 3.1.275.
Apemantus sees the servants as panders
because they bring the usurers' gold to
the poverty-struck rogues. (Ironically, the
gold is equivalent to the prostitute rather
than the money that pays for her ser-
vices.) *Want* quibbles on the senses 'financial need' and 'sexual desire'.

ALL SERVANTS What are we, Apemantus?

APEMANTUS Asses.   60

ALL SERVANTS Why?

APEMANTUS That you ask me what you are, and do not
know yourselves. Speak to 'em, Fool.

FOOL How do you, gentlemen?

ALL SERVANTS Gramercies, good Fool. How does your   65
mistress?

FOOL She's e'en setting on water to scald such chickens as
you are. Would we could see you at Corinth.

APEMANTUS Good; gramercy.

Enter Page, with two letters

FOOL Look you, here comes my master's page.   70

PAGE Why, how now, captain? What do you in this wise
company? How dost thou, Apemantus?

---

59 ALL SERVANTS] F (*Al.*). *Similarly 'All.' through rest of scene, except l.* 181, '*Ser.*'   69.1 *with two
letters*] OXFORD SHAKESPEARE (*following* BEVINGTON, '*He shows two letters*' *after l.* 76); *not in* F
70, 97 master's] F; mistress' THEOBALD   72 Apemantus] F (*Apermantus*)

---

59 ALL SERVANTS The non-naturalistic and
repeated device in this episode of having
all the servants say the same line perhaps
signals a comic and grotesque kind of
theatrical game-playing.

60 Asses The shift from *bawds* to *Asses* has its
own logic: neither personally enjoys the
commodity he trades in or carries (for the
ass, compare 10.49). This is presumably
what the Servants can't work out for
themselves, so compounding the reasons
why they are asses (ll. 62–3).

65 Gramercies many thanks (Shakespearian)

67 setting on putting on the fire to boil (and
see next note)
scald Chickens were scalded to remove the
feathers. Scalding applies to the likes of
the servants as (a) inflamed with desire
(*setting on* could also mean 'sexually
arousing'), (b) fleeced, stripped of money,
(c) made to suffer venereal disease, (d)
treated for venereal disease by sweating in
a heated tub. 1 *Honest Whore* 2.109 refers
to fretting 'at the loss of a little scald hair',
a clear allusion to venereal disease, and
Old Law 3.2.78–9 refers to 'my three court
codlings that look parboiled | As if they
came from Cupid's scalding-house'.

68 Would . . . Corinth i.e. I wish you could
vist our brothel, but it's too up-market for
you. 'Lais, an harlot of Corinth . . . was
for none but lords and gentlemen that

might well pay for it. Whereof came up a
proverb that it was not for every man to go
unto Corinth' (Erasmus, *Apophthegmes*,
trans. Nicholas Udall (1542), ii. 342).
Dent (M202) confirms the proverb. In the
'Life of Alcibiades' Lais is said to have
been Alcibiades' daughter, and is mentioned in a marginal note next to another
saying '*Timandra the courtesan buries
Alcibiades*'. Middleton nowhere refers to
'Corinth'; Shakespeare does in *Comedy of
Errors*, and in 1 *Henry IV* has 'Corinthian'.

69 gramercy The thanks are for speaking to
the Servants—and for insulting them.
Shakespearian.

70 master's Many editors follow Theobald in
emending here and at l. 97 to 'mistress'',
for consistency with l. 66. A repeated
error might arise if the manuscript abbreviated the word to 'Ms', as was common
(Malone).

71 captain A joking title, without implying
military rank, though perhaps referring
to the Fool's 'rank' within the brothel.
OED's earliest example of the sense (*sb.*
12).

72 thou Given the subservient role and youth
of the Page, this is insultingly over-
familiar. Compare his 'you' to the Fool as
'captain'.
Apemantus F's spelling here, '*Apermantus*', is associated with Middleton.

APEMANTUS Would I had a rod in my mouth, that I might answer thee profitably.

PAGE Prithee, Apemantus, read me the superscription of these letters. I know not which is which.   75

APEMANTUS Canst not read?

PAGE No.

APEMANTUS There will little learning die then that day thou art hanged. This is to Lord Timon, this to Alcibiades.   80
Go, thou wast born a bastard, and thou'lt die a bawd.

PAGE Thou wast whelped a dog, and thou shalt famish a dog's death. Answer not; I am gone.   *Exit*

APEMANTUS E'en so: thou outrunn'st grace. Fool, I will go with you to Lord Timon's.   85

FOOL Will you leave me there?

APEMANTUS If Timon stay at home. (*To Servants*) You three serve three usurers?

ALL SERVANTS Ay. Would they served us.

APEMANTUS So would I: as good a trick as ever hangman served thief.   90

FOOL Are you three usurers' men?

ALL SERVANTS Ay, Fool.

FOOL I think no usurer but has a fool to his servant. My

---

75 PAGE] F4; *Boy.* F   81, 82 wast] F (was't)   81 thou'lt] F (thou't)   84 so:] HIBBARD (*subs.*);
~ˌ F   89 Ay. Would] CAPELL; I would F   94 has] F (ha's)

73–4 **Would . . . profitably** i.e. the only fit reply would be to thrash you. From Proverbs 26: 3–4, 'a rod [belongeth] to the fool's back. Answer not a fool according to his foolishness, lest thou also be like him', and Isaiah 11: 4, 'he shall smite the earth with the rod of his mouth, and with the breath of his lips he shall slay the wicked'; quoted in *Two Gates* 87.1, with the marginal note 'Meaning Christ, *the rod of his mouth, which is his word*'.

74 **profitably** so as to improve you

75 **superscription** address. Elsewhere in Shakespeare only in an un-Shakespearian scene of *1 Henry VI* (4.1.53). There are at least three instances in Middleton. The closest in phrasing is 'Read but the superscription' (*Puritan Widow* 1.1.141).

82–3 **famish a dog's death** Proverbial: 'Die a dog's death' (Dent D509), altered to indicate starvation.

84 **E'en . . . grace** 'twisting the Page's *gone* to mean "spiritually ruined", "damned"' (Hibbard). Apemantus pretends that his reply would have been aimed not at trading insults but at reforming a sinner. 'E'en so' usefully stands as a separate utterance to bring out the new meaning Apemantus gives to *gone*, though there is no punctuation after 'so' in F.

87 **If . . . home** i.e. there will be a fool at Timon's house as long as he is there

90–1 **So . . . thief** Based on the standard idiom 'to serve a trick'.

94 **I . . . servant** The construction is distinctly Middletonian; 'no [noun] but has a [noun]' is found three times in his works (*Nice Valour* 3.3.28–9, *Lady's* 1.1.24, *Five Gallants* 1.1.86) but nowhere in Shakespeare, who does not even write 'but has a' or 'but hath a'.

94 **I think** I think there is

---

mistress is one, and I am her fool. When men come to   95
borrow of your masters they approach sadly and go away
merry, but they enter my master's house merrily and go
away sadly. The reason of this?

VARRO'S SERVANT I could render one.

APEMANTUS Do it then, that we may account thee a   100
whoremaster and a knave, which notwithstanding thou
shalt be no less esteemed.

VARRO'S SERVANT What is a whoremaster, Fool?

FOOL A fool in good clothes, and something like thee. 'Tis
a spirit; sometime't appears like a lord, sometime like   105
a lawyer, sometime like a philosopher with two stones
more than 's artificial one. He is very often like a knight;
and generally in all shapes that man goes up and down in
from fourscore to thirteen, this spirit walks in.

VARRO'S SERVANT Thou art not altogether a fool.   110

FOOL Nor thou altogether a wise man. As much foolery as I
have, so much wit thou lack'st.

APEMANTUS That answer might have become Apemantus.

ALL SERVANTS Aside, aside, here comes Lord Timon.

Enter Timon and Steward

APEMANTUS Come with me, Fool, come.   115

---

105 sometime't] F (sometime t')   107 more] F (moe)

94–5 **My mistress is one** A procuress could be
seen as a usurer in the sexual economy.
Compare ll. 57–8, and see note.

97–8 **go away sadly** After a visit to a brothel a
man would have spent his money and
might have picked up a disease, but also,
according to the well-known post-
classical Latin dictum, '*Post coitum omne
animal triste est*': after coition every
animal is sad.

100–1 **that . . . knave** i.e. that you may show
yourself to be not only a knave (as
a usurer's servant) but a 'whoremaster'
with knowledge of brothels as well

101 **whoremaster** whoremonger, man who
uses prostitutes
notwithstanding even if you don't

104 **A fool in good clothes** Actors too were
accused of dressing above their status as
'servants' to their company's patron (and

the Fool is a generic actor's role).

104–5 **'Tis a spirit** (in that it is able to take on
different guises)

106 **philosopher** alchemist (see following
note)
two stones i.e. two testicles. But the *artificial one* is the 'philosopher's stone' of the
alchemists, supposedly capable of turning base metals to gold. Compare *2 Henry
IV* 3.2.319–20, 'I'll make him a philosopher's two stones to me'.

108 **goes up and down in** (a) walks about in,
(b) gets and loses erections in, (c) thrusts
up and down in during the sexual act. The
lower age-limit of thirteen brings out the
sexual meanings.

110 **not altogether a fool** Proverbial (Dent
A231.1). And compare *Lear* 4.146, 'This
is not altogether fool'.

113 **become** done credit to

FOOL I do not always follow lover, elder brother, and
woman: sometime the philosopher.

Exeunt Apemantus and Fool

STEWARD (*to Servants*)
Pray you, walk near. I'll speak with you anon.

Exeunt Servants

TIMON
You make me marvel wherefore ere this time
Had you not fully laid my state before me,   120
That I might so have rated my expense
As I had leave of means.

STEWARD   You would not hear me.
At many leisures I proposed.

117.1, 118.1 *Exeunt Apemantus and Fool . . . Exeunt Servants*] F (*'Exeunt.' after l.* 118)   123 pro-
posed] F2;   propose F1

116–17 **lover . . . woman** Seen as easy
sources of employment for a Fool because
foolish in themselves. Love is proverbially
without reason (Dent L517). Tilley cites
Sharpham, *Cupid's Whirligig* (1607): 'The
younger brothers (according to the old
wives' tales) always proved the wisest
men' (B687). Women were proverbially
inconstant (Dent W698), and '"because"
is a woman's reason' (B179).
118 **walk near** withdraw but stay nearby
119–227 TIMON . . . *Exeunt* This passage is
one of those involving the Steward that
seems to have been supplied mostly by
Middleton, though Shakespeare's hand is
also present (Holdsworth). It is impossible
to reconstruct the genesis of the passage
with confidence.
  'Vantages' at l. 124 is Shakespearian.
Other distinctively Shakespearian parts
are ll. 159–69 ('Heavens . . . given')
and 198–225 ('They answer . . . sink').
Holdsworth notes as Shakespearian: l.
161 ('englutted'), l. 167 ('couched'), and
ll. 205–6 ('hard fractions', 'half-caps',
'cold-moving nods'). The 'd' spelling of
'Ventidius' at ll. 214 and 216 (here 'Ventiddius') is evidently Shakespeare's, and,
as elsewhere, it is probably Shakespeare
who uses the low number of talents ('five'
at ll. 220 and 223). Shakespeare evidently
anticipated a scene in which Ventidius is
petitioned for money; Middleton was not
to supply it, though at 7.3–9 he assumes
the episode has happened.

Holdsworth identifies strong Middleton
parallels for ll. 134–43, and Jackson
explains 'wasteful cock' (l. 157) with
reference to him (see notes). The lines
between the two Shakespearian sections
(ll. 170–97) set up Middleton's scenes in
which Timon's men visit Lucullus,
Lucius, and Sempronius. The first two
have already been named in a Middleton
scene (Sc. 2), and Sempronius is named
for the first time here. Here as elsewhere
Middleton uses high numbers of talents
('fifty' at l. 187, 'A thousand' at l. 193).
The scene's last couplet is probably also
by Middleton (see note).
119–22 **You . . . means** The accusation
against the Steward and his later confrontation with the servants of the creditors recall the parable of the rich man and
the Unjust Steward in Luke 16: 1–13 (see
Appendix B).
119–20 **marvel . . . not** astonished as to why
you haven't previously
120 **state** financial position
121 **rated my expense** estimated my
expenditure
122 **As . . . means** in line with what my
means allowed
123 **leisures** unoccupied moments
  proposed presented for notice, offered for
acceptance. Usually transitive, in which
case Timon interrupts, but an absolute or
intransitive use is possible.

TIMON   Go to.
Perchance some single vantages you took
When my indisposition put you back,   125
And that unaptness made your minister
Thus to excuse yourself.
STEWARD   O my good lord,
At many times I brought in my accounts,
Laid them before you; you would throw them off,
And say you summed them in mine honesty.   130
When for some trifling present you have bid me
Return so much, I have shook my head and wept,
Yea, 'gainst th'authority of manners prayed you
To hold your hand more close. I did endure
Not seldom nor no slight checks when I have   135
Prompted you in the ebb of your estate
And your great flow of debts. My lovèd lord—
Though you hear now too late, yet now's a time.

---

126 your] F1; you F2   128 accounts] F (accompts)   130 summed] OXFORD SHAKESPEARE
(Wells); sound F1; found F2   137 lovèd] CAMBRIDGE; lou'd F1; deare lov'd F2

123 **Go to** come off it
124 **single** slight, poor
   vantages opportunities, occasions. Not in
   Middleton.
125 **indisposition** disinclination; preoccupation with other matters. Not elsewhere in
   Shakespeare or Middleton. Both have *disposition*; Shakespeare has *indisposed*.
126–7 **that . . . yourself** you made that
   unaptness [of mine] an agent who
   excused you thus. Compare *Triumphs of
   Truth* l. 182, 'Error's minister, that sought
   still to blind thee'. The parallel supports F,
   in which *minister* is a noun. *Yourself* is
   partly emphatic for 'you', but also reflex-
   ive in that Timon claims that the Steward
   is indirectly persuading himself.
126 **unaptness** See note to l. 40.
130 **summed . . . honesty** i.e. trusted me to
   calculate them. Perhaps a displacement of
   the proverbial idea that 'The face is (or is
   not) the index of the mind' (Dent F1).
   summed The summing of accounts is
   translated into, and deferred by, the sum-
   marization of the Steward's character.
   Before Stanley Wells suggested 'summed'
   ('sumd' misread 'sound'), editors usually
   followed F2's weaker correction 'found'.

A Middleton parallel strengthens
'summed': 'all the works | Of motherly
love in me, shown to thy youth | When it
was soft and helpless, are summed up | In
thy most grateful mind' (*Triumphs of
Truth* ll. 137–40).
133 **'gainst th'authority of manners** contrary to the rules of politeness; i.e. to the
   point of being rude
134 **close** Both 'closed' and 'close to your
   chest'.
135 **Not seldom nor no slight** i.e. frequent
   and major
   checks rebukes
135–43 **when . . . dues** One of the passages
   Holdsworth identifies as strongly Middletonian, on account of the metaphor of
   ebb and flow (*Roaring Girl* 2.1.318–29,
   etc.), the idiom 'my loved lord' (at least
   five times, but not in Shakespeare), and,
   most particularly, the collocation of 'I'd
   stop his mouth' (with reference to debt)
   with the words *half* and *present* at *Roaring
   Girl* 4.1.183–8.
136 **Prompted you in** reminded, urged you of
137 **flow** incoming tide
138 **now's a time** i.e. better late than never

The greatest of your having lacks a half
To pay your present debts.

TIMON   Let all my land be sold.   140

STEWARD

'Tis all engaged, some forfeited and gone,
And what remains will hardly stop the mouth
Of present dues. The future comes apace.
What shall defend the interim, and at length
How goes our reck'ning?   145

TIMON

To Lacedaemon did my land extend.

STEWARD

O my good lord, the world is but a word.
Were it all yours to give it in a breath,
How quickly were it gone.

TIMON   You tell me true.

STEWARD

If you suspect my husbandry of falsehood,   150

---

150 of] HIBBARD (*conj.* Cambridge); or F

139–40 **The . . . debts** This corresponds to 'you hear now too late' rather than 'now's a time'. Perhaps Timon interrupts before the Steward can elaborate on 'now's a time'.

139 **The greatest of your having** i.e. the greatest estimate of what you still possess
  having . . . half The similar sounds of *have* and *half* reinforce the point.
  lacks falls short of

140 **present** immediate, urgent

141 **engaged** mortgaged
  forfeited confiscated because the loan raised by mortgaging was not repaid on time

142 **stop the mouth** Suggests both feeding and silencing. A proverbial phrase (Dent M1264).

143–5 **The . . . reck'ning** There may be a suggestion of military invasion, especially as Athens and Sparta (see note to l. 146) were often at war—as they are in Plutarch's 'Life of Alcibiades', and as it is suggested they have been at 10.59.

144 **the interim** in the immediate future
  at length in the long term

145 **our reck'ning** (a) the 'bottom line' of our accounts, (b) our ability to settle debts. With a possible suggestion of the final reckoning, God's judgement on the dead.

146 **To . . . extend** The line has strong undercurrents of disbelief and sense of loss. Features such as inversion of syntax, the contrasting register and syllabic value of 'Lacedaemon', alliteration, and other qualities of sound, go some way to explaining the effect.
  Lacedaemon Sparta (over 200 km or 125 miles from Athens)

147 **the . . . word** Based on the proverb 'The world is nought', with the vocal similarity of *world* and *word* reinforcing the point. 'The world is but a word' depends not on the intrinsic primacy of language, but on the function of performative speech, such as in gift-giving, as a socially meaningful act.

150 **husbandry** stewardship, financial management
  of Blake defends F's 'or' as reflecting a use equivalent to 'and' combined with a hendiadys for 'false husbandry' (5.3.1(a)), but there is no convincing parallel, and a compositorial substitution is more likely.

Call me before th'exactest auditors
And set me on the proof. So the gods bless me,
When all our offices have been oppressed
With riotous feeders, when our vaults have wept
With drunken spilth of wine, when every room   155
Hath blazed with lights and brayed with minstrelsy,
I have retired me to a wasteful cock,
And set mine eyes at flow.

TIMON   Prithee, no more.

STEWARD

'Heavens,' have I said, 'the bounty of this lord!
How many prodigal bits have slaves and peasants   160
This night englutted! Who is not Timon's?
What heart, head, sword, force, means, but is Lord
    Timon's?

---

161 Timon's] F; Lord Timon's ALEXANDER (*conj.* Steevens)

---

151 **auditors** For the sense 'scrutineer of accounts' compare *1 Henry IV* 2.1.57. The sense is unusual in the drama, and the word may metatheatrically invoke the play's audience in its more usual sense.

152 **So** as I hope

153 **our offices** i.e. the servants' work-areas, the kitchens, etc.
oppressed crowded out, thronged, overwhelmed (Crystal). *Oppressed with* is in Shakespeare but not Middleton.

154 **feeders** i.e. the attendants on Timon's guests, both their masters' feeders in the sense 'dependants', and feeders at Timon's expense in that they are 'eaters'. The two senses are connected, as *OED* makes clear: 'one who eats at another's expense . . . a servant' (2b, citing *As You Like It* 2.4.98; see also *Nice Valour* 3.1.67).
vaults Either 'arched wine-cellars' (as were often placed below great halls) or 'covered drains'. The latter, less fitting with *offices* and *room*, is more consistent with weeping spilt wine. Lucian has Plutus say of Timon's profligacy: 'no matter how fast I pour in, the thing will not hold water; every gallon will be out almost before it is in; the bore of the *waste-pipe* is so large, and never a plug'. Middleton refers to 'destruction's vaults, [i.e. drains] | Full of old filth, proceeding from new slime' (*Solomon Paraphrased*, 18.39–40). He associates 'the vaults [i.e. cellars]

within our monasteries' with storage of the excessive wealth of Plutus, in *Game at Chess* 5.3.125 (see note to 1.278).

155 **spilth** spillage. *OED*'s only example of the word before 1822.

156 **minstrelsy** i.e. the loud and rowdy songs, music, story-telling or joking of minstrels, itinerant professional entertainers. Not in Middleton.

157–8 **I . . . flow** Jackson compares *Phoenix* 6.92–3, a passage that elucidates the sense of *cock* (spout, tap) and, as here, correlates it with the eyes as source of tears: 'one tear from an old man is a great matter; the cocks of age are dry'. The emblematic association between butler and spigot might here be extended, ironically, to a steward: compare 'Spigot the butler' in Thomas Heywood's *Woman Killed With Kindness*.

157 **me** myself

158 **And . . . flow** The weeping is both provoked by the waste of the spilt wine and analogous to it. Roles become inverted, with the Steward now flowing to excess and Timon vainly urging 'no more'.

160 **prodigal bits** excessive bits of food. *Prodigal* is transferred from the eaters to the food.

161 **Timon's** i.e. Timon's friend, dependant, or devotee; an object at the disposal of Timon; a body and being sustained by Timon's food

---

Great Timon! Noble, worthy, royal Timon!'
Ah, when the means are gone that buy this praise,
The breath is gone whereof this praise is made.   165
Feast won, fast lost; one cloud of winter show'rs,
These flies are couched.

       He weeps

TIMON   Come, sermon me no further.
No villainous bounty yet hath passed my heart.
Unwisely, not ignobly, have I given.
Why dost thou weep? Canst thou the conscience lack   170
To think I shall lack friends? Secure thy heart.
If I would broach the vessels of my love
And try the argument of hearts by borrowing,
Men and men's fortunes could I frankly use
As I can bid thee speak.

STEWARD   Assurance bless your thoughts!   175

TIMON
And in some sort these wants of mine are crowned
That I account them blessings, for by these
Shall I try friends. You shall perceive how you
Mistake my fortunes. I am wealthy in my friends.—

---

167 *He weeps*] BEVINGTON; *not in* F

---

166 **Feast . . . fast** Compare notes on the echoically paired words in ll. 139 and 147. All three lines are the Steward's.

166 **fast lost** (a) quickly lost, (b) lost so that there is a fast instead of a feast

167 **flies** The sense 'parasites' was probably not firmly established until Jonson named the parasite 'Mosca', Italian for 'fly', in Jonson's *Volpone* (1606).
     are couched lie hidden; are put down
     sermon Nowhere else used as a verb in Shakespeare and Middleton.

168 **No . . . heart** i.e. I have not been generous for villainous motives
     villainous (a) vicious, wretched, (b) slavish (anticipating *ignobly*, l. 169)

169 **Unwisely . . . given** Compare Othello's self-characterization, 'one that loved not wisely but too well' (*Othello* 5.2.353).
     not ignobly Generosity was considered a characteristic quality of the nobility. *Ignobly* is not in Middleton.

170 **conscience** sound judgement (Onions). *OED*'s only example of sense 3, 'Reason-ableness, understanding, "sense"'.

171 **Secure** (a) reassure, (b) close up. The latter refers to the tears as a leak, anticipating and contrasting with *broach the vessels*, l. 171, and so develops the symmetry noted at l. 158.

172 **broach the vessels** The image is of tapping a barrel. Compare *Roaring Girl* 11.222, 'Vessels older ere they're broached'. See also ll. 157–8. The *vessels* are now Timon's 'friends', supposedly filled with love for him as they are actually filled with his wine.

173 **try** test
     argument summary (as might be printed at the beginning of a book); statement; evidence

174 **frankly** as freely (Shakespearian)

175 **Assurance . . . thoughts** may your thoughts be blessed by being right

176 **crowned** (a) given dignity, as with a regal crown; perhaps also (b) made wealthy, as with crowns as coins

Within there, Flaminius, Servilius!   180

> *Enter three Servants: Flaminius, Servilius, and a Third*
> *Servant*

ALL SERVANTS My lord, my lord.

TIMON I will dispatch you severally, (*to Servilius*) you to
Lord Lucius, (*to Flaminius*) to Lord Lucullus you—
I hunted with his honour today—(*to Third Servant*) you
to Sempronius. Commend me to their loves, and I am   185
proud, say, that my occasions have found time to use 'em
toward a supply of money. Let the request be fifty talents.

FLAMINIUS As you have said, my lord.   ⌈*Exeunt Servants*⌉

STEWARD Lord Lucius and Lucullus? Hmh!

TIMON

Go you, sir, to the senators,   190
Of whom, even to the state's best health, I have
Deserved this hearing. Bid 'em send o'th' instant
A thousand talents to me.

STEWARD   I have been bold,
For that I knew it the most general way
To them, to use your signet and your name;   195
But they do shake their heads, and I am here
No richer in return.

TIMON   Is't true? Can 't be?

STEWARD

They answer in a joint and corporate voice

---

180 Flaminius] ROWE; *Flauius* F   180.1–2 *Flaminius . . . Servant*] ROWE (*subs.*); *not in* F
188 *Exeunt Servants*] ROWE; *not in* F

---

180 **Flaminius** F's '*Flauius*' is wrong in that
(a) Flavius is the Steward, who is already
on stage, (b) at l. 188 F's speech-prefix is
for '*Flam.*'.
182 **severally** different ways
186 **occasions** circumstances, needs. Also at
7.15 and 11.10. Compare *Widow* 3.3.105,
'It makes me bold to speak my occasions
to you'.
187 **toward** as a help toward
supply See note to l. 23.
fifty talents A vast sum: see note to 1.97.
191 **even . . . health** i.e. as far as is compatible with the state's ability to support him
without coming to harm. Or implies that
Timon's deserving is based on his having
actually strengthened the state, as with

Othello's claim to 'have done the state
some service' (*Othello* 5.2.348).
192 **o'th' instant** at once
193 **been bold** gone as far as
194 **For that** because
general common, usual
197 **No richer** Shakespearian.
198 **joint and corporate voice** This is the only
pre-18th century use of the sense (*OED*,
corporate, ppl. a. 5, of a body politic, as distinct from *forming* a body politic). The use
of adjectival hendiadys makes the meaning clear. For the idiom, compare *Troilus*
2.2.192, 'joint and several dignities'.
'Joint and' is not in Middleton. 'Corporate' is a malapropism for 'corporal' once
in Shakespeare, but is not in Middleton.

That now they are at fall, want treasure, cannot
Do what they would, are sorry, you are honourable,   200
But yet they could have wished—they know not—
Something hath been amiss—a noble nature
May catch a wrench—would all were well—'tis pity;
And so, intending other, serious, matters,
After distasteful looks and these hard fractions,   205
With certain half-caps and cold-moving nods
They froze me into silence.

TIMON   You gods reward them!
Prithee, man, look cheerly. These old fellows
Have their ingratitude in them hereditary.
Their blood is caked, 'tis cold, it seldom flows.   210
'Tis lack of kindly warmth they are not kind;
And nature as it grows again toward earth
Is fashioned for the journey dull and heavy.
Go to Ventidius. Prithee, be not sad.
Thou art true and honest—ingenuously I speak—   215
No blame belongs to thee. Ventidius lately

---

199 treasure] F2; Treature F1   208 cheerly] F (cheerely)   211 warmth,] F (~,)   214, 216 Ventidius] F (*Ventiddius*)   215 ingenuously] F (Ingeniously)

199 **at fall** at a low ebb
  want lack
201 **not—** The inconclusive break is marked by the line's missing tenth syllable (Wright, p. 182).
203 **catch** accidentally suffer
  a wrench In *Old Law* 3.2.95 but not in Shakespeare.
204 **intending** (a) pretending, or (b) turning to
205 **distasteful** showing aversion. *OED*'s earliest example of obsolete sense 3. The earliest instance of the word in *OED*, though *OED* does not record Samuel Daniel's *The Queen's Arcadia* (performed 30 August 1605, printed 1606) in *Complete Works*, ed. A. B. Grosart, 5 vols. (1881–6), vol. iii, l. 891. Another example is *Nice Valour* 3.2.51.
  hard (a) harsh, (b) difficult to understand
  fractions fragments (of utterances). The word occurs in *Troilus* 5.2.161, but not in Middleton.
206 **half-caps** half-doffed caps (suggesting reluctance and the slowness of age). *OED*'s only example of this sense.

cold-moving (a) stiffly moving, (b) conveying coldness
209 **hereditary** as it were 'inherited' with age. Old men are seen as sharing a sterile metaphorical kinship with each other rather than the 'kindly warmth' of families and humanity. Compare 14.10 and 275. For the usage, see *Winter's Tale* 1.2.76–7, 'the imposition cleared | Hereditary ours'. The word is not in Middleton.
210 **caked** congealed. The line provides *OED*'s earliest instance of the verb.
211 **'Tis** it's on account of
  kindly natural. Puns on *kind*, 'caring, generous'. Both words are associated with kinship.
212 **nature** human life
  earth i.e. the grave. Perhaps also the ground, in that old people grow bent.
213 **dull** inert, unresponsive
  heavy sluggish
214, 216 **Ventidius** The 'd' spelling (see collation) is elsewhere associated with Shakespeare.

Buried his father, by whose death he's stepped
Into a great estate. When he was poor,
Imprisoned, and in scarcity of friends,
I cleared him with five talents. Greet him from me.   220
Bid him suppose some good necessity
Touches his friend, which craves to be remembered
With those five talents. That had, give't these fellows
To whom 'tis instant due. Ne'er speak or think
That Timon's fortunes 'mong his friends can sink.   225

STEWARD

I would I could not think it. That thought is bounty's foe:
Being free itself, it thinks all others so.

Exeunt ⌈severally⌉

Sc. 5   *Enter Flaminius, with a box under his cloak, waiting to*
speak with a lord (Lucullus). From his master, enters a
Servant to him

SERVANT   I have told my lord of you. He is coming down to
you.

224 Ne're] F (Neu'r)   227.1 *severally*] OXFORD SHAKESPEARE; *not in* F
    5.0.1 *Enter . . . cloak,*] OXFORD SHAKESPEARE; *Flaminius* F   0.2 *lord (Lucullus). From*] *Lord*ₐ
from F   *(Lucullus)*] ROWE (*subs.*); *not in* F

217–18 **stepped | Into** See note to 10.12.
221 **good necessity** genuine need
222 **which . . . remembered** The hint of per-
    sonification in *craves* conflates the *necess-
    ity* with Timon himself, who is the more
    straightforward referent. For the slippage
    between the quality and the person it
    applies to, compare ll. 226–7. Or, more
    simply, *which* means 'who' (Abbott 265).
    remembered kept in mind as entitled to
    recompense
223 **With** i.e. by the return of
225 **'mong** Generally un-Middletonian,
    though there is an example in *Bloody
    Banquet* 4.2.14.
226–7 **I would . . . so** Middleton has 'I would
    I could persuade my thoughts | From
    thinking thee a brother' in *Nice Valour* at
    4.1.23–4, and 'I would I could not' in *Nice
    Valour* at 5.3.139 and *Widow* at 1.2.169.
    The personification of Bounty is found in
    Middleton pageants. The 'Entertainment
    for Sir William Cockayne' ends with 'For
    bounty did intend it always so', with
    rhymes on 'flow', 'go', and 'below'. There
    is a similar moralizing couplet with

rhyme-word 'so' at the end of 2.1 in *Measure*, a passage probably added by Middle-
ton: 'Mercy is not itself that oft looks so. |
Pardon is still the nurse of second woe.'
'Mercy' and 'bounty' are key words in
Measure and *Timon* respectively. Both
couplets occur at a point in the action
where the principle in question is beginning to come under extreme pressure.
226 **That . . . foe** Timon's false belief that his
    friends are generous makes generosity
    dangerous.
227 **free** generous. But playing on the
    proverb 'thought is free'.
    it i.e. bounty, hence the bountiful
    person
Sc. 5 (3.1) This and the following scenes
    showing Timon's moneylenders reject his
    appeals for support make up a single
    sequence written by Middleton. There are
    particularly strong resemblances with
    episodes in his earlier city comedies figur-
    ing usurers and creditors. The first three
    build as satire by repeating the same idea,
    as with the present-bearing visits of the
    would-be heirs in Jonson's *Volpone* 1.1.

FLAMINIUS I thank you, sir.

    Enter Lucullus

SERVANT Here's my lord.

LUCULLUS (*aside*) One of Lord Timon's men? A gift, I warrant.   5
Why, this hits right; I dreamt of a silver basin and ewer
tonight.— Flaminius, honest Flaminius, you are very
respectively welcome, sir. (*To his Servant*) Fill me some
wine.   *Exit Servant*
And how does that honourable, complete, free-hearted   10
gentleman of Athens, thy very bountiful good lord and
master?

FLAMINIUS His health is well, sir.

LUCULLUS I am right glad that his health is well, sir. And
what hast thou there under thy cloak, pretty Flaminius?   15

FLAMINIUS Faith, nothing but an empty box, sir, which in
my lord's behalf I come to entreat your honour to supply,
who, having great and instant occasion to use fifty
talents, hath sent to your lordship to furnish him,
nothing doubting your present assistance therein.   20

9 *Exit Servant*] CAPELL; *not in* F   11 bountiful] F2; bonntifull F1

0.1–2 **Enter . . . Lucullus)** The key word
is 'waiting'. Compare *Dissemblers*
1.2.99–100, 'like an idle serving-man
below, | Gaping and waiting for his mas-
ter's coming'. The time might afford
comic stage business with the box, so that
the audience knows about the object that
will be hidden from Lucullus. The empty
box particularly recalls Kyd's *Spanish
Tragedy*, where Pedringano expects that
his pardon from execution will be found in
a box that is in fact empty. Middleton
reworks the joke in 3.5 of *Revenger's*,
probably written at about the same time
as *Timon*.

0.2 **From his master** Most meaningful dramatically if it refers to the servant, who
has just 'told my lord of you'. But F's
punctuation suggests, with strained
phrasing, that it refers to Flaminius.

3.1 *Lucullus* Plutarch includes the 'Life of
Lucius Lucullus' and refers to Lucullus in
the 'Life of Marcus Antonius' and 'Life of
Sulla'. Though Middleton treats Lucullus
and Lucius as separate roles, they may
originally have been conceived as a single
'Lucius Lucullus'.

5–14 **A gift . . . glad that his health is well, sir**
A passage dense with Middleton idiom.
Compare *Five Gallants* 2.1.82–3, 'Gentlemen, you are all most respectively
welcome'; *Michaelmas* 1.2.57, 'a fair,
free-breasted gentleman' and 3.2.17–18,
'a good, free-hearted, honest, affable kind
of gentleman'; and *Puritan Widow* 3.4.28,
'the most free-heartedst gentleman'
(Holdsworth). *Respectively* and *free-
hearted* are un-Shakespearian.

6 **hits** hits the mark, achieves the objective.
Compare *Revenger's* 4.2.110, 'It hits as I
could wish'. The present line is *OED*'s
earliest example of the sense (*v.* 16).
ewer pitcher

7 **tonight** last night

8 **respectively** respectfully, particularly

10 **complete** perfect, fully accomplished
free-hearted generously inclined

13 **His health** (as opposed to his finances)

17 **supply** fill

18–19 **fifty talents** Far too great a sum to be
carried in a box!

20 **nothing . . . therein** A 'standard expression of the friendship style' adopted
between merchants (Magnusson, p. 136).
nothing not at all

LUCULLUS La, la, la, la, 'nothing doubting' says he? Alas,
  good lord! A noble gentleman 'tis, if he would not keep so
  good a house. Many a time and often I ha' dined with him
  and told him on't, and come again to supper to him of
  purpose to have him spend less; and yet he would   25
  embrace no counsel, take no warning by my coming.
  Every man has his fault, and honesty is his. I ha' told him
  on't, but I could ne'er get him from't.

  Enter Servant, with wine

SERVANT Please your lordship, here is the wine.

LUCULLUS Flaminius, I have noted thee always wise.   30
  (*Drinking*) Here's to thee!

FLAMINIUS Your lordship speaks your pleasure.

LUCULLUS I have observed thee always for a towardly
  prompt spirit, give thee thy due, and one that knows what
  belongs to reason; and canst use the time well if the time 35
  use thee well. (*Drinking*) Good parts in thee! (*To his
  Servant*) Get you gone, sirrah.   *Exit Servant*
  Draw nearer, honest Flaminius. Thy lord's a bountiful
  gentleman; but thou art wise, and thou know'st well
  enough, although thou com'st to me, that this is no time 40
  to lend money, especially upon bare friendship without
  security. (*Giving coins*) Here's three solidares for thee.

---

31 *Drinking*] CAPELL; *not in* F   36 *Drinking*] THEOBALD (*subs.*); *not in* F   42 *Giving coins*]
BEVINGTON (*subs.*); *not in* F

21 **La** Expresses derision or disdain. No doubt
   an affectation, especially as repeated.
23 **good** i.e. lavish
25 **have him** urge him to
27 **Every man has his fault** Proverbial (Dent
   M116).
   honesty generosity
31 (*Drinking*) **Here's to thee!** Flaminius is
   probably not given a drink after being led
   to expect one (though Capell's direction
   reads '*drinking, and giving Wine to him*').
32 **speaks your pleasure** i.e. is kind to say
   so. With an ironic undertow, 'can say
   whatever you please'; compare *Witch*
   2.2.94–5, 'How great people may speak
   their pleasure, madam!'
33 **towardly** (a) forward, promising (as in
   Michaelmas 4.1.32, 'You have a towardly

   son and heir'), (b) dutiful, helpful,
   friendly (as Crystal prefers)
34 **prompt** ready and willing
   give thee thy due Proverbial (Dent D634).
34–5 **what . . . reason** i.e. how to act wisely
   (or prudently)
35 **time . . . time** opportunity . . . times
36 **Good parts in thee!** to your fine qualities!
   (a toast)
37–8 **Get . . . Flaminius** The orders establish
   a (false) confidentiality. *Sirrah* is a dismissive address to an inferior.
41 **upon bare friendship** i.e. without security
42 **solidares** An invented term for a coin of
   small value (based on Latin *solidus*; compare Italian *soldo*, a coin worth less than
   an English penny).

227

Good boy, wink at me, and say thou saw'st me not. Fare
thee well.

FLAMINIUS

Is't possible the world should so much differ,   45
And we alive that lived?

He throws the coins back at Lucullus

                    Fly, damnèd baseness,
To him that worships thee.

LUCULLUS Ha! Now I see thou art a fool, and fit for thy
master.   *Exit*

FLAMINIUS

May these add to the number that may scald thee.   50
Let molten coin be thy damnation,
Thou disease of a friend, and not himself.
Has friendship such a faint and milky heart
It turns in less than two nights? O you gods,
I feel my master's passion! This slave   55
Unto this hour has my lord's meat in him.
Why should it thrive and turn to nutriment,

46 lived] F3; liued (= -èd) F   *He . . . Lucullus*] CAPELL (*subs.*); *not in* F   49 *Exit*] F (*Exit L.*)
56 this hour] POPE; his Honor F

43 **wink at** turn a blind eye towards. As in
'this knave will wink at small faults'
(*Quiet Life* 1.1.227).
45 **differ** i.e. have changed so much
46 **that lived** who were alive then
baseness worthlessness (punning on the
'base' metal of lesser coins)
50 **these** i.e. the coins he has thrown
51–8 **Let . . . poison** The wicked are by tradition punished in hell by a version of
their sins, in this case usurers being boiled
in or drinking molten lead. The opening
speech of *Revenger's* collocates references
to poison, damnation, and an image of
melting and consuming a usurer's accu-
mulated money (1.1.26–9). Other Middleton parallels are strong: 'wet damnation'
(*Revenger's* 3.5.60, describing liquor
entering the mouth), 'disease of Justice'
(*Phoenix* 5.1.159–62), 'flow in too much
milk and have faint livers' (*Revenger's*
5.2.3), 'one | That has a feeling of his
master's passions' (*Lady's* 4.4.29–30),
'that breast | Is turned to quarlèd poison'
(*Revenger's* 4.4.6–7), etc. (Holdsworth).
Nutriment is not in Shakespeare, but in

Solomon Paraphrased 1.112 Destruction
hopes to eat the sinner's flesh and make
'Thy vice her nutriment'.
52 **disease . . . himself** The false friend is a
diseased double, a source of infection
rather than support. This bold image is
varied and reworked more fully in *Nice
Valour* 5.2.20–2: 'falsehood, | That broth-
erly disease, fellow-like devil, | That plays
within our bosom and betrays us'.
54 **turns** (a) curdles, (b) changes
55 **passion** grief; suffering
56 **this hour** Editors often follow F's 'his
Honor', but Lucullus is a slave to his
self-interest, not his honour. Steevens
resolved this difficulty by punctuating
'Unto his honour' as a parenthesis, which
is syntactically possible but rhetorically
unconvincing. 'Unto this hour' is exactly
the point that needs emphasis: the food is
still in Lucullus' stomach.
57 **thrive** i.e. avoid sickness from the *poison*
of the body it is in. It is of course Lucullus
who thrives on the *nutriment*, though an
implied transitive 'Why should it thrive
[him]' is syntactically unlikely.

When he is turned to poison?
O, may diseases only work upon't;
And when he's sick to death, let not that part of nature   60
Which my lord paid for be of any power
To expel sickness, but prolong his hour.   *Exit*

Sc. 6   *Enter Lucius, with three Strangers*

LUCIUS Who, the Lord Timon? He is my very good friend,
and an honourable gentleman.

FIRST STRANGER We know him for no less, though we are
but strangers to him. But I can tell you one thing, my
lord, and which I hear from common rumours: now Lord   5
Timon's happy hours are done and past, and his estate
shrinks from him.

LUCIUS Fie, no, do not believe it. He cannot want for money.

SECOND STRANGER But believe you this, my lord, that not
long ago one of his men was with the Lord Lucullus to   10
borrow so many talents—nay, urged extremely for't, and
showed what necessity belonged to't, and yet was denied.

LUCIUS How?

SECOND STRANGER I tell you, denied, my lord.

LUCIUS What a strange case was that! Now before the gods,   15
I am ashamed on't. Denied that honourable man? There
was very little honour showed in't. For my own part, I
must needs confess I have received some small kindnesses
from him, as money, plate, jewels, and suchlike trifles—
nothing comparing to his; yet had he not mistook him   20

6.3 FIRST STRANGER] F (I). *Similarly formatted as a numeral without a name for all three Strangers throughout the scene in* F.   II so many] F; fifty THEOBALD   20 he not] OXFORD SHAKESPEARE (*conj.* Johnson); hee F

59 **diseases only** nothing but diseases
60 **nature** i.e. his physical body
62 **but** but only to
    hour time of death
Sc. 6 (3.2) Attributed to Middleton.
0.1 *Lucius* Perhaps an old man; see note to l. 36.
    Strangers i.e. 'foreigners' who are not corrupted by the ways of Athens (as the name 'Hostilius' at l. 60 strongly suggests), and/or people who do not know Timon (as ll. 3–4 suggest)
3 **know him for** i.e. have heard that he is
II **so many** Probably an evasive 'a certain

number of', though could be 'such a lot of'. The phrase is similarly used where a precise number might be expected in *Michaelmas* 5.1.17, where an inventory of an estate specifies 'So many acres of good meadow'.
12 **belonged** pertained
16–17 **Denied . . . in't** The repetition *honourable . . . honour* makes Lucius sound vacuous, though one would indeed have been thought to gain honour by helping someone honourable.
20 **his** i.e. Lucullus'
    mistook him made a mistake

and sent to me, I should ne'er have denied his occasion so
many talents.

    Enter Servilius

SERVILIUS (*aside*) See, by good hap yonder's my lord. I have
sweat to see his honour. (*To Lucius*) My honoured lord!

LUCIUS Servilius! You are kindly met, sir. Fare thee well.   25
Commend me to thy honourable, virtuous lord, my very
exquisite friend.

    ⌈*He starts to leave*⌉

SERVILIUS May it please your honour, my lord hath sent—

LUCIUS Ha! What has he sent? I am so much endeared
to that lord, he's ever sending. How shall I thank him,   30
think'st thou? And what has he sent now?

SERVILIUS ⌈*presenting a note*⌉ He's only sent his present
occasion now, my lord, requesting your lordship to
supply his instant use with so many talents.

LUCIUS

I know his lordship is but merry with me.   35
He cannot want fifty—⌈*reading again*⌉ five hundred
talents.

25, 35, 57 LUCIUS] F2 (*Luci.*); *Lucil.* F1   27.1 *He starts to leave*] BEVINGTON (*subs.*); *not in* F
29 has] F (ha's)   32 *presenting a note*] This edition (*conj.* Steevens); *not in* F   He's] F (Has)
36 fifty—] OLIVER; ~ ∧ F   *reading again*] This edition; *not in* F

---

21 **his occasion** him in his need

23 **hap** chance

24 **sweat** sweated (with anxiety, or physical
exertion). As Lucius tries to depart immediately on meeting Servilius, the location
is probably a public place. Servilius may,
then, have been looking everywhere for
Lucius. (Perhaps Lucius got wind of
Timon's troubles before the Strangers told
him.)

25 LUCIUS F1's '*Lucil.*' here and at ll. 35 and
57 reintroduces the name of the servant
Timon helps in Sc. 1, but this is inconsistent both with the entry of '*Lucius*' at the
beginning of Sc. 6, with '*Lucius*' as spelt
in full in the speech-prefix at 6.8, and
with the references elsewhere in the play
to Timon sending for help from Lucius.
But see note to 5.3.1.

You are kindly met I'm delighted to meet
you

29–30 **endeared to** obliged to; affectionate
towards. As elsewhere, the term is suitably suggestive of financial enrichment.
Compare 2.224, and *Chaste Maid* 5.4.75,
'I am so endeared to thee'.

32 *presenting a note* This is suggested by
the unstipulated 'so many' (l. 35),
and Lucius' confused but somehow
informed knowledge of the sum two lines
later.

32–3 **He's . . . occasion** What is 'sent' is
merely words *about* something (Timon's
needs) rather than an object (a present).

34 **use** need

34 **so many** as many (as *his present occasion*).
Or 'this many'. See note to l. 11.

35 **merry with me** having a joke at my
expense

36 **want** lack (and so 'need')

fifty . . . talents The dash and stage direction are editorial. 'Fifty-five hundred' was

SERVILIUS

But in the mean time he wants less, my lord.
If his occasion were not virtuous
I should not urge it half so faithfully.

LUCIUS

Dost thou speak seriously, Servilius?   40

SERVILIUS Upon my soul, 'tis true, sir.

LUCIUS What a wicked beast was I to disfurnish myself
against such a good time when I might ha' shown myself
honourable! How unluckily it happened that I should
purchase the day before for a little part, and undo a great   45
deal of honour! Servilius, now before the gods I am not
able to do, the more beast, I say. I was sending to use Lord
Timon myself—these gentlemen can witness—but I

---

45 before for] F; before HANMER   47 beast, I] F; beast I, I COLLIER 1853 (*conj.* Collier MS)

---

evidently not a current way of saying 'five
thousand five hundred'. Probably, then,
Lucius is looking at a note in which at first
thinks he reads 'fifty', in arabic numerals,
only to realize that there are not one but
two zeroes. Even five hundred talents is
a huge sum, though biblical texts cite as
many as 10,000 talents (e.g. Matthew 18:
24), and sums of hundreds and even
thousands of talents are mentioned in
Plutarch. Perhaps the sudden inflation
from *fifty* (as at 5.18) to *five hundred* is
grotesque comedy. If Lucius makes a mistake through poor eyesight, this might
converge with the repetitive, cliché-
ridden diction in suggesting that he, like
misers such as Lucre and Hoard in *Trick*, is
an old man.

37 **But . . . lord** Presumably Servilius lowers
the request in the hope of getting at least
something.

38 **occasion** need
virtuous i.e. brought about by acts of
virtue

39 **faithfully** confidently, sincerely

42–6 **What . . . honour** Echoes the response
to a similar request in *Mad World*
2.4.26–8: 'FOLLYWIT Push! Money,
money, we come for money. | SIR BOUN-
TEOUS Is that all you come for? Ah, what a
beast was I to put out my money t'other
day!' The phrase 'What a beast was I to' is

also found in *Trick* 2.1.126 (Holdsworth).

45 **purchase** Probably in the usual modern
sense, but evasively lacks an object.
Onions and *OED* gloss 'strive', in which
case *part* refers to the possession sought
(*OED, Part, sb.* 7b). Crystal adds the alternative 'make a bargain, invest'.
part amount; i.e. spent sum of money
(perhaps with some suggestion of *OED,
Part, sb.* 16, 'parting, separation', recorded only in *1 Jeronimo*, 1605). See also
previous note. Lucius uses evasive expressions. Hanmer's omission of 'for', though
plausible, does not notably improve the
sense.
undo i.e. ruin my chance of acquiring

47 **beast** Collier's addition of 'I' normalizes
the idiom, but Lucius' speech is again
mildly elliptical.

47–8 **I was . . . witness** A doubtful claim,
and certainly not one the audience can
witness.

47 **use** A loaded word (and one that appears
more often in *Timon* than any other
Shakespeare play). The idiom is not
entirely cynical: Simonides in *Old Law*
says 'Cleanthes, if you want money
tomorrow use me' (1.1.317), i.e., as here,
'borrow from'. But the cynical implication and the association with moneylend-
ing are never far away, and are to the
point here.

---

would not, for the wealth of Athens, I had done't now.
Commend me bountifully to his good lordship; and I hope   50
his honour will conceive the fairest of me because I have
no power to be kind. And tell him this from me: I count it
one of my greatest afflictions, say, that I cannot pleasure
such an honourable gentleman. Good Servilius, will you
befriend me so far as to use mine own words to him?   55
SERVILIUS Yes, sir, I shall.

LUCIUS

I'll look you out a good turn, Servilius.   *Exit Servilius*
True as you said: Timon is shrunk indeed;
And he that's once denied will hardly speed.   *Exit*

FIRST STRANGER

Do you observe this, Hostilius?

SECOND STRANGER   Ay, too well.   60

FIRST STRANGER

Why, this is the world's soul, and just of the same piece

57 *Exit Servilius*] JOHNSON; '*Exit Seruil.*' *after l.* 56 in F

49 **would not** could not wish
50–7 **Commend . . . Servilius** The idioms are
distinctively Middletonian (Holdsworth).
Compare in particular 'I count . . .
gentleman' with *Michaelmas* 2.3.120–1,
'It is my greatest affliction at this
instant, I am not able to furnish you', in
another scene where financial aid is
being sought. *Affliction* is favoured by
Middleton.
50 **bountifully** A highly ironic word in the
circumstances. Elsewhere in Middleton
but not Shakespeare.
51 **conceive the fairest** think the best
52–4 **I . . . gentleman** A refusal expressed in
the 'pleasuring friends' style adopted in
connection with financial transactions
(Magnusson, p. 136). The diction originated in courtly language before it was
picked up as a way of consolidating bonds
of trust between merchants. Here, Timon
really might confer gentlemanly *honour*
on his creditor, because he is a noble lord;
but neither courtly friendship nor commercial trust operates when the borrower
is bankrupt.
53 **pleasure** oblige. Middletonian, but also at
Merry Wives 1.1.225.
57 **I'll . . . turn** Based on the proverb 'One
good turn deserves another' (Dent T616).
59 **hardly speed** prosper only with difficulty
60–84 FIRST . . . **conscience**   This   choric

episode has sometimes been cut (for
instance, by Bridges-Adams in 1928).
60 **Hostilius** A Roman name; from the Latin
hostis, 'stranger'. Reminiscent of other
emblematic names based on Latin or Italian roots in Middleton, such as Vindice
and Guardiano.
61–3 **Why . . . dish** With possible sexual
quibbles in *piece* and *spirit*, both allusive of
the penis, and *dips in the same dish*
(Gordon Williams, *piece, spirit, dip, dish*).
They unobtrusively suggest that sharing
Timon's food is as incompatible with
friendship as sharing his mistress. Compare the joke about the place at table
marked with the sign of Virgo in *No Wit*
3.78–9, 'Virgo had been a good dish for
you, had not one of my tenants been
somewhat busy with her' (Holdsworth);
also *Five Gallants* 1.1.128–30, 'as in one
pie twenty may dip their sippets, so upon
one woman forty may consume their
patrimonies'. Such implications jostle
against the echo of Christ's Last Supper
and his betrayal by Judas (Matthew 26:
23; see note to l. 63), and the Stranger's
pious tone.
61 **the world's soul** Translates *anima mundi*,
the scholasticists' and Platonists' term for
the animating principle of the world
(*OED*, *soul*, 7c): i.e. the source of its spiritual essence and (for Bruno and others)

Is every flatterer's spirit. Who can call him his friend
That dips in the same dish? For, in my knowing,
Timon has been this lord's father
And kept his credit with his purse,　　　　　　　　　65
Supported his estate; nay, Timon's money
Has paid his men their wages. He ne'er drinks,
But Timon's silver treads upon his lip;
And yet—O see the monstrousness of man
When he looks out in an ungrateful shape!—　　　　70
He does deny him, in respect of his,
What charitable men afford to beggars.

THIRD STRANGER
　　Religion groans at it.

FIRST STRANGER　　　　　For mine own part,
I never tasted Timon in my life,
Nor came any of his bounties over me　　　　　　　75
To mark me for his friend; yet I protest,
For his right noble mind, illustrious virtue,
And honourable carriage,

62 spirit] THEOBALD; sport F　68 treads] F; trades KLEIN *conj.*

the cause of its movement through space.
The Stranger ironizes the term by turning
the cosmological sense of *world* to the
social sense.

61 **just of the same piece** cut from exactly the
same cloth. 'One piece makes several
suits' (*Hengist* 3.3.76); 'there went but a
pair of shears between us' (*Measure*
1.2.27–8); passage attributed to
Middleton).

62 **spirit** Theobald's emendation confirms
the relation between *the world's soul* and
the individual person.

63 **That . . . dish** Recalls Matthew 26: 23,
'He that dippeth his hand with me in the
dish, he shall betray me' (Christ referring
to Judas). Quoted in *Two Gates* xvi.II, with
a cross-reference to Psalms 41: 9, 'Yea,
my familiar friend, whom I trusted, which
did eat of my bread, hath lifted up the heel
against me', and with marginal notes
'Betraying' and 'Whom I vouchsafe to
come to my table' (Holdsworth, 'Biblical
Allusions').

in my knowing to my knowledge

65 **kept his credit** kept him in credit

68 **treads** i.e. presses

69–70 **O . . . shape** Based on the proverb
'Ingratitude is monstrous' (Dent I66.1).
Monstrousness suggests physical as well as
spiritual deformity; hence *shape*.

70 **looks out** shows himself

71 **in respect of his** with respect to his own
possessions (i.e. what came from Timon
himself). 'When the philosopher Diogenes
wanted money, he was wont to say *that he
re-demanded the same of his friends, and not
that he demanded it*' (Montaigne, 'Of
Friendship', in *Essays*, I.204).

73 **Religion groans at it** Middleton personifies
Religion elsewhere, and writes 'How
virtue groans at this' in *Nice Valour*
I.1.245.

74 **tasted Timon** i.e. had experience of
Timon's bounty. The substance of Timon
is his wealth, but *tasted* connects with the
imagery of Christ's sacrifice (l. 63) and
eating (especially l. 68).

75–6 **Nor . . . friend** The image is probably
of a shower, but there may be a sexual
undercurrent, with *come over* 'allusive of
coitus' (Gordon Williams, p. 75), and
friend as 'sexual partner'.

75 **over** down on

78 **carriage** conduct

Had his necessity made use of me
I would have put my wealth into donation   80
And the best half should have returned to him,
So much I love his heart. But I perceive
Men must learn now with pity to dispense,
For policy sits above conscience.   *Exeunt*

Sc. 7   *Enter Timon's Third Servant, with Sempronius,*
         another of Timon's friends

SEMPRONIUS

Must he needs trouble me in't? Hmh! 'Bove all others?
He might have tried Lord Lucius or Lucullus;
And now Ventidius is wealthy too,
Whom he redeemed from prison. All these
Owes their estates unto him.

SERVANT   My lord,   5
They have all been touched and found base metal,
For they have all denied him.

SEMPRONIUS   How, have they denied him?
Has Ventidius and Lucullus denied him,

7.0.1 *Timon's*] CAPELL; *a* F

80 **donation** a deed of gift. Cotgrave, Dictio-
nary (1611), explains French *donation
entre vifs* as 'a deed of gift executed in the
donor's lifetime'. Steevens and Malone
suggested the Stranger offers to consider
his wealth as though it had been a donation *from* Timon; the *best half* can then be
said to be *returned* to Timon even though
the Stranger claims to have received no
actual gift. But *returned* can mean simply
'sent back in response to the request'
without implying the return of a gift, or
'transferred': as Harold Jenkins comments on 'returned' at *Hamlet* 1.1.94 (in
the context of a *moiety*), 'A loose use, not
to be taken as implying that Fortinbras
would have got *back* possessions originally
his' (Arden edn, 1980). The more obvious
meaning of l. 83 can therefore stand.

84 **policy** cynical calculation
   conscience Pronounced as three syllables,
   to complete a rhyming couplet.

Sc. 7 (3.3) Attributed to Middleton.

0.1 **with Sempronius** In this scene the servant and the 'friend' are already in dialogue as the scene begins. Sempronius
was the name of a Roman statesman.

0.2 **another of Timon's friends** Compare
Fair Quarrel 1.1.36.1: '*Enter a "Friend" of
the Colonel's and "another of" Captain
Ager's*' (internal quotation marks added).

3–4 **now . . . prison** Similarly in the comedy
Timon, ll. 1639–40: 'O ye ingrateful, have
I freed thee | From bonds in prison to
requite me thus, | To trample o'er me in
my misery?'

3 **Ventidius** He earlier offered to repay his
debt (2.4–7). Both passages are evidently
by Middleton. Ventidius might count on
Timon's refusal in Sc. 2 and/or smell disaster now (Nuttall, pp. 30–1). A tactical
shift such as this would itself be
Middletonian.

6 **touched** tested for purity. The sense
'tapped for money' was not current.
   base metal OED records this as the earliest
instance of the expression. There are five
comparable instances elsewhere in Middleton (Holdsworth). The earliest would
appear to be the adjectival 'slave to
sixpence, *base-mettled* villain' (1 *Honest
Whore* 8.54); the compound is first
recorded in OED no later than 1683.

And does he send to me? Three? Hmh!
It shows but little love or judgement in him.   10
Must I be his last refuge? His friends, like physicians,
Thrive, give him over; must I take th' cure upon me?
He's much disgraced me in't. I'm angry at him,
That might have known my place. I see no sense for't
But his occasions might have wooed me first,   15
For, in my conscience, I was the first man
That e'er receivèd gift from him.
And does he think so backwardly of me now
That I'll requite it last? No.
So it may prove an argument of laughter   20
To th' rest, and I 'mongst lords be thought a fool.
I'd rather than the worth of thrice the sum
He'd sent to me first, but for my mind's sake.
I'd such a courage to do him good. But now return,
And with their faint reply this answer join: 25
Who bates mine honour shall not know my coin.   *Exit*

12 Thrive] F; Thrice KNIGHT (*conj.* Johnson)   13 He's] F (Has)   21 I 'mongst lords] DELIUS; 'mong'st Lords F1; 'mongst Lords I F2   23 He'd] F (Had)

11–12 **like . . . over** Proverbially, 'Physicians enriched give over their patients' (Dent P274.1; Webster, *Duchess of Malfi* 3.5.7–8.); i.e. abandon them, give up on them. The idiom is cryptically compressed, but the proverbial background makes the meaning clear. *Thrive* must mean 'prosper on his money'. Emendation to 'Thrice' is supported by 'Three' in l. 9, and by Christ's anticipation that Peter would deny him 'thrice' in Matthew 26: 34, as fulfilled in 26: 75. Matthew 26 is a strong influence on Middleton's scenes (Holdsworth, 'Biblical Allusions'). But the parallel is inexact, involving three creditors denying once rather than one three times. In defence of F, compare *Penniless Parliament* ll. 332–5: 'it shall be lawful for bakers to *thrive* by two things . . . *physicians* by other men's harms'.

14 **That** who
  known my place i.e. put me first
14–15 **for't** | **But** for it to be otherwise than that
15 **occasions** See note to 4.186.
15–18 **wooed . . . receivèd,   gift . . . back-** wardly There seems to be a homoerotic undercurrent. *Backward* refers to 'Italian' homosexual acts in *Dissemblers* 1.4.83–5.

18 **backwardly** (a) unfavourably; (b) in a low manner; (c) in reverse order of priority (Crystal). See previous note. The adverb is not elsewhere in pre-1642 drama (*Literature Online*).
20 **argument of** subject-matter for; reason for
21 **'mongst lords** Either 'above all other lords', qualifying 'I', or 'by lords', as predicate to 'thought'. The first reading seems preferable. It is made possible by Delius's emendation of F, as adopted here (see collation), but is excluded by F2's alternative emendation, which places 'I' after ''mongst lords'.
22 **I'd** Either 'I had' or 'I would' (Blake 4.3.7.6.e).
23 **but . . . sake** i.e. if only on account of my good will to him
24 **courage** desire
25 **faint reply** spiritless reply (in contrast with *courage*, l. 24)
26 **bates** abates, undervalues

SERVANT Excellent. Your lordship's a goodly villain. The
devil knew not what he did when he made man politic—
he crossed himself by't, and I cannot think but in the end
the villainies of man will set him clear. How fairly this   30
lord strives to appear foul! Takes virtuous copies to be
wicked, like those that under hot ardent zeal would set
whole realms on fire; of such a nature is his politic love.
This was my lord's best hope. Now all are fled
Save only the gods. Now his friends are dead.   35
Doors that were ne'er acquainted with their wards
Many a bounteous year must be employed
Now to guard sure their master;
And this is all a liberal course allows:
Who cannot keep his wealth must keep his house.   40

Exit

27–33 **Excellent . . . love** Middleton parallels
include *Five Gallants* 4.3.72–6, 'The devil
scarce knew what a portion he gave his
children when he allowed 'em large impu-
dence to live upon and so turned 'em into
th'world. Surely he gave away the third
part of the riches of his kingdom; rev-
enues are but fools to't'; and *No Wit*
9.394–401, 'amorous sparks . . . fire . . .
blaze', 'You knew what you did,
wench, when you', and 'politic love'
(Holdsworth). 'Politic love' is found
nowhere else in pre-1642 literature (*Literature Online*). The passage in *No Wit* also
has an analogue to 'whole realms' in 'any
emperor's court in Christendom'. Compare also 'set whole realms on fire' with
'sets whole hearts on fire', *Dissemblers*
3.1.229, and 'Such as these venom whole
realms', *Meeting of Gallants* ll. 65–6.

28 **politic** cunning in self-interest

29 **crossed himself** (a) thwarted himself, (b)
crossed himself off the list of debtors
(hence *set him clear*, 7.30), (c) made the
Christian sign of the cross

29 **but** but that

30 **set him clear** (a) make him appear innocent, (b) clear his debts. *Him* is evidently
the devil who, as in Jonson's *Devil is an Ass*
(1616), turns out to be a mere innocent as

compared with humanity.

30–1 **How . . . foul** Sempronius uses fair (virtuous) appearances as a means to *be* foul.
The Servant's phrasing is paradoxical,
but *appear* evidently means 'manifest
himself'.

31–2 **Takes . . . wicked** he copies virtuous
behaviour in order to be wicked. *Takes . . .
copies* is literally 'copies out examples of
edifying writing'.

32 **those** i.e. religious fanatics. Often thought
to allude specifically to the 1605 Catholic
Gunpowder Plot to blow up King James in
Parliament. This passage echoes 'the kind
of analogies drawn between the plot and
the ultimate conflagration of the world at
the Last Judgement' (Soellner, p. 204).
under hiding behind; subject to

33 **politic** self-interested and cunning

36 **wards** locks (literally the notched part
that accepts the right key)

37 **Many** for many
bounteous plentiful, prosperous (for the
world at large)

38 **sure** securely

39 **this . . . allows** Paradoxically, liberal conduct has led to stricture. *Liberal* is both
'generous' and 'unconstrained'.

40 **keep . . . keep his house** retain . . . stay
indoors (to avoid arrest for debt)

Sc. 8 *Enter Varro's two Servants, meeting others, all*
         ⌈*Servants of* ⌉ *Timon's creditors, to wait for his coming*
         out. Then enter ⌈*a Servant of* ⌉ *Lucius, Titus, and*
         Hortensius

VARRO'S FIRST SERVANT

  Well met; good morrow, Titus and Hortensius.

TITUS The like to you, kind Varro.

HORTENSIUS

  Lucius, what, do we meet together?

LUCIUS' SERVANT

  Ay, and I think one business does command us all,

  For mine is money.

TITUS   So is theirs and ours.   5

         Enter Philotas

LUCIUS' SERVANT And Sir Philotas too!

PHILOTAS Good day at once.

LUCIUS' SERVANT Welcome, good brother.

  What do you think the hour?

PHILOTAS   Labouring for nine.

LUCIUS' SERVANT

  So much?

8.0.1 *two Servants*] CAPELL; *man* F   0.2 *Servants of*] ROWE; *not in* F   0.3 *a Servant of*] MAL-
ONE; *not in* F   0.3 *Titus,*] ROWE; *not in* F   I FIRST SERVANT] CAPELL; *man* F   4 LUCIUS' SER-
VANT] *Luci.* F. *Similarly throughout the scene*   5.1, 6 *Philotas . . .* Philotas] F (*Philotus . . .*
Philotus)   6 And‸ Sir‸] F; and, sir, OLIVER

Sc. 8 (3.4) Attributed to Middleton. The location returns to Timon's house, or the
entrance to it.

0.1–3 *Servants of . . . a Servant of* See note
to 4.9.1. Titus, Hortensius, and Philotas
(l. 5.1) might similarly be the names of
the servants' masters. But if they are personal names, the men could be, like
Lucius' Servant, in service with the lords
who have refused Timon aid.

  I **Hortensius** The name alludes to a Roman
orator at the time of Cicero who defended
corrupt nobles, including one called
Varro. He is mentioned in Plutarch's 'Life
of Marcus Antonius' and 'Life of Sulla'.
Compare also Hortensio in *Taming of the
Shrew*; similarly, *Lucius* and *Titus* are both
roles in *Titus Andronicus*.

5.1 ***Philotas*** Here and at l. 6 modernized to
the correct spelling from F's '*Philotus*'.
Philotas is a physician in Plutarch's 'Life

of Marcus Antonius' who receives gifts of
silver and gold pots from Mark Antony (p.
981). Another Philotas was topical when
the play was written. Samuel Daniel's
closet tragedy *Philotas* (performance suppressed 1604, published 1605) told of the
torture and execution of Philotas, an
esteemed soldier, for supposedly conniv-
ing with conspirators against Alexander
the Great. Daniel was charged with
covertly defending the rebellion against
Queen Elizabeth by the Earl of Essex (to
whom Middleton had in 1597 dedicated
Solomon Paraphrased). An allusion is possible, though it is hard to calculate its
intent or effect.

  6 **Sir** Perhaps a mock address relating to the
use of masters' names for servants.

  7 **at once** to you all

  9 **Labouring for** going up to. The single,
hour hand laboriously climbs the dial.

PHILOTAS   Is not my lord seen yet?

LUCIUS' SERVANT   Not yet.   10

PHILOTAS

I wonder on't; he was wont to shine at seven.

LUCIUS' SERVANT

Ay, but the days are waxed shorter with him.

You must consider that a prodigal course

Is like the sun's,

But not, like his, recoverable. I fear   15

'Tis deepest winter in Lord Timon's purse; that is,

One may reach deep enough, and yet find little.

PHILOTAS I am of your fear for that.

TITUS

I'll show you how t'observe a strange event.

Your lord sends now for money?

HORTENSIUS   Most true, he does.   20

TITUS

And he wears jewels now of Timon's gift,

For which I wait for money.

HORTENSIUS It is against my heart.

LUCIUS' SERVANT Mark how strange it shows.

---

15 recoverable. I fear₍ₐ₎] JOHNSON; ~, I ~: F

11 **shine** rise (like the sun)
12 **waxed** grown
13–14 **a prodigal . . . sun's** i.e. a spendthrift way of life is like the sun's seasonally declining course; *prodigal course* meaning riotous spending occurs three times in *Bloody Murders*: ll. 147, 160, and 338.
15 **his** its (the sun's)
   recoverable not elsewhere in Middleton or Shakespeare. *OED* defines it as 'capable of being retraced', this line being its only example of this sense. 'Restorable' is more likely. Next year the sun's summer course will be restored or retraced.
16–17 **'Tis . . . little** Plays on *deepest* as referring to (a) the depth of winter, (b) the extent to which the purse is empty. Steevens–Reed plausibly suggested a reference to animals digging through winter snow in search of food.
18 **of your fear** An unusual idiom, varying 'of your mind'.
19 **observe** see and interpret
   a strange event a strange outcome, consequence, eventuality. Following from the

imagery of the sun, this also suggests an unusual astronomical event. Compare *Plato's Cap* ll. 388–9, 'many strange events shall happen and befall this year in those houses where the maid is predominant', where *predominant* plays on the astrological sense.
20–2 **Your . . . wait for money** This absurd picture of the circulation of commodities and money resembles *Five Gallants*: 'Why, this is the right sequence of the world: a lord maintains her, she maintains a knight, he maintains a whore, she maintains a captain. So, in like manner, the pocket keeps my boy, he keeps me, I keep her, she keeps him; it runs like quicksilver from one to another. 'Sfoot, I perceive I have been the chief upholder of this gallant all this while' (3.1.134–41).
24 **how strange it shows** Continues the image of a 'strange event'. The idiom is distinctively Middleton's; compare 'How strange this shows' (*Revenger's* 3.4.43, *Roaring Girl* 8.46; no other examples in the period in *Literature Online*).

Timon in this should pay more than he owes,	25

And e'en as if your lord should wear rich jewels
And send for money for 'em.

HORTENSIUS

I'm weary of this charge, the gods can witness.
I know my lord hath spent of Timon's wealth,
And now ingratitude makes it worse than stealth.   30

VARRO'S FIRST SERVANT

Yes; mine's three thousand crowns. What's yours?

LUCIUS' SERVANT   Five thousand, mine.

VARRO'S FIRST SERVANT

'Tis much deep, and it should seem by th' sum
Your master's confidence was above mine,
Else surely his had equalled.

> *Enter Flaminius*

TITUS   One of Lord Timon's men.

LUCIUS' SERVANT

Flaminius! Sir, a word. Pray, is my lord   35
Ready to come forth?

FLAMINIUS   No, indeed he is not.

TITUS

We attend his lordship. Pray signify so much.

FLAMINIUS

I need not tell him that; he knows you are
Too diligent.   ⌈*Exit*⌉

> *Enter Steward, in a cloak, muffled*

LUCIUS' SERVANT

Ha, is not that his steward muffled so?   40
He goes away in a cloud. Call him, call him.

31, 32 VARRO'S FIRST SERVANT] *Varro*. F   39 *Exit*] STEEVENS; *not in* F

25 **in this** i.e. by owing money to the person who received a gift that was itself paid for with the loan
should has to

26–7 **And e'en . . . 'em** Reminiscent of double con-tricks as in *Mad World*, where Follywit disguises himself as (a) a thief, to rob his grandfather Sir Bounteous, and (b) a lord, to trick Sir Bounteous into compensating him for supposedly having been robbed while Sir Bounteous's guest.

29 **of** some of

30 **stealth** stealing. As in 'close stealths, cun-

ning filches', *Five Gallants* 5.1.15.

32 **much deep** i.e. a very deep debt

37 **attend** wait for expectantly

38 **that; he knows** Hibbard repunctuates 'that he knows.'; i.e. 'you need not tell him what he knows'.

39.1 **in a cloak, muffled** i.e. with his face concealed by his cloak

41 **in a cloud** (a) muffled from sight, (b) in a state of trouble and anxiety. The phrase was proverbial in sense (a), usually indicating secret intrigue or dissimulation (Dent C443.1).

TITUS (*to Steward*) Do you hear, sir?

VARRO'S SECOND SERVANT (*to Steward*) By your leave, sir.

STEWARD   What do ye ask of me, my friend?

TITUS

    We wait for certain money here, sir.

STEWARD   Ay,   45

    If money were as certain as your waiting,

    'Twere sure enough.

    Why then preferred you not your sums and bills

    When your false masters ate of my lord's meat?

    Then they could smile and fawn upon his debts,   50

    And take down th'int'rest into their glutt'nous maws.

    You do yourselves but wrong to stir me up.

    Let me pass quietly.

    Believe't, my lord and I have made an end.

    I have no more to reckon, he to spend.   55

LUCIUS' SERVANT

    Ay, but this answer will not serve.

STEWARD

    If 'twill not serve 'tis not so base as you,

    For you serve knaves.   *Exit*

VARRO'S FIRST SERVANT How? What does his cashiered

    worship mutter?   60

---

43 VARRO'S SECOND SERVANT] F (2. *Varro.*); 1. *Var. Serv.* MALONE; *Both Var. Serv.* DYCE   57 If]
F4; If't FI   58 *Exit*] ROWE; *not in* F   59, 61 VARRO'S FIRST SERVANT . . . VARRO'S SECOND SER-
VANT] F (1.*Varro. . . .* 2.*Varro.*)

45 **certain money** particular sums of money.
In the Steward's reply, *certain* is 'sure,
guaranteed'. If Titus similarly implied
'money we are certain we will get before
leaving', the effect might be menacing
(Klein).

48 **preferred** brought forward

50 **Then** Either 'at that time' (in which case
'his debts' and 'th' int'rest' refer to the
entertainment that gave rise to them) or
'if you had done so' (in which case 'his
debts' and 'th' int'rest' become alternatives to the entertainment).

50–1 **fawn upon . . . glutt'nous maws** Spurgeon (p. 198) notes that this fits with
Shakespearian imagery of dogs. But *gluttonous* is un-Shakespearian and found in
Middleton, for example 'Gluttonous feast'
(*Owl's Almanac* l. 1275, collocated with
'cramming of your guts'); 'gluttonous
surfeits' (*Owl's Almanac* l. 1349, collocated

with 'invest'). The image of financial
interest being greedily devoured echoes
words from a song by Thomas Ravenscroft
that Middleton had recently included in
Trick 4.5.1, 'Let the usurer cram him, in
interest that excel'.

51 **take down** swallow (as in *Weapons*
1.1.244)
maws stomachs

52 **You . . . up** you merely harm yourselves
by provoking me

54 **made an end** settled our affairs, agreed to
part

55 **I . . . spend** With wordplay on *have no
more*: the Steward is *no longer under obligation* to do accounts, Timon *possesses nothing* to spend.

56 **serve** suffice, do. The Steward alters the
meaning to 'act as a servant'.

60 **worship** Used ironically: the Steward no
longer commands deference.

VARRO'S SECOND SERVANT No matter what; he's poor, and
that's revenge enough. Who can speak broader than he
that has no house to put his head in? Such may rail
against great buildings.
    Enter Servilius

TITUS O, here's Servilius. Now we shall know some   65
answer.

SERVILIUS If I might beseech you, gentlemen, to repair some
other hour, I should derive much from't; for, take't of
my soul, my lord leans wondrously to discontent. His
comfortable temper has forsook him. He's much out of   70
health, and keeps his chamber.

LUCIUS' SERVANT
Many do keep their chambers are not sick,
And if it be so far beyond his health
Methinks he should the sooner pay his debts
And make a clear way to the gods.

SERVILIUS   Good gods!   75

TITUS
We cannot take this for answer, sir.

FLAMINIUS ⌈*within*⌉
Servilius, help! My lord, my lord!
    Enter Timon, in a rage

TIMON
What, are my doors opposed against my passage?
Have I been ever free, and must my house

---

76 answer] F; an answer ROWE

---

62 **broader** more freely and contempuously.
As in 'speak out, and e'en proclaim |
With loud words and broad pens'
(*Revenger's* 1.2.9–10).
63 **has no house to put his head in** Proverbial
(Dent H784.1).
64 **great buildings** Alludes to the fashion
amongst the rich of building spectacular
'prodigy houses', as satirized in Jonson's
poem 'To Penshurst'. The phrase occurs
twice in Middleton.
67 **repair** return
68 **derive** gain
   of on
70 **comfortable temper** cheerful disposition
71 **keeps** stays in
72 **Many . . . sick** See note to 7.41.

72 **are** who are
73 **it be** things are (with *it* indefinite). Or
refers to Timon's (in)ability to come out of
his chamber.
75 **clear** (a) unimpeded, (b) innocent. Compare 7.30.
76 **answer** Sometimes emended to 'an
answer', on grounds of metre.
77.1 **in a rage** Of four other instances of this
phrase in stage directions cited by Dessen
and Thomson, two are in Middleton
plays: *Puritan Widow* 3.2.19.1, *Women
Beware* 4.3.0.4.
78 **opposed against my passage** closed to prevent me passing through. *Opposed against*
is Middletonian (*Peacemaker* l. 316).
79 **free** generous (playing on 'at liberty')

Be my retentive enemy, my jail?   80
The place which I have feasted, does it now,
Like all mankind, show me an iron heart?

LUCIUS' SERVANT

Put in now, Titus.

TITUS   My lord, here is my bill.

LUCIUS' SERVANT

Here's mine.

⌈HORTENSIUS⌉   And mine, my lord.

VARRO'S ⌈FIRST *and*⌉ SECOND SERVANTS   And ours, my lord.

PHILOTAS All our bills.   85

TIMON

Knock me down with 'em, cleave me to the girdle.

LUCIUS' SERVANT Alas, my lord.

TIMON Cut my heart in sums.

TITUS Mine fifty talents.

TIMON

Tell out my blood.

LUCIUS' SERVANT   Five thousand crowns, my lord.   90

---

84 HORTENSIUS] CAPELL (*subs.*); I.*Var*. F   84 VARRO'S . . . SERVANTS] CAPELL (*subs.*); 2.*Var*. F

80 **retentive** confining
81 **The place which** Shifting the pronoun from *where* to *which*, Timon speaks of the house as if it were one of his friends.
82 **an iron heart** Proverbially unlikely to melt (Dent H310.1). *Iron* also suggests the bars of a prison, and perhaps contrasts with gold; there may be a suggestion too of the Ovidian Iron Age. *An iron heart* is in Middleton at *Solomon Paraphrased* 13.142.
83 **Put in** i.e. present your bill
83–97 **My lord . . . owes 'em** The contest to present bills echoes *Trick* 4.3.27–36, 48–9, and 60–6. *Cleave*, referring to splitting a person's body, is at *Michaelmas* 1.2.107, 'cleave the heir in twain'; 5.3.92, 'my deeds have cleft me, cleft me'; and *Yorkshire* 4.35, 'Your syllables have cleft me'. 'Cut my heart in pieces' occurs as 'Cut my heart in two pieces' in *Mad World* 2.6.18. Similar jokes about *desperate* debts occur in *Michaelmas* 3.4.166–75 and elsewhere in Middleton (Holdsworth).
84 HORTENSIUS . . . SERVANTS F attributes the first speech to Varro's First Servant and the second to his Second Servant,

but (a) Varro's Servants are presenting the same claim ('And ours, my lord'); (b) Hortensius also evidently presents his bill. The compositor presumably misinterpreted copy in which the prefixes were not clearly marked. Perhaps '1 Var. 2 Varro' was written against the second speech.
85 **bills** notes of debt. But Timon understands the weapon: an axe or blade with a long handle (such as might be used by a prison warder: compare the imprisoning 'iron heart' he imagines his house as having). In *Nice Valour* 4.1.315, 'Welsh bills' plays on *bills* as documents and weapons. There is a similar pun in *Michaelmas*, where 'our *writs*, like wild-fowl, fly abroad, | And then return . . . With clients like dried straws between their *bills*' (1.1.58–60).
88 **Cut my heart in sums** In Lucian, Plutus charges Timon of having 'cut me into a thousand pieces'. Here Timon, as Plutuslike embodiment of wealth, turns Plutus' reproach on to his creditors.
     sums pieces of fixed value; sums of money
90 **Tell** count

TIMON

Five thousand drops pays that. What yours? And yours?

VARRO'S FIRST SERVANT My lord—

VARRO'S SECOND SERVANT My lord—

TIMON Tear me, take me, and the gods fall upon you.   *Exit*

HORTENSIUS Faith, I perceive our masters may throw their   95
caps at their money. These debts may well be called
desperate ones, for a madman owes 'em.   *Exeunt*

Sc. 9   *Enter Timon and Steward*

TIMON They have e'en put my breath from me, the slaves.
Creditors? Devils!

STEWARD My dear lord—

TIMON What if it should be so?

STEWARD My lord—   5

TIMON

I'll have it so. My steward!

STEWARD   Here, my lord.

TIMON

So, fitly! Go bid all my friends again:

94 *Exit*] F (*Exit Timon.*)
  9.0.1 *and Steward*] ROWE (and *Flavius*); *not in* F   7 So, fitly!] F (~ ̩ ~?)

94 **Tear me** This brings Timon's first great
outbreak of rage to its climax. Kean
emphasized the image by tearing open his
vest (and so also anticipated Timon stripping off his clothes in Sc. 12).

95–6 **throw their caps at** A proverbial gesture
expressing the impossibility of catching
up (Dent C62).

97 **desperate** A 'desperate debt' was one that
a creditor had no hope of recovering.
There are several instances of the phrase
in Middleton, including some written earlier than *Timon* (J. C. Maxwell, 'Desperate
Debts', *Notes and Queries*, 212 (1967), p.
141). Timon himself as a *madman* is *desperate* in the sense 'violently reckless'.

Sc. 9 (3.4 continued / 3.5) Attributed to Middleton. The action follows almost straight
on from the previous scene. Many editions continue the same scene, but there
is a cleared stage, and a probable shift
of location from outdoors to indoors, or
from an ante-room to an inner room.
Timon's departure and Hortensius'
speech at the end of Sc. 8 allow the
impression that a brief spell of time has

passed. Now Timon can quickly master
his outward rage.

1 **e'en . . . me** made me utterly breathless;
taken even my breath from me (drawing
on the proverb 'air is free')

2 **Creditors** In view of the riposte 'Devils!',
perhaps *Creditors* plays on the idea that
they are men of *credit* in the sense 'honour, good reputation'.

4 **What . . . so** Timon is pondering the plan
he has devised.

7 **So, fitly!** i.e. 'that's just the way', with
Timon either still thinking about his plan
(compare 'so' in l. 4 and l. 6) or perhaps
responding to the Steward's prompt
answer. Usually printed 'So fitly?' as in F,
which imposes the second interpretation.
A Middleton parallel is 'Mass, fitly' in
Revenger's Tragedy 2.1.54, which supports
the present punctuation, but occurs as a
response to someone entering on cue. For
'fitly' as approval for one's own thoughts
of a fitting revenge, compare *Bloody Banquet* 3.3.57–8, 'Now could I poison him
fitly, aptly, rare. | My vengeance speaks
me happy'.

Lucius, Lucullus, and Sempronius—all luxurs, all.
I'll once more feast the rascals.

STEWARD   O my lord,
You only speak from your distracted soul.   10
There's not so much left to furnish out
A moderate table.

TIMON   Be it not in thy care.
Go, I charge thee, invite them all. Let in the tide
Of knaves once more. My cook and I'll provide.

Exeunt ⌐severally⌐

Sc. 10 *Enter three Senators at one door, Alcibiades meeting
          them, with attendants*

FIRST SENATOR (*to another Senator*)
My lord, you have my voice to't. The fault's bloody.
'Tis necessary he should die.
Nothing emboldens sin so much as mercy.

SECOND SENATOR
Most true; the law shall bruise 'em.

8 all luxurs] OXFORD SHAKESPEARE (*conj.* Fleay); *Vllorxa* F1; *not in* F2; Ventidius WHITE
14.1 *severally*] OXFORD SHAKESPEARE; *not in* F
10.4 SECOND SENATOR] F (2). F *similarly uses a numeral only for the Senators throughout the scene,
except at ll.* 1, 24, 38, *and* 58, *where it is followed by* '*Sen.*' 'em] F; him HANMER

8 **luxurs** debauchees. All three instances in *OED* are from Middleton; compare also the character Lussurioso in *Revenger's*. Compositor B evidently did not recognize this otherwise unexampled word. He took 'All luxors' as 'Vllorxa', and set it in italic as though it were another name.

11 **to furnish out** as to supply

12 **Be . . . care** don't you worry about that

13–14 **the tide | Of knaves** Echoes the 'great flood of visitors' of 1.42. Compare also *Puritan Widow* 1.4.23–4, 'The tide runs to bawds and flatterers' (Holdsworth).

Sc. 10 (3.5 / 3.6) Alcibiades' unexpected appearance before the Senate, like the preceding scenes, is attributed to Middleton, though the germ of the interest in the banishment of the military leader from the city might have come from Shakespeare's reading of Plutarch. The theme of credit and debt in previous scenes is altered to that of obligation in return for service.

0.1–2 *meeting them* Indicates entrance from another door. Alcibiades may not

actually enter until after l. 5. The attendants are evidently Senate officials.

1–3 **My . . . mercy** Holdsworth compares *Revenger's* 2.3.95–100 and notes other Middleton references to sin being bold. The sequence of dialogue is similar to that in a passage in *Measure* attributable to Middleton, where Escalus says, with reference to another prisoner's fate, 'It grieves me for the death of Claudio, | But there's no remedy', acknowledging that 'Pardon is still the nurse of second woe' (2.1.268–75); this scene too takes place in a court-room with the representatives of justice as the speakers. Proverbially, 'Pardon makes offenders' (Dent P50).

1 **voice to't** vote for it
fault crime

3 **emboldens sin** For the collocation, compare *Solomon Paraphrased* 18.118, 'sin-bold'.

4 **bruise** crush, smash, mangle. Occurs in *Solomon Paraphrased* 1.28, referring to God's punishment, and *Measure* 2.1.6, 'bruise to death' (in a scene Middleton

ALCIBIADES

Honour, health, and compassion to the senate!   5

FIRST SENATOR   Now, captain.

ALCIBIADES

I am an humble suitor to your virtues;
For pity is the virtue of the law,
And none but tyrants use it cruelly.
It pleases time and fortune to lie heavy   10
Upon a friend of mine, who in hot blood
Hath stepped into the law, which is past depth
To those that without heed do plunge into't.
He is a man, setting his feat aside,
Of comely virtues;   15
Nor did he soil the fact with cowardice—

14 feat] F (Fate)

elsewhere evidently revised; see note to 10.1–3), referring to the law's punishment.

'**em** Sometimes emended 'him', but ' 'em' seems right as a Middletonian contraction and is an unlikely error for 'him'. The sense 'them' is possible, referring to Alcibiades and his friend (cynically suggesting that Alcibiades' banishment is already determined, which runs against the tenor of the scene) or, more likely, that the Second Senator understands 'sin' as an abstraction for 'sinners'.

5 **Honour, health, and** A 'double trochee' that 'may help to convey anger, scorn, or some other intense emotion' (Wright, p. 198).

6 **Now** Either 'now then' or an expression of surprise at Alcibiades' presumptuous greeting calling for 'compassion'.

7 **your virtues** Slightly but critically ambiguous between 'your virtuous selves' and 'the virtues in you'. Alcibiades goes on to suggest the latter: the senators are virtuous only if they ignore the letter of the law and show pity. But see next note.

8 **virtue** (a) essence, (b) goodness (the latter most clearly bringing out Alcibiades' aggressively conditional use of compliment)

9 **none . . . cruelly** The near-tautology carries the potential for a dangerously subversive accusation.
   it i.e. the law

10–11 **lie heavy | Upon** oppress. Compare

'old age lies heavy on our back' (*Solomon Paraphrased* 2.73).

11 **a friend of mine** This figure does not appear in the play. Commentators have occasionally indicated that he is Timon, a mistake no doubt prompted by an understandable wish to weave up a loose end (and perhaps unconsciously stimulated by the echo of 'Timon' to be found in 'time and' in the previous line). See Introduction, p. 51 and pp. 71–2.

12 **stepped into** Compare 'My ignorance has stepped into some error' (*Dissemblers* 4.3.117), followed by an image of justice as an oppressive weight as in l. 10: 'let me feel my sin | In the full weight of justice' (ll. 119–20). In figurative contexts Shakespeare has *step* with *in*, but not with *into*.
   past depth out of depth (as in water)

14 **feat** deed, crime (perhaps also suggesting *fate*). F's 'Fate' is probably a Middleton spelling of *feat*, which seems to be the main sense. In *Yorkshire* 6.18, 'The Scithians in their marble hearted fates' (original spelling) are said to be responsible for 'deeds' that are 'acted' in 'their relentless natures'; here too the primary sense is *feats* or deeds, with the emphasis on acts of violence. Related in etymology to *fact*, and here virtually identical in sense (see next note).

16 **fact** crime. The usual sense in Middleton; for instance used twice in the trial of Junior for rape in *Revenger's*: 'The fact is great' (1.2.20), 'sparing toward the fact' (1.2.58).

An honour in him which buys out his fault—
But with a noble fury and fair spirit,
Seeing his reputation touched to death,
He did oppose his foe;   20
And with such sober and unnoted passion
He did behave his anger, ere 'twas spent,
As if he had but proved an argument.

FIRST SENATOR

You undergo too strict a paradox,
Striving to make an ugly deed look fair.   25
Your words have took such pains as if they laboured
To bring manslaughter into form, and set quarrelling
Upon the head of valour—which indeed
Is valour misbegot, and came into the world

---

17 An] JOHNSON; And F   22 behave] ROWE; behooue F

17 **An . . . fault** It is characteristic of Middleton's contribution that honour should be seen as having the power to buy.

19 **reputation touched to death** Exactly the same words in a similar context occur in *Yorkshire* at 2.158 (Holdsworth). *Literature Online* identifies no other instance.
touched (a) hit, wounded, (b) infected through contagion, besmirched
to death mortally

21–3 **And . . . argument** This extenuation contrasts with the man's 'hot blood' at l. 11, making it potentially specious (Klein).

21 **sober** Meaning he was not 'drunk with rage' (*Game at Chess* 2.2.152; contrasted with 'Sober sincerity'), or perhaps that he was not literally drunk, or both. The first sense is supported by *OED*, which identifies this line as the earliest example of *sober* as 'free from extravagance or excess' (*a.* 10a).
unnoted inconspicuous, restrained

22 **behave** manage, control. F's 'behooue' is Compositor B's regular spelling of *behove* (five instances, as against none of 'behoue'), so the error is no more than an o/a misreading. Neither Middleton nor Shakespeare uses *behove* with a personal pronoun as subject. The line has a strong parallel in a passage attributed to Dekker in *Bloody Banquet* 1.3.81–2: 'in thy rescue | His noble rage so manfully behaved'. The idea is also in *Solomon Paraphrased*

15.112, 'The foaming anger which his thoughts suppress'.

23 **argument** proposition for formal debate (such as Alcibiades himself is engaged in, as the Senator's reply indicates).

24–5 **You . . . fair** This neatly answers Alcibiades' accusation that the senators risk interpreting the law too strictly. *Too strict a paradox* suggests one so rigorous by the rules of rhetoric that it is absurd to apply it to real life. *Paradox* is not elsewhere in Middleton, but 'What a strange paradox I run into' is collocated with 'hard fate' (see l. 73) in a passage in *Fair Quarrel* attributed to Rowley (2.2.56–8).

24 **undergo** undertake

27 **form** formal acceptance. As in *Phoenix* 12.8–9, 'I'll strive to bring this act into such form | And credit amongst men'. Compare *OED* 15, 'Behaviour according to prescribed or customary rules', though this does not fit these contexts exactly. Other possibly relevant senses are 'beauty, comeliness' (*OED* 1e), 'due shape, good order' (8), and 'according to the rules' (*in form*, 11b). *Bring into form* is not in *OED*. It occurs again in *Phoenix* at 9.161, 'to bring you into form'.

28 **Upon the head** (a) in the category (*OED, head, sb.* 27, citing this line), or (b) as the crowning instance
which i.e. *quarrelling*
indeed in fact

When sects and factions were newly born.   30
He's truly valiant that can wisely suffer
The worst that man can breathe, and make his wrongs
   his outsides,
To wear them like his raiment carelessly,
And ne'er prefer his injuries to his heart
To bring it into danger.   35
If wrongs be evils and enforce us kill,
What folly 'tis to hazard life for ill!

ALCIBIADES
  My lord—

FIRST SENATOR You cannot make gross sins look clear.
  To revenge is no valour, but to bear.

ALCIBIADES
  My lords, then, under favour, pardon me   40
If I speak like a captain.
Why do fond men expose themselves to battle,
And not endure all threats, sleep upon't,
And let the foes quietly cut their throats
Without repugnancy? If there be   45

---

30 **factions** Pronounced as three syllables.

31–5 **He's . . . danger** A Stoic sentiment, as expounded in Seneca, 'On Anger', in *Moral Essays* III.37. Seneca disputes Aristotle's view that anger is necessary to do battle, and compares anger with drunkenness.

32 **breathe** (a) speak, utter; or (b) inhale, take in
outsides outer garments. The plural is not in Shakespeare, but Middleton refers to 'satin outsides' (*Roaring Girl* 10.283), and contrasts 'the outsides of true worth' with 'the mind' (*Lady's* 1.1.177–8).

33 **carelessly** casually

34 **prefer** advance, promote
heart Seen as (a) seat of feelings, (b) the organ (in the centre of the body, in contrast with *outsides*; the vital organ of life).

36 **wrongs** (as suffered)

38 **gross sins** Compare *Dissemblers* 4.3.135–6, 'A sin . . . More gross than flattery'.
gross (a) palpable, obvious, (b) serious
clear innocent. With some suggestion of 'transparent' (i.e. invisible) or 'illustrious', in contrast with *gross*.

39 **revenge** Here stressed on the first syllable.
but to bear i.e. but rather, to endure wrongs is valour (Blake 6.3.4, 'Ellipsis through parallelism'). The rhyme *clear / bear* is Middletonian (*Solomon Paraphrased* 2.77–8).

40 **under favour** by your leave. The exact phrase is not recorded in *OED* before c.1645 (see entry for *regular, a., adv.,* and *sb.,* 2a), but occurs in *Puritan Widow* at 4.2.291 and 5.4.53. The first is Pieboard's address to the Sheriff in a situation comparable with that of Alcibiades. Pieboard intervenes to save the soldier Skirmish as he is led to execution for apparently killing Corporal Oath in a brawl. Also in *Volpone* 5.2.45–6.

42 **fond men** men foolishly

43 **upon't** i.e. when threatened

45 **repugnancy** resistance, fighting back. Not elsewhere in Middleton or Shakespeare. But compare *Solomon Paraphrased* 2.99, 'Repugnant earth, repugnant heaven resist'; *Revenger's* 1.3.100, where Castiza is said to be 'repugnant' to seduction; and *Hamlet* 2.2.474, where Priam's sword is 'Repugnant to command'.

Such valour in the bearing, what make we
Abroad? Why then, women are more valiant
That stay at home if bearing carry it,
And the ass more captain than the lion, the fellow
Loaden with irons wiser than the judge,   50
If wisdom be in suffering. O my lords,
As you are great, be pitifully good.
Who cannot condemn rashness in cold blood?
To kill, I grant, is sin's extremest gust,
But in defence, by mercy, 'tis most just.   55
To be in anger is impiety,
But who is man that is not angry?
Weigh but the crime with this.

SECOND SENATOR   You breathe in vain.

ALCIBIADES   In vain?
His service done at Lacedaemon and Byzantium
Were a sufficient briber for his life.   60

FIRST SENATOR
What's that?

ALCIBIADES   Why, I say, my lords, he's done fair service,
And slain in fight many of your enemies.
How full of valour did he bear himself
In the last conflict, and made plenteous wounds!

49 fellow] F; felon JOHNSON *conj.*   61 Why, I] F2; Why FI; I POPE   he's] F (ha's)

46 **bearing** enduring (of wrongs). Leads on
to quibbles on childbearing and on being
underneath in sexual intercourse (l. 48).
46–7 **what make we | Abroad** what's the
point of us soldiers venturing out
48 **carry it** wins the day (with wordplay on
bearing)
49 **fellow** Johnson's conjecture 'felon' is
plausible but unnecessary.
50 **irons** The sense 'fetters' is not in
Shakespeare, but is found in *Revenger's*
4.2.129 and elsewhere in Middleton.
52 **pitifully good** good by showing pity
53 **condemn . . . blood** in cold blood (with
detached impartiality) condemn a rash
deed
54 **gust** outburst, violent blast (Crystal). As
in 'gust(s) of envy' ('Sun in Aries' l. 57,
and *Honourable Entertainments* 6.64). In
view of the parallels, the alternative
gloss 'relish, taste, inclination' seems less
likely.

55 **by mercy** if seen mercifully (or possibly
'by your merciful leave')
56 **To . . . impiety** Compare note to ll. 31–5.
57 **angry** i.e. subject to anger. Possibly three
syllables: 'angery'.
60 **sufficient** adequate (and specifically as
said of someone with adequate financial
capacity)
briber Found in *Microcynicon* 6.28
(Holdsworth). The line is *OED*'s only
example of sense 5, 'A thing that bribes, a
price paid'.
61 **What's that** The Senator's attention is
roused presumably by the word 'briber'.
Why, I say Holdsworth suggests that F's
apparent omission of 'I' may be right, citing other omissions of nominative pronouns in Middleton. But in those cases
the pronoun can usually be inferred from
its appearance in the preceding lines.
64 **plenteous wounds** Contrast the image of
the 'plenteous bosom' at 2.120–1 and

248

SECOND SENATOR

He has made too much plenty with 'em.   65
He's a sworn rioter; he has a sin
That often drowns him and takes his valour prisoner.
If there were no foes, that were enough
To overcome him. In that beastly fury
He has been known to commit outrages   70
And cherish factions. 'Tis inferred to us
His days are foul and his drink dangerous.

FIRST SENATOR

He dies.

ALCIBIADES Hard fate! He might have died in war.
My lords, if not for any parts in him—
Though his right arm might purchase his own time   75
And be in debt to none—yet, more to move you,
Take my deserts to his and join 'em both.
And for I know
Your reverend ages love security,
I'll pawn my victories, all my honour to you   80
Upon his good returns.
If by this crime he owes the law his life,

---

65 'em] F2; him F1

14.187. *Plenteous* is sufficiently uncommon for the echo to be intentional: in Middleton's and Shakespeare's works it elsewhere occurs more than once in one play only (*Phoenix*, twice). *Plenteous wounds* occurs in *Meeting of Gallants* l. 7. *Literature Online* reveals no other example in the period.

65 **He . . . 'em** i.e. he has made an excess of wounds, not only on the battlefield
with 'em This collocation is much more common in Middleton than Shakespeare, so the attribution of the scene to Middleton happens to support F2's emendation of F1's 'with him'.

66 **rioter** Frequent in Middleton, but not found in Shakespeare (Holdsworth).
a sin i.e. drunkenness (as *drowns* indicates)

71 **cherish factions** encourage factional violence
inferred alleged

73 **Hard fate!** Also as an unqualified interjection at *Chaste Maid* 3.1.19, but not in any idiom in Shakespeare.

74 **parts** (a) good qualities, (b) limbs (the sense taken up in *right arm*, l. 75)

75 **purchase** Introduces a sequence of words and images relating to money: *in debt* (l. 76), *security* (l. 79), *pawn* (l. 80), *returns* (l. 81), *owes* (l. 82).
time natural lifespan

78 **for** because

79 **security** Refers to both financial and military security.

81 **Upon . . . returns** as pledge that he will repay your mercy. Also suggests both reformation and returns from battle. Middleton, but not Shakespeare, uses 'returns' as a noun elsewhere (*Michaelmas* 1.1.56, *Revenger's* 5.1.9, both with wordplay), and writes a parallel phrase in 'upon a good return' (*Weapons* 5.1.141–2).

Why, let the war receive't in valiant gore,
For law is strict, and war is nothing more.

FIRST SENATOR
We are for law; he dies. Urge it no more, 85
On height of our displeasure. Friend or brother,
He forfeits his own blood that spills another.

ALCIBIADES
Must it be so? It must not be.
My lords, I do beseech you know me.

SECOND SENATOR How?

ALCIBIADES
Call me to your remembrances.

THIRD SENATOR What? 90

ALCIBIADES
I cannot think but your age has forgot me.
It could not else be I should prove so base
To sue and be denied such common grace.
My wounds ache at you.

FIRST SENATOR Do you dare our anger?
'Tis in few words, but spacious in effect: 95
We banish thee for ever.

ALCIBIADES Banish me?
Banish your dotage, banish usury
That makes the senate ugly.

---

83 **receive . . . gore** i.e. receive the equivalent to it in the blood of enemies that he will valiantly spill

84 **nothing more** not at all otherwise

86 **On height of our** at risk of our highest

89–94 **My lords . . . ache at you** There are several parallels with *Chaste Maid* 5.1.13–21, especially 'My wound aches at thee', where the parallel is (contrary to Oliver) without any other known example. 'My wounds ache at you' and the riposte 'Do you dare our anger' also echo *Five Gallants* 3.3.7–10, 'my wound ached, and I grew angry' (Holdsworth).

89 **know me** acknowledge my importance and merit

How? Might (a) respond to the defiance of 'It must not be', or (b) ask what he means

by saying 'I beseech you know me' (as Alcibiades' reply suggests). Alcibiades' reference to the senators' age in l. 91 suggests that 'How?' and 'What?' might be effects of senility: they fail to understand, or are inattentive, or are deaf.

91 **but your age has** but that in your old age you have

92 **else** otherwise

93 **To** as to
grace With religious connotation. 'Law was a curst judge and ready to condemn. But the King of heaven being as full of mercy as of justice, abated the edge of the axe, and to a heavy sentence added a comfortable pardon. The balsamum of grace healed the wounds of the law' (*Two Gates*, Preface 77–81).

FIRST SENATOR

  If after two days' shine Athens contain thee,
  Attend our weightier judgement; and, not to swell our
     spirit,   100
  He shall be executed presently.   *Exeunt all but Alcibiades*

ALCIBIADES

  Now the gods keep you old enough that you may live
  Only in bone, that none may look on you!
  I'm worse than mad. I have kept back their foes
  While they have told their money and let out   105
  Their coin upon large interest, I myself
  Rich only in large hurts. All those for this?
  Is this the balsam that the usuring senate
  Pours into captains' wounds? Banishment!
  It comes not ill; I hate not to be banished.   110
  It is a cause worthy my spleen and fury,
  That I may strike at Athens. I'll cheer up
  My discontented troops, and lay for hearts.

---

100 our] F; your CAPELL   101 *all but Alcibiades*] CAPELL (*subs.*); *not in* F   113 lay] F; play JOHNSON *conj.*

---

99 **shine** sunshine. *OED* does not record this sense (*sb.* 3) before 1622. Compare *No Wit*, 'How soon the comfortable shine of joy | Breaks through a cloud of grief!' Alcibiades is denied such comfort.

100 **Attend** expect
  not to swell to avoid swelling. Perhaps suggests a swelling sore that is lanced by the execution.
  our The emendation 'your' is plausible, but the Senator may be warning of the senate's swelling indignation against Alcibiades.
  spirit hostility, anger, rage (Crystal; only instance in the Shakespeare canon of this sense)

101 **presently** immediately

102 **keep you old enough** i.e. keep you alive until you are so old

102–3 **live . . . bone** i.e. be mere living skeletons (too ugly to be looked at)

105 **they** i.e. the senators
  told counted
  let out in contrast with 'kept back', l. 104.

108 **balsam** balm, a resinous ointment used as an antiseptic and to heal wounds. In Shakespeare only once, in the trisyllabic form 'balsamum' (*Comedy of Errors* 4.1.89). In *Phoenix* 5.1.317 Middleton writes of pouring *balsam* 'into this thirsty vein'. For balsam(um) as mercy (alluding to its symbolic use in Christian ritual), see note to 'grace', l. 93.
  usuring Middletonian

111 **worthy** befitting

113 **lay** Johnson's suggestion of 'play' is plausible, but 'lay' can be supported. Oliver explains as 'waylay, set an ambush' (*OED v.*[1] 18b). Perhaps instead simply 'make arrangements' (*v.*[1] 38c). In either case there is a pun on the sense 'wager' (*v.*[1] 12). This gives further puns on *hearts* as (a) men of courage, (b) the suit in cards; and on *at odds* as (a) in conflict, (b) at odds in the gambling sense. Malone compared *Lust's Dominion*, in Thomas Dekker, *Dramatic Works*, ed. F. Bowers, vol. iv (1976), 2.2.102–3: 'He *takes up* Spanish *hearts* on trust, to pay them | When he shall finger Castile's crown'.

'Tis honour with most lands to be at odds.
Soldiers should brook as little wrongs as gods.   *Exit*   115

Sc. 11   *Enter diverse of Timon's friends, ⌈amongst them
Lucullus, Lucius, Sempronius, and other Lords and
Senators,⌉ at several doors*
FIRST SENATOR   The good time of day to you, sir.
SECOND SENATOR   I also wish it to you. I think this
honourable lord did but try us this other day.

---

114 most] F; worst HIBBARD
11.0.1 *of Timon's*] HINMAN (*subs.*); *not in* F   0.1–3 *amongst . . . Senators*] SISSON (*subs., also
including Ventidius*); *not in* F   1 FIRST SENATOR] F (1). *Similarly formatted as a numeral without a
name for all the Senators in Sc.* 11.

---

114 **'Tis . . . odds** Presumably, the greater
the enemy the greater the honour. Malone conjectured that 'lands' should read
'lords'. Hibbard emends 'most' to 'worst'.
115 **brook** endure
Sc. 11 (3.6 / 3.7) This structurally central
scene is evidently of mixed authorship.
There is a similar mock-banquet in the
anonymous *Timon* (see note to l. 84.2).
Shakespeare clearly drafted the central
section of the mock-grace. Middleton
supplied, probably subsequently, an
opening to link up with the previous
action dealing with the creditors, and finished the scene, concluding this strand in
the plot and providing a break between
Timon's enraged exit and his entry in Sc.
12 outside the walls of Athens. The section predominantly by Shakespeare might
begin at l. 25 or l. 38, and probably ends
with Timon's exit at l. 104; within it, Middleton may have contributed a passage
around ll. 64–8.
0.1 *Enter* Some editors follow Capell in pre-
scribing music here instead of at l. 24.1.
0.1 *diverse* various
0.2 **Lucullus, Lucius, Sempronius** These are
not named in the scene in F, but are the
'friends' who are going to be invited at
9.8. Some editors (such as Sisson and Hibbard) introduce the names into speech-
prefixes. It makes sense in terms of both
cogency of plot and economy in the use of
actors for the named figures to be the
First, Second, and Third Lords of Sc. 1 and
Sc. 2, and the equivalent senators subsequently. But it is hard to tell which is
which. The Second Senator's excuse that
'my provision was out' at 11.15–16 recalls

Lucius' excuse at 6.44–6; and Lucius is
indeed the second lord whom Timon's
servants approach. However, the First
Senator's claim that Timon's request was
for 'a thousand pieces' does not match
the loan requested of Lucullus, the
lord/senator in the first of these scenes.
The First Senator may, then, be Sempronius. But the identities are insecure and
probably had not been determined—compare note to 2.126—and Ventidius might
also be present. See also following note.
1 FIRST SENATOR The stage directions in F call
for '*Friends*' at the beginning of the scene
and '*the Senators, with other Lords*' when
they re-enter after l. 104; it is '*the Senators*' who leave at the end of the scene.
The overlap between 'friends', 'lords', and
'senators' is also found in Sc. 2, where the
speech-prefixes are for '*Lord*'. This is
also the usual and least confusing way of
expanding the plain numerals for speech-
prefixes in Sc. 11. However, identifying
them as senators in this scene establishes
greater consistency with the stage directions in Sc. 11, and with the stage directions and speech-prefixes for senators in
all scenes with unnamed dignitaries after
Sc. 2. By this arrangement, Sc. 10 and Sc.
11 show the two main protagonists in
confrontation with the same group as
they defy Athens and prepare to leave it.
However, a different theatrical logic
would suggest that the senators might be
predominantly old and at least some
of Timon's friends more young and
attractive.
good time of day A greeting (as also at
Richard III 1.1.123 and 1.3.18).

FIRST SENATOR Upon that were my thoughts tiring when we
    encountered. I hope it is not so low with him as he made   5
    it seem in the trial of his several friends.
SECOND SENATOR It should not be, by the persuasion of his
    new feasting.
FIRST SENATOR I should think so. He hath sent me an
    earnest inviting, which many my near occasions did urge   10
    me to put off, but he hath conjured me beyond them, and
    I must needs appear.
SECOND SENATOR In like manner was I in debt to my
    importunate business, but he would not hear my excuse.
    I am sorry when he sent to borrow of me that my   15
    provision was out.
FIRST SENATOR I am sick of that grief too, as I understand
    how all things go.
SECOND SENATOR Every man here's so. What would he have
    borrowed of you?   20
FIRST SENATOR A thousand pieces.
SECOND SENATOR A thousand pieces?
FIRST SENATOR What of you?
SECOND SENATOR He sent to me, sir—
        Loud music
    Here he comes.   25
        Enter Timon and attendants
TIMON With all my heart, gentlemen both; and how fare you?

---

19 here's] F (heares)   24.1 *Loud music*] CAPELL ('*Flourish*' *before entry at l.* 25.1); *not in* F

4 **tiring** exhausting themselves. Perhaps
because the Senator is old. As of thoughts
also in *Phoenix* 12.18: 'tire my inven-
tions'. The alternative is 'feeding', said
especially of a bird of prey tearing flesh,
as in *Venus and Adonis* l. 56, but there is
nothing in the context to support this
metaphor. *OED* explains as 'exercising
themselves', inconclusively citing only
Cymbeline 3.4.94, which is also ambiguous. Middleton nowhere has the present participle, except adjectivally in
'tiring-house'.
6 **several** various
9 **I should think so** (agreeing with the
Second Senator)
10 **which** (the object of *urge*)
    many my my many

10 **near occasions** pressing engagements
11–12 **conjured . . . appear** Compare 1.7 and
note.
13 **in debt** i.e. obliged, committed
16 **out** i.e. exhausted (or 'out on loan')
17 **grief** (a) illness, (b) offence, (c) sorrow
17–18 **as . . . go** considering how I now
understand everything to be working out
(assuming that Timon was merely testing
his friends). The phrase is slippery, almost
suggesting 'because I understand the
plight of those who have lost everything'.
19 **here's** Modernized from F's 'heares'.
Some editors print 'hears'.
21 **pieces** gold coins
26 **With all my heart** The greeting is perhaps
in response to the First and Second
Senators bowing.

FIRST SENATOR Ever at the best, hearing well of your lordship.

SECOND SENATOR The swallow follows not summer more
willing than we your lordship.

TIMON (*aside*) Nor more willingly leaves winter, such   30
summer birds are men.—Gentlemen, our dinner will not
recompense this long stay. Feast your ears with the music
a while, if they will fare so harshly o'th' trumpets' sound;
we shall to't presently.

FIRST SENATOR I hope it remains not unkindly with your   35
lordship that I returned you an empty messenger.

TIMON O sir, let it not trouble you.

SECOND SENATOR My noble lord—

TIMON Ah my good friend, what cheer?

The banquet brought in

SECOND SENATOR My most honourable lord, I am e'en sick of 40
shame that, when your lordship this other day sent to
me, I was so unfortunate a beggar.

TIMON Think not on't, sir.

SECOND SENATOR If you had sent but two hours before—

TIMON Let it not cumber your better remembrance.—   45
Come, bring in all together.

Enter Servants with covered dishes

46.1 *Enter . . . dishes*] OXFORD SHAKESPEARE; *not in* F; F's *direction at l.* 39.1 *moved here* DYCE

27 **hearing** as we are when we hear
28–31 **The . . . men** Proverbially, 'Swallows,
like false friends, fly away upon the
approach of winter' (Dent S1026; see also
1.102–3).
33 **harshly** Quibbles on *harsh* as referring to
the sound of trumpets and to the taste of
food (hence 'Feast' and 'fare'). '[S]o
harshly' is in *Hamlet* 3.1.3; 'harshly' is
not in Middleton.
34 **to't presently** very shortly begin eating
35–6 **it . . . that** your lordship doesn't still
regard it as *unkindly* towards you that.
With this interpretation, *unkindly* means
'unnatural with respect to our relationship', euphemistic for 'treacherous',
'malicious'. This is consistent with
Women Beware 1.2.197, 'And could you
deal so unkindly with my heart'. May also
suggest 'your lordship doesn't still feel
unkindly because'. The syntax conflates
'remains with your lordship' and
'unkindly with your lordship'. This line is

OED's only example of *remain* meaning
'to stick in the mind' (*v.* 6b).
36 **returned you** sent you back
39 **what cheer**? How are you? The question is
presumably pointed, in that the Senator
is shamefaced rather than cheerful. By
dramatic irony the words also cue the
preparations for the banquet; compare
the comment on the banquet as 'Royal
cheer' at l. 48. The Senator's response
that he is '*sick* of shame' brings together
the connotations of shame, ill health, and
ill-fittedness for festive eating.
39.1 *The banquet brought in* Editors often
relocate this direction to after l. 46, but it
may indicate a table with place-settings,
etc., ready for the dishes themselves, and
stools.
40 **e'en** utterly
42 **a beggar** i.e. someone more fit to beg himself than be asked for money
45 **cumber . . . remembrance** trouble your
memory of better things

SECOND SENATOR All covered dishes.

FIRST SENATOR Royal cheer, I warrant you.

THIRD SENATOR Doubt not that, if money and the season
    can yield it.   50

FIRST SENATOR How do you? What's the news?

THIRD SENATOR Alcibiades is banished. Hear you of it?

FIRST *and* SECOND SENATORS Alcibiades banished?

THIRD SENATOR 'Tis so, be sure of it.

FIRST SENATOR How, how?   55

SECOND SENATOR I pray you, upon what?

TIMON My worthy friends, will you draw near?

THIRD SENATOR I'll tell you more anon. Here's a noble feast
    toward.

SECOND SENATOR This is the old man still.   60

THIRD SENATOR Will't hold, will't hold?

SECOND SENATOR It does; but time will—and so—

THIRD SENATOR I do conceive.

TIMON Each man to his stool with that spur as he would to
    the lip of his mistress. Your diet shall be in all places alike.   65
    Make not a City feast of it, to let the meat cool ere we can
    agree upon the first place. Sit, sit.
        They sit

67.1 *They sit*] OXFORD SHAKESPEARE; *not in* F

47 **covered dishes** The covers keep the con-
tents hot and, as the First Senator's
response suggests, create anticipation of
a spectacular display of extravagant
foods. The entry of servants carrying
'covered dishes', and the phrase itself, are
found in *Mad World* 2.1.167.1.

48 **Royal** Perhaps recalls the ethos of the
royal sport of hunting in Sc. 2.
    cheer entertainment, fare

49–50 **if . . . it** if money can buy it and if
it's in season. There may be a hint that
the feast will be the fruit of an unnatural sexual union between money and
nature.

59 **toward** about to take place

60 **the old man** the man we know of old

61 **hold** continue, prove true

62 **time   will**—Perhaps   intimating   the
proverb 'time will tell truth'.

63 **conceive** understand

64 **stool** Even in wealthy households, stools

or benches were usual for guests to sit on.
A chair was given only to the most important people.

64 **spur** urgent speed, eagerness (as when
a horse is spurred). Middleton repeatedly   associates   spurs   with   sexual
excitation.

65 **Your . . . alike** you'll have the same food
no matter where you sit. Timon observes
no discriminations by social rank or
degree of favour. It would be common for
low-ranking guests to be given poorer fare
at the foot of the table. Timon's guests are
perhaps ambitious not only to feed well
but also to sit near him as a mark of his
favour to them.

66 **City feast** feast given by dignitaries of the
City of London. The phrase puts London
and the play's Athens into equivalence.

66–7 **to . . . place** Implies both that social
precedence is contested in the City and
that all matters are subject to debate.

The gods require our thanks:

> You great benefactors, sprinkle our society with
> thankfulness. For your own gifts make yourselves   70
> praised; but reserve still to give, lest your deities be
> despised. Lend to each man enough that one need not
> lend to another; for were your godheads to borrow of
> men, men would forsake the gods. Make the meat be
> beloved more than the man that gives it. Let no   75
> assembly of twenty be without a score of villains. If
> there sit twelve women at the table, let a dozen of them
> be as they are. The rest of your foes, O gods—the
> senators of Athens, together with the common tag of
> people—what is amiss in them, you gods, make   80
> suitable for destruction. For these my present friends,
> as they are to me nothing, so in nothing bless them;
> and to nothing are they welcome.—

---

78 foes] WARBURTON; *Fees* F   79 tag] COLLIER 1853 (*anon. conj. in* Rann); *legge* F; lag ROWE

68 **The . . . thanks** Following Shakespeare's earlier editors, this edition preserves F's setting of these words on a separate type-line, which suggests a formal induction to the prayer.

69–98 **You great . . . o'er** Holdsworth identifies a cluster of Shakespearian diction here: 'reserve still to give', 'common tag of people', 'mouth-friends', 'trencher-friends', 'cap-and-knee slaves', 'minute jacks', 'Crust'. There is also a hint of the Shakespeare image cluster associating flattery with the licking of a dog (compare note to 14.253–71).

69–83 **You . . . welcome** Timon's grace is printed in italics in F, suggesting a set piece. The indentation in this edition preserves the effect.

69–71 **sprinkle . . . praised** Both petitions equivocate between imploring the grace to acknowledge the gods' gifts and petitioning for the gifts themselves. Both imply that the gods virtually have to thank themselves, especially as *sprinkle* in context suggests a sacrificial ceremony of thanks to the gods, and in terms of Christian ritual invokes the sprinkling of water to symbolize cleansing and blessing in the Catholic mass.

69 **society** social gathering

71 **reserve still** always hold something back
to give Either (a) to give at a later date, or

(b) in giving.

74 **forsake** (a) refuse, (b) renounce

77 **twelve . . . table** Another variant of the Last Supper theme?

78 **be as they are** i.e. be no better than women generally are. Or 'avoid pretending to be better than they are'. Probably based on proverbial 'Be it as it is' (Dent B112.1).
foes F's '*Fees*' makes very strained sense as 'tenanted property'; the Riverside gloss extending this sense, 'those holding their lives in fee from you', is not supported by *OED*. A single-letter misreading is more likely.

79 **tag** rabble. As in *Coriolanus* 3.1.246–7, 'Will you hence | Before the tag return', which supports the emendation of F's '*legge*'. Most earlier editors from Rowe emended to 'lag', which *OED* glosses 'The lowest class' (*sb.* 1, 3), but there is no other known example of such a sense, and Shakespeare nowhere uses *lag* as a noun.

81 **suitable** Used in the familiar modern sense; *OED* cites this line as the earliest instance of it (*a.* 3).
present friends Puns on 'present-friends', friends for the sake of presents.

82–3 **to nothing . . . welcome** They are (a) not welcome to anything, and (b) welcome to the nothingness in the dishes.

Uncover, dogs, and lap.

> *The dishes are uncovered, and seen to be full of steaming*
> *water ⌈and stones⌉*

SOME SENATORS What does his lordship mean?   85
SOME OTHER SENATORS I know not.

TIMON

May you a better feast never behold,
You knot of mouth-friends. Smoke and lukewarm water
Is your perfection. This is Timon's last,
Who, stuck and spangled with your flatteries,   90
Washes it off, and sprinkles in your faces
Your reeking villainy.

> ⌈*He throws water in their faces*⌉
>   Live loathed and long,
Most smiling, smooth, detested parasites,

84.1–2 *The . . . water*] JOHNSON (*subs.*); *not in* F   84.2 *and stones*] STEEVENS *conj.*; *not in* F
85–6 SOME SENATORS . . . SOME OTHER SENATORS] F (*Some speake. . . . Some other.*)   90 with
your] WARBURTON; you with F   flatteries] F; flattery DYCE (*conj.* W. S. Walker)   92 *He . . .
faces*] JOHNSON (*subs.*); *not in* F

84 **dogs** The word repeatedly associated
with Apemantus as snarler is here applied to those whom he attacked as
flatterers. See W. Empson, *The Structure of
Complex Words* (1952), pp. 175–84, and
Spurgeon.

84.2 *stones* Stone-throwing at l. 99 is highly
probable in view of the comment at l. 114.
It imitates in parody the custom of show-
ering guests with sweetmeats (Bradbrook,
p. 14). Lucian's Timon threatens his visitors with stones, and later says he will
'lay as many stones as I can on heaps
together, and dung amongst them as
thick as hail'. In the comedy *Timon*,
Timon throws stones painted as imitation
artichokes. More elemental stones and
water can be seen as equivalent to the
bread and wine of the Communion.
Christ's first miracle was to turn water to
wine, and in the desert Satan tempted
Christ to 'command this stone that it be
made bread' (John 2: 1–11; Luke 4: 3).

88 **knot** group, band
mouth-friends (a) friends in lip-service
only, (b) friends when it comes to eating.
The line supplies *OED*'s only example of
the word, but compare Shakespearian
compounds such as *mouth-honour*
(*Macbeth* 5.3.29); also *trencher-friends*

(l. 95), which affirms the idea of friends
eating food.

88 **Smoke** steam (characteristically insubstantial and diffusing to nothing). *Smoke*
is also 'mere talk'.
lukewarm Klein finds an allusion to Reve-
lation 3: 16, 'because thou art lukewarm
. . . I will spew thee out of my mouth'.

89 **perfection** (a) finishing touch, (b) perfect
representation. No doubt with ironic
echoes of the word as used in the Book of
Job as an attribute of God, and in side-
notes to the Geneva Bible as the state
towards which the Christian life leads; for
instance to 1 Thessalonians 3: 12: 'the
perfection of a Christian life consisteth in
two things, to wit, in charity toward all
men, and inward purity of the heart'. See
also 2.81–4 n.
last Evidently alludes to the Last Supper of
Christ.

90 **stuck and spangled** Both verbs apply to
fixing jewels or ornaments. *Spangles* were
sequins.
flatteries F's plural conflicts with 'it' in
l. 91, but is consistent with 'stuck and
spangled' in suggesting a metaphor of
plural glittering ornaments.

92 **reeking** (a) steaming, (b) stinking
93 **smooth** oily, ingratiating

257

Courteous destroyers, affable wolves, meek bears,
You fools of fortune, trencher-friends, time's flies,   95
Cap-and-knee slaves, vapours, and minute-jacks!
Of man and beast the infinite malady
Crust you quite o'er.
  ⌈*A Senator is going*⌉
       What, dost thou go?
Soft, take thy physic first. Thou too, and thou.
  ⌈*He throws stones at them*⌉
Stay, I will lend thee money, borrow none.   100
    Exeunt Senators, leaving caps and gowns
What, all in motion? Henceforth be no feast
Whereat a villain's not a welcome guest.
Burn house! Sink Athens! Henceforth hated be
Of Timon man and all humanity!   *Exit*
  Enter the Senators with other Lords
FIRST SENATOR How now, my lords?   105

98 *A Senator is going*] OXFORD SHAKESPEARE (*subs.*); *not in* F 99.1 *He . . . them*] HINMAN
(*subs.*); *not in* F; *Throwing the Dishes at them* ROWE 100.1 *Exeunt Senators*] ROWE (*drives 'em
out*); *not in* F *leaving caps and gowns*] OXFORD SHAKESPEARE; *not in* F

95 **fools** dupes, playthings. *Fools of fortune*
was proberbial (Dent F617.1).
 trencher-friends, time's flies Echoes
Robert Greene, *Never Too Late*, in *Life and
Complete Works*, ed. A. B. Grosart, 15 vols.
(1885–96), viii. 130: 'time-pleasers and
trencher-friends'.
 trencher-friends friends in feasting,
parasites
 flies (only about in fair weather, and
attracted to food)
96 **Cap-and-knee** cap-doffing and knee-
bending; bowing and scraping
 vapours insubstantial things
 minute-jacks over-punctilious time-
servers. *OED*'s only example of the word.
Compare *Richard III* telling Buckingham
that 'like a jack, thou keep'st the stroke |
Betwixt thy begging and my meditation'
(*Richard III* 4.2.117–18). The *jack* was the
mechanical human figure that struck the
bell on medieval clocks—normally every
hour or quarter-hour rather than every
minute. As in *Richard III*, *jack* is also
'knave'.
97–8 **Of . . . o'er** Compare this and 'general
leprosy' at 12.30 with *Hamlet* 1.5.64–72,

where 'leperous distilment' leads to 'the
vile and loathsome crust'.
98 **Crust** (as with a scab)
 quite o'er all over
99 **Soft** wait
 physic medicine
104 **man and all humanity** Apparently
recognizes the ambiguity of *man* as either
'humanity' or only the male members of
it.
 Exit Here Kelvin Han Yee as Timon pulled
down purple curtains to reveal the bare
brick wall of the theatre, making a strong
transition from Athens to the woods and
effectively anticipating 'O thou wall . . .'
at 12.1 (Thick Description company, San
Francisco, 1993).
104.1–11.114 *Enter . . . stones* Loosely based
on the comedy *Timon*, where the guests
say: 'O my head!', 'O my cheek!', 'Is this a
feast?', 'Truly, a stony one'. Phelps cut
this passage, to sustain the momentum
of Timon's fury into the next scene.
Schlesinger made it a a highly comic coda
to the first part of the play, resuming the
action with Timon's soliloquy in Sc. 12
after the interval.

SECOND SENATOR

Know you the quality of Lord Timon's fury?

THIRD SENATOR

Push! Did you see my cap?

FOURTH SENATOR   I have lost my gown.

FIRST SENATOR He's but a mad lord, and naught but
  humours sways him. He gave me a jewel th'other day,
  and now he has beat it out of my hat.   110

  Did you see my jewel?

THIRD SENATOR   Did you see my cap?

SECOND SENATOR

Here 'tis.

FOURTH SENATOR Here lies my gown.

FIRST SENATOR   Let's make no stay.

SECOND SENATOR

Lord Timon's mad.

THIRD SENATOR   I feel't upon my bones.

FOURTH SENATOR

One day he gives us diamonds, next day stones.

                                              Exeunt

Sc. 12 *Enter Timon*

TIMON

Let me look back upon thee. O thou wall
That girdles in those wolves, dive in the earth,

106 the] rhe F   111–12 THIRD SENATOR . . . SECOND SENATOR] CAPELL (3 *L<ord>*. . . . 2 *L<ord>*.);
2 . . . 3 F   114.1 *Exeunt*] F (*Exeunt the Senators.*)

106 **quality** nature
107 **Push!** A strong exclamation characteristic of Middleton.
108 **but a mad lord** a completely mad lord
109 **humours** extremes of temperament, wild fancies
110–11 **hat . . . cap** Anchronistic for ancient Greece.
111–12 THIRD . . . SECOND Capell's reversal of F's speech-prefixes, accepted here, makes it the Third Senator who has lost his cap, as at l. 107, giving a logical and comic repetition. The labelling of anonymous senators, etc., often seems to have been casual or even careless.
113 **upon my bones** A literalizing alteration of *in my bones*, 'intuitively'.

Sc. 12 (4.1) The important transition of Timon leaving Athens, consisting entirely of Timon's first tirade against the city and humanity, is strongly Shakespearian. It anticipates Shakespeare's command over the rest of the play—with the exception of the episodes with the Steward. In most modern productions an interval usually falls immediately before or after this scene.
1 **wall** The city wall of Athens. City walls were conventionally represented by the tiring-house wall at the rear of the stage. Timon would have entered through a door in it.
2 **That . . . wolves** Paradoxical: city walls were usually thought to keep wild beasts

And fence not Athens! Matrons, turn incontinent!
Obedience fail in children! Slaves and fools,
Pluck the grave wrinkled senate from the bench   5
And minister in their steads! To general filths
Convert o'th' instant, green virginity!
Do't in your parents' eyes. Bankrupts, hold fast!
Rather than render back, out with your knives,
And cut your trusters' throats. Bound servants, steal!   10
Large-handed robbers your grave masters are,
And pill by law. Maid, to thy master's bed!
Thy mistress is o'th' brothel. Son of sixteen,
Pluck the lined crutch from thy old limping sire;
With it beat out his brains! Piety and fear,   15
Religion to the gods, peace, justice, truth,
Domestic awe, night rest, and neighbourhood,

12.6 steads! . . . filths‸] CAPELL; ~, . . . ~. F   13 Son] F2; Some F1

out, separating civic society from the world of savage nature. The line would have offered the actor in the Jacobean public theatre an opportunity to invoke the galleries of spectators within the theatre walls, which would have extended from the tiring-house wall. This would make a theatrical point of the paradox: the audience is at once with Timon outside the walls of Athens and enclosed by the theatre walls, perhaps implicated as 'wolves'.

2 **That girdles** It is probably the relative construction that causes the verb to shift from second person ('girdlest') to the third person, as in *Julius Caesar* 3.1.30, 'Casca, you are the first that rears your hand'. Alternatively, the final 't' may be missing for reasons of euphony.
   wolves Also said of Timon's false friends in Lucian.
   dive *OED*'s latest example of sense 2, 'To sink deeply . . . to penetrate into any body'.

3 **Matrons** married women (as bearers of female dignity)
   incontinent sexually unrestrained

4 **Obedience fail** Probably a subjunctive ('let obedience fail . . .'), in contrast with the probable imperatives in the surrounding lines addressed to the people concerned. (As an imperative, 'fail to obey' could be fulfilled only through obedience.) But the

distinction is far from clear-cut: Timon *might* be saying 'let matrons turn incontinent', etc., or commanding personified Obedience to fail in children.
   fools idiots

5 **the bench** the bench-seats in Senate (hence the place and office of the Senate)

6 **minister** execute their duties
   steads places
   general common, publicly available
   filths filthy whores

7 **green** i.e. fresh, young, innocent

8 **Do't . . . eyes** i.e. copulate in front of your parents
   hold fast i.e. refuse to repay

10 **Bound** i.e. under a binding contract to serve, indentured

11 **Large-handed** grasping, rapacious. This line provides *OED*'s one instance of the sense, and the earliest instance of any sense.

12 **pill** plunder

13 **Thy . . . brothel** Implies either that marriage is a form of prostitution, or that the wife is unfaithful or, as at 14.113–15, 'a bawd'.

14 **lined** padded

15 **fear** reverential dread

17 **Domestic awe** reverential obedience in the home
   night rest security and calm at night (also 'sleep')
   neighbourhood neighbourliness

Instruction, manners, mysteries, and trades,
Degrees, observances, customs, and laws,
Decline to your confounding contraries,   20
And yet confusion live! Plagues incident to men,
Your potent and infectious fevers heap
On Athens, ripe for stroke! Thou cold sciatica,
Cripple our senators, that their limbs may halt
As lamely as their manners! Lust and liberty,   25
Creep in the minds and marrows of our youth,
That 'gainst the stream of virtue they may strive
And drown themselves in riot! Itches, blains,
Sow all th'Athenian bosoms, and their crop
Be general leprosy! Breath infect breath,   30
That their society, as their friendship, may
Be merely poison!
          ⌈*He tears off his clothes*⌉
                    Nothing I'll bear from thee
But nakedness, thou detestable town;

---

21 yet] F; let HANMER (*similarly* Shadwell)   32 *He tears off his clothes*] BEVINGTON (*subs.*); *not in* F

18 **Instruction** directions, orders (i.e. lines of social authority); authoritative teaching
   manners Primarily 'customary ways of doing things'; also 'polite behaviour, civilities'.
   mysteries skills of crafts and professions; i.e. knowledge perpetuated and kept under control by the system of trade guilds.
   trades occupations with trade guilds
19 **Degrees** social ranks
   observances following of customary rules and duties
20 **Decline** sink. Perhaps alludes to the sun, whose setting causes darkness.
   confounding self-destroying
21 **yet** still. Timon wishes confusion itself to remain active despite its own effects of general death and destruction, which might otherwise lead to a cessation of all things. Hanmer's emendation 'let' might be right, but is not strongly justified.
   confusion ruin, destruction. The first of four occurrences in this sense.
   incident to apt to fall on
23 **for stroke** to be struck
24 **halt** limp

25 **liberty** licentiousness, wild behaviour
26 **marrows** Proverbially 'burnt' or 'melted' by lust.
27 **'gainst . . . strive** From Ecclesiasticus 4: 28 (Bishops'), 'strive thou not against the stream, but for righteousness take pains . . .'. Proverbial (Dent S927).
28 **riot** debauchery (and perhaps, in the metaphor, tumult or turbulence caused by opposing the *stream of water*)
   blains sores, blisters
29 **Sow** sow yourselves in, scatter through
   bosoms The image is of sowing as in the 'bosom' of the earth. Contrast 14.187.
31 **their society** i.e. the company of Athenians; associating with them
32 **merely** unadulterated
   He . . . clothes This would be theatrically straightforward and effective if Timon were wearing a gown in classical Greek style.
   thee In line with this strikingly contemptuous use of the singular form of pronoun for the city, Timon demotes Athens to a 'detestable town' (l. 33).
33 **detestable** The stress falls on the first and third syllables.

Take thou that too, with multiplying bans.
Timon will to the woods, where he shall find   35
Th'unkindest beast more kinder than mankind.
The gods confound—hear me you good gods all—
Th'Athenians, both within and out that wall;
And grant, as Timon grows, his hate may grow
To the whole race of mankind, high and low.   40
Amen.   *Exit*

Sc. 13 *Enter Steward, with two or three Servants*
FIRST SERVANT

Hear you, master steward, where's our master?
Are we undone, cast off, nothing remaining?
STEWARD

Alack, my fellows, what should I say to you?
Let me be recorded: by the righteous gods,
I am as poor as you.
FIRST SERVANT   Such a house broke,   5

13.1 FIRST SERVANT] F (1). *Similarly formatted as a numeral without a name for all the Servants in* Sc. 13.

34 **Take thou that too** Timon probably throws a garment back through the stage door where he entered. Or *that* may be nakedness itself.
bans curses
36, 39–40 **Th' . . . mankind, And . . . low** The account of Timon in Painter's *Palace of Pleasure* is titled 'Of the strange and beastly nature of Timon of Athens, enemy to mankind'.
36 **kinder than mankind** Plays on *kind* as 'caring, affectionate' and 'showing kinship'.
37 **confound** destroy
38 **out** without. The Athenians in question would be those dwelling in the suburbs, or travellers from Athens such as Timon will encounter. In either case, this extension of his curse undermines the opposition between walled city and woods, and anticipates 'the whole race of mankind'.
39 **grows . . . grow** lives, grows older . . . expand, extend
41 **Amen** This suggests that Timon's delivery of ll. 37–41 assumes a ritualistic gesture of prayer. See note to 14.449.
Sc. **13 (4.2)** Servants were dependent for housing and food as well as income, so

dismissal could leave them destitute. Holdsworth suggests that Middleton may have written ll. 1–29, but the language has Shakespearian features such as the noun *deck* and the verb to *leak*; see also notes to l. 2 and l. 17. Perhaps Middleton added touches. The rest of the scene is probably by Middleton.
2 **undone . . . remaining** Echoes in figurative terms Timon's divestment in the previous scene. For the phrasing, compare *King John* 5.7.35, 'Dead, forsook, cast off'.
undone (a) ruined, (b) unbuttoned
cast off (a) dismissed, ejected; (b) taken off (as of a garment)
5–6, 16 **Such . . . fall'n, STEWARD . . . house** Possibly added by Middleton. Compare 'You are true and necessary implements of mischief' (*Mad World* 1.1.62–3); *house* follows at l. 66. Shakespeare never uses *implements* of people, nor qualifies the word adjectivally. Nor does he refer to a house as breaking or broken, but Middleton has 'To break up house' (*Revenger's* 2.1.183) and 'Our house commonly breaks' (*Weapons* 3.1.43).
5 **house** household
broke broken up; bankrupt

So noble a master fall'n? All gone, and not
One friend to take his fortune by the arm
And go along with him?

SECOND SERVANT   As we do turn our backs
From our companion thrown into his grave,
So his familiars to his buried fortunes   10
Slink all away, leave their false vows with him
Like empty purses picked; and his poor self,
A dedicated beggar to the air,
With his disease of all-shunned poverty,
Walks like contempt alone. More of our fellows.   15

Enter other Servants

STEWARD
All broken implements of a ruined house.

THIRD SERVANT
Yet do our hearts wear Timon's livery.
That see I by our faces. We are fellows still,
Serving alike in sorrow. Leaked is our barque,
And we, poor mates, stand on the dying deck   20
Hearing the surges threat. We must all part
Into this sea of air.

STEWARD   Good fellows all,
The latest of my wealth I'll share amongst you.
Wherever we shall meet, for Timon's sake
Let's yet be fellows; let's shake our heads and say,   25
As 'twere a knell unto our master's fortunes,

---

7 **his fortune** i.e. him in his misfortune
10 **his familiars to** Shifts from 'his intimate friends' to 'those familiar with'.
   buried fortunes Timon's *fortunes* as 'luck' are figuratively *buried*. But it was his material *fortunes* that his friends were familiar with. The idea of buried treasure is developed in the next scene.
12 **picked** from which the money has been stolen
13 **dedicated beggar to the air** i.e. beggar dedicated to life in the open air
15 **contempt** i.e. the personification of those subject to contempt
17 **Yet . . . livery** Compare 'Lover's Complaint' l. 195, 'Kept hearts in liveries'.
18 **fellows** comrades

19 **Leaked** This line provides *OED*'s earliest example of *leak* as 'To have sprung a leak' (*v.* 3).
   barque boat
20 **mates** (a) subordinate naval officers (the full expression was *master's mate*), (b) fellows
   dying i.e. sinking
21 **threat** threaten. Alternatively, 'the surges' threat', the threat of the surges.
   part (a) separate, (b) die
22 **this sea of air** For the servants, the open air of homelessness is as dangerous as the sea into which the ship sinks. Their ship was Timon's house.
23 **latest** last

'We have seen better days.'
>   *He gives them money*
>   Let each take some.
Nay, put out all your hands. Not one word more.
Thus part we rich in sorrow, parting poor.
>   *Embrace, and the Servants part several ways*
O, the fierce wretchedness that glory brings us!   30
Who would not wish to be from wealth exempt,
Since riches point to misery and contempt?
Who would be so mocked with glory as to live
But in a dream of friendship,
To have his pomp and all what state compounds   35
But only painted, like his varnished friends?
Poor honest lord, brought low by his own heart,
Undone by goodness! Strange, unusual blood
When man's worst sin is he does too much good!
Who then dares to be half so kind again?   40
For bounty, that makes gods, does still mar men.
My dearest lord, blessed to be most accursed,
Rich only to be wretched, thy great fortunes
Are made thy chief afflictions. Alas, kind lord!
He's flung in rage from this ingrateful seat   45
Of monstrous friends;
Nor has he with him to supply his life,

---

27 *He gives them money*] ROWE (*subs.*); *not in* F   29.1 *the Servants*] CAMBRIDGE (*before 'embrace'*); *not in* F   33 as to] ROWE; or to F; or so STAUNTON (*conj.* White)   41 does] F4; do F1   47 has] F (ha's)

---

27 **We have seen better days** Proverbial (Dent
D121.2); appropriate to the funeral of a
master.
28 **put out all** all put out
29 **part** There may be a suggestion of the
sense 'share'.
30 **fierce** violent, excessive
32 **point** lead
33 **as to** See collation. In the text as emended,
the idiom 'be so . . . as to . . .' is Middletonian: *Hengist* 4.2.150–51, *Old Law*
3.1.332.
34 **But in a dream** in a mere dream
35 **what state compounds** that goes into the
making of worldly splendour. *What* is
'that which'. *OED*'s earliest example of
obsolete *compound*, *v.* 5, 'To make up,
constitute, or compose, as ingredients or

elements do'.
36 **But only painted** existing only as a
painted image
    varnished glossily painted; implying
'specious, pretended'
38 **blood** temperament; passion. Steevens
compares *Yorkshire* 4.62, ' 'tis our blood to
love what we're forbidden'.
40 **again** a second time
41 **bounty . . . men** i.e. bounty is a defining
attribute of gods, but ruins humans
42 **to be** only to be
45 **He's flung** Probably 'he has flung
himself'.
45–6 **ingrateful . . . monstrous** Compare
6.69–70 and note.
45 **seat** centre, stronghold
47 **to** i.e. that with which to

Or that which can command it.
I'll follow and enquire him out.
I'll ever serve his mind with my best will.   50
Whilst I have gold I'll be his steward still.   *Exit*

Sc. 14   *Enter Timon in the woods, ⌜half naked, and with a spade⌝*

TIMON

O blessèd breeding sun, draw from the earth
Rotten humidity; below thy sister's orb

14.0.1 *half naked, and*] OXFORD SHAKESPEARE; *not in* F   0.1–2 *with a spade*] BEVINGTON; *not in* F

48 **command it** i.e. ensure the necessities life are obtained (referring to money)

50 **serve his mind** be obedient to his wishes. Similarly *Lady's* 4.1.57, 'serve his mind all his life after'.

Sc. 14 (4.3–5.2) Swinburne described this scene as 'the dark divine service of a darker Commination Day': *Study of Shakespeare* (1880), p. 215. It is mostly by Shakespeare. Middleton clearly added the Steward episode (ll. 457.1–536.1); perhaps also a short passage at ll. 66–9 (see also notes to l. 9 and ll. 151–3). He probably transcribed and/or added touches to the Poet and Painter episode (see note to ll. 536.2–650.1), and perhaps, with less intervention, to the Thieves and Apemantus passages (see Appendix C for Middleton forms). Another possible short addition is at ll. 721–3.
    The sustained episodic structure based on a series of visits to a virtually static main character is without close parallel. For discussion of scene division, see note to l. 536.1, and Introduction, pp. 9–11.

0.1 *Enter Timon* Later in the scene he retreats to and re-enters from his cave. He might enter from it here. A cave might have been represented naturalistically as a stage property, or conventionally by a door in the rear stage wall, or a curtain in front of a door, or the trap in the stage floor. The trap would (a) allow the cave and the hole where Timon finds gold to be the same place; (b) enable Timon to guard his gold when he retreats to his cave; (c) place him downstage relative to the Poet and Painter when he comments to the audience at 14.565–89. Dessen and Thomson cite stage directions in which a character ascends from or descends into

a cave, suggesting use of the trap. But a property, door, or curtain to the rear of the stage is perhaps more likely: see note to 16.0.2.

0.1 *in the woods* Stage trees were sometimes used, though rarely to represent extensive woods or forests. A stage tree, however, would equate with Timon's 'tree which grows here in my close' (l. 740). Use of the property has sometimes reminded modern audiences of the tree in Beckett's *Waiting for Godot*.

1–23 **O . . . mankind** A speech of difficult meaning and puzzling transitions, with textual cruxes. The example of the twinned brothers shows nature corrupted by 'several fortunes'. Humanity's susceptibility to circumstance and lack of intrinsic virtue show the 'villainy' that makes human nature 'cursèd'. That in turn justifies Timon's opening call on the sun to breed poisonous infection instead of things beneficial and 'blessèd'. The wished-for distortion of the sun's 'breeding' connects with the distortion of the 'procreation, residence, and birth' of the brothers. There may be a submerged pun between 'sun' and 'son'. In the comedy *Timon*, Timon has a speech to the sun as Titan beginning l. 1857.

1 **blessèd breeding sun** Compare *Rape of Lucrece* l. 1837, 'By heaven's fair sun that breeds the fat earth's store'. Timon negates such ideas. *Breeding* can apply also to the belief that 'the sun breeds maggots in a dead dog' (*Hamlet* 2.2.183). Here the sun breeds infection.

2 **Rotten** putrid
    below . . . orb i.e. throughout the corruptible part of creation. *Thy sister* is the moon, for in classical mythology the

Infect the air. Twinned brothers of one womb,
Whose procreation, residence, and birth
Scarce is divident, touch them with several fortunes,   5
The greater scorns the lesser. Not nature,
To whom all sores lay siege, can bear great fortune
But by contempt of nature.
Raise me this beggar and deject that lord,
The senator shall bear contempt hereditary,   10

9–13 Raise . . . lean.] F (*but see following notes*); It . . . lean. | Raise . . . honour. OXFORD
SHAKESPEARE   9 deject] HUDSON (*conj.* Arrowsmith); deny't F; denude THEOBALD; demit
OXFORD SHAKESPEARE (*conj.* Staunton)   10 senator] ROWE; Senators F

goddess of the moon, Diana, was sister to
the god of the sun, Apollo. Her sphere or
orbit (*orb*) was supposed to divide the
mutable world from the heavens.

3–6 **Twinned . . . lesser** Montaigne cites
Plutarch's example of the man who said
of his brother 'I care not a straw the more
for him, though he came out of the same
womb as I did'. Montaigne notes that 'this
commixture, dividence, and sharing of
goods, this joining of wealth to wealth,
and that the riches of one shall be the
poverty of the other, doth exceedingly dis-
tract all brotherly alliance and lovely conjunction' ('Of Friendship', in *Essays*, I.
197). *Divident* (l. 5) strongly suggests that
Timon's lines are a harsh variant of this
passage.

3 **Twinned** twin. *OED*'s earliest instance
of the adjective. Shakespeare used it
again in *Winter's Tale* ('twinned lambs',
1.2.69) and *Cymbeline* ('twinned stones',
1.6.36).

4 **residence** i.e. period of gestation in the
womb. Not a usual sense of the word.

5 **divident** divisible; i.e. distinguishable. A
rare word. The passage is *OED*'s only
example of this sense (*adj.* 2: 'Divided,
separate'), and the earlier of its two
examples of the adjective. See note to ll.
3–6.
   touch them if they are touched
   several different

6–7 **Not nature . . . can bear** it is not in
human nature to bear. The following
notes take human nature as the referent,
but there is probably also a wider glance
at things in the natural world and at
nature itself.

7 **To whom** i.e. to humanity in its raw,
natural condition

8 **nature** i.e. (a) the natural human state,
devoid of the benefits of *great fortune*; (b)
kinship and familial origins, a person's
own kind

9 **Raise me** promote, elevate. The mood
is subjunctive, equivalent to 'if you
raise'. *Me* is redundant except as a
mark of emotional investment in what
is said.
   deject cast down from high estate. Emendation of F's 'deny't' is necessary because
denying advancement to a lord does not
make him subject to the 'contempt'
directed at the poor. Arrowsmith supported 'deject' by citing Middleton examples of a contrast between *raise* and *deject*
in the sense required here. *Deject* is also
used by Shakespeare, though not in the
same sense. It seems preferable to *demit*,
which neither author uses, even though
the latter gives an easier misreading.
Arrowsmith's Middleton parallels occur
in works written in the same period as
Timon ('I both deject my foe, and raise my
state', *Trick* 2.2.80; 'Would I be poor,
dejected, scorned of greatness . . . No, I
would raise my state', *Revenger's*
2.1.90–4; see also *Revenger's* 1.1.124–6,
'deject him . . . mount'). Middleton may
have added the single verse-line or less, in
which case it may have replaced something illegible or otherwise unsatisfactory
in Shakespeare's draft.

10 **The senator** i.e. the man formerly a senator; the 'lord' of l. 9. Rowe emended to the
singular, in line with the exemplary
nature of the figures in this passage.
   bear endure
   hereditary as if he were born to it. Similarly *native*, l. 11. Social rank is radically
unstable, but the attitude of mind still
assumes a fixed social hierarchy.

The beggar native honour.
It is the pasture lards the beggar's sides,
The want that makes him lean. Who dares, who dares
In purity of manhood, stand upright
And say 'This man's a flatterer'? If one be,   15
So are they all, for every grece of fortune
Is smoothed by that below. The learnèd pate
Ducks to the golden fool. All's obliquy;
There's nothing level in our cursèd natures
But direct villainy. Therefore be abhorred   20
All feasts, societies, and throngs of men.
His semblable, yea, himself, Timon disdains.

---

12 beggar's] ROWE; Brothers F; Weather's WARBURTON   13 lean] F3 (leane); leaue FI
15 say] F2; fay FI   18 obliquy] F (obliquie); Obloquy ROWE; oblique POPE

---

12 **It . . . sides** Compare *As You Like It* 3.2.27:
'good pasture makes fat sheep'.
  pasture feeding, sustenance (as of live-stock).
  lards that fattens
  beggar's F reads 'Brothers'. Timon takes
two instances of 'divident' fortune: (a)
the twin brothers who have contrasting
fortunes (ll. 3–6), (b) the lord and beggar
whose fortunes are reversed (ll. 9–13). I
previously argued for dislocation in the
order of the lines (*Textual Companion*,
p. 505), but the difficulty can be narrowed
to F's 'Brothers' in this line. This reverts
to the first example (twin brothers) where
it should more logically expound the
second. A repeat of the key word in the
parable of reversed fortune, 'beggar's',
seems required. As the passage is sket-
chily written, the error could derive from
Shakespeare's hand. But, as it provided
the compositor with difficult copy (hence
four other editorial emendations in six
lines), 'Brother's' could equally be a
misreading.
13 **him** i.e. the other one (the former lord)
  lean The emendation of F's 'leaue' establishes the antithesis, and is generally
accepted. A simple u/n error in F.
13–15 **Who . . . flatterer** Suggests that the
accuser's integrity would be sullied by his
partiality in singling out any one person.
14 **In . . . upright** A potentially phallic
image, but the contrast (or the lack of it)
between man and beast is more to the
point.
16 **grece** a step in a flight of stairs; here, more

specifically, those standing on the step.
17 **smoothed** (a) made smooth and easy,
(b) flattered
17–18 **The . . . fool** Compare Sir Thomas
More, *Utopia*, in *Complete Works*, vol. iv,
ed. Edward Surtz and J. H. Hexter (1965),
p. 157: 'a blockhead, who has no more
intelligence than a log and who is as dishonest as he is foolish, keeps in bondage
many wise men and good men merely for
the reason that a great heap of gold coins
happens to be his'.
17 **pate** head (as both seat of intellect and the
part of the body that bows)
18 **golden** Suggests both wealth and the
figure of an idol.
  obliquy deviousness; lack of straightforward or *level* dealing. A trisyllabic variant
of *obliquity*. *OED* identifies no other example of the word. It occurs in Thomas
Thomas's *Dictionarium Linguae Latinae et
Anglicanae* (1588?; 7th edn. 1606) under
Traduco–'infamie and obliquie'—but this
may be a misprint for 'obloquie' (abuse,
verbal detraction), as Rowe conjectured
here. Whereas the context in Thomas
supports emendation, Rowe's reading
loses the consistency with 'nothing level'.
Obliquy might work as a portmanteau
or suggest 'obloquy' through wordplay.
Pope's emendation 'oblique' (supported
by *OED*) produces a metrical irregularity
he resolved by expanding 'All's' to 'All is';
this seems a weak normalization of F.
20 **direct** downright; straight, 'level'
22 **His semblable** anything that resembles
him

Destruction fang mankind. Earth, yield me roots.
   He digs
Who seeks for better of thee, sauce his palate
With thy most operant poison.
   He finds gold

                 What is here?   25
Gold? Yellow, glittering, precious gold?
No, gods, I am no idle votarist:
Roots, you clear heavens. Thus much of this will make
Black white, foul fair, wrong right,
Base noble, old young, coward valiant.   30
Ha, you gods! Why this, what, this, you gods? Why, this
Will lug your priests and servants from your sides,

23.1 *He digs*] ROWE; *not in* F   25 *He finds gold*] BEVINGTON; *not in* F

23 **fang** seize with fangs. The image of a beast (a dog?) leads on to the contrasting idea of a diet that avoids savagery.
   roots As food, roots would usually be root vegetables such as turnips or parsnips. Timon might refer to wild roots such as the edible tuber pignut (*Conopodium majus*), or to the wild parsnip (*Pastinaca sativa*), which John Gerard's *Herbal* (1597) calls 'not fit to be eaten', or to even less nutritious tree-roots.

23.1 *He digs* The opened trapdoor in the middle of the stage would probably be used.

24–8 **Who . . . heavens** Timon's prayer is answered, though against his intention and ironically. Compare Bassanio's description of 'gaudy gold' as 'Hard food for Midas' (*Merchant of Venice* 3.2.101–2). Timon's self-abasement is rewarded with riches. It is he, not those who seek for wealth, who gets gold, the earth's most operant poison. The irony depends on biblical teachings, particularly 'the desire of money is the *root* of all evil, which while some lusted after they erred from the faith and pierced themselves with many sorrows' (1 Timothy 6: 10).

24 **of** from

25 **operant** potent

25 *He finds gold* Though not in F, a stage direction with these words appears at the equivalent place in the comedy *Timon*.

26 **Gold . . . gold** Wright (p. 178) cites this as an example of lines whose metre has 'an extraordinary expressive force' and that

'appear to have gone beyond iambic pentameter to become accentual five-stress lines' (p. 178). There are missing unstressed syllables before 'Gold' and 'Yellow'; 'glittering' is pronounced as two syllables. Compare *Macbeth* 2.2.17, beginning with Lady Macbeth's 'Ay.' and continuing with Macbeth's 'Hark!—Who lies i'th' second chamber?'

27–8 **No . . . heavens** Presumably a petition that the gold should not be gold after all.

27 **idle** ineffective; insincere. Perhaps plays on *idol*.
   votarist one bound by vow to a religious way of life

28 **Roots . . . heavens** This parallels the moment in Kyd's *Spanish Tragedy* where Hieronimo implores the 'sacred heavens' to give him justice for his son's murder; his prayer is answered by an 'unexpected miracle' when a letter identifying the murderers falls from above (3.2.1–2). The heavens in *Spanish Tragedy* are ruled by the spirit of revenge. The 'clear heavens' in *Timon* answer the prayer for edible roots by providing money, the root of evil.
   clear innocent, blameless. With reference to the skies, unclouded. And so, transparent in their dealings.

28–44 **Thus . . . nations** Compare Jonson, *Volpone* 1.1.22–4: 'Riches, the dumb god, that . . . mak'st men do all things; | The price of souls'.

28–9 **make | Black white** Proverbial (Dent B440).

Pluck stout men's pillows from below their heads.
This yellow slave
Will knit and break religions, bless th'accursed,   35
Make the hoar leprosy adored, place thieves,
And give them title, knee, and approbation
With senators on the bench. This is it
That makes the wappered widow wed again.
She whom the spittle house and ulcerous sores   40
Would cast the gorge at, this embalms and spices
To th' April day again. Come, damned earth,
Thou common whore of mankind, that puts odds
Among the rout of nations; I will make thee

39 wappered] SINGER 1856 (*conj.* Malone); wappen'd F

33 **Pluck . . . heads** Compare Jonson, *Volpone* 2.6.87–8: ''Tis but to pluck the pillow from his head, | And he is throttled'. In Jonson the victim is supposedly sick rather than *stout* ('robust'). Here the implication is perhaps 'kill even stout men easily'.

36 **hoar** Refers to the pale greyish colour of leprous skin. The bitter assonance with *adored* is all the more effective after *abhorred*, l. 20. The word *whore* seems to lurk in the background. Timon almost immediately turns to women's sexual activity (ll. 38–42). *Whore* itself comes into the open—applying to the earth itself as source of the gold—at l. 43.

36 **leprosy** Long thought to be a punishment for promiscuity, as when Pistol calls Doll Tearsheet 'the lazar [leper] kite of Cressid's kind' in *Henry V* 2.1.74.
place thieves appoint thieves to office

37 **knee** the right to be knelt to

39 **wappered** sexually worn-out. F's 'wappen'd' is not otherwise known. *Wappered* is also extremely rare, known in the period only through 'unwappered' in a scene in *Two Noble Kinsmen* attributed to Shakespeare ('we come towards the gods | Young and unwappered, not halting under crimes | Many and stale', 5.6.9–11). From this context, *unwappered* would appear to mean 'fresh, innocent'. The general sense of *wappered*, as in 19th century use, is 'fatigued, wearied'.

40 **She** This turns out to be the object of 'embalms and spices'.
the . . . sores i.e. those in hospital and

with ulcerous sores (the whole for the parts, followed by the metonymic parts for the whole)

41 **cast the gorge** vomit
embalms and spices Balm is an aromatic ointment that might be thought to restore the body from sexual disease (or at least give it a medicinal fragrance), and spices were also used as cosmetic perfumes.

42 **damned earth** i.e. the gold, so described for the sinfulness Timon attributes to it, and also because it dwells buried under the ground, suggesting the traditional location of hell. F's monosyllable 'damn'd' indicates a missing syllable at the caesura, an acceptable licence of metre emphasizing the starkness of damnation.

43 **common whore** Alters the traditional figure of the earth as a common (general, universal) mother (as at l. 178), debasing the connotations of *common*. *Whore* is appropriate as a reference to *earth* as mother earth, and so land, in that land can be bought and sold, reflecting a real or imagined debasement of land as a result of its increasing treatment as a commodity in the period. But this *whore* is more specifically the gold Timon has unearthed. Whether as land or gold, she is seen as a woman who provokes warfare and is sexually available to the victor. The depiction of the earth as whore anticipates the arrival of the whores Timandra and Phrynia with Alcibiades.
puts odds creates conflict

44 **rout** rabble

Do thy right nature.
> *March afar off*
>   Ha, a drum! Thou'rt quick;   45
But yet I'll bury thee.
> *He buries gold*
>   Thou'lt go, strong thief,
When gouty keepers of thee cannot stand.
> *He keeps some gold*
Nay, stay thou out for earnest.
> *Enter Alcibiades, with ⌈soldiers marching to⌉ drum and*
> *fife, in warlike manner; and Phrynia and Timandra*

ALCIBIADES   What art thou there? Speak.

TIMON

A beast, as thou art. The canker gnaw thy heart
For showing me again the eyes of man.   50

ALCIBIADES

What is thy name? Is man so hateful to thee
That art thyself a man?

TIMON

I am Misanthropos, and hate mankind.

45 Thou'rt] F (Th'art)   46 *He buries gold*] BEVINGTON; *not in* F   Thou'lt] F (Thou't)   47.1 *He keeps some gold*] POPE (*subs.*); *not in* F   48.1 *soldiers marching to*] POPE (*subs.*); *not in* F

45 **Thou'rt quick** Lucian's Timon similarly
describes the sudden arrival of visitors
after he finds gold as 'quick work'.
  quick sudden (to bring about strife). Also,
punningly, 'alive', anticipating *bury*.
46 **go** walk on, keep going
47 **keepers** (a) owners, (b) jailers
48 **for earnest** as a pledge for the rest
48 *soldiers* Not specified in F, but the drum
implies soldiers representative of an army
marching to the beat. See Introduction,
pp. 115–16.
  drum and fife Instruments associated
with soldiers. The effect here would be all
the more impressive because there has
been little music in the preceding
episodes.
  fife Shrill wind instrument played like a
flute.
  Phrynia and Timandra See note to l. 80.
Timandra is mentioned in Plutarch (see
Introduction, p. 18). Phrynia is based on
Phryne, 'an Athenian courtesan so
exquisitely beautiful that when her judges
were proceeding to condemn her for
numerous and enormous offences, a sight

of her bosom (which as we learn from
Quintilian, had been artfully denuded by
her advocate) disarmed the court of its
severity, and secured her life from the sentence of the law' (Steevens, elaborating
on Quintilian, *Institutio oratoria* II.xv.9).

49 **A beast** 'Whosoever is delighted in solitude is either a wild beast or a god':
Francis Bacon, 'Of Friendship', quoting
Aristotle, *Politics*, in *Essays*, ed. John
Pitcher (1985), p. 138. The essay is not in
the 1597 edition. In the 1598 English
edition with commentary of *Politics*, 'wild
beast' is 'wicked wretch'.
  canker canker-worm (with the heart seen
as a flower-bud); or 'cancer'
53 **Misanthropos** Greek for 'man-hater'. The
italicization in F is no more than usual for
proper names. From Plutarch's marginal
note in 'Life of Antony' (see Appendix B),
and 'Life of Alcibiades', p. 218: 'Timon
surnamed Misanthropus, as who would
say Loupgarou [literally, 'werewolf' or
'wild wolf'], or the man-hater'. There is
no earlier known example of the word
'misanthrope' in English, which is why

For thy part, I do wish thou wert a dog,
That I might love thee something.

ALCIBIADES   I know thee well,   55
But in thy fortunes am unlearned and strange.

TIMON

I know thee too, and more than that I know thee
I not desire to know. Follow thy drum.
With man's blood paint the ground gules, gules.
Religious canons, civil laws, are cruel;   60
Then what should war be? This fell whore of thine
Hath in her more destruction than thy sword,
For all her cherubin look.

PHRYNIA   Thy lips rot off!

TIMON

I will not kiss thee; then the rot returns
To thine own lips again.   65

ALCIBIADES

How came the noble Timon to this change?

TIMON

As the moon does by wanting light to give.
But then renew I could not like the moon;
There were no suns to borrow of.

ALCIBIADES

Noble Timon, what friendship may I do thee?   70

'Misanthropos' is explained in the second half of the line.

55 **something** somewhat
56 **But . . . strange** Contrast ll. 92–5.
    strange unacquainted
58 **not** do not
59 **gules** Heraldic term for red.
61 **fell** dreadful, savage
62 **destruction** Both physical (disease) and moral (damnation).
63 **Thy lips rot off** Alludes to an effect of syphilis.
64–5 **I . . . again** Timon implies that Phrynia's curse could only be fulfilled by his kissing her (perhaps so that she would pass her disease to him to be cured herself, as was thought possible). As he refuses to do so, he claims that the curse of rotten lips recoils back to the lips of the speaker. Compare *Richard III* 1.3.238, 'Thus have

you breathed your curse against yourself'.
66–9 **How . . . borrow of** Capell described this passage as 'A most exalted conception, rising by just degrees, and in the end over-whelming us; for who can read the hemistich [the short l. 69 suggesting a universal depletion of light] and not be lost in astonishment?' (in Vickers, ed., *Critical Heritage*, vi. 244). Middleton may have been responsible. Holdsworth cites a number of parallels. For instance, Tailby in *Five Gallants*, when asked, 'How cheer you, sir?', replies 'Faith, like the moon, more bright; | Decreased in body, but remade in light' (2.1.297–8). Tailby's brightness is his newly-acquired money. Alcibiades' apparent ignorance of Timon's fortune here, partly contradicted in the following lines, is significant for the role and the plot; see Introduction, pp. 71–2.

TIMON None but to maintain my opinion.

ALCIBIADES What is it, Timon?

TIMON Promise me friendship, but perform none. If thou
wilt promise, the gods plague thee, for thou art a man. If
thou dost not perform, confound thee, for thou art a man.   75

ALCIBIADES

I have heard in some sort of thy miseries.

TIMON

Thou saw'st them when I had prosperity.

ALCIBIADES

I see them now; then was a blessèd time.

TIMON

As thine is now, held with a brace of harlots.

TIMANDRA

Is this th'Athenian minion, whom the world   80
Voiced so regardfully?

TIMON   Art thou Timandra?

TIMANDRA Yes.

TIMON

Be a whore still. They love thee not that use thee.
Give them diseases, leaving with thee their lust.
Make use of thy salt hours: season the slaves   85

74–5 promise . . . not perform] HIBBARD; not promise . . . performe F

---

73 **Promise . . . perform** From the proverb
'to promise much and perform little'
(Dent P602). As Hibbard first realized,
Alcibiades needs to promise but not perform in order to fulfil Timon's expectation
and receive his curses; hence the transposition of 'not', which F prints before
'promise'.

76 **in some sort** to some extent

77 **Thou . . . prosperity** i.e. it was when I was
prosperous that I suffered miseries

79 **held with a brace of** (a) spent with a pair
of, (b) held together with a clamp made of
(suggesting that Alcibiades has a whore
on each arm)

80 **Athenian minion** darling of Athens. But
as *minion* is also a derogatory term for a
woman, it brings Timon into equivalence
with the speaker. Her name Timandra,
which Timon speaks in the next line, has
the same effect. In Sc. 4 the Page was

bearing letters from the brothel to Timon
and Alcibiades; one might choose to infer
that Timandra was Timon's whore
(compare 'They love thee not that use
thee', l. 83).

81 **Voiced so regardfully** spoke about so
respectfully. Timandra's diction is evidently affected: 'Voiced' is *OED*'s only
example of *voice*, *v*. 3b, and 'regardfully' is
OED's earliest example of the word
(though *Literature Online* identifies an
earlier instance in Robert Chambers's
Palestina of 1600).

83 **Be a whore still** Proverbially, 'Once a
whore, always a whore' (Dent W321).

84 **lust** Seen as expended and deposited in
the whore's body, like semen (and the
trade-off for her giving them diseases).

85 **salt hours** hours of lechery (also anticipating *season*, as with salt)
season prepare (and see previous note)

For tubs and baths, bring down rose-cheeked youth
To the tub-fast and the diet.

TIMANDRA   Hang thee, monster!

ALCIBIADES

Pardon him, sweet Timandra, for his wits
Are drowned and lost in his calamities.
I have but little gold of late, brave Timon,   90
The want whereof doth daily make revolt
In my penurious band. I have heard and grieved
How cursèd Athens, mindless of thy worth,
Forgetting thy great deeds, when neighbour states
But for thy sword and fortune trod upon them—   95

TIMON

I prithee, beat thy drum and get thee gone.

ALCIBIADES

I am thy friend, and pity thee, dear Timon.

TIMON

How dost thou pity him whom thou dost trouble?
I had rather be alone.

ALCIBIADES   Why, fare thee well.
Here is some gold for thee.

TIMON   Keep it. I cannot eat it.   100

ALCIBIADES

When I have laid proud Athens on a heap—

TIMON

Warr'st thou 'gainst Athens?

---

87 tub-fast] THEOBALD (*conj.* Warburton); Fubfast F

86 **tubs and baths** sweating-tubs and hot baths; treatments for venereal disease. *OED*'s earliest illustration of *bath, sb.*[2] 11, the usual present-day sense of the domestic receptacle.

87 **tub-fast** sexual abstinence (fasting) during treatment with the sweating-tub
diet i.e. dry food, as another part of the therapy (Gordon Williams)

89 **lost** (as at sea)

91 **want** lack. The soldiers are mutinying for lack of pay.

95 **thy sword and fortune** From this, Timon seems to have played a military role as well as financing the wars. Plutarch gives

no such indication, though he relates that Alcibiades' close friend the philosopher Socrates fought in battle, and his account of Timon compares him with the soldier Antony. In Lucian, a flatterer presents him with a decree that untruly claims 'he fought with distinction last year at Acharnae cutting two Peloponnesian companies to pieces', and calls him an 'indefatigable promoter of his country's good'.

trod upon them would have trodden upon them. A victor symbolically *trod upon* a vanquished foe. And see 2.139–40.

101 **on a heap** in ruins

ALCIBIADES   Ay, Timon, and have cause.

TIMON The gods confound them all in thy conquest, and
    thee after, when thou hast conquered.

ALCIBIADES Why me, Timon?   105

TIMON That by killing of villains thou wast born to conquer
    my country.
    Put up thy gold.
        He offers Alcibiades gold
                Go on; here's gold; go on.
    Be as a planetary plague when Jove
    Will o'er some high-viced city hang his poison   110
    In the sick air. Let not thy sword skip one.
    Pity not honoured age for his white beard;
    He is an usurer. Strike me the counterfeit matron;
    It is her habit only that is honest,
    Herself's a bawd. Let not the virgin's cheek   115

---

106 wast] F (was't)   108 *He offers Alcibiades gold*] OXFORD SHAKESPEARE; *not in* F

103–7 **The gods . . . country** F sets as verse,
dividing after 'Conquest' and 'Villains',
but the lines are irregular and lack the
simple alterations that might establish
metre (for instance 'And after, thee, when
thou hast conquerèd'). It seems best to
regard the passage as prose that Compositor B has set as rough verse to accord with
the surrounding verse.

103 **in thy conquest** in being conquered by
you

108 **Put up** put away

109–11 **Be . . . air** 'This passage looks as
though it has been influenced by Thomas
Nashe's description of the Fall of
Jerusalem and of the wickedness of
London in his *Christ's Tears over Jerusalem*
(1593), a pamphlet written during a very
bad outbreak of the plague in 1592–3'
(Hibbard): 'You usurers and engrossers of
corn, by your hoarding up of gold and
grain till it is mould, rusty, moth-eaten,
and almost infects the air with the stench,
you have taught God to hoard up
your iniquities and transgressions, till
mouldiness, putrefaction, and mustiness
enforceth him to open them; and, being
opened, they so poison the air with their
ill savour, that from them proceedeth this
perilsome contagion. The land is full of
adulterers, and for this cause the land
mourneth. The land is full of

extortioners, full of proud men, full of
hypocrites, full of murderers. This is the
cause why the sword devoureth abroad,
and the pestilence at home' (*Works*, ed.
McKerrow, 5 vols. (1904–10), ii. 158).
The widespread belief that plague was
God's punishment on a city derives from
Jeremiah 25: 29, an apocalyptic passage
that, as in this speech, adds the threat of
the *sword*: 'Lo, I begin to plague the city,
where my name is called upon, and
should you go free? You shall not go quit:
for I will call for a sword upon all the
inhabitants of the earth, saith the Lord of
hosts' (quoted in *Two Gates* 89.I).

109 **planetary plague** plague or disaster
caused by malign planetary influence

110 **Will** determines to

111 **sick** infected, infectious
skip omit

113 **me** The pronoun is either redundant
except for lending emotional impact
(compare l. 11), or 'for me'.

114 **habit** dress; demeanour
honest decent, respectable (of the dress);
sexually faithful (of the matron)

115 **a bawd** For 'prostituting' her children
in the marriage market or for social
advancement?

115–19 **Let . . . traitors** According to Deuteronomy 20: 13–14, when a city is cap-
tured the victor should 'smite all the

Make soft thy trenchant sword; for those milk-paps
That through the window-bars bore at men's eyes
Are not within the leaf of pity writ;
But set them down horrible traitors. Spare not the babe
Whose dimpled smiles from fools exhaust their mercy.   120
Think it a bastard whom the oracle
Hath doubtfully pronounced the throat shall cut,

117 window-bars] STEEVENS 1778 (*conj.* Johnson); window Barne F; window, bared, HIBBARD
122 the throat] F; thy throat POPE

males thereof with the edge of the sword'
but spare 'the women and the children'.
This is here conflated with Roman laws
which 'Admit no virgin immature to die'
(Jonson, *Sejanus* 5.860; published 1605;
perhaps a point of reference here). Timon
confines the question to virgins, urging
that no sexually mature woman deserves
mercy on account of virginity.

115 **the virgin's cheek** streaked with tears?

116 **Make soft** Refers to the effect on the
wielder of the sword; but the sword is
phallic, and potential rape is also an issue.
trenchant cutting, sharp-pointed
milk-paps nipples (*OED*'s only instance).
Timon presents an emblematic image of a
woman whose body gives conflicting signals as to her sexual status. The 'virgin's
cheek' commends her to mercy, but the
erotic display of nipples betrays her as a
whore (actually or by inclination or by
perception). *Milk-paps* suggests lactation,
in which case she is less likely a virgin;
contrast Luke 23: 29, 'Blessed are . . . the
paps that never gave suck' (a passage
against female fertility that is relevant to
the play more widely). The purpose of
breasts in feeding infants becomes a sign
of women's propensity not to be virgins,
so confirming Timon's savage view that
all women should be put to the sword. He
turns the benign and nurturing connotations of *milk* into evidence of guilt, just as
he revokes the associations of white with
innocence when he takes the white beard
as a sign of a usurer at ll. 112–13.

117 **window-bars** open-work squares of a
bodice (?). This, Steevens's emendation of
F's 'window Barne', is generally accepted,
though Hibbard prefers 'window, bared,',
which is also possible. *OED* records no
(other) instance of *window-bar* before
1677, where it refers, literally, to bars on a
window. A somewhat earlier example is

in John Phillips's *Satire against Hypocrites*
(1655), 'And on the window-bars in
swarms they hung'. The word is on the
analogy of *window-work*, for which *OED*
has a 1594 quotation unambiguously in
the sense of open lacework over the
breasts. *Bar* could refer to an ornamented
band of cloth. But the literal sense of
window-bars may also apply if the breasts
are seen inside a barred window, perhaps
of a brothel (compare Bardolph's face
seen through the 'red lattice' of an
implied brothel in *2 Henry IV* 2.2.72).
Oliver cites the proverb 'A woman that
loves to be at a window is like a bunch of
grapes on the highway' (Tilley W647);
this, however, is unlikely to be relevant as
Tilley records only one instance, in 1666.

118 **leaf of pity** Alludes to the biblical Book
of Life, whereby 'the dead were judged of
those things which were written in the
books, according to their works' (Revela-
tion 20: 12). The implication of *leaf* is that
in Timon's book of judgement there is
little space indeed for the list of those to be
spared punishment.

119 **set** write
horrible traitors Sexual betrayal of man,
betrayal of virtue, and betrayal of the
woman's claim to be a virgin, all seem to
be implied. Timon makes these faults
equivalent to betrayal of the state, pun-
ishable by death.

120 **exhaust** draw forth

121 **whom** of whom (or 'who'?). The irregular syntax feeds into the ambiguity.

122 **doubtfully** ambiguously (see next note).
The oracles of Greek and Roman literature notoriously issued prophecies that
could be and were interpreted the wrong
way.
the throat shall cut The prophecy does not
specify whether the child will be victim or
agent. Alcibiades is urged to think himself
the eventual victim unless he cuts the

And mince it sans remorse. Swear against objects.
Put armour on thine ears and on thine eyes
Whose proof nor yells of mothers, maids, nor babes,   125
Nor sight of priests in holy vestments bleeding,
Shall pierce a jot. There's gold to pay thy soldiers.
Make large confusion, and, thy fury spent,
Confounded be thyself. Speak not. Be gone.

ALCIBIADES *(taking the gold)*

Hast thou gold yet, I'll take the gold thou giv'st me,   130
Not all thy counsel.

TIMON

Dost thou or dost thou not, heaven's curse upon thee!

PHRYNIA *and* TIMANDRA

Give us some gold, good Timon. Hast thou more?

TIMON

Enough to make a whore forswear her trade,
And to make whole a bawd. Hold up, you sluts,   135

---

130 *taking the gold*] BEVINGTON; *not in* F   giv'st] POPE; giuest F   133 PHRYNIA *and* TIMANDRA] F
(*Both.*). *Similarly at ll.* 149 *and* 167.   135 whole] THEOBALD (*conj.* Warburton); Whores F;
whore POPE; wholesomeness OXFORD SHAKESPEARE (Taylor)

child's throat while he can. Pope's emendation of 'the' to 'thy' removes a pointed
ambiguity.

123 **mince it** chop it in pieces
  sans without
  Swear against i.e. take an oath to be
  unmoved by
  objects objections. 'Quasi-legal' (Sisson,
  p. 174).
124–7 **Put . . . jot** The only 'weapon' of the
  victims is their appeal to pity.
125 **Whose proof** the tested strength of
  which (referring to *armour*)
  nor yells neither the yells
128 **large** wholescale
  confusion ruin, havoc, destruction
129 **Confounded** brought to confusion and
  loss of purpose; destroyed. Also an impre-
  cise curse, as in 'to hell with you'.
130 **Hast thou gold yet** if you still have gold.
  F's punctuation is followed. Alternatively,
  'Hast thou gold yet?' is a question.
133 PHRYNIA *and* TIMANDRA F's '*Both.*' here
  and at ll. 149 and 167 leaves no doubt.
  The effect is unnaturalistic and perhaps
  sardonic.
135 **And . . . bawd** Whether and how this

line should be emended is finely balanced.
The most plausible readings are:

  And to make whores a bawd: This, the
Folio reading, means most obviously that
whores would use the gold to set up in
business running a brothel themselves.
The difficulties are: 'To make a whore . . .
And to make whores' is rhetorically weak;
'make whores a bawd' turns plural to
singular; the example of a whore turning
bawd shows gold neither reforming
whores   nor   even   making   them
respectable. Johnson suggested inverted
word-order: that gold would enable a
bawd to stop making *whores*. This
'wrenches the syntax beyond belief'
(Oliver), and it is hard to think of a spoken
delivery that would make the sense
communicable.

  And to make wholesomeness a bawd: By
this reading, if a whore would forswear
her trade (bad to good), the personification of wholesomeness would turn bawd
(good to bad). Among Shakespeare parallels is 'Mercy to thee would prove itself a
bawd' (*Measure* 3.1.152). The reading is
based on a word not found elsewhere in
Shakespeare or Middleton. It creates a

Your aprons mountant.

He throws gold into their aprons

You are not oathable,
Although I know you'll swear, terribly swear,
Into strong shudders and to heavenly agues
Th'immortal gods that hear you. Spare your oaths;
I'll trust to your conditions. Be whores still,   140
And he whose pious breath seeks to convert you,
Be strong in whore, allure him, burn him up.

136 *He . . . aprons*] BEVINGTON; *not in* F

hexameter, which is suspect particularly because 'to make' is redundant to the sense. A more radical emendation would be to assume that the error is partly a repetition of 'to make' from the previous line, and so to substitute 'to make whores' for one of several Shakespearian trisyllabic nouns appropriate to innocent virtue: wholesomeness, honesty (especially attractive in view of Hamlet's comment on the power of beauty to 'transform honesty from what it is to a bawd': *Hamlet* 3.1.114), bashfulness (associated with virginity and imputed to be lost in *Midsummer Night's Dream* 3.2.286–7; also compare 'Make bold her bashful years with your experience', *Richard III* Add. Pass. K. 39), blessedness (compare virginity as 'single blessedness', *Midsummer Night's Dream* 1.1.78), loveliness (personified, associated with virginity, and urged to be 'used' in procreation, in Sonnet 4), tenderness, etc. But the mechanics of error arising from these conjectures are not straightforward.

And to make whole a bawd: This extends the idea in the previous line that even those with a commercial interest in sex would reform. Repetition of *make* is now effective because of the change in its force ('to make a whore . . . to make whole').

135 **whole a bawd** The reading might invite the sexually suggestive mishearing 'hole [vagina] abhorred' (compare l. 184).

136 **aprons mountant** lifted-up aprons. *Mountant* is a coinage on the analogy of heraldic terms such as *couchant* and *rampant*, suggesting that the lifted skirts are emblems of prostitution. It probably puns on sexual 'mounting', and may also sug-

gest that the aprons gather 'amounts' of money. For the gesture, compare *Pericles* 19.63, where a visitor to the brothel 'will line your apron with gold', and *No Wit* 1.78–9 where, 'because gold | Is such a heavy metal' the men 'eased our pockets | In wenches' aprons'. Phrynia and Timandra's aprons taking the gold make the whores 'like parody Danaës' impregnated by Zeus' shower of gold (Gordon Williams, p. 28). The analogy with the sexual act might be made evident on the stage. Lucian too alludes to Danaë when Timon says: 'well might Zeus take the shape of gold; where is the maid that would not open her bosom to receive so fair a lover gliding through the roof?'

136 **oathable** able to keep an oath. *OED*'s only instance of this word.

138 **shudders . . . agues** i.e. dismay and physical pain. Both words suggest, quibblingly, both orgasm and effects of venereal disease.

shudders *OED*'s only instance of the noun before the 19th century.

139 **Spare** withhold

140 **trust . . . conditions** (a) take your quality on trust, (b) trust what your occupations indicate (that as whores they are not to be trusted)

still constantly

142 **Be strong in whore** Perhaps an ironic echo of St Paul's admonition to 'Be strong in the Lord' as a militant Christian who is 'able to stand against the assaults of the devil' (Ephesians 6: 10–11).

burn him up refers to both the flames of lust and their effect, venereal disease. The idea develops from the phrase 'a hot whore', as in Marlowe, *Doctor Faustus* A.2.1.148, adding the idea of disease.

Let your close fire predominate his smoke;
And be no turncoats. Yet may your pain-sick months
Be quite contrary, and thatch your poor thin roofs   145
With burdens of the dead—some that were hanged,
No matter. Wear them, betray with them; whore still;
Paint till a horse may mire upon your face.
A pox of wrinkles!

PHRYNIA *and* TIMANDRA Well, more gold; what then?
Believe't that we'll do anything for gold.   150

TIMON Consumptions sow
In hollow bones of man, strike their sharp shins,
And mar men's spurring. Crack the lawyer's voice,

---

144 pain-sick] OXFORD SHAKESPEARE (*conj.* Becket); paines six F

143 **close fire** (a) the enclosed fire of your lust (virtually 'hot cunt'), (b) secret venereal disease
predominate his smoke prevail over his vacuous pieties. Also suggests 'control the outcome of his steaming in the sweating-tub'. For *smoke*, compare 'Sweet smoke of rhetoric', *Love's Labour's Lost* 3.1.61. Proverbially, 'No smoke without some fire' (Dent S569), and 'fire is quenched in its own smoke' (F261.1), but these contribute little to the meaning. The line provides *OED*'s earliest example of *predominate* in this sense (*v.* 3, 'dominate over, prevail over, control').

144 **be no turncoats** i.e. stay true to being whores
pain-sick months F's 'paines six months' has not been adequately explained, and probably results in part from -e/-es misreading.

145 **quite contrary** entirely opposed to your well-being and continuance as whores. And just the opposite in character: i.e. making the whores sick instead of active, cold (*thin roofs*) instead of hot.
thin roofs i.e. hairless scalps (a supposed symptom of venereal disease). Alludes to house roofs with worn-out thatches.

146 **burdens of the dead** i.e. wigs made from the hair of the dead. Compare Sonnet 68, ll. 5–7: 'Before the golden tresses of the dead, | The right of sepulchres, were shorn away | To live a second life on second head'.

147–8 **whore . . . horse** The similarity in sound between these words is probably not incidental. See note to l. 36.

148 **Paint** apply cosmetics
mire upon get stuck in (as if in mud). *OED*'s earliest example of this sense (*v.*[1] 3). Though not part of the literal meaning, there is an underlying and perverse suggestion of the horse defecating on the whore's face.

149 **A pox of** a pox on, to hell with

149–50 **Well . . . for gold** The whores offer to fulfil Timon's instructions—or to listen to his tirade as though abusing them gave him sexual pleasure.

151–3 **Consumptions . . . spurring** Middleton may have added a touch here. The exact phrase *hollow bones* is in *Revenger's* 1.1.6, with the same implications, but nowhere else in pre-1642 drama (*Literature Online*). The sexual innuendo in *spur* (see note to ll. 64) is Middletonian. Compare also 'thy bones are hollow', etc., in *Measure* 1.2.54, in a passage now attributed to Middleton. *Consumptions* occurs twice in Middleton, in conjunction with *marrow* (*Penniless Parliament* l. 130; compare *hollow bones*) and with copulation (*Plato's Cap* l. 373).

151 **Consumptions** consuming diseases (especially sexual ones)

152 **hollow bones** The anticipated result of *Consumptions*. Syphilis makes bones brittle and fragile.
sharp shins Again the anticipated result: perhaps painful nodes on the shins. Perhaps the text should read 'strike sharp their shins'.

153 **spurring** (a) horse-riding, (b) copulation
Crack . . . voice An ulcered larynx is another effect of syphilis.

That he may never more false title plead,
Nor sound his quillets shrilly. Hoar the flamen   155
That scolds against the quality of flesh
And not believes himself. Down with the nose,
Down with it flat; take the bridge quite away
Of him that his particular to foresee
Smells from the general weal. Make curled-pate ruffians
   bald,   160
And let the unscarred braggarts of the war
Derive some pain from you. Plague all,
That your activity may defeat and quell
The source of all erection. There's more gold.
Do you damn others, and let this damn you;   165
And ditches grave you all!

PHRYNIA *and* TIMANDRA
  More counsel with more money, bounteous Timon.

TIMON
  More whore, more mischief first; I have given you
    earnest.

156 scolds] ROWE; scold'st F

154 **title** claim to possession
155 **quillets** verbal niceties, quibbles; the 'nice sharp quillets of the law' of *1 Henry VI* 2.4.17.
  Hoar make greyish-white (with syphilis). With an incidental echo of *whore*: see notes to ll. 36 and 147–8.
  flamen priest. The Latinism is perhaps a concession to the setting in classical Greece, but may have been chosen to avoid censorship. The 17th-century annotator of the Meisei copy of the Folio saw the point, commenting on ll. 153–7: 'Injustice and atheism among men' (Yamada, p. 215).
156 **quality of flesh** i.e. characteristic of the flesh in being prone to sexual desire.
157 **himself** Refers to either his own words or the evidence of his own body.
  Down with the nose Syphilis causes collapse of the nose-bridge.
158 **flat** completely; to flatness
159 **his particular to foresee** to provide for his own self-interest.
160 **Smells . . . weal** Johnson suggested an underlying image of a hound that parts from the pack by following a different scent.

160 **from the general weal** i.e. (a) at odds with the well-being of society at large, or (b) apart from society as a whole
  curled-pate ruffians curly-headed swaggerers
161 **unscarred braggarts** i.e. boastful cowards
163 **quell** destroy
164 **The . . . erection** i.e. the male sexual impulse
166 **ditches grave you all** Grave is probably optative subjunctive: 'let ditches grave you all' (Blake 4.3.3.a). Timon might gesture to the hole he has himself been digging. His call for the whores' bodies to be dumped in ditches excludes them from Christian burial, and confirms their status as common but disregarded beings. The ditches are perhaps a humiliating equivalent to the whores' publicly-available sexual organs; compare *Michaelmas* 3.1.222–4, 'if ditches were not cast once a year, and drabs once a month, there would be no abiding i'th' city', and *Macbeth* 4.1.31.
168 **earnest** a down-payment

ALCIBIADES

 Strike up the drum towards Athens. Farewell, Timon.

 If I thrive well, I'll visit thee again.   170

TIMON

 If I hope well, I'll never see thee more.

ALCIBIADES I never did thee harm.

TIMON Yes, thou spok'st well of me.

ALCIBIADES Call'st thou that harm?

TIMON

 Men daily find it. Get thee away,   175

 And take thy beagles with thee.

ALCIBIADES   We but offend him. Strike!

                          Drum beats. Exeunt all but Timon

TIMON (*digging*)

 That nature, being sick of man's unkindness,

 Should yet be hungry! Common mother—thou

 Whose womb unmeasurable and infinite breast

 Teems and feeds all, whose selfsame mettle   180

176.1 *Drum beats*] JOHNSON (*subs.*); *not in* F   *all but Timon*] JOHNSON (*subs.*); *not in* F   177 *digging*] JOHNSON; *not in* F

171 **If I hope well** if my hopes come about

172–3 **I . . . me** Might allude to (a) Luke 6: 26, 'Woe be to you when all men speak well of you, for so did their fathers to the false prophets' (followed by a text significant in relation to Timon, 'But I say unto you which hear, love your enemies; do well to them which hate you'); (b) the proverb 'Praise by evil men is dispraise' (Dent P540).

175 **find it** discover the truth of it

176 **beagles** dogs good at hunting by scent. The implication is 'bitches who sniff out their male prey'. In a gentler vein, Sir Toby calls Maria 'a beagle true bred' because she follows and 'adores' him (*Twelfth Night* 2.3.173–4).

177–8 **That . . . hungry** *Nature* refers to Timon's own needs. He is metaphorically sick through a surfeit of 'man's unkindness', but physically hungry, and digs the earth for 'one poor root' (l. 187). There may be some suggestion that *nature* as the earth is both sick and eager to stimulate more human unkindness in yielding gold.

178–85 **Common . . . shine** In this passage of lyrical saturnalia, Timon attributes the sinfulness of 'man' to the same substance

(*mettle*) as the poison and deformity found elsewhere in created beings. Man's vain self-image corresponds to the alluring and unexpected colorations in poisonous animals, and also to the blindness of the 'venomed worm'.

178 **Common mother** Proverbially, 'earth is the common mother of us all' (Dent E28.1). Timon's view of the earth as *womb* (l. 179) is conditioned for an audience by the fact that he is extracting a substance, gold, from it. He may indeed be standing half-hidden within the trapdoor hole, as was Pennington in the 1999 RSC production (see Illustration 8).

180 **Teems** breeds with prolific fertility. 'Teeming earth' occurs in *1 Henry IV* 3.1.26, collocated with *womb*, and Jonson's *Volpone* 1.1.2, in Volpone's soliloquy worshipping his gold, the 'son of Sol' (compare l. 185).

mettle spirit, 'stuff' in the non-material sense. The suggestion also of material substance is strong. The alternative modern equivalent 'metal' is relevant as Timon is digging a metal from the ground, and the colours attributed to the toad, adder, and newt are metallic.

Whereof thy proud child, arrogant man, is puffed
Engenders the black toad and adder blue,
The gilded newt and eyeless venomed worm,
With all th'abhorrèd births below crisp heaven
Whereon Hyperion's quick'ning fire doth shine—   185
Yield him who all the human sons doth hate,
From forth thy plenteous bosom, one poor root.
Ensear thy fertile and conceptious womb;

186 the] F; thy POPE (*similarly* Shadwell)   doth] CAPELL; do's ROWE; do F

181 **puffed** inflated (with pride)
182–3 **Engenders . . . worm** See Introduction, p. 60. The colours are neither naturalistic nor associated with the animals in question. They might describe the eyes rather than the skin, anticipating the *eyeless* and uncoloured *worm*. *Black* and *blue* are words Shakespeare elsewhere uses to describe eyes. Reptiles are elsewhere described as *gilded*: in *As You Like It* 4.3.109 ('A green and gilded snake'), and *Lear* 24.82 ('This gilded serpent'). *Gilded* may suggest the gleam of reflected light on smooth scales. There may be a thematic link between *gilded* as a false appearance and *eyeless*. Further, as an offspring of the earth, the gilded newt connects with the gold Timon has found. See also note to ll. 178–85.
182, 183 **toad . . . newt** Both were thought poisonous.
183 **eyeless venomed worm** The blindworm proper is not poisonous (and neither blind nor a worm). But the poisonous (and well-sighted) adder was sometimes also called the 'blindworm'. The comparison and contrast between 'arrogant man' and the humble worm was commonplace.
184 **abhorrèd births** Timon perhaps views *all* births as abhorred, correlating them with the specific births of deformed, poisonous, and prodigious creatures. Janet Adelman plausibly suggests wordplay on *ab-whored*, 'come from a whore', reflecting disgust towards mother earth: *Suffocating Mothers* (1992), p. 173. Compare notes to l. 36 and l. 135.
crisp shining, bright, clear (Crystal). *OED* cites this line, finding one earlier instance of the sense in Golding's translation of *Metamorphoses*. Shakespeare's two other uses of the word both contrast a 'crisp' river with the 'hollow bank' or 'green land' through which it flows (*1 Henry IV* 1.3.105, *Tempest* 4.1.130).

185 **Hyperion's** i.e. the sun's. In Greek mythology he was the sun's father, or sun-god.
quick'ning life-giving
186 **who . . . hate** who hates all the human sons. Emendation of F's 'do' to 'doth' is necessary to establish that the primary meaning is not 'whom all the human sons hate'.
the Pope's emendation 'thy' is attractive.
187 **plenteous bosom** fertile womb. Perhaps also the equivalent of breasts, as the source of nutriment. Contrast Francis Quarles, *Emblems* (1635), Book 1, Emblem 12: 'What, never filled? Be thy lips screwed so fast | To th'earth's full breast? For shame, for shame, unseize thee! | Thou tak'st a surfeit where thou shouldst but taste, | And mak'st too much not half enough to please thee'. See 2.120–1 note.
188 **Ensear . . . womb**   Compare Lady Macbeth's rhetorical unsexing of herself (*Macbeth* 1.5.39–49), and Lear's invocation of nature, 'Into her womb convey sterility. | Dry up in her the organs of increase' (*Lear* 4.271–2). Lear's speech is closely comparable with Timon's in temper and language, including 'teem' at l. 274. Timon, however, is less resolute: first 'Yield' (l. 186), then 'Ensear' (l. 188), then 'Go great' (l. 190). Perhaps he digs before 'Ensear' and again before 'Go great', switching his imprecation as though seeking the one that will work. After finding the root he returns to imagery of infertility: 'Dry up thy marrows . . .' (l. 194).
Ensear 'Dry up' (see l. 194), cause to wither away. Reverses the sun's effect on the earth in l. 185. With possible violent connotations of cauterization with hot irons, as of a wound rather than a womb; compare l. 668. The only example of this variant of *sear* in *OED*.

Let it no more bring out ingrateful man.
Go great with tigers, dragons, wolves, and bears;   190
Teem with new monsters whom thy upward face
Hath to the marbled mansion all above
Never presented.
  He finds a root
      O, a root! Dear thanks.
Dry up thy marrows, vines, and plough-torn leas,
Whereof ingrateful man with liquorish draughts   195
And morsels unctuous greases his pure mind,
That from it all consideration slips!
  Enter Apemantus
More man? Plague, plague!

APEMANTUS

I was directed hither. Men report
Thou dost affect my manners, and dost use them.   200

193 *He finds a root*] BEVINGTON; *not in* F 195 liquorish] F (Licourish)

188 **conceptious** apt to conceive, prolific.
 OED's one example of the word.

190 **great** pregnant

191 **Teem with** breed prolifically
 upward upturned

192 **marbled mansion** i.e. the heavens (perhaps suggesting their depiction in the
 domed roof of a Renaissance Catholic
 church or chapel or, more immediately,
 the decorated 'heavens' or canopy of the
 theatre stage). *Marbled* suggests both the
 opulence of a building and luminosity
 of the sky. Compare *Cymbeline* 5.5.181,
 where Jupiter is implored to 'Peep
 through thy marble mansion'.

193 **O, a root** A moment of potentially comic
 bathos after the powerful and extravagant
 imagery of the previous lines. As a stage
 property, the root is likely to be the same
 as that Apemantus enjoys in Sc. 2,
 though a far less nutritious tree-root is
 possible.

194 **marrows** vital pulp, hence vital strength
 of the earth as a female body.
 leas fields

195–6 **Whereof . . . mind** Drink and food, the
 products of the earth, are here seen as
 making 'ingrateful man' intoxicated and
 decadent—a recollection, perhaps, of
 Timon's own feasting.

195 **Whereof** from which

liquorish (a) pleasing to taste, (b) lust-
 inducing. F spells 'Licourish'; *OED*'s
 lemma is 'Lickerish, liquorish'. The latter
 is preferred because the context also
 admits 'liquor-like', i.e. liquid and alco-
 holic. Compare *liquorishness*, meaning
 'fond of liquor', first recorded in *OED* in
 1789 and castigated as an 'etymologizing
 sense-perversion'.
 draughts drinks: (a) potions, (b)
 swallowings

196 **unctuous** rich in fat
 greases (a) makes gross and lewd, (b)
 makes slippery (see next line)

197 **consideration** ability to think reflectively

197.1 **Enter Apemantus** He evidently produces food at l. 285. He brought a root to
 the banquet in Sc. 2; now that Timon eats
 roots he perversely claims to bring better
 fare. It may be no better than Capell's
 crust or Johnson's another root (see collation to l. 285); but alternatively he might
 manifestly enter with a picnic, as in
 Doran's 1999 production.

198–398 **More . . . them.** Some productions
 have conveyed an inexplicable need
 Apemantus and Timon have for each
 other in this episode (as perhaps Timon
 expresses at ll. 288–9). Apemantus is the
 one visitor who at first dominates the
 dialogue.

200 **affect** (a) like, (b) assume, imitate

TIMON

'Tis then because thou dost not keep a dog
Whom I would imitate. Consumption catch thee!

APEMANTUS

This is in thee a nature but infected,
A poor unmanly melancholy, sprung
From change of fortune. Why this spade, this place,   205
This slave-like habit, and these looks of care?
Thy flatterers yet wear silk, drink wine, lie soft,
Hug their diseased perfumes, and have forgot
That ever Timon was. Shame not these woods
By putting on the cunning of a carper.   210
Be thou a flatterer now, and seek to thrive
By that which has undone thee. Hinge thy knee,
And let his very breath whom thou'lt observe
Blow off thy cap. Praise his most vicious strain,
And call it excellent. Thou wast told thus.   215
Thou gav'st thine ears, like tapsters that bade welcome,
To knaves and all approachers. 'Tis most just
That thou turn rascal. Hadst thou wealth again,
Rascals should have't. Do not assume my likeness.

TIMON

Were I like thee, I'd throw away myself.   220

---

203 infected] F; affected ROWE   205 fortune] ROWE (*similarly* Shadwell), SOUTHERNE MS (*in copy of* F4); future F   212 has] F (ha's)

202 **Consumption** See note to l. 151.
203 **but infected** i.e. merely infected for now, not intrinsically so. Rowe emended to 'but affected'.
204 **unmanly** i.e. effeminate. But 'beast-like' is also possible: Dekker refers to 'brutish and unmanly passions': *'Wonderfull Yeare', 1603*, ed. G. B. Harrison (1924), p. 42.
205 **change of fortune** F's 'change of future' is without precedent or parallel.
206 **habit** costume, get-up. Compare l. 240.
208 **perfumes** Metonymic for 'perfumed mistresses'.
210 **putting . . . carper** assuming the expertise of a professional fault-finder. *Cunning* is 'knowledge, skill', with a suggestion of the skills of a particular trade.

212 **Hinge** bend. *OED*'s earliest example of the verb in any sense.
213 **observe** obsequiously follow
214 **strain** characteristic
215 **Thou wast told thus** that's just what they told you. Perhaps punning on *tolled*, 'enticed, lured into a trap'. Not, apparently, 'you were warned'.
216 **tapsters** barmen in inns (who would greet all comers). Contrast the porter of 3.10.
218 **turn rascal** turn into a lean and solitary deer. An image of Timon's condition in the woods, and anticipating *Rascals* as 'rogues' in the next line.
219 **Rascals should have't** i.e. it should be had not by a rascal (deer) but by rascals (rogues)

APEMANTUS

Thou hast cast away thyself being like thyself—
A madman so long, now a fool. What, think'st
That the bleak air, thy boisterous chamberlain,
Will put thy shirt on warm? Will these moist trees
That have outlived the eagle page thy heels   225
And skip when thou point'st out? Will the cold brook,
Candied with ice, caudle thy morning taste
To cure thy o'ernight's surfeit? Call the creatures
Whose naked natures live in all the spite
Of wreakful heaven, whose bare unhousèd trunks   230
To the conflicting elements exposed
Answer mere nature; bid them flatter thee.
O, thou shalt find—

TIMON   —a fool of thee. Depart.

APEMANTUS

I love thee better now than e'er I did.

TIMON

I hate thee worse.

224 moist] F; moss'd HANMER

221–32 **Thou . . . thee** This moralization of
nature recalls Duke Senior's contrast
between the 'painted pomp' of court and
the 'icy fang' of the wind in the woods
where he is dwelling, which offers 'no flattery' (*As You Like It* 2.1.1–17). That
passage also refers to 'the toad, ugly and
venomous' and 'running brooks'.

222 **think'st** thinkest thou; do you think

223 **chamberlain** personal servant. The literal sense of a servant in charge of private
chambers ironically reinforces the point
that Timon lives outdoors.

224 **put . . . warm** Warming his master's
clothes by the fire was a usual part of a
personal servant's duties.

moist As an indication of the tree's age,
Hanmer's emendation 'moss'd' is more
plausible than some commentators (Sisson, Hulme, Oliver) have allowed. But F's
reading is consistent with the imagery—it
contrasts with the dryness of a warm
shirt and anticipates the 'cold brook'—
and so it has been retained.

225 **outlived the eagle** From the proverbial
expression 'an eagle's old age' (Dent E5).
page thy heels follow at your heels like a
(young) page

226 **skip** jump to it

226 **point'st out** indicate something you want

227 **Candied** sugar-frosted, crusted. The line
is *OED*'s earliest example of *candy, v.* 4,
'To cover or incrust with crystalline substance, as hoar-frost, etc.'. The association with *taste* shows that there is also a
connotation of sweetness, as in 'let the
candied tongue lick absurd pomp' (*Hamlet*
3.2.58; compare 'willing misery | Out-
lives in certain pomp', ll. 243–4 below). In
this case the sweetness is lacking.
caudle thy morning taste refresh the bad
taste in your mouth in the morning with
a caudle (a warm, spiced medicinal
drink). *OED*'s earliest example of *caudle* as
a verb.

228–32 **Call . . . nature** Compare *Lear*
11.25–9: 'Poor naked wretches . . . How
shall your houseless heads and unfed
sides . . . defend you | From seasons such
as these?', and 8.3, 'Contending with the
fretful element'.

229 **live in** (as equivalent to their house)

230 **wreakful** vindictive

231 **conflicting** The only instance of this
word in Shakespeare or Middleton.

232 **Answer** have to face
mere absolute, unmitigated

233 **a fool of thee** you to be a fool

284

APEMANTUS	Why?	
TIMON	Thou flatter'st misery.	235

APEMANTUS

I flatter not, but say thou art a caitiff.

TIMON

Why dost thou seek me out?

APEMANTUS   To vex thee.

TIMON

Always a villain's office, or a fool's.
Dost please thyself in't?

APEMANTUS   Ay.

TIMON   What, a knave too?

APEMANTUS

If thou didst put this sour cold habit on   240
To castigate thy pride, 'twere well; but thou
Dost it enforcèdly. Thou'dst courtier be again
Wert thou not beggar. Willing misery
Outlives incertain pomp, is crowned before.
The one is filling still, never complete;   245
The other at high wish. Best state, contentless,
Hath a distracted and most wretched being,

244 Outlives,] JOHNSON; ~: F

235 **misery** i.e. Timon himself
236 **caitiff** wretch
238 **villain's office** job for a menial. The notion of rogue is perhaps reserved for *knave*, in the next line.
239 **knave** See note to 1.264.
240 **sour** harsh
  habit Both 'appearance, manner', and a reference to Timon's scanty garb, seen as self-punitive, like a penitent's or a hermit's.
241 **castigate** *OED*'s earliest example of the verb.
243–4 **Willing ... pomp** Johnson's removal of F's colon after 'Out-liues' seems right. It is 'Willing misery' that is 'crowned before', and so 'at high wish'. Hulme (pp. 84–5) accepts F, taking *Outlives* to be intransitive. She explains that incertain pomp, 'crowned before the end of the story, is always seeking again the moment of completion, the high-flood of honour'. But, in the absence of any refer-ence to losing this crown, with F's punc-tuation 'is crowned before' is contradicted by 'never complete'.
243 **Willing misery** voluntary poverty (in contrast with Timon's enforced poverty)
244 **incertain** insecure, susceptible to change
  is crowned i.e. finds fulfilment
245 **The ... complete** Compare *Cymbeline* 1.6.49–51: 'The cloyèd will, | That satiate yet unsatisfied desire, that tub | Both filled and running . . .'. Alludes to the punishment of the Danaïds, who were condemned in Hades perpetually to keep filling a jar with an empty bottom (Horace, *Odes*, 3.11.23–9).
  The one i.e. *incertain pomp*
246 **at high wish** Probably an alteration of 'at high water'.
  Best state, contentless the greatest pros-perity, if it is without contentment. The earliest example in *OED* of *contentless*.
247 **distracted** confused, deranged

Worse than the worst, content.
Thou shouldst desire to die, being miserable.

TIMON

Not by his breath that is more miserable.   250
Thou art a slave whom fortune's tender arm
With favour never clasped, but bred a dog.
Hadst thou like us from our first swathe proceeded
The sweet degrees that this brief world affords
To such as may the passive drudges of it   255
Freely command, thou wouldst have plunged thyself
In general riot, melted down thy youth
In different beds of lust, and never learned
The icy precepts of respect, but followed
The sugared game before thee. But myself,   260
Who had the world as my confectionary,
The mouths, the tongues, the eyes and hearts of men

---

255 drudges] F (drugges)   256 command] ROWE; command'st F

248 **the worst, content** the least prosperity, if it brings contentment

249 **miserable** i.e. both poor *and* unhappy. For Apemantus, Timon's misery lies in his present state. For Timon, Apemantus' misery lies in his wretched birth and neglect by Fortune.

250 **by his breath that** by the persuasion of one who

252 **bred** i.e. whom fortune bred

253–71 **Hadst . . . thee** Spurgeon finds in this passage a strong example of a recurrent Shakespearian image cluster reflecting his 'strong and individual tendency to return under similar emotional stimulus to a similar picture or group of associated ideas', these here being ice, sugar, licking, tongues, dogs, and flattery (p. 199).

253 **swathe** swaddling-clothes (of infancy)

253–4 **proceeded . . . degrees** i.e. passed up the sweet steps on fortune's ladder (*sweet* because leading upward). And see following note.

254 **degrees** (a) steps (compare 'He then unto the ladder turns his back, | Looks in the clouds, scorning the base degrees | By which he did ascend', *Julius Caesar* 2.1.25–7); (b) stages in a process (compare 'the third degree of drink', *Twelfth Night* 1.5.130, and 'perjury, in the high'st degree', *Richard III* 5.5.150); (c) social ranks (see 12.19); (d) university degrees (with *proceeding* in the sense 'permitted to

advance from one degree to a higher one')

255–6 **such . . . command** i.e. such a high state as has the power to freely command the world's passive drudges. *May* is 'has the power or ability to'.

255 **drudges** Sometimes thought to play on *drugs*, as the ambiguous Folio spelling 'drugges' suggests. A student who had proceeded through his degree to become a Doctor of Medicine (see note to l. 254) would be able to prescribe drugs.

257 **riot** wild revelling, debauchery

258 **different** varying in kind

259–60 **icy . . . sugared** The contrast as it were recognizes and separates out the suggestions of sweetness in the earlier 'candied with ice' (l. 227). *Sugared* suggests that the sweetness is only an outer coating.

259 **precepts of respect** (a) commands issued by those in authority, (b) rules for maintaining a position of respect, (c) soundly-judged moral principles

259–60 **followed . . . game** hunted the sugared prey (i.e. his objects of sexual pursuit)

261 **confectionary** the place where sweetmeats are made, stored, or sold. Or perhaps the sense is 'confectioner'. *OED* recognizes the ambiguity, and perhaps should have allowed also for the only sense that certainly predates *Timon*, the sweetmeat itself.

At duty, more than I could frame employment,
That numberless upon me stuck, as leaves
Do on the oak, have with one winter's brush   265
Fell from their boughs, and left me open, bare
For every storm that blows—I to bear this,
That never knew but better, is some burden.
Thy nature did commence in sufferance, time
Hath made thee hard in't. Why shouldst thou hate men?   270
They never flattered thee. What hast thou given?
If thou wilt curse, thy father, that poor rag,
Must be thy subject, who in spite put stuff
To some she-beggar and compounded thee
Poor rogue hereditary. Hence, be gone.   275
If thou hadst not been born the worst of men
Thou hadst been a knave and flatterer.

APEMANTUS Art thou proud yet?

TIMON Ay, that I am not thee.

APEMANTUS I that I was   280
　No prodigal.

TIMON　　　　 I that I am one now.
Were all the wealth I have shut up in thee
I'd give thee leave to hang it. Get thee gone.
That the whole life of Athens were in this!
Thus would I eat it.
　　　He bites the root

---

272 rag] F (ragge); rogue JOHNSON *conj.*   285 *He bites the root*] ROWE (*Eating a root*); *not in* F

263 **At duty** at my service
　frame employment devise employment
　for
264–7 **as . . . blows** Compare *Cymbeline*
　3.3.60–4: 'Then was I as a tree | Whose
　boughs did bend with fruit; but in one
　night | A storm or robbery, call it what
　you will, | Shook down my mellow hang-
　ings, nay, my leaves, | And left me bare to
　weather'.
265 **winter's brush** violent winter squall.
　This sense of *brush* (*OED sb.* 3), 'hostile
　meeting, collision, forceful encounter'
　(Crystal), is entirely distinct from the
　action of the sweeping-brush, though the
　idea of winter sweeping leaves from the
　trees might be present too.
269 **thy . . . sufferance** i.e. you endured
　hardship from the beginning

272 **rag** The term leads on to the image of sex
　as 'stuffing' in the next lines.
273 **in spite** out of spite
273–4 **put stuff | To** copulated with, 'stuffed'
274 **compounded** begot
275 **hereditary** by heredity
276 **worst** lowest. The previous lines lead in
　to this sense, but, as with *miserable*
　(l. 249), the word may have another
　meaning, here 'most evil'. Apemantus is
　probably said to be both too poor *and* too
　bad to be even a knave and flatterer
278 **yet** still
281 **I that . . . now** Timon presumably offers,
　gives, or throws gold, though Apemantus
　does not respond.
282 **shut up** (as in a locked room or box)
284 **That** would that

APEMANTUS (*offering food*) Here, I will mend thy feast.   285
TIMON

First mend my company: take away thyself.

APEMANTUS

So I shall mend mine own by th' lack of thine.

TIMON

'Tis not well mended so, it is but botched;

If not, I would it were.

APEMANTUS   What wouldst thou have to Athens?

TIMON

Thee thither in a whirlwind. If thou wilt,   290

Tell them there I have gold. Look, so I have.

APEMANTUS

Here is no use for gold.

TIMON   The best and truest,

For here it sleeps and does no hirèd harm.

APEMANTUS Where liest a-nights, Timon?

TIMON Under that's above me. Where feed'st thou a-days,   295
Apemantus?

APEMANTUS Where my stomach finds meat; or rather,
where I eat it.

TIMON Would poison were obedient, and knew my mind!

APEMANTUS Where wouldst thou send it?   300

---

285 *offering food*] SISSON (*subs.*); *not in* F; *offering him another <root>* JOHNSON; *Throwing him a crust* CAPELL   286 my] ROWE (*similarly* Shadwell); thy F

285 *offering food* See note to l. 197.1.

285–317 **Here . . . dog** In Pope's edition these lines were relegated to a footnote as inferior.

285–6 APEMANTUS . . . **thyself** Based on Plutarch: 'Apemantus said unto the other, "O here is a trim banquet, Timon." Timon answered again, "Yea," said he, "so thou wert not here".'

285, 288 **mend . . . mended** improve . . . repaired

286 **my company** Klein supports F's 'thy company', glossing 'the company you provide', but the reading is strained, and Apemantus' reply 'So shall I mend my own' assumes that his own company has not been mentioned by Timon.

288 **it . . . botched** The suggestion seems to

be that Apemantus cannot be properly sufficient to himself because he depends on Timon.

289 **If . . . were** Presumably meaning that if Apemantus were to find his own company mended, Timon would wish it to become botched. This cryptic line might be taken to hint at a need to be needed in Timon himself.

What wouldst thou have (a) what message would you send; or (b) what would you want to happen. Timon takes as 'what would you like to go'.

292 **use** employment (with a glance at the sense 'increase through usury'?)

295 **that's** that that is

297–8 **or . . . it** A joking reference to Apemantus' picnic.

TIMON To sauce thy dishes.

APEMANTUS The middle of humanity thou never knewest,
but the extremity of both ends. When thou wast in thy
gilt and thy perfume, they mocked thee for too much
curiosity; in thy rags thou know'st none, but art despised   305
for the contrary. There's a medlar for thee; eat it.

TIMON On what I hate I feed not.

APEMANTUS Dost hate a medlar?

TIMON Ay, though it look like thee.

APEMANTUS An thou'dst hated meddlers sooner, thou   310
shouldst have loved thyself better now. What man didst
thou ever know unthrift that was beloved after his means?

TIMON Who, without those means thou talk'st of, didst
thou ever know beloved?

APEMANTUS Myself.   315

TIMON I understand thee: thou hadst some means to keep
a dog.

APEMANTUS What things in the world canst thou nearest
compare to thy flatterers?

TIMON Women nearest; but men, men are the things   320
themselves. What wouldst thou do with the world,
Apemantus, if it lay in thy power?

306, 308, 310 medlar . . . medlar . . . meddlers] F (medler . . . Medler . . . Medlers)

302–3 **The . . . ends** Though the episode is
Shakespearian, potentially significant is
Middleton's pun on his own name as
'*Thomas Medius et Gravis Tonus*' ('Thomas,
in a moderate and weighty voice'; *Ghost of
Lucrece* ll. 18–19), claiming a serious poetics of the 'middle of humanity'. Proverbially, 'Virtue is found in the middle'
(Dent V80). The reference to moderation
and extremes of experience and behaviour develops from the discussion of eating, and so might allude to the digestive
tract: the *middle* is the nurturing stomach, hence the *extremity of both ends* the
consuming mouth and the defecating
anus.

305 **curiosity** (a) delicacy, fastidiousness, (b)
desire for novelty

306 **the contrary** i.e. of *curiosity*
medlar A kind of fruit eaten when rotten;
with a pun in 14.310 on *meddlers*.

306–7 **eat . . . hate** 'dubious' as a pun

(Cercignani, *Shakespeare's Works and
Elizabethan Pronunciation* (1981),
p. 158)

309 **Ay . . . thee** Ironic, in that Timon claims
to hate Apemantus too.

312 **unthrift** a dissolute spendthrift, a good-
for-nothing
after his means Most straightforwardly,
'to the extent that he was able to be generous'. Alternatively, 'after his means were
depleted'.

320 **Women nearest; but men,** This punctuation is based on F's 'Women neerest, but
men:'. Sisson prefers 'Women nearest but
men—', i.e. women are nearest to flatterers apart from men. This is not an intrinsically more accurate representation of
F, where the colon can admissibly be
rhetorical rather than logical, and it is
rhetorically weaker.

320–1 **the things themselves** One meaning is
that, whereas women *resemble* Timon's

289

APEMANTUS Give it the beasts, to be rid of the men.

TIMON Wouldst thou have thyself fall in the confusion of
    men, and remain a beast with the beasts?   325

APEMANTUS Ay, Timon.

TIMON A beastly ambition, which the gods grant thee
    t'attain to. If thou wert the lion, the fox would beguile
    thee. If thou wert the lamb, the fox would eat thee. If
    thou wert the fox, the lion would suspect thee when   330
    peradventure thou wert accused by the ass. If thou wert
    the ass, thy dullness would torment thee, and still thou
    lived'st but as a breakfast to the wolf. If thou wert the
    wolf, thy greediness would afflict thee, and oft thou
    shouldst hazard thy life for thy dinner. Wert thou the   335
    unicorn, pride and wrath would confound thee, and
    make thine own self the conquest of thy fury. Wert thou
    a bear, thou wouldst be killed by the horse. Wert thou a

flatterers, men actually and intrinsically *are* such flatterers. But Apemantus' question invited Timon to compare his flatterers with 'things' such as dogs, so men are also these 'things themselves'.

323 **to . . . men** Both 'so that men will no longer own the world' and 'as reward to the beasts for destroying men'.

324 **fall in** Critically ambiguous between (a) participate in (whereby the beasts overthrow mankind), or (b) degenerate (into a beast) as part of.
confusion overthrow, destruction

328–42 **If . . . absence** An incantatory passage (as brought out in Scofield's 1965 performance). The content is reminiscent of beast fables of Aesop, and, in the opening examples, Innocent Gentillet's exposition of Machiavelli: 'the fox is cunning enough to keep himself from snares, but he is too weak to guard himself from wolves; and the lion is strong enough to guard himself from wolves, but he is not subtle enough to guard himself from nets' (trans. from *Anti-Machiavel*, 1576, ed. C. Edward Rathé (Genève, 1968), 12th Maxim, p. 396, based on *The Prince*, Ch. 18). Machiavelli recommends acting as both man and beast, and as beast to imitate the qualities of both the lion and the fox. Timon extends the catalogue to

argue that every beast suffers from the savagery of other beasts, describing animal behaviour in human-like terms (suspect, accuse, breakfast, dinner, jurors, etc).

328–9 **beguile thee** defeat you by guile, outwit you

332 **dullness** stupidity
still all the time

333–5 **lived'st . . . shouldst hazard** Abbott notes that these subjunctives 'imply inevitability and compulsion' because they coincide in form with the indicative (362; compare 361).

335–7 **Wert . . . fury** Pliny's well-known account of the unicorn, perhaps actually based on the rhinoceros, described a very ferocious beast with a horse's body, the head of a deer, feet of an elephant, tail of a boar, and a single black horn about four feet long. Conrad Gesner, in the influential zoological study *Historia animalium* (1551–87), explains how pride and wrath were thought to be its undoing: '. . . he [the unicorn] and the lion being enemies by nature, as soon as the lion sees the unicorn he betakes him to a tree. The unicorn in his fury . . . running at him, sticks his horn fast in the tree' (cited by Hanmer).

336 **confound** destroy

338 **bear** (said to be hated by horses)

horse, thou wouldst be seized by the leopard. Wert thou a
leopard, thou wert german to the lion, and the spots of   340
thy kindred were jurors on thy life; all thy safety were
remotion, and thy defence absence. What beast couldst
thou be that were not subject to a beast? And what a
beast art thou already, that seest not thy loss in
transformation!   345

APEMANTUS If thou couldst please me with speaking to me,
thou mightst have hit upon it here. The commonwealth
of Athens is become a forest of beasts.

TIMON How, has the ass broke the wall, that thou art out of
the city?   350

APEMANTUS Yonder comes a poet and a painter. The plague
of company light upon thee! I will fear to catch it, and
give way. When I know not what else to do, I'll see thee
again.

TIMON When there is nothing living but thee, thou shalt   355
be welcome. I had rather be a beggar's dog than
Apemantus.

APEMANTUS

Thou art the cap of all the fools alive.

349 has] F (ha's)

340 **german** closely related
   spots crimes (of the lion). Quibbling on
   the leopard's physical spots. Compare the
   pun at 17.34–5.
341–2 **all . . . absence** Oliver takes this to
   summarize all the options rather than
   referring only to the leopard. But both the
   sense and the legal metaphor in *defence*
   follow from the predicament of the leopard, which must escape arrest because
   it cannot expect acquittal in court. The
   syntax, 'wert thou a leopard . . . all thy
   safety *were*' might also support a single
   sentence.
   were remotion would depend on keeping
   well away. *Remotion* is (a) removal, departure; (b) remoteness (Crystal).
343 **a beast** i.e. (a) a creature without reason, and (b) in effect a beast already, in
   that there is (to Timon) no transformation
   involved in becoming one
344–5 **in transformation** i.e. if you were
   transformed

347 **hit upon it here** i.e. succeeded by saying
   that
348 **a forest of beasts** Compare Titus'
   description of Rome as 'a wilderness of
   tigers' (*Titus Andronicus* 3.1.53).
351 **Yonder . . . painter** This disconnected
   remark anticipates the episode beginning
   at l. 536.2, which is not imminent.
   Apemantus might merely be warning
   that other asses have also broken the
   walls of Athens and are on their way.
   But the comment looks like a loose end
   resulting from a change in intention as
   Shakespeare wrote, or from a subsequent
   resequencing of episodes (see Introduction, pp. 148–9). The line might have
   been deleted if and when the play reached
   the stage. Bridges-Adams (prompt book,
   1928) altered to a 'Parcel of Soldiers',
   anticipating the Banditti at l. 397.1.
353 **give way** retire; yield to others
358 **cap** top example (punning on the fool's
   coxcomb)

TIMON

Would thou wert clean enough to spit upon.

APEMANTUS

A plague on thee!—Thou art too bad to curse.   360

TIMON

All villains that do stand by thee are pure.

APEMANTUS

There is no leprosy but what thou speak'st.

TIMON   If I name thee.

I'll beat thee, but I should infect my hands.

APEMANTUS

I would my tongue could rot them off.   365

TIMON

Away, thou issue of a mangy dog!

Choler does kill me that thou art alive.

I swoon to see thee.

APEMANTUS   Would thou wouldst burst!

TIMON   Away, thou tedious rogue!   370

⌈*He throws a stone at Apemantus*⌉

I am sorry I shall lose a stone by thee.

APEMANTUS   Beast!

360–1 Thou . . . TIMON All] F (*subs.*); *speech-prefix before 'Thou'* POPE 1728 (*conj.* Theobald, *Shakespeare Restored*, 1726)   364 I'll] F (Ile); I'd HANMER   370.1 *He . . . Apemantus*] CAPELL (*subs.*); *not in* F

---

360 **A plague on thee** It can be interpreted (a) that Apemantus curses Timon in the most conventional terms then, realizing his failure, gives up, seeking to outbid him instead by claiming he is too bad to curse; or (b) that 'A plague on thee' is comically self-contradictory with 'Thou art too bad to curse'. Some editors reassign these words to Timon, so that Timon curses and Apemantus responds by putting Timon beyond being cursed. F splits the line into two apparent verse-lines divided after 'thee'. The supposed error would therefore consist simply of placing the speech-prefix for Apemantus a line too early, the 'line' here being the fragmented unit as printed in F. F's two-line setting of the speech therefore defines circumstances in which the misassignation would happen easily. But F's splitting has little demonstrative force, in that it is not particular to this speech only. The dividing of short lines runs throughout the passage (see

Lineation Notes), and is clearly motivated by Compositor B's need to make the text as printed stretch towards the page-break marked in his copy (see Introduction, p. 130). In defence of F, 'Thou art too bad to curse' is effective as a direct riposte to Timon's charge that Apemantus is too dirty to be spat on.

362 **leprosy** Might refer specifically to the detritus that drops off the leprous body.

364 **I'll . . . but** I would beat thee, were it not that

365 **tongue** i.e. words

367 **Choler . . . alive** i.e. my anger that you are alive is killing me. An extreme excess of *choler* as one of the bodily 'humours' was indeed thought capable of making the heart burst (compare 17.28–9).

368 **to see** at seeing

372–5 **Beast . . . rogue!** These monosyllables bring the exchange of insults to a reductive end, with Timon seen as the beast and Apemantus as the man tainted by low

TIMON Slave!

APEMANTUS Toad!

TIMON Rogue, rogue, rogue!   375

> I am sick of this false world, and will love naught
> But even the mere necessities upon't.
> Then, Timon, presently prepare thy grave.
> Lie where the light foam of the sea may beat
> Thy gravestone daily. Make thine epitaph,   380
> That death in me at others' lives may laugh.
> > *He looks on the gold*
> O, thou sweet king-killer, and dear divorce
> 'Twixt natural son and sire; thou bright defiler
> Of Hymen's purest bed; thou valiant Mars;
> Thou ever young, fresh-loved, and delicate wooer,   385
> Whose blush doth thaw the consecrated snow

381.1 *He looks on the gold*] POPE (*subs.*); *not in* F   383 son and sire] ROWE; Sunne and fire F
385 fresh-loved] fresh, loued F   loved] POPE; loued (= -èd) F

---

birth. Timon's repeated 'rogue' is perhaps
painfully feeble with exhaustion, making
the transition to his suicidal 'I am sick of
this false world'.

377 **even . . . upon't** the very barest necessities of it. Probably refers not only to the
basic needs of life, but to death as life's
most necessary outcome.

378 **presently** immediately

381 **That . . . laugh** Suggests the 'grin' of a
skull or figure of Death on the gravestone.
That so that
in me i.e. as it presents itself in me, in the
example of me

382–93 **O . . . empire** An example of 'the
characteristic form of Renaissance
parody, the mock-encomium', comparable with *Volpone*'s sincere but authorially
ironized worship of gold in the opening
passage of *Volpone* (William E. Slights,
'*Genera Mixta* and *Timon of Athens*',
Studies in Philology, 74 (1977), 39–62;
pp. 52–3).

382 **king-killer** *OED*'s only example of this
compound dating from before the execution of Charles I, though there is another
instance in Thomas Heywood's *Troia Brit-
tanica* (1609), 15.47. Shakespeare has one
other instance of *killer*—again in a compound referring to an especially opprobri-
ous form of murder: *child-killer*, in *Richard*

Duke of York 2.2.112.
dear Both 'held in affection' (compare
sweet) and 'expensive'.
divorce The sense 'That which causes
divorce' (*OED sb.* 2) is Shakespearian.
OED cites only *Venus and Adonis* l. 932 and
this line.

383 **sire** father. F's 'Sunne and fire' combines
a common confusion between forms of
son and *sun* with a common misreading of
long 's' as 'f'. By association, 'Sunne' may
be influenced by 'bright', and 'fire' by
'defiler'. F makes little sense, and Timon
clearly runs through the usual sequence
of patriarchal males: king, father,
husband.
bright defiler An oxymoron.

384 **Hymen** Greek and Roman god of
marriage.
Mars The Roman god of war is here
invoked on account of his adultery with
Venus, goddess of love.

385 **fresh-loved** newly in love; newly loved.
Previous editors have taken this to be two
separate adjectives, but the compound
makes much better sense of *loved*. F has a
comma, which in F's punctuation is
sometimes equivalent to a hyphen.
delicate graceful

386 **blush** Plays on the lustre of gold and the
flush of the young wooer.

386–7 **the . . . lap** Compare *Coriolanus*

That lies on Dian's lap; thou visible god,
That sold'rest close impossibilities
And mak'st them kiss, that speak'st with every tongue
To every purpose; O thou touch of hearts: 390
Think thy slave man rebels, and by thy virtue
Set them into confounding odds, that beasts
May have the world in empire.

APEMANTUS   Would 'twere so,
But not till I am dead. I'll say thou'st gold.
Thou wilt be thronged to shortly.

TIMON   Thronged to?

APEMANTUS   Ay.   395

TIMON
Thy back, I prithee.

APEMANTUS   Live, and love thy misery.

TIMON
Long live so, and so die. I am quit.
    Enter ⌈at a distance⌉ the Banditti, Thieves

APEMANTUS
More things like men. Eat, Timon, and abhor them. *Exit*

397.1 *Enter . . . Banditti*] OXFORD SHAKESPEARE; *after 'Exit Apeman.', l.* 398, *in* F   *at a distance*]
OXFORD MIDDLETON; *not in* F   *Thieves*] POPE; *not in* F   398 APEMANTUS] F (*Ape.*); *not in* HANMER
More] F (Mo)   them] ROWE;   then F   *Exit*] F (*Exit Apeman.*)

5.3.65–7, 'chaste as the icicle | That's
candied by the frost from purest snow |
And hangs on Dian's temple'. 'Candied'
(F 'curdied'), harks back to l. 227.

387 **Dian** Roman goddess of chastity. There
is a suggestion too of Danaë, whom
Jupiter seduced as a shower of gold in her
lap.
   visible god In contrast with Christ as
'image of the invisible God' by whom
'were all things created' (Colossians 1:
15–16).

388 **sold'rest** Soldering was often a metaphor
for sexual union.
   close closely together (qualifying *sold'rest*)
   impossibilities i.e. things otherwise
incapable of union or irreconcilable

389 **with every tongue** (a) with the tongue of
every speaker, (b) in every language

390 **touch of hearts** (a) touchstone of hearts,
(b) influence that 'touches' or moves
hearts

391 **Think** choose to believe that
   virtue power. Gold's capacity to produce

impossible union is turned now to produce *confounding odds*.

392 **confounding odds** mutually destructive
strife

392–3 **that . . . empire** Compare Apemantus'
similar wish at l. 325. There, Timon criti-
cizes Apemantus for his ambition to
'remain a beast with the beasts'.

394 **not till I am dead** Though Apemantus is
not thinking of suicide or immediate
death, he does not appear in the play
again after his exit at l. 398.

396 **Thy back** i.e. turn your back to me,
depart. As entrances and exits were by
doors in the rear stage wall, a departing
actor would turn his back on most of the
audience too.

397 **quit** (a) at evens, (b) rid of him

397.1 *Enter . . . Thieves* These might logi-
cally be some of the deserters from
Alcibiades' army mentioned at ll. 90–2.
   Banditti Italian for 'bandits, outlaws'.

398 APEMANTUS Some editors follow Hanmer
in removing the speech-prefix so that
Timon continues to speak. But presum-

FIRST THIEF Where should he have this gold? It is some poor
fragment, some slender ort of his remainder. The mere   400
want of gold and the falling-from of his friends drove him
into this melancholy.

SECOND THIEF It is noised he hath a mass of treasure.

THIRD THIEF Let us make the assay upon him. If he care not
for't, he will supply us easily. If he covetously reserve it,   405
how shall 's get it?

SECOND THIEF True, for he bears it not about him; 'tis hid.

FIRST THIEF Is not this he?

OTHER THIEVES Where?

SECOND THIEF 'Tis his description.   410

THIRD THIEF He, I know him.

ALL THIEVES ⌈*coming forward*⌉ Save thee, Timon.

TIMON Now, thieves.

ALL THIEVES
    Soldiers, not thieves.

TIMON   Both, too, and women's sons.

ALL THIEVES
    We are not thieves, but men that much do want.   415

TIMON
    Your greatest want is, you want much of meat.

---

399 FIRST THIEF] F (1). *Similarly a numeral without a name for all the Thieves.*   401 falling-from
of] F (falling from of)   409 OTHER THIEVES] KNIGHT (*subs.*); *All.* F   412 ALL THIEVES] F (*All.*).
Similarly at ll. 414 and 415.   coming forward] OXFORD SHAKESPEARE; *not in* F

ably Apemantus, after parting from
Timon, meets the Banditti as he crosses
the stage to leave.

399 **Where should he have** (a) from where
can he have obtained, (b) where might he
keep

400 **ort** left-over (usually of food)
mere absolute

401 **falling-from** falling off. Blake (5.4.2,
'From') suggests reading F's 'from of' as
'from off', as in 'you must cut this flesh
from off his breast' (*Merchant of Venice*
4.1.299). This makes Timon's rejection of
his friends the cause of his melancholy,
but it is more likely that the friends'
behaviour is said to be the cause.

403 **noised** rumoured

404 **assay** (a) test (as for the presence and
quality of gold in an alloy), (b) assault

406 **shall 's** shall us, for 'shall we' (Abbott
215). Colloquial, but not always demotic;

said, for instance, by Hermione in
Winter's Tale 1.2.179.

409 **OTHER THIEVES** An editorial modification
of F's '*All.*'. Sometimes emended to the
Third Thief.

410 **'Tis** i.e. it matches

413 **Now** A non-committal greeting.

414 **Soldiers, not thieves** See note to l. 397.1.
Both . . . sons Timon implies that the distinction scarcely matters, as all men are
bad. *Women's sons* is proverbial ('To be
born of woman', Dent W637), here suggesting 'members of sinning humanity',
alluding to Eve's transgression. Contrast
14.492–3.

415 **much do want** are very needy (but also
'are very greedy')

416 **much of meat.** F has 'much of meat:'.
Sisson unnecessarily ends the sentence
after 'much' instead of 'meat'.
meat Food generally; not necessarily
flesh.

Why should you want? Behold, the earth hath roots.
Within this mile break forth a hundred springs.
The oaks bear mast, the briers scarlet hips.
The bounteous housewife nature on each bush   420
Lays her full mess before you. Want? Why want?

FIRST THIEF

We cannot live on grass, on berries, water,
As beasts and birds and fishes.

TIMON

Nor on the beasts themselves, the birds and fishes;
You must eat men. Yet thanks I must you con   425
That you are thieves professed, that you work not
In holier shapes; for there is boundless theft
In limited professions. (*Giving gold*) Rascal thieves,
Here's gold. Go suck the subtle blood o'th' grape
Till the high fever seethe your blood to froth,   430
And so scape hanging. Trust not the physician;
His antidotes are poison, and he slays
More than you rob. Take wealth and lives together—
Do, villains, do, since you protest to do't,
Like workmen. I'll example you with thievery.   435

---

428 *Giving gold*] BEVINGTON (*subs.*); *not in* F   433 More] F (Moe)   434 villains] This edition;
Villaine F; villainy (*as object of* 'Do') ROWE   protest] F; profess G. Taylor *conj. in* OXFORD SHAKE-
SPEARE   434–5 do't, | Like workmen.] POPE; ~. | Like ~, F

419–21 **The . . . you** Nature is presented as
  fecund and erotic, with probable wordplay on *hips* as fruits of the rose and
  body-part.
419 **mast** acorns (fed to swine)
421 **mess** serving of food
423 **As** as do
425 **thanks I must you con** I must offer
  thanks to you
428 **limited professions** (a) regulated trades,
  (b) less forthright admissions. Timon
  challenges the view that guilds effectively
  controlled trades and imposed fair standards. *Limited* contrasts with *boundless*.
429 **subtle** (a) fine, delicate; (b) treacherous
  blood o'th' grape wine. The phrase
  became common in the 17th century, but
  was unusual at the time of *Timon*. The
  image of sucking blood suggests a leech
  (a) in the pejorative sense 'extortioner',
  (b) as used in medical blood-letting (the

blood-sucker here doesn't cure the patient
  but induces a *high fever*).
430 **high fever** The suggestion of drunkenness merges into that of fatal disease (and
  see previous note).
  seethe (a) boil; (b) dissipate; (c) ferment,
  foam
431 **so scape hanging** (by dying of fever first)
431–3 **Trust . . . rob** See note to 7.11–12.
433 **Take wealth and lives** steal wealth and
  end lives
434 **villains** F's 'Villaine' is inconsistent with
  workmen and, just as important, *you* (a *villain* would usually be addressed *thou*). The
  present emendation gives a more metrical
  line than Rowe's (see collation), and
  continues the idea that theft is a kind of
  murder.
  protest profess; vow
435 **example you with** give you precedent
  for

The sun's a thief, and with his great attraction
Robs the vast sea. The moon's an arrant thief,
And her pale fire she snatches from the sun.
The sea's a thief, whose liquid surge resolves
The moon into salt tears. The earth's a thief,   440
That feeds and breeds by a composture stol'n
From gen'ral excrement. Each thing's a thief.
The laws, your curb and whip, in their rough power
Has unchecked theft. Love not yourselves. Away,
Rob one another. There's more gold. Cut throats;   445
All that you meet are thieves. To Athens go,
Break open shops; nothing can you steal
But thieves do lose it. Steal less for this I give you,
And gold confound you howsoe'er. Amen.

---

444 Has] F (Ha's)   448 less] F; not less ROWE; no less COLLIER

436–44 **The sun's . . . theft** Evidently based
on the Greek Anacreon's Ode 19 (variously numbered): 'Fruitful earth drinks
up the rain, | Trees from earth drink that
again, | The sea drinks the air, the sun |
Drinks the sea, and him the moon' (trans.
Thomas Stanley, 1625–88). According to
George Puttenham, Ronsard's French
version (which is extant) had been translated into English in the 16th century.

436 **attraction** action of drawing to itself (i.e.
drawing up moisture). The line provides
OED's earliest example of sense 5.

437 **arrant** notorious

439–40 **The . . . tears** Alludes to the then
current view that tides were caused by the
sea drawing moisture from the moon.
Compare *Richard III* 2.2.69–70, 'That I,
being governed by the wat'ry moon, |
May send forth plenteous tears to drown
the world'; also *Midsummer Night's Dream*
2.1.103–4, where the moon, 'Pale in her
anger washes all the air'.

439 **resolves** melts, dissolves

440–2 **The earth's . . . excrement** Perhaps
suggested by John Marston's *The Malcontent* (published 1604): 'this earth is . . .
the very muck-hill on which the sub-
lunary orbs cast their excrements': ed.
G. K. Hunter (1975), 4.5.110–13.

441 **composture** compost. *OED*'s earliest
example of the word, and only example in
this sense. But there is an earlier instance

in another sense in John Beaumont's
Metamorphosis of Tobacco (1602): 'And in
the sweet composture of a dock | Drinks
to his lady's dog and mistress' smock'.

442 **excrement** Could refer to any matter
secreted by plants or animals, but the
sense 'faeces' is probably dominant.

443 **your curb and whip** The implied image is
of controlling an unruly horse, though
criminals were also whipped.

444 **Has unchecked theft** have unlimited
power to steal. The singular 'Has' is
prompted by the previous word, 'power'.
Most modern editions agree that
unchecked is an adjective (first instance in
OED dated 1469). *OED* sees it as a unique
example of the verb *uncheck*, 'To fail to
check', which is also possible.

447 **Break . . . steal** Wright (p. 177) cites this
line and 17.37 as examples of a missing
syllable after the caesura creating 'a more
condensed style and strong effects of
sharpness or gravity'.

448–9 **Steal . . . howsoe'er** even if you steal
less on account of this gold I give you,
may the gold ruin you whatever you do.
For subjunctive followed by *and,* and
its confusability with the imperative,
see Abbott 364. For *howsoe'er*, compare
Abbott 47 and 403.

449 **Amen** A word Timon has borrowed (or
stolen) from Apemantus; compare 2.70
(Apemantus) and 12.41 (Timon).

THIRD THIEF He's almost charmed me from my profession   450
by persuading me to it.

FIRST THIEF 'Tis in the malice of mankind that he thus
advises us, not to have us thrive in our mystery.

SECOND THIEF I'll believe him as an enemy, and give over my
trade.   455

FIRST THIEF Let us first see peace in Athens. There is no time
so miserable but a man may be true.   *Exeunt Thieves*
    Enter the Steward to Timon

STEWARD O you gods!
Is yon despised and ruinous man my lord,
Full of decay and failing? O monument   460
And wonder of good deeds evilly bestowed!
What an alteration of honour has desp'rate want made!
What viler thing upon the earth than friends,
Who can bring noblest minds to basest ends!
How rarely does it meet with this time's guise,   465
When man was wished to love his enemies!
Grant I may ever love and rather woo

450, 469 He's] F (Has)   456 There] F; *2 Thief.* There WARBURTON   457 *Exeunt*] F (*Exit*)
459 yon] F (yon'd)

450 **He's** F's 'Has', as a contraction of 'he
has', is a Middleton characteristic coming
just before his contribution of the Steward episode (Holdsworth). But the lines
seem otherwise Shakespearian, having
echoes, for instance, of the exchange
between the executioners of Clarence in
Richard III. Middleton probably transcribed this section or part of it, perhaps
to reorganize the scene or join the two
authorial sections.

452 **in the malice of** out of hatred for

453 **mystery** profession

454–5 **I'll . . . trade** The Thief trusts Timon's
exhortations to steal so little that he offers
to quit his 'trade'.

454 **believe him as an enemy** i.e. disbelieve
him (as an enemy is not to be
trusted)

456–7 **Let . . . true** Implies either (a) he too
will become *true* (honest) once peace
returns (peace being a *miserable* time for
banditti), or (b) he will not quit his trade
(peace being unlikely) but remain *true*
to his calling. Neither reading is wholly
convincing. Perhaps, as Warburton
emended, the First Thief proposes

delay and another Thief replies that one
can be honest at any time, even now.

459 **despised and ruinous** Compare Isaiah's
prophecy that the Messiah will be
'despised and rejected' (Isaiah 53: 2, as
quoted in *Two Gates* xi.I).
ruinous ruined. The suggestion of a building is continued in *decay* and *monument*.
But Middleton also applied the adjective to
an impoverished *man*: a character in
Weapons is called Sir Ruinous Gentry.

461 **wonder** astonishing example
evilly bestowed Both 'bestowed on evil
people' and 'badly bestowed'.

462 **desp'rate** extreme; causing spiritual
despair

465 **it** i.e. the time recalled in the next line.
Oliver takes the referent to be 'the fact that
friends destroy noble minds such as
Timon's', reading *rarely* as an ironic 'splen-
didly', but this seems strained, and leaves
the relation with the next line obscure.
meet accord
guise custom, fashion

466 **wished** desired
love his enemies As in Christ's command-
ment (Matthew 5: 54).

Those that would mischief me than those that do!
He's caught me in his eye. I will present
My honest grief unto him, and as my lord   470
Still serve him with my life.—My dearest master.

TIMON
Away! What art thou?

STEWARD   Have you forgot me, sir?

TIMON
Why dost ask that? I have forgot all men;
Then if thou grant'st thou'rt a man, I have forgot thee.

STEWARD
An honest poor servant of yours.

TIMON   Then I know thee not.   475
I never had honest man about me; ay, all
I kept were knaves to serve in meat to villains.

STEWARD The gods are witness,
Ne'er did poor steward wear a truer grief
For his undone lord than mine eyes for you.   480

He weeps

TIMON
What, dost thou weep? Come nearer then; I love thee
Because thou art a woman, and disclaim'st
Flinty mankind whose eyes do never give
But thorough lust and laughter. Pity's sleeping.
Strange times, that weep with laughing, not with
    weeping!   485

---

474 grant'st‸ thou'rt a man,] POPE; grunt'st, th'art a man. F   479 Ne'er] F (Neu'r)
480.1 *He weeps*] BEVINGTON; *not in* F

468 **would mischief** intend to harm
472 **Have you forgot me** Potentially ambiguous to Timon, as the expression could be that of an 'honest poor servant' (l. 475) requesting reward or reminding his master of his obligations to him. Timon avoids this implication by taking the question literally.
477 **knaves** Puns on the senses 'rogues' and 'servants'. There is a similar ambiguity in *villains*, which refers to Timon's rich friends but could mean 'coarse peasants'.
479 **wear** The *grief* expressed in the Steward's tears is worn like the badge that identified the household to which a servant was bound.

481–2 **I . . . woman** Middleton's *Timon's* validation of 'woman' here contrasts with Timon's misogyny in the main Shakespearian part of the scene.
483 **Flinty** Based on the proverbial hardness of flint (Dent H311) and the proverb 'To fetch water out of a flint' (Dent W107).
   give yield tears. Perhaps also the eyes are metonymic for the man who withholds generosity.
484 **thorough** A disyllabic form of *through*.
   Pity's sleeping The eyes of Pity are closed in sleep, so tears must come from a different source.

STEWARD

I beg of you to know me, good my lord,

T'accept my grief,

    He offers his money

                    and whilst this poor wealth lasts

To entertain me as your steward still.

TIMON Had I a steward

So true, so just, and now so comfortable?   490

It almost turns my dangerous nature wild.

Let me behold thy face. Surely this man

Was born of woman.

Forgive my general and exceptless rashness,

You perpetual sober gods! I do proclaim   495

One honest man—mistake me not, but one,

No more, I pray—and he's a steward.

How fain would I have hated all mankind,

And thou redeem'st thyself! But all save thee

I fell with curses.   500

Methinks thou art more honest now than wise,

For by oppressing and betraying me

Thou mightst have sooner got another service;

For many so arrive at second masters

Upon their first lord's neck. But tell me true—   505

---

487 *He offers his money*] BEVINGTON (*subs.*); *not in* F   491 wild] F (wilde); mild HANMER

486 **I . . . me** Compare 'Have you forgot me', l. 472, and note. The sense in which the Steward wishes to be recognized is now clear.

487 **this poor wealth** This is most obviously the remnant of the Steward's savings (offered as it were as reverse payment for his continuing to serve Timon), but could refer instead (or as well) to his living body.

488 **entertain** employ

490 **comfortable** comforting

491 **wild** The meaning seems to be that Timon's dangerous propensity to wildness (distraction, madness) is almost unleashed, that he is close to losing entirely his remaining self-control. Some editors accept Hanmer's 'mild'.

492–3 **Surely . . . woman** From Job 14: 1, where 'man that is born of woman' describes the human condition. Timon finds that being born of woman has, in the Steward's case, left traces in his 'womanish' behaviour.

494 **exceptless** indiscriminate. *OED*'s only instance of the word.

496–7 **One . . . steward** The Steward contrasts with the biblical Unjust Steward, who is wise but worldly and dishonest (see Appendix B, extract 3).

497 **No more, I pray** A telling sign that Timon actually wants humanity to accord with his idea of universal wickedness?

498 **fain** willingly

499 **thou redeem'st thyself** Refers to the Protestant emphasis on individuals' responsibility for their own salvation. Timon wills the gods to damn all mankind (his curse being an ironic prayer), but the Steward exempts himself.

502 **oppressing** trampling down, molesting

503 **service** employment as servant

505 **Upon . . . neck** (a) by mounting on his first master's shoulders, (b) having subjugated him, (c) having betrayed him to execution or broken his neck

For I must ever doubt, though ne'er so sure—
Is not thy kindness subtle, covetous,
If not a usuring kindness, and, as rich men deal gifts,
Expecting in return twenty for one?

STEWARD

No, my most worthy master, in whose breast　　　　510
Doubt and suspect, alas, are placed too late.
You should have feared false times when you did feast.
Suspect still comes where an estate is least.
That which I show, heaven knows, is merely love,
Duty and zeal to your unmatchèd mind,　　　　515
Care of your food and living; and, believe it,
My most honoured lord,
For any benefit that points to me,
Either in hope or present, I'd exchange
For this one wish: that you had power and wealth　　　　520
To requite me by making rich yourself.

TIMON

Look thee, 'tis so. Thou singly honest man,
　　He gives the Steward gold
Here, take. The gods, out of my misery,
Has sent thee treasure. Go, live rich and happy,
But thus conditioned: thou shalt build from men,　　　　525

508 If not a] F; A POPE   522.1 *He gives the Steward gold*] OXFORD SHAKESPEARE (*subs.*); *not in* F; *He offers gold* BEVINGTON   524 Has] F (Ha's)

507 **subtle** treacherous. Perhaps part of a compound, *subtle-covetous*, 'covetous to the point of treachery'.

508 **If not a** Usually taken to be Compositor B's near-repetition of 'Is not' from the previous line, which is especially likely as the repetition of 'kindness' would encourage eye-skip. But the hexameter does not in itself invite emendation, and the sense in F is unobjectionable.
usuring Middletonian; not in Shakespeare.

509 **twenty for one** Varies Middleton's usual phrase 'two for one'.

511 **suspect** suspicion

513 **still** always

514 **merely** entirely, purely

518–20 **For . . . For** The first 'For' becomes redundant as the sentence structure shifts.

521 **To . . . yourself** Might mean either that Timon's renewed riches would be the source of reward, or (more likely) that the Steward would regard Timon's enrichment as reward in itself.
requite Here stressed on the first syllable.

522 **Look thee, 'tis so** Phelps established a strong moment here by having a pause before it. Whereas Timon had given Apemantus coins from his wallet, he presented the Steward with 'his store of gold in an urn' (prompt book).

524 **Has** The preceding word 'misery' influences the verb to become singular.

525 **But thus conditioned** bound only by this condition. Compare *Bloody Banquet* 4.3.204, 'so conditioned'. *Conditioned* is not in Shakespeare.
from away from

Hate all, curse all, show charity to none,
But let the famished flesh slide from the bone
Ere thou relieve the beggar. Give to dogs
What thou deniest to men. Let prisons swallow 'em,
Debts wither 'em to nothing; be men like blasted woods,   530
And may diseases lick up their false bloods.
And so farewell, and thrive.

STEWARD

O, let me stay and comfort you, my master.

TIMON If thou hat'st curses,

Stay not. Fly whilst thou art blest and free.   535
Ne'er see thou man, and let me ne'er see thee.

Exit Steward. ⌈*Timon withdraws into his cave*⌉
Enter Poet and Painter

PAINTER As I took note of the place, it cannot be far where
he abides.

POET What's to be thought of him? Does the rumour hold
for true that he's so full of gold?   540

536.1 *Exit . . . cave*] COLLIER 1853; *Exit.* F; *Exeunt severally* THEOBALD

527 **famished** Not elsewhere in Middleton.

527–9 **flesh slide from the bone . . . prisons swallow 'em** For the correlation of starvation to 'the bone' with the 'swallow' of the prison, compare *Puritan Widow* 3.4.53–5: 'if I fall into the hungry swallow of the prison, I am like utterly to perish, and with fees and extortions be pinched clean to the bone'.

529 **Let . . . 'em** Debtors were often imprisoned.

530 **be men** let men be
blasted blighted, withered

531 **lick up** i.e. consume. Hints that the diseases are like a dog licking a sick man's sores or wounds; compare the dogs that consume food that would preserve men in ll. 528–9.

535 **free** i.e. free from curses

536.1 *Exit . . . cave* For the cave as stage property, see note to l. 1. F's '*Exit.*' applies to the Thieves and, with qualification, to Timon. It may establish a cleared stage, or Timon may remain visible in his cave, a liminal space that might be regarded as either on or off stage (compare the direction '*Exit and stays behind the hangings*' in James Shirley's *The Grateful Servant*, 1629). The actual or notional representa-

tion of the cave maintains continuity of action even if the stage is cleared of actors. Capell introduced an act break, but provided no exit and began Act 5 with '*Before* Timon's *Cave. Enter* Poet, *and* Painter; TIMON *behind, unseen*'. This implicitly recognizes the continuity in F. Subsequent editors have been less circumspect.

Phelps reintroduced continuity of presence by deleting the Poet and Painter episode and having the Steward remain on stage. The action flowed straight into the episode with the senators, who entered to meet the Steward after a pregnant pause.

536.2–650.1 *Enter . . . Exeunt* Middleton probably added touches during transcription. Jackson notes Middleton's linguistic preferences in ll. 539–45 (does, has) and ll. 610–17 (three instances of y', e'en). See also notes to ll. 541–4, 545, 550, 556–7, 579, and 592. Middleton's contribution of the Steward's visit to Timon raises questions relating to the sequence of episodes. See Introduction, pp. 148–9.

540 **full of gold** The idiom also occurs in *All's Well* 4.3.217, 'the Count's a fool, and full of gold'.

PAINTER Certain. Alcibiades reports it. Phrynia and
   Timandra had gold of him. He likewise enriched poor
   straggling soldiers with great quantity. 'Tis said he gave
   unto his steward a mighty sum.

POET Then this breaking of his has been but a try for his   545
   friends?

PAINTER Nothing else. You shall see him a palm in Athens
   again, and flourish with the highest. Therefore 'tis not
   amiss we tender our loves to him in this supposed distress
   of his. It will show honestly in us, and is very likely to load   550
   our purposes with what they travail for, if it be a just and
   true report that goes of his having.

POET What have you now to present unto him?

PAINTER Nothing at this time, but my visitation; only I will
   promise him an excellent piece.   555

POET I must serve him so too, tell him of an intent that's
   coming toward him.

PAINTER Good as the best. Promising is the very air o'th'
   time; it opens the eyes of expectation. Performance is
   ever the duller for his act, and but in the plainer and   560

---

541 Phrynia] ROWE 1714; *Phrinica* F   542 Timandra] F2; *Timandylo* F1   545 has] F (ha's)

541–4 **Phrynia . . . sum**   Probably a
Middleton addition. This would explain
the errors in naming the whores: F's
'*Phrinica* and *Timandylo*' are inconsistencies likely to derive from Middleton
misremembering names Shakespeare
introduced from classical sources. As
Middleton here refers to 'poor straggling
soldiers', he elsewhere, in *Dissemblers*,
refers to 'a poor straggling Gypsy'. Shakespeare's only use of 'straggling' is in a
non-dramatic context (*Rape of Lucrece* l.
428), and is not adjunct with 'poor'. It is
Middleton who refers to soldiers as 'poor'
(*Puritan Widow* 3.5.50, *Tennis* l. 600).

543 **straggling** vagrant, vagabond
   soldiers As the Banditti call themselves at
   l. 414.

545 **breaking** bankruptcy. Middletonian
   (*Weapons* 1.1.49).
   try test. The line supplies *OED*'s only
   example of this sense (*sb.* 2). Compare
   4.173.

547–8 **a . . . highest** Alludes to Psalms 92:
   11: 'The righteous shall flourish like a
   palm-tree'.

550 **show honestly in us** show us to be honest. Possibly a Middleton idiom. Compare
   Quiet Life 3.1.72, 'It shows a generous
   condition in you'; *Women Beware*
   3.2.24–5, 'to show | Perfection once in
   woman'. But these examples use a noun
   rather than an adverb.

551 **what they travail for** A transparent cir-
   cumlocution for Timon's gold. Similarly
   'his having' in the next line (for which
   compare 4.139).
   travail Both 'labour' and 'travel'.

556–7 **tell . . . him** Possibly Middletonian;
   compare *Women Beware* 1.2.221,
   'Methought I heard ill news come toward
   me'.

558 **Good as the best** as good as could be;
   excellent

558–64 **Promising . . . it** See note to l. 73.

558 **air** Metaphoric for 'style, manner'; also
   the medium of words as breath; empti-
   ness; and the medium of life.

558–9 **th' time** the times, the present

560 **for his act** (a) when it comes to the act of
   performance, or perhaps (b) as a result of
   the act of promising. *His* could be the

simpler kind of people the deed of saying is quite out
of use. To promise is most courtly and fashionable.
Performance is a kind of will or testament which argues a
great sickness in his judgement that makes it.

Enter Timon from his cave, unobserved

TIMON (*aside*) Excellent workman, thou canst not paint a   565
man so bad as is thyself.

POET (*to Painter*) I am thinking what I shall say I have
provided for him. It must be a personating of himself,
a satire against the softness of prosperity, with a
discovery of the infinite flatteries that follow youth and   570
opulency.

TIMON (*aside*) Must thou needs stand for a villain in thine
own work? Wilt thou whip thine own faults in other men?
Do so; I have gold for thee.

POET (*to Painter*) Nay, let's seek him.   575
Then do we sin against our own estate
When we may profit meet and come too late.

PAINTER True.
When the day serves, before black-cornered night,

564.1 *unobserved*] POPE; *not in* F

neuter pronoun ('its'), or, especially with
sense (a), there could be an element of
personification.

561 **the deed of saying** doing what has been
promised
561–2 **quite out of use** completely
unpractised
562 **courtly** *OED*'s earliest example of the
word used in a pejorative sense
563–4 **Performance . . . it** A paradox, as a
will or testament is more similar to a
promise than a performance. Ambiguous
also in that *a great sickness in his judgement*
comes close to meaning 'that, in his
judgement, he is suffering a mortal sickness', but in context must mean 'that his
judgement is seriously impaired'.
564.1 *Enter . . . unobserved* See note to l.
536.1.
568 **provided** planned
568–71 **opulency** The terms *personating* and *discovery* (as of a curtain drawn
back to reveal a tableau behind it) suggest
that the poem will be couched in terms of
an allegorical theatrical display. *[Y]outh
and opulency* suggests youth in the specific

circumstance of opulence, and might
recall the figure of misled Youth in
morality plays such as Robert Wever's
mid 16th-century *Lusty Juventus*. The present passage provides the earliest examples in *OED* of both *personating* (as either
verbal noun, as here, or adjectival participle) and *opulency*. However, *opulency*
occurs earlier, in Henry Chettle's *Pierce
Plainness* (1595), in a miser's 'execrable'
orison praising gold as 'the chiefest good'
(sig. G2).
572 **stand for** act as a model for, be represented as
a villain i.e. one of the flatterers. The
satire against 'infinite flatteries' is itself
an act of flattery.
573 **whip . . . men** From proverbial 'To find
fault with others and do worse oneself'
(Dent F107).
576 **Then do** (redundant to the sense)
estate prosperity
577 **may profit meet** are able to meet profit.
579 **serves** is available
black-cornered night night full of dark
corners. The Painter perhaps expresses
himself in terms of paintings. *OED*'s only

Find what thou want'st by free and offered light.   580
Come.

TIMON (*aside*)

I'll meet you at the turn. What a god's gold,
That he is worshipped in a baser temple
Than where swine feed!
'Tis thou that rigg'st the barque and plough'st the foam,   585
Settlest admirèd reverence in a slave.
To thee be worship, and thy saints for aye
Be crowned with plagues, that thee alone obey.
Fit I meet them.

    He comes forward to them

POET

Hail, worthy Timon!

PAINTER   Our late noble master!   590

TIMON

Have I once lived to see two honest men?

POET

Sir, having often of your open bounty tasted,

---

587 worship] ROWE; worshipt F   589.1 *He . . . them*] CAPELL (*subs.*); *not in* F

example of *black-cornered*. Shakespeare
has no instance of 'cornered'. Middleton
has 'four-cornered', in conjunction with
'Pale-mantled night' three lines before
and 'blackness' nine lines later (*Solomon
Paraphrased* 8.2), which suggests that he
added a touch here, perhaps to create a
rhyming couplet.

582 **meet . . . turn** confront you when you
turn the corner; i.e. take you by surprise.
Timon may be concealed behind a stage
pillar, or refer to a corner of the stage.
Other relevant senses of *turn* are 'subtle
device', 'opportunity', 'sudden veer of a
hunted hare'.

What a god's gold If the sentence is read
as an exclamation, the sense is a sarcastic
'What a fine god gold is!' As a question, it
would be 'What sort of a god is gold?' F
punctuates with a question mark after
'feede' (l. 584). As this could be used for
an exclamation mark, it could stand for
either interpretation.

583 **a baser temple** i.e. the human body
(ironizing I Corinthians 6: 19, 'your body
is the temple of the Holy Ghost'), specifi-

cally the Painter's body. Shakespeare,
Middleton, and other writers often refer to
the sinful body as a ruined, defiled, or
debased temple.

585 **thou** i.e. gold. The 'informal' form of the
pronoun may register contempt, though
thou was also used in addresses to supernatural beings such as a 'god'.

rigg'st the barque sets the rigging on the
ship (presumably a trading vessel).

plough'st *OED*'s earliest example of this
poeticism (*plough*, *v*. 4).

586 **admirèd reverence** an expression of
reverential wonder

587 **saints** i.e. devout followers, including the
living such as the Poet and Painter

aye ever

588 **that thee alone obey** The referent is *thy
saints*.

591 **once** i.e. really

592 **Sir . . . tasted** See note to 1.275–85. As
the idiom seems Middletonian, and as
there are some indications of minor
Middleton additions to this scene, he
might have added the present line.

open open-handed, generous.

Hearing you were retired, your friends fall'n off,
Whose thankless natures—O abhorrèd spirits,
Not all the whips of heaven are large enough—   595
What, to you,
Whose star-like nobleness gave life and influence
To their whole being! I am rapt, and cannot cover
The monstrous bulk of this ingratitude
With any size of words.   600

TIMON

Let it go naked; men may see't the better.
You that are honest, by being what you are
Make them best seen and known.

PAINTER   He and myself
Have travelled in the great show'r of your gifts,
And sweetly felt it.

TIMON   Ay, you are honest men.   605

PAINTER

We are hither come to offer you our service.

TIMON

Most honest men. Why, how shall I requite you?
Can you eat roots and drink cold water? No.

POET *and* PAINTER

What we can do we'll do to do you service.

TIMON

You're honest men. You've heard that I have gold,   610
I am sure you have. Speak truth; you're honest men.

---

601 go‸ naked;] *punctuation follows* THEOBALD; go. / Naked‸ F   604 travelled] F (trauail'd)
605 men] F2; man FI   609 POET *and* PAINTER] F (*Both.*). *Similarly throughout rest of scene.*
610, 611 You're . . . you're] F (Y'are . . . y'are)   610 You've] F (Y'haue)

---

593 **were retired** had withdrawn from society. Very euphemistic.
  fall'n off become estranged, dropped away
594–5 **Whose . . . enough** The syntax is left uncertain, as the Poet breaks off in pretended indignation.
596 **to you** i.e. *thankless* to you
597 **influence** The supposed astrological effect of celestial bodies on humans, here seen as beneficent.
598–606 **I . . . service** There is probably a homoerotic undercurrent to the language.

598 **I am rapt** As the Painter said the Poet was at 1.19.
600 **size** (a) quantity, (b) glutinous wash applied to prepare paper or canvas for painting
601 **Let . . . better** Proverbially, 'The truth shows best being naked' (Dent T589).
604 **travelled** F's spelling 'trauail'd' is ambiguous: also *travailed*, toiled. 'Felt' (l. 605) suggests that the image of journeying in a shower of rain is primary.
609 **What . . . service** The repetition of 'do' suggests the speakers' obsequious anxiety.

PAINTER

  So it is said, my noble lord, but therefor
  Came not my friend nor I.

TIMON

  Good honest men. (*To Painter*) Thou draw'st a
     counterfeit
  Best in all Athens; thou'rt indeed the best;   615
  Thou counterfeit'st most lively.

PAINTER   So so, my lord.

TIMON

  E'en so, sir, as I say. (*To Poet*) And for thy fiction,
  Why, thy verse swells with stuff so fine and smooth
  That thou art even natural in thine art.
  But for all this, my honest-natured friends,   620
  I must needs say you have a little fault.
  Marry, 'tis not monstrous in you, neither wish I
  You take much pains to mend.

POET *and* PAINTER   Beseech your honour
  To make it known to us.

TIMON   You'll take it ill.

POET *and* PAINTER Most thankfully, my lord.   625

TIMON Will you indeed?

POET *and* PAINTER Doubt it not, worthy lord.

TIMON

  There's never a one of you but trusts a knave
  That mightily deceives you.

POET *and* PAINTER   Do we, my lord?

TIMON

  Ay, and you hear him cog, see him dissemble,   630
  Know his gross patchery, love him, feed him,

---

615 thou'rt] F (th'art)

612 **therefor** on that account
614 **counterfeit** (a) life-like picture, (b) forgery. The latter idea, that the Painter dissimulates, is brought out in *counterfeit'st* in l. 616.
616 **lively** lifelike
617 **fiction** (a) artistic invention, (b) deceit
618 **swells with stuff** (a) swells with ideas (like a swollen river?), (b) is inflated with padding (like a garment?)

smooth smoothly flowing (but also 'flattering')
619 **even** absolutely
    natural in thine art Praise of the Poet's verisimilitude half-conceals the sense 'instinctively duplicitous'.
622 **monstrous** Compare l. 599.
628 **never . . . trusts** not a single one of you that doesn't trust
630 **cog** cheat, flatter
631 **patchery** knavery

Keep in your bosom; yet remain assured
That he's a made-up villain.

PAINTER I know none such, my lord.

POET Nor I.   635

TIMON

Look you, I love you well. I'll give you gold,
Rid me these villains from your companies.
Hang them or stab them, drown them in a draught,
Confound them by some course, and come to me,
I'll give you gold enough.

POET *and* PAINTER   Name them, my lord, let's know them.   640

TIMON

You that way and you this, but two in company;
Each man apart, all single and alone,
Yet an arch-villain keeps him company.
(*To one of them*) If where thou art two villains shall not
  be,
Come not near him. (*To the other*) If thou wouldst not
  reside   645
But where one villain is, then him abandon.
Hence; pack! ⌈*Throwing stones*⌉ There's gold. You came
for gold, ye slaves. (*To one of them*) You have work for
me; there's payment. Hence! (*To the other*) You are an

---

642 apart] F3; a part F1   647 *Throwing stones*] This edition; *not in* F; *Beating and driving 'em
out* ROWE

632 **Keep** keep him
  in your bosom close to your heart
633 **made-up** consummate, accomplished
  (*OED*'s one example of the sense, and
  earliest example in any sense)
637 **Rid** if you get rid of (subjunctive, as with
  the following verbs too)
  me Either 'for me' or the emotionally
  emphatic 'ethic dative'.
638 **draught** cesspool, sewer
639 **Confound** ruin, destroy
641 **but . . . company** yet there is still a company of two
646 **But** except
647 **pack** get packing, clear off
  Throwing stones Timon may alternatively strike the Poet and Painter. Stone-
  throwing is consistent with his attack on

the false friends at 11.99, and stones are
an appropriate valueless equivalent to the
gold Timon has dug from the earth. For
stones in Lucian, see note to 11.84.2.
648 **work** a piece of work, i.e. a poem
649–50 **You are an alchemist** Because as a
  poet he transmutes his subject into something finer, as alchemists supposedly
  transmute base metal to gold. Compare
  the contrast between the trickster poet of
  the market place and the Apollonian poet
  associated with gold in the epigram from
  Ovid heading *Venus and Adonis*: '*Vilia
  miretur vulgus: mihi flavus Apollo | Pocula
  Castalia plena ministret aqua*' ('Let what is
  cheap excite the marvel of the crowd; for
  me may golden Apollo minister full cups
  from the Castalian fount').

alchemist; make gold of that. Out, rascal dogs!   650

    Exeunt Poet and Painter; Timon withdraws to his cave

    Enter Steward and two Senators

STEWARD

It is in vain that you would speak with Timon,

For he is set so only to himself

That nothing but himself which looks like man

Is friendly with him.

FIRST SENATOR   Bring us to his cave.

It is our part and promise to th'Athenians   655

To speak with Timon.

SECOND SENATOR   At all times alike

Men are not still the same. 'Twas time and griefs

That framed him thus. Time with his fairer hand

Offering the fortunes of his former days,

The former man may make him. Bring us to him,   660

And chance it as it may.

STEWARD   Here is his cave.—

Peace and content be here! Lord Timon, Timon,

Look out and speak to friends. Th'Athenians

By two of their most reverend senate greet thee.

Speak to them, noble Timon.   665

    Enter Timon out of his cave

TIMON

Thou sun that comforts, burn! Speak and be hanged.

650.1 *Exeunt . . . cave*] STAUNTON (*subs.*); *Exeunt* F 651 is in] F3; is F1 661 chance] F3; chanc'd F1

651–764 **It . . . foot** Some editors make this a new scene (5.2). This episode may owe something to the passage in Plutarch's 'Life of Caius Martius Coriolanus' where Roman ambassadors vainly plead with Coriolanus 'to let him understand how his countrymen did call him home again, and restored him to all his goods, and besought him to deliver them from this war' (p. 251).

652 **set** fixed, directed

  only exclusively

654 **with him** i.e. in his eyes

655 **our . . . promise** the role we promised to play

657 **still** always, consistently

  time and griefs i.e. the griefs of the time

658 **Time with his fairer hand** Though male, Time here seems related to the figure of changeable Fortune: an emblematic figure who inflicts misery with one hand and confers prosperity with the other. The more usual emblematic properties associated with Time, the hourglass, the scythe, and the skull, emphasized his destructive nature. But compare Time's dual capacity in *Winter's Tale* 4.1.8–9 'in one self-born hour | To plant and o'erwhelm custom'.

660 **The . . . make him** may make him the man he formerly was

666 **comforts** For a similar alteration of the second person singular (comfort'st), compare 12.2. Here the form may simply avoid the vocally awkward '-t'st' ending.

  Speak and be hanged Varies the proverb 'Confess and be hanged' (Dent C587).

For each true word a blister, and each false
Be as a cantherizing to the root o'th' tongue,
Consuming it with speaking.

FIRST SENATOR   Worthy Timon—

TIMON
Of none but such as you, and you of Timon.   670

FIRST SENATOR
The senators of Athens greet thee, Timon.

TIMON
I thank them, and would send them back the plague
Could I but catch it for them.

FIRST SENATOR   O, forget
What we are sorry for ourselves in thee.
The senators with one consent of love   675
Entreat thee back to Athens, who have thought
On special dignities which vacant lie
For thy best use and wearing.

SECOND SENATOR   They confess
Toward thee forgetfulness too general-gross;
Which now the public body, which doth seldom   680
Play the recanter, feeling in itself
A lack of Timon's aid, hath sense withal

---

668 cantherizing] F1; Catherizing (*for* cauterizing) F2   669 FIRST SENATOR] F (1.). *Similarly formatted as a numeral without a name from here on for all the Senators in* Scs. 14, 15, *and* 17, *except at* 15.13, '1. *Sen*.'.   680 Which] F; But CAPELL; And HANMER; Where KINNEAR *conj.*   682 sense] ROWE; since F

667–8 **For . . . tongue** Proverbially, 'Report has a blister on her tongue'—because she tells lies (Dent R84).

668 **cantherizing** Probably a portmanteau meaning both (a) *cantharidizing*, 'blistering (as with cantherides, blister-flies)', and (b) *cauterizing*. There is also a suggestion of burning by the sun.

669 **speaking** i.e. the tongue's speaking

673 **catch** Quibbles on contracting a disease and capturing an escaped beast.

674 **What . . . thee** i.e. what we ourselves are sorry for in our treatment of you

675 **consent** agreement, accord, unanimity, compact (Crystal). Also *concent*, harmony or concord of voices, as in *Henry V* 1.2.181, where there is wordplay between the two etymologically distinct words.

677 **dignities** high offices

678 **best** i.e. Timon is best suited to the dignities (and, as garments, they will be worn on special occasions)

use and wearing The doubled-up nouns are an example for the figure of speech called hendiadys, which is associated particularly with Shakespeare.

679 **forgetfulness** neglect, ingratitude

general-gross 'obvious to everyone' (Riverside)

680 **Which** A loose but admissible construction; perhaps 'for which'. The emendation 'Where' (i.e. 'whereas') would assume a relatively simple error, resulting from confusion between superscript 'ch' after 'w' (= which) with 're' (= where). This would avoid an awkward repetition of 'Which' in the line.

682 **withal** moreover

Of it own fall, restraining aid to Timon;
And send forth us to make their sorrowed render,
Together with a recompense more fruitful   685
Than their offence can weigh down by the dram;
Ay, even such heaps and sums of love and wealth
As shall to thee blot out what wrongs were theirs,
And write in thee the figures of their love,
Ever to read them thine.

TIMON   You witch me in it,   690
Surprise me to the very brink of tears.
Lend me a fool's heart and a woman's eyes,
And I'll beweep these comforts, worthy senators.

FIRST SENATOR

Therefore so please thee to return with us,
And of our Athens, thine and ours, to take   695
The captainship, thou shalt be met with thanks,
Allowed with absolute power, and thy good name
Live with authority. So soon we shall drive back
Of Alcibiades th'approaches wild,
Who, like a boar too savage, doth root up   700
His country's peace.

683 fall] F; fail CAPELL; fault HANMER

683 **it** its
  fall Has appropriate spiritual connotations of loss of grace, suitably undermined by the literal fall that threatens Athens. See collation for alternative readings.
  restraining through withholding
684 **sorrowed render** sorrowful payment of account. *OED*'s earliest example of adjectival *sorrowed* (under *sorrow*, v. 3).
686 **weigh down** The image is of a set of scales.
  by the dram i.e. when measured with most exacting accuracy. A dram was an eighth or a sixteenth of an ounce, so a several-thousandth of a talent (see note to 1.97). *Dram* is from *drachma*, which, like *talent*, was a measure used in the Greek world.
687 **heaps . . . wealth** The confusion of love and money harks back to Timon's initial predicament. The promise of wealth in return for leadership is puzzling, in that the senators surely need Timon's gold. Perhaps this is another instance of a gift that anticipates a far greater gift in

return. Perhaps the speaker is the same figure as Second Lord who spoke 1.280–1.
688 **theirs** committed by them
689 **write in thee** Timon's body or heart is seen as an account book in which the 'figures' of love can be written.
  figures (a) images, expressions; (b) numbers, arithmetic
690 **Ever to** i.e. so that you will always be able to
  witch bewitch, enchant
691 **Surprise me** overcome me with emotion
693 **these comforts** this comforting news; these joys
694 **so please thee** if you please
696 **captainship** leadership. Timon is being invited to be, in the words of the 17th-century annotator of the Meisei copy of F, 'captain for defence of the state against Alcibiades'.
697 **Allowed** invested
699 **Of . . . wild** The otherwise unnecessary inversion perhaps reinforces 'drive back'.
700 **Who . . . up** From Psalms 80: 13 (Bishops'): 'The wild boar out of the wood doth root it up'.

SECOND SENATOR   And shakes his threat'ning sword
  Against the walls of Athens.
FIRST SENATOR   Therefore, Timon—
TIMON
  Well, sir, I will; therefore I will, sir, thus.
  If Alcibiades kill my countrymen,
  Let Alcibiades know this of Timon: 705
  That Timon cares not. But if he sack fair Athens,
  And take our goodly agèd men by th'beards,
  Giving our holy virgins to the stain
  Of contumelious, beastly, mad-brained war,
  Then let him know, and tell him Timon speaks it   710
  In pity of our agèd and our youth,
  I cannot choose but tell him that I care not;
  And—let him take't at worst—for their knives care not
  While you have throats to answer. For myself,
  There's not a whittle in th'unruly camp   715
  But I do prize it at my love before
  The reverend'st throat in Athens. So I leave you
  To the protection of the prosperous gods,
  As thieves to keepers.
STEWARD (*to Senators*)   Stay not; all's in vain.
TIMON
  Why, I was writing of my epitaph.   720

---

717 reverend'st] F (reuerends)   720 Why, ... epitaph.] POPE (*subs.*);   ~ˌ . . . ~, F

703 **I will . . . I will** The first 'I will' apparently agrees to assume the captainship of Athens. The second issues a perverse 'I command' in that role. The speech that follows deflates the conventions of the speech of defiance, replacing the challenge with 'I care not'. 'For myself . . .' (l. 714) replaces the leader's assertions of willingness to sacrifice himself in the cause.

707 **take . . . beards** (both violent and insulting)

708–9 **stain . . . war** i.e. rape

709 **contumelious** insolent; i.e. disrespectful of holiness and virginity
  beastly bestial

713 **take't at worst** put the worst interpretation on it. Compare *Five Gallants* 3.1.90,

'You take me still at worst'. Varies proverbial 'Take it as you list' (Dent T27).

713 **care** i.e. I care

714 **answer** i.e. for the knives to cut (with wordplay on 'to respond vocally')

715 **whittle** clasp-knife
  th'unruly camp (of Alcibiades' soldiers)

716 **But I do prize it at** that I do not value as meriting

719 **As thieves to keepers** as I would leave thieves to the protection of prison guards (who might well admit executioners, or turn out to be executioners themselves, as in *Richard III*, *Richard II*, *King John*, etc.).

720–1 **Why . . . tomorrow** Timon continues his farewell and anticipation that he will die begun in 'So I leave you . . .'. F's only punctuation is a comma after 'Epitaph',

It will be seen tomorrow. My long sickness
Of health and living now begins to mend,
And nothing brings me all things. Go; live still.
Be Alcibiades your plague, you his,
And last so long enough.

FIRST SENATOR   We speak in vain.   725

TIMON

But yet I love my country, and am not
One that rejoices in the common wrack
As common bruit doth put it.

FIRST SENATOR   That's well spoke.

TIMON

Commend me to my loving countrymen—

FIRST SENATOR

These words become your lips as they pass through them.   730

SECOND SENATOR

And enter in our ears like great triumphers
In their applauding gates.

728 it] F (*some copies*); t F (*others*)

which could be interpreted 'Why I was
writing of my epitaph | It will be seen
tomorrow' (i.e. the reason why . . . will
be seen . . .). The usual punctuation, as
accepted in this edition, makes the line
Timon's call to be left alone, because he
has preoccupying work to finish by (literally!) a deadline. 'Of' is redundant to the
sense (Abbott 178).

721–3 **My . . . things** Probably added by Middleton. Compare *Hengist* 3.1.39–42: 'For-
getfulness, | 'Tis the pleasing'st virtue
anyone can have | That rises up from
nothing, for by the same, | Forgetting all,
they forget from whence they came'. The
idiom 'sickness of' followed by an abstraction is in Middleton's vein; compare 'sickness of affection' (*Lady's* 2.2.96). There is
a similar echoic collocation of 'thing',
'nothing', and 'bring' in *Triumphs of
Truth* ll. 303–4. Holdsworth compares
Middleton passages such as *Lady's*
5.2.89–90, 'health | After long sickness',
and *Changeling* 3.4.161–2, 'Let me go poor
unto my bed with honour, | And I am
rich in all things'.

723 **And . . . things** Echoes, with altered
meaning, the words of St Paul: 'yet alway

rejoicing: as poor, and yet make many
rich; as having nothing, and yet possess-
ing all things' (2 Corinthians 6: 10). St
Paul's theme of personal poverty as a
source of communal richness is immediately relevant to Timon, though Timon
'rejoices in the common wrack' (l. 727).
In the comedy *Timon*, Timon says the
opposite: 'Nothing (I say) nothing | All
things are made nothing' (1776–7). *Nothing* is also a key word in *Lear* (1.81–2,
2.31–5, 4.125–8, etc.).

723 **nothing** nothingness, oblivion

725 **last so long enough** i.e. survive in that
state for a long time before dying.

727 **the common wrack** general destruction.

728 **common bruit** popular rumour
it Hinman describes the variant 't' as a
typesetting error corrected to 'it' (i. 298).

730 **become** befit, grace

731 **great triumphers** i.e. great men entering
the city at a triumphal welcome. The
Roman practice of according a triumph
to victorious generals was imitated
in Renaissance civic welcomes for
dignitaries.

732 **applauding** Applies to the imagined
crowds at the gates, suggesting crowd and
gates as fused elements of a ceremonial

TIMON   Commend me to them,
  And tell them that to ease them of their griefs,
  Their fears of hostile strokes, their achës, losses,
  Their pangs of love, with other incident throes   735
  That nature's fragile vessel doth sustain
  In life's uncertain voyage, I will some kindness do them.
  I'll teach them to prevent wild Alcibiades' wrath.

FIRST SENATOR (*aside*)
  I like this well; he will return again.

TIMON

  I have a tree which grows here in my close   740
  That mine own use invites me to cut down,
  And shortly must I fell it. Tell my friends,
  Tell Athens, in the sequence of degree
  From high to low throughout, that whoso please
  To stop affliction, let him take his haste,   745
  Come hither ere my tree hath felt the axe,
  And hang himself. I pray you do my greeting.

STEWARD (*to Senators*)
  Trouble him no further. Thus you still shall find him.

TIMON

  Come not to me again, but say to Athens,
  Timon hath made his everlasting mansion   750

---

spectacle. Shakespeare provides several early examples of the verb *applaud* in *OED*, where the present line is the only pre-18th century illustration of the adjectival participle.

734–8 **Their . . . wrath** Capell noted the concentration of hexameters in this passage.

735 **throes** pangs, agonies

736 **nature's fragile vessel** i.e. the human body (seen as a container for the soul)
  fragile *OED*'s earliest example that is *not* in the moral sense 'Liable to err or fall into sin'

740–7 **I . . . himself** Timon's sardonic joke is based on Plutarch (see following note). But Bradbrook identifies the passage as an equivalent to episodes where 'the figure of Despair appeared with rope and knife' in morality plays (pp. 27–8), also citing *Faerie Queene* I.ix.33–4.

740 **close** enclosure, yard. The word, perhaps unexpected in relation to Timon's cave,

echoes the 'little yard at my house' in Plutarch, where Timon is speaking in the market place. The cryptic 'use' that leads Timon to propose felling the tree is similarly a relic from the source: in Plutarch Timon says 'I mean to make some building on the place'.

743 **degree** social precedence, class

744 **please** would like

745 **take his haste** hurry up

747 **do** i.e. convey

748 **still** always

749–58 **Come . . . reign** See Introduction, pp. 85–6.

750 **mansion** dwelling. There may be an allusion, by way of contrast, with John 14: 2–3, 'In my father's house are many mansions; and if I go to prepare a place for you, I will come again and receive you even unto myself'. If so, the line recalls the Great Bible translation, as quoted here.

Upon the beachèd verge of the salt flood,
Who once a day with his embossèd froth
The turbulent surge shall cover. Thither come,
And let my gravestone be your oracle.
Lips, let four words go by, and language end. 755
What is amiss, plague and infection mend.
Graves only be men's works, and death their gain.
Sun, hide thy beams. Timon hath done his reign.

⌈Exit ⌈*into his cave*⌉

FIRST SENATOR
His discontents are unremovably
Coupled to nature. 760
SECOND SENATOR
Our hope in him is dead. Let us return,
And strain what other means is left unto us
In our dear peril.
FIRST SENATOR   It requires swift foot.   *Exeunt*

Sc. 15 *Enter two other Senators, with a Messenger*
⌈THIRD⌉ SENATOR
Thou hast painfully discovered. Are his files
As full as thy report?

---

755 four] F; sour ROWE 758.1 *Exit*] F (*Exit Timon.*) *into his cave*] DYCE; *not in* F
15.1, 13 ⌈THIRD⌉ SENATOR] SISSON; I F. F *numbers anew in this scene, identifying the Senator at l.*
5 *as '2' and that at l.* 14 *as '3'.*

---

751 **the beachèd . . . flood** A lyrical phrase
that echoes *Midsummer Night's Dream*
2.1.85, 'the beachèd margin of the sea'.
752–3 **Who . . . cover** See Introduction, p.
85.
752 **Who** The referent is merged between
'beachèd verge', 'mansion', and Timon
himself.
embossèd foaming. Often said of an
exhausted hunted animal foaming at the
mouth.
753 **Thither come** But contrast the words on
the epitaph at 17.74.
755 **four words** See Introduction, pp. 85–6.
Rowe's emendation 'sour' is unnecessary.
language i.e. Timon's use of speech.
Michael Kevin (Oregon Shakespeare Festival, 1978) bit out his tongue at the end of
the scene.
757 **their** i.e. men's (though it is not impossible that the referent is 'Graves')

758.1 *Exit* Timon's final departure from the
stage.
760 **Coupled to nature** i.e. part of his essential character
762 **strain** apply beyond their accustomed
use (as of stretching sinews, etc.).
763 **dear** extreme
764 *Exeunt* F's directions '*Exit Timon.*' at l.
758 and '*Exeunt.*' here indicate that the
Steward leaves at the same time as the
Senators. But it would be possible for him
to follow Timon or depart in another
direction from the Senators, so suggesting
that he attended on Timon's death and
buried him.
Sc. 15 (5.3) Attributed to Shakespeare.
Occasionally omitted on stage, e.g. by
Bridges-Adams (1928).
1, 13 **THIRD SENATOR** In F the Senators are
numbered in the order in which they
speak in the scene. But the first two to

315

MESSENGER   I have spoke the least.
  Besides, his expedition promises
  Present approach.
⌈FOURTH⌉ SENATOR
  We stand much hazard if they bring not Timon.   5
MESSENGER
  I met a courier, one mine ancient friend,
  Whom, though in general part we were opposed,
  Yet our old love made a particular force
  And made us speak like friends. This man was riding
  From Alcibiades to Timon's cave   10
  With letters of entreaty which imported
  His fellowship i'th' cause against your city,
  In part for his sake moved.
        Enter the other Senators
⌈THIRD⌉ SENATOR   Here come our brothers.
⌈FIRST⌉ SENATOR
  No talk of Timon; nothing of him expect.
  The enemy's drum is heard, and fearful scouring   15
  Doth choke the air with dust. In, and prepare.
  Ours is the fall, I fear, our foe's the snare.   *Exeunt*

---

speak are '*two other Senators*'—that is, other than the two who have visited Timon, who enter at l. 13. Sisson's emendations create consistency with the previous scene.

1 **painfully discovered** (a) painstakingly reconnoitred, (b) told painful news
  files (of troops)

2 **least** lowest estimate
3 **his expedition** the speed of his march
4 **Present approach** an immediate advance to attack
5 **stand much hazard** will be at great risk
6 **one** one who is
  ancient long-standing; former
7 **Whom** with whom
  in general part as regards which side we're on
8 **particular** personal (in contrast with *general*, which refers to the political realm)
  force Suggests both the *old love*'s enforcement of the present friendship, and that this temporary alliance is like a little

army. In the next line *friends* could also mean 'military allies'.

11 **imported** Suggests something between 'conveyed, communicated' (*OED v.* 3), 'involved as a consequence' (*v.* 4), and 'induced' (not supported by *OED*, but compare the rare 'induce (a person *to do* something)', *import*, *v.* 8, first recorded 1649).

12 **His ... city** There is no other evidence that Alcibiades wages war partly on Timon's behalf, though he may have wished to persuade Timon so.

13 **moved** taken up, set on foot
15 **fearful** terrible; inducing fear
  scouring (a) roving with hostile purpose; or (b) military scourging or 'cleansing' operations. Editors usually propose (a), but (b) seems specially appropriate as Athens is presented as a corrupt state.

17 **our foe's the snare** i.e. our foe's role is to set the snare into which we fall. Alternatively 'our foes the snare', with no possessive apostrophe; i.e. our foes are the snare.

Sc. 16 *Enter a Soldier, in the woods, seeking Timon*
SOLDIER
By all description, this should be the place.
Who's here? Speak, ho! No answer?
⸤*He discovers an inscribed tomb*⸣
                                          What is this?
'Timon is dead, who hath outstretched his span.
Some beast read this; there does not live a man.'

16.2 *He . . . tomb*] BEVINGTON (*subs.*) (*conj.* Collier MS); *not in* F; *A Rude Tomb seen* CAPELL
(*before the scene's opening entry*)   3–4 Timon . . . man] F; *not in* OXFORD SHAKESPEARE   4 read]
F (reade); rear'd THEOBALD (*conj.* Warburton)

Sc. 16 (5.4) The scene was relegated to a footnote in Pope's edition, and has often been
omitted in performance. Johnson com-
mented, 'There is something elaborately
unskilful in the contrivance of sending a
soldier, who cannot read, to take the epitaph in wax, only that it may close the
play by being read with more solemnity in
the last scene.' Charles Knight and others
attributed the scene to another dramatist,
but recent studies restore it to Shakespeare. It presents Timon's burial as a
shocking enigma. The physicality of the
grave as source of the words that are
transported to Alcibiades gives concrete
expression to Timon's death, an equivalent in stage properties to the words
themselves.

0.1 *Enter . . . Timon* The Soldier probably
enters at one door and crosses to the door
or stage property that represents Timon's
cave. The Soldier must be the *courier* of
15.6–13.

2 *He discovers . . . tomb* This episode is a
clue that the cave may have been represented by a curtain hanging in front of a
door, because the required staging seems
to be that of a 'discovery': a curtain
drawn back now to reveal the primitive
monument of Timon's tomb. Compare
the discovery in Prospero's equivalent
dwelling, his cell: '*Here Prospero discovers
Ferdinand and Miranda, playing at chess*'
(*The Tempest* 5.1.173.1–2). The text calls
for an inscription that needs to be copied,
which implies a visible and apparently
immovable structure. In this way
the scene produces a spectacle that
announces to the audience that Timon is
dead. In the modern theatre, less formal-
ized staging can be preferred; in Doran's
1999 RSC production, the trapdoor hole
in which Timon dug and discovered gold

became his grave; as in Benthall's production at the Old Vic in 1956, the epitaph
was written on a piece of driftwood that
the Soldier could carry away without the
intervention of wax.

3–4 **Timon . . . man** These lines are not itali-
cized or indicated as quotation in F.
Warburton emended 'read' to 'rear'd',
which helps ll. 3–4 to be understood as
the Soldier's own words rather than the
words he reads on the grave. Johnson
defended 'read', taking the couplet as the
Soldier's own words: 'for it must be read,
and in this place it cannot be read by
man'. But the line is in the vein of
Timon's misanthropy, and the rhyming
couplet has the formality of an inscription. Most commentators agree that it is
an epitaph. It differs from the lines read
from the Soldier's wax copy at 17.71–4.
Textual Companion, pp. 506–7, suggests
that the present epitaph was abandoned
and superseded as the writing of the
play's final scenes progressed, and that
these two lines should therefore be deleted
from the text. 'What's on the tomb | I
cannot read', puzzling just after the Soldier has apparently just read an epitaph,
could then be explained as a later addition
replacing the reading of the epitaph.
However, as a superfluity of epitaphs
seems oddly appropriate to the play and
the character, it seems best to leave the
text unemended if possible. *Interpreter* (l.
8), if taken in the sense 'translator', supports Oliver's suggestion that there is a
second, unread inscription that is not in
the Soldier's native language, or is, for
some other reason, illegible to him.
Plutarch records two epitaphs, the first
reported to be written by Timon himself,
the second by the poet Callimachus. Textually, these are conflated in the play into

Dead, sure, and this his grave. What's on this tomb   5
I cannot read. The character I'll take with wax.
Our captain hath in every figure skill,
An aged interpreter, though young in days.
Before proud Athens he's set down by this,
Whose fall the mark of his ambition is.   *Exit*   10

Sc. 17 *Trumpets sound. Enter Alcibiades with his powers,*
        before Athens

ALCIBIADES

Sound to this coward and lascivious town
Our terrible approach.
        Sounds a parley. The Senators appear upon the walls
Till now you have gone on and filled the time
With all licentious measure, making your wills
The scope of justice. Till now myself and such   5

the epitaph of 17.71–4. Functionally, they correspond here with the epitaph read by the Soldier and the one copied by him. How Timon came to be buried within the tomb is left a mystery, but see note to 14.764.

3 **outstretched his span** i.e. lived too long. Proverbially, 'Life is a span' (Dent L251). *Outstretched* is Shakespearian, but not in Middleton.

4 **Some beast read this** Implies 'being able to read this doesn't prove that you are not a beast'. Or an impatient absurdity: 'it's more likely that a beast will be capable of reading this than that a truly human man will do so'.

6 **The . . . wax** Either the Soldier takes a wax impression of the letters or copies them on to a wax tablet by hand. The latter would be more straightforward on stage (and would avoid creating a mirror image of the letters).

7 **figure** kind of writing
8 **aged** experienced
  interpreter Perhaps specifically 'translator'.
9 **Before . . . down** To *set down before* is to encamp before and besiege. The Soldier's *captain* is clearly Alcibiades. *Set down* and *mark* (ll. 9–10) seem also to glance, perhaps illogically, at writing.

9 **by this** by now
10 **Whose** Refers to Athens.
   mark target
Sc. 17 (5.5) Attributed to Shakespeare (but see notes to ll. 10–13).
0.2 *before Athens* See note to l. 2.1.
 1 **Sound** i.e. proclaim by trumpet-call
   lascivious The accusation could properly be levelled against Alcibiades himself (Klein).
 2 **terrible approach** terrifying advance to the attack
2.1 *upon the walls* As in Sc. 12, the tiring-house wall behind the stage would represent the city wall. The senators would appear in the upper acting space, a gallery above the wall continuing the gallery occupied by members of the audience. The staging is standard for siege scenes, as in *King John* 2.1, *Henry V* 3.3, and *Coriolanus* 1.4, in all of which the non-combatant representatives of the city appear 'upon the walls'.
 4 **all licentious measure** every degree and kind of licentiousness
4–5 **making . . . justice** i.e. enacting justice as it pleases you; excluding the rule of law from actions that gratify your own desires
 5 **scope** determining limit

As slept within the shadow of your power
Have wandered with our traversed arms, and breathed
Our sufferance vainly. Now the time is flush
When crouching marrow, in the bearer strong,
Cries of itself 'No more'; now breathless wrong   10
Shall sit and pant in your great chairs of ease,
And pursy insolence shall break his wind
With fear and horrid flight.

FIRST SENATOR   Noble and young,
When thy first griefs were but a mere conceit,
Ere thou hadst power or we had cause of fear,   15
We sent to thee to give thy rages balm,
To wipe out our ingratitude with loves
Above their quantity.

SECOND SENATOR   So did we woo

17.6 slept] F; stepped HIBBARD (*conj.* Danchin)

6 **slept** Either 'dwelt' or 'remained inert'. The senators' *power* might be seen as like the sun, with those wronged by it (as a group distinct from the rest of Athenians) living in the *shadow* of night. Or the senators' *power* is itself a shadow they cast over their victims. Hibbard emends to 'stepped', which is more consistent with 'wandered'.

7 **traversed arms** folded arms (a sign of melancholy). The sense 'weapons held crossed (as in military drill)' is also possible, implying soldiers who passively exercised restraint. *OED* cites this line as the earliest instance of *traversed* as 'Placed or laid across; crossed; transverse' (*ppl. a.* 1).
breathed spoken about.

8 **sufferance** sufferings, grievances
vainly in vain
flush in full flood. *OED*'s earliest example of this sense (*a.*¹ 1a).

9 **crouching** The position of cringing subservience is transformed into the position from which the *bearer* springs forward.
marrow (source of vitality and strength).

10 **of itself** of its own accord

10–13 **No . . . flight** Possibly Middletonian; see following notes.

10–11 **No . . . ease** Punctuated following F: 'no more:'. By this reading, *breathless wrong* (i.e. wrongdoers) shall *pant* with fear. Alternatively, the *cry* includes all of

'No more now . . . chairs of ease': the wrongdoers can now no longer rest their senile breathlessness in the chairs of ease.

11 **chairs of ease** Not, apparently, a set phrase: this is the earliest known example. In *Game at Chess* 'chair of ease' was later used metaphorically for a sinecure (3.1.47), and also specifically to mean a chair designed to avoid putting pressure on an anal fistula (4.2.3). Here evidently implies both undemanding places of high office and comfortable chairs for flatulent old gentlemen.

12 **pursy** fat and short-winded. Probably puns on 'having a full purse'; compare 'thinking his purse had been as pursy as his body', *Puritan Widow* 1.4.22–3.
insolence overbearing pride (i.e. those so characterized).
break his wind gasp for breath; fart

13 **horrid** horrifying

14 **griefs** grievances
conceit thought, concept

16 **sent** sent messages

18 **Above their quantity** greater in quantity than they were
their i.e. either Alcibiades' *griefs* (l. 14) or his *rages* (l. 16)
So likewise. This speech strongly correlates the senators' *ingratitude* to Alcibiades with that to Timon.

Transformèd Timon to our city's love
By humble message and by promised means.   20
We were not all unkind, nor all deserve
The common stroke of war.

FIRST SENATOR   These walls of ours
Were not erected by their hands from whom
You have received your grief; nor are they such
That these great tow'rs, trophies, and schools should fall   25
For private faults in them.

SECOND SENATOR   Nor are they living
Who were the motives that you first went out.
Shame that they wanted cunning, in excess,
Hath broke their hearts. March, noble lord,
Into our city with thy banners spread.   30
By decimation and a tithèd death,
If thy revenges hunger for that food
Which nature loathes, take thou the destined tenth,
And by the hazard of the spotted die

---

23 their] F2; rheir F1   28 wanted‿ cunning,] F2 (*subs.*); ~, ~‿ F1

---

20 **means** terms; compromises; wealth

21–9 **We . . . hearts** As the play is vague about the identities of the senators, it is unclear whether these senators' attempts to exculpate themselves are justified. But theatrical logic and economy point to their being the same figures who angered Alcibiades and denied Timon aid.

21 **unkind** unnaturally cruel; alien to the nobility of senators or the fellow-feeling of humans

22 **common** i.e. indiscriminate
stroke Suggests both violence and punishment. Compare phrases such as 'stroke of God', 'stroke of justice', etc.

23 **their hands** the hands of those men

24 **grief** grievances
they i.e. those men

25 **trophies** monuments
schools public buildings

26 **private** personal, individual

27 **motives** i.e. instigators of the grievances
that for which

28 **Shame . . . excess** F1 unhelpfully puts the whole line in parentheses and marks a mid-line comma after 'wanted'. F2 adjusts by removing the comma and beginning the parenthesis before 'that'.
wanted lacked

28 **cunning** i.e. sufficient cleverness to forestall Alcibiades' revolt
in excess An excess of a passion was believed capable of making the heart burst. Hence *in excess* must qualify *Shame* rather than *cunning*.

31 **decimation . . . death** Both expressions mean 'execution of one person in ten'. *Decimation* is nowhere else in Shakespeare, and 'probably derives from Plutarch's description of Antonius' punishment of his soldiers at the siege of Phraata' (Honigmann; 'Life of Marcus Antonius', p. 987, with the marginal note 'Decimation a martial punishment'). It was on this Parthian campaign that Antony and his soldiers suffered famine and 'were compelled to live off herbs and roots', an episode Shakespeare recalled in *Antony and Cleopatra* 1.4.56–71.

32–3 **that . . . loathes** The revenge is seen as unnatural because directed against Alcibiades' own country—or perhaps because metaphorically cannibalistic.

34–5 **spotted die . . . Let die the spotted** The singular of *dice* puns with *Let die*, 'put to death'. *Spotted* shifts from 'having dots' to 'tainted, guilty'. The contrivance of the language perhaps suggests a euphemistic,

Let die the spotted.

FIRST SENATOR   All have not offended.   35
For those that were, it is not square to take,
On those that are, revenge. Crimes like lands
Are not inherited. Then, dear countryman,
Bring in thy ranks, but leave without thy rage.
Spare thy Athenian cradle and those kin   40
Which, in the bluster of thy wrath, must fall
With those that have offended. Like a shepherd
Approach the fold and cull th'infected forth,
But kill not all together.

SECOND SENATOR   What thou wilt,
Thou rather shalt enforce it with thy smile   45
Than hew to't with thy sword.

FIRST SENATOR   Set but thy foot
Against our rampired gates and they shall ope,
So thou wilt send thy gentle heart before
To say thou'lt enter friendly.

SECOND SENATOR   Throw thy glove,
Or any token of thine honour else,   50
That thou wilt use the wars as thy redress,
And not as our confusion, all thy powers
Shall make their harbour in our town till we
Have sealed thy full desire.

ALCIBIADES (*throwing a glove*) Then there's my glove.

37 revenge] F; revenges STEEVENS 1778   44 all together] F (altogether)   49 thou'lt] F
(thou't)   54 *thowing a glove*] OXFORD SHAKESPEARE (*subs.*); *not in* F

evasive, or embarrassed quality (as is evident in the BBC production). Pope dis-
approved, relegating 'And by . . . die
spotted' to a footnote.

36 **were** lived before (an unexpected intima-
tion that much time has lapsed)
square right, just

37 **On . . . lands** See note to 14.447.
are still live
revenge Some editors follow Steevens
in emending to 'revenges', mainly for
reasons of metre, but a syllable is often
omitted at a caesura.

37–8 **Crimes . . . inherited** crimes are not
inherited as lands are

39 **in . . . without** within the walls . . . outside them

41 **bluster** wild storm

43 **cull th'infected forth** select out the infected. *OED* records *cull* in the sense 'selective
killing to improve stock' only from 1934,
so this sense is highly implausible. But
there is an echo between *cull* and *kill* in
the next line.

44 **What** whatever

47 **rampired** (a) strengthened (as with ram-
parts), (b) blocked with earth piled behind
them

48 **So** provided that

49 **Throw thy glove** if you throw your glove
(subjunctive). The dependent phrase continues to 'confusion', l. 52.

50 **token** pledge

53 **make their harbour** be given safe
repose

54 **sealed** i.e. formally satisfied (as with seal-
ing a document)

Descend, and open your unchargèd ports.   55
Those enemies of Timon's and mine own
Whom you yourselves shall set out for reproof
Fall, and no more; and to atone your fears
With my more noble meaning, not a man
Shall pass his quarter or offend the stream   60
Of regular justice in your city's bounds
But shall be remedied to your public laws
At heaviest answer.
BOTH SENATORS 'Tis most nobly spoken.
ALCIBIADES Descend, and keep your words.   65

⌐*Trumpets sound. Exeunt Senators from the walls and*
enter below⌐
Enter Soldier, with a tablet of wax

SOLDIER
My noble general, Timon is dead,
Entombed upon the very hem o'th' sea;

---

55 Descend] F2; Defend F1   62 remedied] F; render'd DYCE (*conj.* Chedworth); remanded
HIBBARD   to] F1; by F2   64 BOTH SENATORS] F (*Both.*)   65.1 *Trumpets sound.*] OXFORD SHAKE-
SPEARE; *not in* F   65.1–2 *Exeunt . . . below*] MALONE (*subs.*); *not in* F   65.3–66 *Soldier . . .* SOL-
DIER] THEOBALD; *a Messenger . . . Mes.* F   65.3 *with a tablet of wax*] BEVINGTON (*subs.*); *not in* F

---

55 **Descend** F1's 'Defend' is nonsensical, as
opening the gates does not defend them.
The error need be no more than misreading of long 's' as 'f'. Compare l. 65.
unchargèd ports unassailed gates. *OED*'s
only instance of *uncharged* in this sense.
The adjectival form is not elsewhere in
Shakespeare, but *uncharge* (verb) occurs
in *Hamlet* 4.7.66.
57 **reproof** ignominy, blame
58 **atone** reconcile
59 **meaning** intentions
man soldier
60 **pass his quarter** leave his allotted place
offend violate
62 **shall** i.e. it shall
remedied Pronounced as two syllables,
as *remedy* sometimes is elsewhere in
Shakespeare. The syntax of the line is
acceptably elliptic. *Remedied* is often
emended 'rendered', which might be
right. Hibbard's alternative 'remanded' is
un-Shakespearian and unmetrical.
to in accordance with (*OED*, *to*, *prep.*,
conj., *adv.* 20)
63 **At heaviest answer** according to the
severest punishment allowed.

65.1 **Exeunt . . . walls** In the Jacobean theatre the descent from the upper acting
area was by off-stage ladders behind the
tiring-house wall. Unless the senators
ignore Alcibiades, they must exit, and,
unless there is a pause in the action while
they descend, they will be off stage
when the soldier arrives. A flourish of
trumpets would drown the noise of the
senators descending (as elsewhere in
Shakespeare), and might allow time for
them to enter ceremonially before the
Soldier arrives. Compare the exit from
above and apparent re-entry below of the
Earl of Warwick and his followers in
Richard Duke of York at the end of 5.1, and
Richard's similar descent in *Richard II*
3.3.182–4. The senators' movement out
of the city is a reversal of the ceremonial
entry of the Duke into the city at the end
of *Measure*.
65.3 **Soldier** F reads '*a Messenger*' and has
the speech-prefix '*Mes.*', but he is clearly
the Soldier of Sc. 16.
67 **hem** edge

And on his gravestone this insculpture, which
With wax I brought away, whose soft impression
Interprets for my poor ignorance.   70
   Alcibiades reads the epitaph

ALCIBIADES

'Here lies a wretched corpse, of wretched soul bereft.
Seek not my name. A plague consume you wicked
   caitiffs left!
Here lie I, Timon, who alive all living men did hate.
Pass by and curse thy fill—but pass, and stay not here
   thy gait.'
These well express in thee thy latter spirits.   75
Though thou abhorred'st in us our human griefs,
Scorned'st our brains' flow and those our droplets which
From niggard nature fall, yet rich conceit
Taught thee to make vast Neptune weep for aye
On thy low grave, on faults forgiven. Dead   80

77 brains'] F (Braines); brine's HANMER

68 **insculpture** carved inscription. *OED*'s earliest example of the word, though Middleton refers to '*insculption* on a tomb' (*Revenger's* 1.2.13). Despite his 'poor ignorance', the Soldier speaks an elevated language befitting his serious subject matter.

70 **Interprets** Figuratively speaking, the impression 'interprets' the original by communicating the letters in altered physical form. It so performs a task equivalent to the literal interpretation that the Soldier cannot perform.

71–4 **Here . . . gait** These are two separate epitaphs in Plutarch. The first two lines are those attributed to Timon, the second pair to the poet Callimachus. Joined together, they conflict oddly in that 'Seek not my name' is contradicted in 'Here lie I, Timon'. Sisson proposes that the first two lines should be deleted as a rejected first draft, but the desire to resolve the difficulties and contradictions in the epitaphs is probably misguided. See note to 16.3–4.

72 **caitiffs** wretches, villains

74 **stay not here thy gait** do not break your footsteps to linger here

75 **latter** belonging to the more recent part of your life

76 **griefs** hardships, sufferings

77 **brains' flow** i.e. tears
   our droplets i.e. our small tears, in contrast with the weeping of 'vast Neptune', l. 79. The diminutive would be striking: this is *OED*'s only instance of *droplets* before 1788. The element *drop* is picked up in *fall*.

78 **niggard nature** parsimonious human nature. The phrase is Spenserian. In *Faerie Queene* II.xii.50 'niggard Nature' contrasts with lavish art. Timon's 'rich conceit' (ingenuity, imagination; i.e. the faculty of artistic creativity) leads him to find a lavish mourner in a world of nature separate from the human, making an extravagant and 'conceited' art out of nature.
   rich The play's last image of wealth

79–80 **to . . . grave** Refers to the tide regularly wetting the beach where Timon lies buried.

79 **aye** ever

80 **On . . . on** upon . . . on account of
   faults Either (a) the faults of Timon's friends and the senators—*forgiven* by Alcibiades, not Timon, or (b) Timon's failing, i.e. contempt for human weaknesses.

Is noble Timon, of whose memory
Hereafter more. Bring me into your city,
And I will use the olive with my sword,
Make war breed peace, make peace stint war, make each
Prescribe to other as each other's leech.   85
Let our drums strike.   *Drums. Exeunt*

FINIS

86 *Drums.*] BEVINGTON; *not in* F

83 **olive** olive branch (as emblem of peace)
84 **stint** put an end to
85 **leech** physician. Also the worm used in medical bloodletting; hence 'cure'—but also 'bloodsucker'. War purges corruption by spilling blood, peace draws away the blood of violence. The two are perhaps disturbingly symbiotic (R. Berry,

Shakespearean Structures (1981), pp. 99–119). It is also disturbing that the final image is an unpleasant variant on the theme of consuming blood.

86 *Exeunt* It might be effective for the impression of the epitaph to be left on stage.

ALTERATIONS TO LINEATION

1.7	Hath . . . merchant] POPE; *as two lines divided after* 'attend' F
19–20	You . . . lord] POPE; *as prose* F
65	Feigned . . . mount] ROWE; *as two lines divided after* 'throned' F
146	This . . . long] ROWE; *as two lines divided after* 'mine' F
152	My . . . promise] POPE; *as two lines divided after* 'thee' F
156	Vouchsafe . . . lordship] POPE; *as two lines divided after* 'labour' F
179–80	Look . . . chid] POPE; *as one line* F
183	Good . . . Apemantus] ROWE; *as two lines divided after* 'thee' F
186	Why . . . not] POPE; *as prose* F
210	O . . . bellies] POPE; *as verse divided after* 'lords' F
212	So . . . labour] POPE; *as two lines divided after* 'apprehend'st it' F
225	Then thou liest] POPE; *as verse* F
237–8	That . . . merchant] THEOBALD; *as verse divided after* 'lord' F
251–5	So . . . monkey] CAPELL; *as prose* F
259	In . . . in] ROWE; *as two lines divided after* 'pleasures' F
271–2	No . . . friend] POPE; *as verse divided after* 'bidding' F
273–4	Away . . . hence] POPE; *as verse divided after* 'dog' F
276	He's . . . in] CAPELL; *as two lines divided after* 'humanity' F
2.2–3	It . . . peace] CAPELL; *as two lines divided after* 'age' F
23–4	No . . . welcome] CAPELL; *as one line* F
51–2	Lest . . . throats] ROWE 1709; *as prose* F
73	Captain . . . now] POPE; *as verse divided after* 'Captain' F
112–13	Please . . . admittance] POPE; *as verse divided after* 'ladies' F
118–21	Hail . . . bosom] F; *as four lines divided after* 'all', 'taste', *and* 'freely' POPE; *divided after* 'all', 'senses', *and* 'come' THEOBALD; *divided after* 'all', 'senses', *and* 'freely' RANN
124–5	They're . . . welcome] F3; *as prose* F1
142	You . . . ladies] POPE; *as two lines divided after* 'pleasures' F
185	Be . . . news] CAPELL; *as two lines divided after* 'entertained' F
190–1	I'll . . . reward] HANMER; *divided after* 'him' F
192–3	He . . . coffer] STEEVENS; *as one line* F
198–202	That . . . out] CAPELL (*after* Hanmer); *as four lines divided after* 'word', 'for't', *and* 'were' F
205–6	You . . . merits] MALONE; *divided after* 'wrong' F

208	With . . . it] POPE; *as two lines divided after* 'thanks' F
214–17	You . . . to you] JOHNSON; *as prose* F
233–6	What . . . 'em] ROWE; *as prose* F
236	Friendship's . . . dregs] ROWE; *as one verse line* F
4.29	From . . . payment] OXFORD SHAKESPEARE; *as prose* F; *as two lines divided after* 'Isidore' CAPELL
31	'Twas . . . past] OXFORD SHAKESPEARE; *as prose* F
43–4	Do . . . entertained] MALONE; *as one line* F
65–6	Gramercies . . . mistress] POPE; *as verse divided after* 'fool' F
72	How . . . Apemantus] POPE; *as one verse line* F
83	Answer . . . gone] POPE; *as one verse line* F
84–5	E'en . . . Timon's] CAPELL; *as verse divided after* 'grace' F
87–8	If . . . usurers] CAPELL; *as verse divided after* 'home' F
90–1	So . . . thief] POPE; *as verse divided after* 'I' F
111–12	Nor . . . lack'st] POPE; *as verse divided after* 'man' F
118	Pray . . . anon] POPE; *as two lines divided after* 'near' F
178–9	Shall . . . friends] CAPELL; *as three lines divided after* 'perceive' *and* 'fortunes' F
226	I . . . foe] CAPELL; *as two lines divided after* 'it' F
5.55–6	I . . . him] POPE; *divided before* 'has' F
6.61	Why . . . piece] MALONE; *as two lines divided after* 'soul' F
73–4	For . . . life] ROWE; *as one line* F
7.1	Must . . . others] STEEVENS; *as two lines divided after* 'Hmh' F
8.14–15	Is . . . fear] OLIVER (*conj.* W. S.Walker); *as one line* F
16–17	'Tis . . . little] POPE; *as prose* F
28	I'm . . . witness] ROWE; *as two lines divided after* 'charge' F
31	Yes . . . yours] POPE; *as two lines divided after* 'crowns' F
35–6	Flaminius . . . forth] POPE; *as prose* F
38–9	I . . . diligent] OXFORD MIDDLETON; *as one line* F ('diligent' *turned down*). Usually taken as prose.
45–6	Ay . . . waiting] CAPELL; *as one line* F
59–60	VARRO'S . . . worship] *unjustified type-line* F
91	Five . . . And yours] DYCE 1857; *as two lines divided after* 'that' F
9.9–12	O . . . table] POPE; *as prose* F
10.1	My . . . bloody] ROWE; *as two lines divided after* 'to't' F
14–15	He . . . virtues] JOHNSON; *as one line* F
32–3	The . . . carelessly] OXFORD SHAKESPEARE; *as three lines divided after* 'breathe' *and* 'outsides' F; *divided after* 'wrongs' POPE
49–50	And . . . judge] F2; *divided after* 'lion' F1
78–9	And . . . security] OXFORD SHAKESPEARE (*conj.* W. S. Walker); *as one line* F. CAPELL *divides* ll. 78–81 *after* 'love' *and* 'all'.

100	Attend . . . spirit] CAPELL; *as two lines divided after* 'judgement' F
102	Now . . . live] STEEVENS; *as two lines divided after* 'enough' F
11.45–6	Let . . . together] *as verse divided after* 'remembrance' F. *Ambiguous or as verse in most editions, but, e.g.,* HIBBARD *prints as prose.*
14.45	Do . . . quick] POPE; *as two lines divided after* 'nature' F
73	Promise . . . none] POPE; *as one verse line* F
81–2	TIMON . . . Yes] *one type-line* F
83–7	Be . . . diet] POPE; *as prose* F
103–4	The gods . . . conquered] This edition; *as verse divided after* 'conquest' F
106–7	That . . . country] This edition; *as verse divided after* 'villains' F
130–1	Hast . . . counsel] CAPELL; *as prose* F; *divided after* 'yet' POPE
132	Dost . . . thee] CAPELL; *as prose* F
145–7	Be . . . still] CAPELL; *as four lines (near foot of page) divided after* 'thatch', 'dead', *and* 'matter' F
167	More . . . Timon] POPE; *as prose* F
168	More . . . earnest] POPE; *as prose* F
169–70	Strike . . . again] POPE; *as prose* F
280–1	I . . . prodigal] CAPELL; *as one line* F
295–6	Under . . . Apemantus] CAPELL; *as verse divided after* 'me' F
346–8	If . . . beasts] POPE; *as verse divided after* 'please me', 'mightst', 'here', *and* 'become' F
351–4	Yonder . . . again] POPE; *as verse divided after* 'painter', 'thee', 'way', *and* 'do' F
355–7	When . . . Apemantus] POPE; *as verse divided after* 'thee', 'welcome', *and* 'dog' F
358	Thou . . . alive] POPE; *as two lines divided after* 'cap' F
359	Would . . . upon] POPE; *as two lines divided after* 'enough' F
360	A . . . curse] POPE; *as two lines divided after* 'thee' F
361	All . . . pure] POPE; *as two lines divided after* 'villains' F
362	There . . . speak'st] POPE; *as two lines divided after* 'leprosy' F
363–4	If . . . hands] CAPELL; *divided after* 'beat thee' F
365	I . . . off] POPE; *as two lines divided after* 'tongue' F
367–8	Choler . . . thee] ROWE; *divided after* 'me' F
370–1	Away . . . thee] prose? F ('Away . . . shall' *set as unjustified type-line*)
387	That . . . god] ROWE; *as two lines divided after* 'lap' F
398	More . . . them] HANMER; *as two lines divided after* 'men' F
403	It . . . treasure] POPE; *as verse divided after* 'noised' F
407	True . . . hid] POPE; *as verse divided after* 'him' F

415	We . . . want] POPE; *as two lines divided after* 'men' F
454–5	I'll . . . trade] POPE; *as verse divided after* 'enemy' F
469–71	He's . . . life] POPE; *as prose* F
471	My dearest master] POPE; *as one verse-line* F
474	Then . . . thee] CAPELL; *as two lines divided after* 'man' F
481	What . . . thee] ROWE; *as two lines divided after* 'weep' F
539–40	What's . . . gold] POPE; *as verse divided after* 'him' *and* 'true' F
541–4	Certain . . . sum] POPE; *as verse divided after* 'Certain', 'Timandra', 'enriched', 'quantity', *and* 'steward' F
545–6	Then . . . friends] POPE; *as verse divided after* 'of his' F
547–52	Nothing . . . having] POPE; *as verse divided after* 'else', 'again', 'highest', 'loves', 'his', 'us', 'purposes', 'for', *and* 'goes' F
553	What . . . him] POPE; *as verse divided after* 'now' F
554–5	Nothing . . . piece] POPE; *as verse divided after* 'time' *and* 'him' F
556–7	I . . . him] POPE; *as verse divided after* 'too' F
558–64	Good . . . it] POPE; *as verse divided after* 'best', 'time', 'expectation', 'act', 'people', 'use', 'fashionable', 'testament', *and* 'judgement' F
565–6	Excellent . . . thyself] POPE; *as verse divided after* 'workman' *and* 'bad' F
567–71	I . . . opulency] POPE; *as verse divided after* 'thinking', 'him', 'himself', 'prosperity', *and* 'flatteries' F
572–4	Must . . . thee] POPE; *as verse divided after* 'needs', 'work', *and* 'men' F
582–4	I'll . . . feed] CAPELL; *divided after* 'turn' *and* 'worshipped' F
591	Have . . . men] ROWE; *as two lines divided after* 'lived' F
592	Sir . . . tasted] ROWE; *as two lines divided after* 'Sir' F
601	Let . . . better] POPE; *as two lines divided after* 'go' F
606	We . . . service] POPE; *as two lines divided after* 'come' F
607	Most . . . you] POPE; *as two lines divided after* 'men' F
609	What . . . service] POPE; *as two lines divided after* 'can do' F
610	You're . . . gold] POPE; *as two lines divided after* 'men' F
630	Ay . . . dissemble] ROWE; *as two lines divided after* 'cog' F
636	Look . . . gold] POPE; *as two lines divided after* 'Look you' F
641	You . . . company] POPE; *as two lines divided after* 'this' F
666	Thou . . . hanged] HANMER; *as two lines divided after* 'burn' F
670	Of . . . Timon] POPE; *as two lines divided after* 'as you' F
672	I . . . plague] POPE; *as two lines divided after* 'thank them' F
730	These . . . them] POPE; *as prose* F

748	Trouble . . . find him] POPE; *as two lines divided after* 'shall' F
759–60	His . . . nature] CAPELL; *as one line* F
15.3–4	Besides . . . approach] POPE; *as one line* F

NARRATIVE SOURCE MATERIALS

1. From Plutarch's 'Life of Marcus Antonius', translated by Thomas North, pp. 1001–2

[Marginal note:] Antonius followeth the life and example of Timon Misanthropos the Athenian.

Antonius, he forsook the city and company of his friends, and built him a house in the sea by the isle of Pharos, upon certain forced mounts which he caused to be cast into the sea, and dwelt there as a man that banished himself from all men's company, saying that he would lead Timon's life, because he had the like wrong offered him that was before offered unto Timon; and that for the unthankfulness of those he had done good unto and whom he took to be his friends, he was angry with all men and would trust no man.

[Marginal note:] Plato and Aristophanes' testimony of Timon Misanthropos, what he was.

This Timon was a citizen of Athens that lived about the war of Peloponnesus, as appeareth by Plato and Aristophanes' comedies, in the which they mocked him, calling him a viper, and malicious man unto mankind, to shun all other men's companies but the company of young Alcibiades, a bold and insolent youth, whom he would greatly feast and make much of, and kissed him very gladly. Apemantus, wondering at it, asked him the cause what he meant to make so much of that young man alone, and to hate all others. Timon answered him, 'I do it', said he, 'because I know that one day he shall do great mischief unto the Athenians.' This Timon sometimes would have Apemantus in his company, because he was much like of his nature and conditions, and also followed him in manner of life. On a time when they solemnly celebrated the feasts called Choae at Athens—to wit, the feasts of the dead where they make sprinklings and sacrifices for the dead—and that they two then feasted together by themselves, Apemantus said unto the other, 'O, here is a trim banquet, Timon!' Timon answered again, 'Yea,' said he, 'so thou wert not here.' It is reported of him also that this Timon on a time, the people being assembled in the market place about dispatch of some affairs, got up into the pulpit for orations, where the orators commonly use to speak unto the people; and, silence being made, every man listening to hear what he would say, because it was a wonder to see him in that place, at length he began to speak in this manner: 'My lords of Athens, I have a little yard in my house where there groweth a fig tree, on the which many citizens have hanged themselves; and because I mean to make some building on the place, I thought good to let you all understand it that, before the fig tree be cut down, if any of you be desperate, you may there in time go hang yourselves.' He died in the city of Hales, and was buried upon the seaside. Now it chanced so that, the sea getting in, it compassed his tomb round about, that no man could come to it; and upon the same was written this epitaph:

[Marginal note:] The epitaph of Timon Misanthropos.

> Here lies a wretched corpse, of wretched soul bereft.
> Seek not my name. A plague consume you wicked wretches left!

It is reported that Timon himself, when he lived, made this epitaph; for that which is commonly rehearsed was not his, but made by the poet Callimachus:

> Here lie I, Timon, who alive all living men did hate.
> Pass by and curse thy fill: but pass, and stay not here thy gait.

2. Lucian of Samosata, 'Timon, or, The Misanthrope'

The following extracts are from the earliest extant English translation, in *Certain Select Dialogues*, translated by Francis Hickes (1634), sigs. X3–Aa4. Explanatory notes in square brackets have been added editorially.

TIMON [*to Jupiter*] . . . To come to myself, that have set so many Athenians afloat, of miserable beggars have made them wealthy men, and succoured all that craved assistance at my hands, nay, rather poured out my riches by heaps to do my friends good; yet when by that means I grew poor and fell into decay I could never be acknowledged by them, nor they once so much as cast an eye towards me who before crouched and kneeled unto me, and wholly dependent on my beck. . . . Others, if they see me afar off, will turn aside and take another way, a[s] if I were some dismal and unlucky object to be looked upon who, not long before, had been their founder and benefactor. These indignities have made me betake myself to this solitary place, to clothe myself in this leather garment, and labour in the earth for four halfpence a day, here practising philosophy with solitariness and my mattock, and think I shall gain enough by the match in that I shall have no sight of many that are rich men without desert.

[. . .]

JUPITER . . . What an alteration is this! That good man, that rich man, that had so many friends! How came he to be in such a case, miserably distressed, fain to dig and labour for his living . . . ?

MERCURY Some say his bounty undid him, and his kindness, and commiseration towards all that craved of him; but, in plain terms, it was his folly, simplicity, and indiscretion in making choice of his friends, not knowing that he bestow his liberality upon crows and wolves that tare out the very entrails of that miserable man, like so many vultures. He took them for men that loved him well and such as came to him for goodwill, when they took pleasure in nothing but devouring, eating of the flesh to the bare bones; and if there were any marrow remaining within, they would be sure to suck it out clean before they went away, and so leave him withered and quite cut up by the roots . . . This hath made him, as you see, betake himself to his mattock and his pelt, and, forsaking the city for very shame, works in the field for day wages, half mad with melancholy to think upon his misfortunes.

[. . .]

JUPITER . . . But now, Mercury, take Plutus with you and repair to him with all speed, and let Plutus take treasure along with him also, and let them both make their abode with Timon, and not depart with him lightly . . .

[. . .]

MERCURY This it is to be clamorous, importunate, and[1] bold . . . Now must Timon from a poor beggarly wretch be made a rich man again for his exclamation' sake . . .

[. . .]

PLUTUS [*objecting to going*] Because he hath used me ill, Jupiter, drave me out of doors, and cut me into a thousand pieces . . . Should I go again to him, to be scattered among flatterers, parasites, and harlots? . . . But he will ever give over to set me a-running, as it were liquor out of a rotten vessel, and haste to pour me out before I can be all put in . . . I do no more but pour water into the tubs of the Danaides, and vainly seek to fill a concavity that will hold nothing; but before I can get in almost all is run out, the holes of the vessel have so wide a vent that nothing can stop the passage . . . .

[. . .]

[*Mercury and Plutus travel to Timon, finding him attended by Poverty*]

TIMON . . . I hate all alike both gods and men . . .

PLUTUS For God's sake, Mercury, let us be gone; the man is sure more than mad, and will do me a mischief before I shall get from him.

MERCURY Be not self-willed, Timon, I pray you, but lay aside this fierceness and bitterness; stretch out your hands, receive good fortune, be rich again, and chief among the Athenians; live in despite of those ungrateful wretches, and no man happy but thyself.

[1] The 1634 edition prints 'and' twice.

TIMON I tell you plainly, I have no occasion to use you. Trouble me not. This mattock is riches enough for me, and, for all other matters, I think myself best at ease when no man comes near me.

[. . .]

[*Timon's reason for rejecting Plutus*] Because he hath been the means of the infinite miseries that have betid unto me, betrayed me into the hands of flatterers, delivered me up to those that lay in wait for me, stirred up hatred against me, undid me with voluptuous pleasures, caused every man to envy me, and at the last most treacherously and perfidiously forsook me. . . . I desire no more but this: to be a perpetual vexation to all men from the youngest to the oldest everlastingly . . .

[. . .]

PLUTUS . . . I have been the author of all your greatest delights, honour, prerogative, ornaments, and all the delicacies you ever enjoyed. In that you have been respected, reverenced, and affected by all men, it was by my means. If you have been abused by flatterers, the fault is not in me, for I have more cause to say I have been ill used at your hands, in prostituting me basely to lewd and vile persons that bewitched you with praises so to get me into their fingers . . .

MERCURY . . . You, Timon, dig as you did before, and do thou, Plutus, convey treasure unto him under his mattock, for he will hear thee at the first call.

TIMON I am content for this once, Mercury, to be ruled by you, and to be made a rich man again; for what can a man do withal when the gods do so importune him? But consider, I beseech you, what a peck of troubles you plunge me, miserable man, into, that have lately lived most happily, and must now suddenly be endowed with such a mass of gold, without doing any injury, and taking so many cares upon me.

[. . .]

PLUTUS . . . Dig now, Timon, as deep as thou canst; I will give way unto you.

TIMON Come on then, my good mattock, strengthen thyself for my sake, and be not tired with provoking treasure to show himself openly out of the bowels of the earth.—O miraculous Jupiter, and ye friendly Corybantes, and auspicious Mercury, how should so much gold come hither? Or is all this but a dream? I doubt I shall find it to be but coals when I awake. Nay, certainly this is pure gold, ruddy, weighty, and lovely to look upon. . . . Well may I now believe that Jupiter sometime turned himself into a shower of gold, for what virgin would not with open arms embrace so beautiful a lover, falling into the room through the roof of the house? . . . I will resolve upon these rules: to accompany no man, to take notice of no man, and to live in contempt of all men. The title of friend, or guest, or companion, or the altar of mercy, are but mere toys, not worth a straw to be talked of. To be sorry for him that weeps, or help him that wants, shall be a transgression and breach of our laws. I will eat alone as wolves do, and have but one friend in the world to bear me company, and that shall be Timon. All others shall be enemies and traitors . . . Let Timon alone be rich, and live in despite of all other; let him revel alone by himself, far from flattery and odious commendations; let him sacrifice to the gods and make good cheer alone, as a neighbour conjoined only to himself, discarding all other; and let it be further enacted that it shall be lawful for him only to shake himself by the hand, that is, either when he is about to die or to set a crown upon his head; and the welcomest name to him in the world is to be called 'Man-hater'. The notes and ensigns of his conditions shall be austerity, cruelty, frowardness, anger, and inhumanity. If thou see any man in the fire ready to be burned, and he entreat to have it quenched, pour into it pitch and oil. If any man be driven down the stream in a flood and shall stretch out his hands to thee for help, give him a knock on the pate and send him to the bottom, that he may never be able to put up his head again. So shall they receive according to their desert. Timon, the son of Echecratides the Colyttean, hath published this law, and the same Timon in parliament hath confirmed it. So it is, so have we decreed, and will constantly persist therein. Now it would do me good at the heart to have all men take notice of mine abundant riches, for it would be as bad as a hanging to them to hear of it.—But how comes this to pass, good God, upon a sudden? How they come running in every way, as soon as they had recovered, I know not by what means, the scent of gold! Whether were it best for me to ascend this hill and from the higher ground drive them away with stones, or dispense with mine own order for once and enter conference with them to their greater vexation when they shall see themselves despised? It shall be so; I will therefore receive them and tarry their coming. But let me see: who is the foremost man of the company? Who but Gnathonides the flatterer, whose benevolence I craved not long ago, and he held me out a halter, who had many times spewed whole tubfuls at my table. He hath done well in repairing hither so speedily, for he is the first that shall repent it.

GNATHONIDES Have I not always said that the gods would never be forgetful of Timon, so good a man? Hail, Timon, the comeliest of all creatures, the most pleasing of all companions, and the flower of all good fellowship!

TIMON And thou Gnathonides, the most ravenous of all vultures, and the vilest of all men.

GNATHONIDES O sir, you always love to break jests upon your friends. But where shall we meet and sup together? I have brought you here a new song of the last edition which I have lately learned.

TIMON But I will make thee sing a sorrowful elegy under this mattock.

GNATHONIDES What's the matter now? Dost thou strike me, Timon? Bear witness, alas, alas, I warn thee to appear at Mars his hill upon an action of battery.

TIMON If thou tarry a little longer, thou shalt have cause to warn me upon an action of manslaughter.

GNATHONIDES I will none of that. Yet I pray you make me a plaster of gold to lay upon my wound, for I have heard it hath an excellent virtue in staunching blood.

TIMON Art thou here yet?

GNATHONIDES Nay then, I am gone; and little joy shall it be to thee of so courteous a man to become so cruel.

TIMON What bald-pated fellow is this that comes next? It is Philiades, the impurest parasite that ever lived. This knave had from me a whole lordship, and two talents I gave his daughter to her marriage, because he once commended my singing. For when all the company beside were silent, he alone extolled me to the skies, and sware I had a sweeter voice than ever had swan. But when he saw me sickly a while ago and that I came to him to crave his relief, the rascal fell a-beating of me.

PHILIADES O impudency, do you now acknowledge Timon? Would Gnathonides now be his friend and playfellow? Wherefore his reward hath been righteous, in respect of his ingratitude. Whereas I that have been his old acquaintance, brought up with him from a child, and of the same tribe, do yet so moderate myself that I may not seem to be an intruder. Hail, noble Timon, and I beseech you free yourself from these base flatterers that come only to fill their bellies, and are indeed no better than cormorants. No man is to be trusted nowadays; all are unthankful and wicked. I was bringing a talent along with me to help to furnish you with necessaries, but being upon the way I heard of wonderful riches that were come to your hands; whereupon I made the cause of my visitation to be only to give you good counsel, though I know you are indeed with such wisdom that you needed not to be advised by me, but are able to tell Nestor himself what he hath to do.

TIMON It may be so, Philiades; but come a little nearer, that I may see how well I can welcome you with this mattock.

PHILIADES Help, neighbours! This unthankful man hath broke my head because I counselled him for his good.

TIMON Behold a third man, Demeas the rhetorician, with a decree in his hand, who professeth himself to be one of our kindred. I paid to the City for this fellow eleven talents in one day, which he was fined in, and committed until he should make payment, and for pity set him at liberty; yet the other day, when it was his lot to distribute dole money among the Erechthean tribe, and I came to him to crave my share, he said he could not tell whether I were a citizen.

DEMEAS All hail, Timon, a bounteous benefactor towards your kindred, the bulwark of Athens, and the ornament of Greece! The people and both the councils are all assembled, expecting your coming long ago. But first, I pray you hearken to this decree which I have penned down for you: 'For as much as Timon, the son of Echecratides the Colyttean, a man not only honest and virtuous, but so wise and discreet withal that his like again is not to be found in Greece, hath evermore sought the good of the City, and hath got the best prize at combating, wrestling, and running at the Olympian Games in one day, beside the race-chariot and coursing-horses—'

TIMON Why, man, I never went to see the Olympian Games in all my life.

DEMEAS What then? You may see them hereafter. And for such matters as these it is better the mention of them should precede than follow. 'He also fought bravely of late in the quarrel of his country against the Acharnians, and cut in pieces two companies of the Lacedaemonians.'

TIMON What's that? I protest, for my part, because I had no skill in arms, I was never yet enrolled into any military company.

DEMEAS You speak so poorly of yourself; but we might be thought unthankful if we should not remember it. Moreover: 'By publishing decrees, by giving good counsel, and by good command in war, he hath procured no small benefit to the City. For all which considerations, be it enacted by the Council and the people, and the highest court of the City, according to their tribes, and all the multitude in particular and general, that a golden statue shall be erected to Timon in the castle, and placed next to the image of Minerva, holding a thunderbolt in his right hand, and the sunbeams shining about his head; and he be crowned with seven crowns of gold, and this to be publicly proclaimed this day in the new tragedies of Bacchus . . .'

[. . .]

TIMON [*responding to Demeas' plan to marry and call his son Timon:*] I know not whether it will be your fortune ever to come to marriage, friend mine, if this blow with my mattock do but fall aright.

DEMEAS Alas, alas, what meanest thou by this? Dost thou tyrannize, Timon, and beat freemen, that art no true freeman nor citizen thyself?

[. . .]

TIMON . . . What's the reason that Thrasycles hath been so slow in coming to visit me?

THRASYCLES I come not, Timon, with the same intent as other men do, which aim at thy riches, and run themselves out of breath in hope to get silver, gold, and good cheer by thee, expressing a great deal of flattery towards a man so honest and plain as thou art, and so ready to impart anything that is within thy power. As for me . . . for gold I have it in no more estimation than the rubbish that lies upon the seashore. For your sake it is that I am come hither, lest this mischievous and most deceitful possession of riches should corrupt you, which hath oftentimes been the cause of incurable mischiefs to many men. Wherefore, if you will be ruled by me, take it and cast it all into the sea as an unnecessary clog to a good man that is able to discern the riches of philosophy. I mean not into the main sea, good sir, but that you would go into it as far as a man is forked before the going forth of the tide, and suffer no man to see you but myself. Or, if you like not well of this, take another course which perhaps may do better: disburden yourself of it so soon as you can. Leave not one halfpenny, but distribute it to all that stand in need: to one man, five drachmas; to another, a pound; to a third, a talent. But if any philosopher come in your way, you cannot upon your conscience but give him twice or thrice as much as any other. For my part, I crave nothing for myself, but to bestow upon my friends that are in want, and I shall hold myself well satisfied if you will but fill me this satchel, which doth not altogether contain two bushels of Aegina measure; for a philosopher ought to be content with a little, and observe the mean, and never stretch his thoughts wider than his scrip.

TIMON   I commend thee, Thrasycles, for this, in faith. But before I deal with thy scrip, let me try whether I can fill thy head with blows and measure them out with my mattock.

THRASYCLES   O democracy and laws! I am beaten by a rebellious wretch in a free city.

TIMON   Why dost thou complain, my honest Thrasycles? Have I deceived thee in thy measure? I am sure I put in four quarts more than was thy due. But what's the matter of this? They come now tumbling in by heaps. There is Blepsias, and Laches, and Gniphon, and a whole rabble of such rascals as shall be sure to rue for it. I will therefore ascend this rock, and forbear the use of my mattock awhile, which hath made me over-weary, and lay as many stones as I can on heaps together, and dung amongst them as thick as hail.

BLEPSIAS   You may save yourself that labour, Timon, for we will be going.

TIMON   But I hope not without blood or blows.

3. The Parable of the Unjust Steward (Luke 16:1–13; Bishops' Bible)[2]

And he said also unto his disciples, 'There was a certain rich man which had a steward, and the same was accused unto him that he had wasted his goods. And he called him, and said unto him: "How is it that I hear this of thee? Give accounts of thy stewardship, for thou mayest be no longer steward." The steward said within himself: "What shall I do, for my master

---

[2] For 'unrighteous Mammon' in this passage, the Geneva Bible reads 'riches of iniquity'.

taketh away from me the stewardship? I cannot dig, and to beg I am ashamed. I wot what to do, that when I am put out of the stewardship they may receive me into their houses." So, when he had called all his master's debtors together, he said unto the first: "How much owest thou unto my master?" And he said, "An hundred measures of oil." And he said unto him: "Take thy bill, and sit down quickly and write fifty." Then said he to another: "How much owest thou?" And he said, "An hundred measures of wheat." He said unto him: "Take thy bill, and write fourscore." And the lord commended the unjust steward, because he had done wisely. For the children of this world are in their nation wiser than the children of light. And I say unto you, make you friends of the unrighteous Mammon, that when ye shall have need they may receive you into everlasting habitations. He that is faithful in that which is least, is faithful also in much; and he that is unrighteous in the least is unrighteous also in much. So then, if ye have not been faithful in the unrighteous Mammon, who shall trust you in the true treasure? And if ye have not been faithful in another man's business, who shall give you that which is your own? No man can serve two masters; for either he shall hate the one and love the other, or else he shall lean to the one and despise the other. Ye cannot serve God and Mammon.'

TABULATION OF FORMS FAVOURED BY MIDDLETON

In the works of Shakespeare and Middleton, the following forms, listed as they appear in *Timon of Athens*, are markedly favoured by Middleton, though few are exclusive to him. The Folio spellings are reproduced, though with one exception it is the form rather than the spelling that is significant. The exception is 'Oh', as distinct from 'O'.

Long scenes are divided into shorter passages of about fifty lines.

Shakespeare (except ll. 39–42?): 1.1–49
  [ ]

Shakespeare: 1.50–99
  [ ]

Shakespeare: 1.100–49
  1.135 Does

Shakespeare: 1.150–99
  1.171 for't

Shakespeare: 1.200–49
  1.203 he's
  1.232 E'ne
  1.232 does

Shakespeare: 1.250–73
  [ ]

Middleton: 1.274–2.49
  1.276 Hee's
  2.4 has
  2.27 Does
  2.31 does
  2.32 for't
  2.34 on't
  2.39 nere
  2.39 Oh
  2.40 'em
  2.46 for't

Middleton: 2.50–99
  2.59 nere
  2.69 'em

2.70 too't
2.78 'em
2.80 'em
2.80 'em
2.85 Oh
2.91 Oh
2.92 nere
2.93 'em
2.94 nere
2.94 'em
2.99 Oh

Middleton: 2.100–49
   2.101 Oh
   2.101 e'ne
   2.102 er't
   2.124 They'r
   2.124 'em
   2.145 vntoo't
   2.147 for't

Middleton: 2.150–99
   2.162 ne're
   2.177 does
   2.188 ha's

Middleton: 2.200–52
   2.200 for't
   2.203 has
   2.204 e'ne
   2.209 he's
   2.213 Oh
   2.215 does
   2.221 nere
   2.224 mong'st
   2.236 'em
   2.251 Oh

Shakespeare: 3.1–35
   [ ]

Shakespeare mainly?: 4.1–44
   [ ]

Middleton mainly?: 4.45–84
   4.46 ha (for 'have')

4.46 'em
4.63 'em
4.65 does
4.67 She's
4.67 e'ne

Shakespeare mainly?: 4.84–117
4.84 E'ne
4.94 ha's
4.105 sometime t'

Middleton mainly?: 4.118–89
4.186 'em

Middleton mainly?: 4.190–227
4.192 'em
4.217 hee's
4.224 Neu'r

5.1–62: Middleton
5.10 does
5.23 ha (for 'have')
5.24 on't
5.27 has
5.27 ha (for 'have')
5.28 on't
5.28 nere
5.28 from't
5.53 Has
5.56 Has
5.59 vpon't
5.60 he's

Middleton: 6.1–49
6.11 for't
6.12 too't
6.16 on't
6.17 in't
6.21 ne're
6.23 yonders
6.29 ha's
6.30 hee's
6.31 has
6.32 Has (for 'he has')
6.43 ha (for 'have')

Middleton: 6.50–84

    6.64 has
    6.67 Has
    .6.67 ne're
    6.69 oh
    6.71 does

Middleton: 7.1–40

    7.1 in't
    7.1 'Boue
    7.8 Has
    7.9 does
    7.13 Has (for 'he's')
    7.13 in't
    7.13 I'me
    7.14 for't
    7.18 does
    7.21 'mong'st
    7.22 I'de
    7.23 Had (for 'he had')
    7.24 I'de
    7.29 by't
    7.36 ne're

Middleton: 8.1–49

    8.4 do's
    8.11 on't
    8.20 doe's
    8.26 e'ne
    8.27 'em
    8.28 I'me

Middleton: 8.50–97

    8.59 does
    8.61 hee's
    8.63 has
    8.65 Oh
    8.68 from't
    8.70 has
    8.70 he's
    8.81 does
    8.86 'em
    8.97 'em

Middleton: 9.1–10.49
    9.1 e'ene
    10.1 too't
    10.13 intoo't
    10.31 Hee's
    10.34 ne're
    10.43 vpon't

Middleton: 10.50–115
    10.51 Oh
    10.61 ha's (for 'he has')
    10.65 has
    10.65 'em
    10.66 He's
    10.66 has
    10.70 has
    10.77 'em
    10.91 has
    10.104 I'm

Middleton and Shakespeare: 11.1–67
    11.34 too't
    11.40 e'ne
    11.43 on't
    11.62 do's

Shakespeare: 11.68–104
    11.85 do's

Middleton: 11.105–14
    11.108 He's
    11.110 has

Shakespeare: 12.1–41
    [ ]

13.1–29: Shakespeare mainly
    [ ]

13.30–51: Middleton
    13.30 Oh
    13.39 do's
    [13.41 does (emended from F 'do')]
    13.45 Hee's
    13.47 ha's

14.1–49: Shakespeare
  [ ]

14.50–99: Shakespeare (except 14.66–9?)
  14.67 do's

14.100–49: Shakespeare
  [ ]

14.150–99: Shakespeare
  [ ]

14.200–49: Shakespeare (transcribed by Middleton?)
  14.212 ha's
  14.220 I'de
  14.239 in't

14.250–99: Shakespeare (transcribed by Middleton?)
  14.270 in't
  14.283 I'ld
  14.293 do's

14.300–49: Shakespeare (transcribed by Middleton?)
  14.349 ha's

14.350–99: Shakespeare (transcribed by Middleton?)
  14.367 does
  14.377 vpon't

14.400–57: Shakespeare (transcribed by Middleton?)
  14.405 for't
  14.444 Ha's
  14.450 Has (for 'he has')

14.458–99: Middleton
  14.458 Oh
  14.460 Oh
  14.462 has
  14.465 does
  14.469 Has (for 'he has')
  14.479 Neu'r
  14.497 hee's

14.500–36: Middleton
  14.506 ne're
  14.519 I'de
  14.524 Ha's
  14.529 'em

14.530 'em
14.536 Ne're
14.536 ne're

14.537–86: Shakespeare (transcribed by Middleton?)
   14.539 Does
   14.540 hee's
   14.545 Ha's

14.587–649: Shakespeare (transcribed by Middleton?)
   14.617 E'ne
   14.633 he's

14.650–99: Shakespeare
   [ ]

14.700–63: Shakespeare
   [ ]

15.1–16.10: Shakespeare
   16.4 do's
   16.9 hee's

17.1–86: Shakespeare (except ll. 10–13?)
   17.46 too't

MAJOR PRODUCTIONS

Timon of Athens is performed less frequently than most Shakespeare plays, and so a record of major productions can be presented here. This remains a provisional listing. A few productions for which information is unverified have been omitted.

I. British Isles

Locations are in London unless otherwise noted.

1674–8. Adaptation by Thomas Shadwell, *The History of Timon of Athens, the Man-Hater.* Acted Duke's Company, Dorset Garden Theatre. Thomas Betterton as Timon. Mrs Betterton and Mrs Shadwell as Evandra ('mistress') and Melissa ('fiancée').

1707–33. Drury Lane (every year except 1713 and 1727). George Powell, John Mills, R. Bridgewater, and Barton Booth as Timon. Shadwell's version.

1707. Queen's. John Mills as Timon. Shadwell's version.

1714. Smock Alley Theatre, Dublin. Shadwell's version?

1715–16, 1718. Lincoln's Inn Fields. Barton Booth as Timon. Shadwell's version.

1733–4. Covent Garden. William Milward and Thomas Walker as Timon. Shadwell's version.

1735–7, 1740–1. Drury Lane. William Milward as Timon. Shadwell's version.

1736. Goodman's Fields. Shadwell's version.

1741. Goodman's Fields. James Marshall as Timon. Shadwell's version.

1745. Covent Garden. Sacheverel Hale as Timon. Shadwell's version.

1761. Smock Alley Theatre, Dublin. Based on the Shakespeare–Middleton version.

1767. Adaptation by 'James Love' (James Dance). Acted at the Theatre Royal, Richmond. Mr Aickin as Timon.

1771–2. Adaptation by Richard Cumberland. Staged by David Garrick at Drury Lane. Spranger Barry as Timon.

1783. Smock Alley, Dublin. John Philip Kemble as Timon. In a version 'Altered from Shakespeare', evidently Cumberland's, played for Kemble's benefit in his last Dublin season.

1786. Adaptation by Thomas Hull. Acted at Covent Garden. Joseph George Holman as Timon. Hull as the Steward Flavius.

1816–17. Drury Lane. George Lamb manager. Edmund Kean as Timon. Cut version of the Shakespeare–Middleton text, which prevails from now on.

1851, 1856. Sadler's Wells. Samuel Phelps manager and as Timon.

1871. Princes Theatre, Manchester. Charles Calvert manager and as Timon.

1892. Memorial Theatre, Stratford-upon-Avon. Frank Benson manager and as Timon.

1904. Court Theatre. J. H. Leigh manager and as Timon. Directed by Holbrook Blinn. Based on Benson's version.

1921–2. Old Vic. Robert Atkins manager and as Timon. Wilfrid Walter as Alcibiades.

1928. Greenhill Street Picture House, Stratford-upon-Avon. Directed by William Bridges-Adams. Wilfrid Walter as Timon. Produced as the Shakespeare Birthday play.

1929. Maddermarket Theatre, Norwich. Directed by Tyrone Guthrie.

1935. Westminster Theatre. Directed by Nugent Monck. Ernest Milton as Timon. Music by Benjamin Britten.

1947. Birmingham Repertory Theatre. Directed by Willard Stoker. John Phillips as Timon. Modern dress.

1948. Leeds University Union Theatre. Directed by George Wilson Knight, with Knight as Timon. Based on Knight's 1940 Toronto production.

1952. Theatre Royal, Newcastle-upon-Tyne, and Old Vic. Directed by Tyrone Guthrie. Decor Tanya Moiseiwitsch. André Morell as Timon.

1955. Marlowe Society, Cambridge. Directed by Tony White. Peter Woodthorpe as Timon.

1956–7. Old Vic. Directed by Michael Benthall. Ralph Richardson as Timon.

1960. Audio recording. Argo. Marlowe Society. Directed by George Rylands.

1965. Royal Shakespeare Theatre, Stratford-upon-Avon. Directed by John Schlesinger. Sets by Ralph Koltai. Paul Scofield as Timon.

1971. Stratford-upon-Avon. Royal Shakespeare Company production scheduled but cancelled. Director Clifford Williams. Derek Godfrey to have played Timon.

1972. Close Theatre Club, Glasgow, and Abbey Theatre, Dublin. Citizens' Theatre Company. Directed by Keith Hack.

1975. BBC Radio adaptation by Raymond Raikes. Stephen Murray as Timon.

1979. New Vic, Bristol. Directed by Adrian Noble. John Shrapnel as Timon.

1980–2. Other Place, Stratford-upon-Avon; Gulbenkian Studio, Newcastle-upon-Tyne; and [Donmar] Warehouse, London. Directed by Ron Daniels. Richard Pasco as Timon. Music by Guy Woolfenden.

1981. BBC TV and video. Directed by Jonathan Miller. Jonathan Pryce as Timon. Norman Rodway as Apemantus. John Shrapnel as Alcibiades.

1988. Leicester Haymarket. Directed by Simon Usher. Guy Williams as Timon.

1988–9. Drama Department, Bristol University.

1989. Croydon Warehouse and tour. Red Shift Theatre Company. Directed by Jonathan Holloway. Kate Fenwick as a female Timon.

1991. Young Vic, London. Directed by Trevor Nunn. David Suchet as Timon.

1994. Whiteley's Store, Bayswater. Ursa Major Theatre Company. Directed by John Longenbaugh.

1997. Brix Theatre. Andrew Jarvis Theatre Company. Directed by Jarvis. Jarvis as Timon.

1999–2000. Royal Shakespeare Theatre, Stratford-upon-Avon, and Barbican. Directed by Greg Doran. Michael Pennington as Timon, Richard McCabe as Apemantus.

2. Elsewhere in Europe

Eastern Europe

1778. Premiere in German, in Prague.

1852, 1859. Nemzeti Színház, Budapest, Hungary. Lajos Fáncsy as Timon.

1935. Nemzeti Színház, Budapest, Hungary. Directed by Artúr Somlay. Somlay as Timon. Lőrinc Szabó's translation.

1955. Divadlo Vítězného února, Hradec Králové, Czechoslovakia. Directed by Milán Pásek. Kamil Marek as Timon. Bohumil Štěpánek's translation.

1961. Municipal Theatre, Istanbul. Directed by Tunç Yalman. Agâh Hûn as Timon.

1969. Divadlo na zábradlí (Balustrade), Prague, Czechoslovakia. Directed by Jaroslav Gillar. Jan Přeučil as Timon. Translated by Josef Véclav Sládek.

1969. Nemzeti Színház, Budapest, Hungary. Directed by Tamás Major. István Iglódi as Timon.

1973. Film, Yugoslavia. Directed by Tomislav Radic, who wrote the screenplay.

1974. Teatr Ziemi Pomorskieij, Grundziądz, Poland. Directed by Zofia Wierchowicz. Henryck Dłużński as Timon. Andrzej Lis's translation.

1974. Teatrul de Nord Satu Mare, Romania. Directed by Mihai Raicu.

1976. Szigligeti Színház, Szolnok, Hungary. Directed by Gábor Székely. Gyula Piróth as Timon. Lőrinc Szabó's translation.

1977. Slovenska narodno gledališče, Ljubljana, Slovenia. Directed by Zvone Sedlbauer. Danilo Benedičič as Timon. Anuše Sodik's adaptation of Matej Bor's translation.

1978. Teatrul Nottara, Bucharest, Romania. Directed by Dinu Cernescu. George Constantin as Timon. Translation by Dan Duțescu and Leon Levițchi.

1992. Kamaraszínház, Budapest; Kiscelli ruins. Director Imre Csiszár. Péter Bregyán as Timon.

1993. Mahen Theatre, Brno, Moravia, Czech Republic. Directed by Ivan Balad'a. Frantisek Derfler as Timon. Translated by Bohumil Franek.

1994. Narodno Pozoriste, Subotica, Yugoslavia. Directed by Sasa Gabric. Petar Radovanovic as Timon.

2000–1. Radnóti Színház, Budapest, Hungary. Directed by Sándor Zsótér. György Cserhalmi as Timon.

Germany, Austria, Switzerland

1789. Mannheim. Two performances.

1910. Munich. Paul Heyse's translation. Eugen Kilian director. Albert Steinrück as Timon.

1921. Schosspark-Theater, Berlin. Directed by Paul Henckels. Rudolph Klix as Timon. Robert Prochtl's adaptation.

1930. National-Theater, Mannheim. Directed by Richard Dorseiff, in his adaptation. Hans Finohr as Timon.

1930. German radio. Adaptation by Karl Kraus, with Kraus as Timon.

1937. Stadttheater, Basel. Directed by Alfred Braun. Leopold Biberti as Timon.

1943. Schauspielhaus, Zürich. Directed by Leopold Lindtberg. Wolfgang Heinz as Timon. Karl Kraus's adaptation of Dorothea Tieck's translation.

1949. Neues Theater, Düsseldorf. Directed by Hans Schalla. Gerhard Geisler as Timon. Schalla's adaptation of Martin Wieland's translation.

1960. Kammerspiele, Munich. Produced by Fritz Kortner. Romuald Pekny as Timon. Dorothea Tieck's translation.

1963. Schauspielhaus, Städtische Theater, Leipzig. Directed by Heinrich Voigt. Hans-Joachim Hegewald as Timon. Voigt's adaptation of Dorothea Tieck's translation.

1964. Schiller-Theater, Berlin. Directed by Hans Lietzau. Erich Schellow as Timon. Adapted by Lietzau from the translations of Johann Joachim Eschenburg and Dorothea Tieck.

1965. Schauspielhaus, Bochum, for Deutsche Shakespeare-Gesellschaft West conference. Directed by Hanskarl Zeiser. Erich Aberle as Timon. Zeiser's adaptation of Martin Wieland's translation.

1968. Württenbergischer Landesbühne, Esslingen. Directed by Bernd Rademaker.

1972. Volkstheater, Vienna.

1975. Schauspielhaus Zürich. Directed by Bernard Sobel. Hans-Dieter Zeidler as Timon. Eric Fried's translation.

1975. Städtische Theater, Karl-Marx-Stadt (Chemnitz). Directed by Hartwig Albiro. Gerd Preusche as Timon. Eric Fried's translation.

1976. Saarländisches Staatstheater, Saarbrücken. Directed by Günter Penzoldt. Joachim Ansorge as Timon. Penzoldt's adaptation of Karl Georg Montey's translation.

1976. Zweites Deutsches Fernsehen, Munich. Radio broadcast. Directed by Oswald Döpke. Wolfgang Reichman as Timon. Manfred Vogel's translation.

1983. Schauspiel, Frankfurt am Main. Directed by David Mouchtar-Samorai. Peter Roggisch as Timon. Frank Günther's translation.

1990. Schauspielhaus, Bochum. Directed by Frank Patrick Steckel.

1991. Freiburg. Directed by Jürgen Kruste. Jürgen Rohe as Timon. Translated by Dorothea Tieck. Adapted by J. Kruster and Carl Georg Hegemann.

1992. Berlin and tour of Germany. Directed by Martin Lüttge. Translated by Georg John.

1997. Freie Kammerspiele, Cologne. Directed by Kostas Papakastopoulus.

1997, 2000. Bremer Shakespeare Company, Bremen. Directed by Vera Sturm. Performed by three actors. Norbert Kentrup as Timon.

1998. Schülertheater des Kleist Theaters, Frankfurt an der Oder. Directed by Jochen Henke, from his translation.

Northern Europe

1866. Stora Theatern, Kongliga Theatrarne, Stockholm. Adaptation of Carl August Hagberg's translation.

1940. Danmarks Radio, Copenhagen. Radio adaptation by Tavs Neiiendam. Directed by Oluf Bang. Based on Edvard Lembcke's translation.

1969. Göteborg, Sweden. Directed by Ralf Langbacka.

1982. Suomen Kansallisteatteri, Helsinki. Directed by Radu Penciulescu. Pentti Siimes as Timon. Penciulescu's adaptation of Anniki Lasski and Terttu Savola's translation.

1995. Theatergroept ELS, Het Veem Theater, Amsterdam. Directed by Arie De Mol. Kees Scholten as Timon.

1995. Transformatorhuis Toneelgroep Amsterdam. Toneelgroep Amsterdam. Directed by Pierre Audi. Mark Rietman as Timon.

2001. Jaarbeurs, Utrecht. Zuidelijk Toneel Hollandia and Stadsschouwburg. Directed by Paul Koek and Jeroen Willems. Henriëtte Koch as Timon. Translated and adapted by Tom Blokdijk.

France, Italy, and Spain

1961. Théâtre Municipal, Bourges. Directed by Gabriel Monnet. Monnet as Timon. Translated by Pierre and Hélène Gavarry.

1969. Piccolo Teatro di Milano. Directed by Marco Bellocchio. Salvo Randone as Timon. Based on Bellocchio's adaptation of Eugenio Montale's translation.

1973. Teatro Griego de Montjuich, Barcelona. Directed by Ramiro Bascompte, from his own translation.

1974–5. Bouffes-du-Nord, Paris. Directed by Peter Brook. François Marthouret as Timon. Malik Bagayogo as Apemantus. Translation by Jean-Claude Carrière.

1983. Teatro di Roma. Directed by Luigi Squarzina. Gianrico Tedeschi as Timon. Agostino Lombardo's translation.

1991. Théâtre de l'Athénée-Louis Jouvet, Paris. Compagnie Pitoiset. Directed by Dominique Pitoiset. Hervé Pierre as Timon. Translated by Jean-Michel Déprats.

1994. Teatro Español de la Juventud and Manchester University, Benidorm. Directed by Vicente Genovés and David O'Shea. Arturo Muñoz and Duncan Ryall as Timon.

1994–5. Teatro Carignano, Turin, and tour of Italy. Teatro Stabile di Torino. Directed by Walter Pagliaro. Massimo Venturiello as Timon. Renato Oliva's translation.

3. North America

1839. Franklin Theatre, New York. Nathaniel Harrington Bannister manager and as Timon. Two performances.

1910. Fulton Opera House, Lancaster, Pennsylvania, and US tour. Frederick Warde manager and as Timon. Heavily adapted; based on Calvert's text.

1936. Pasadena Playhouse, California. Directed by Lenore Shanewise (the first woman to direct the play), in a season of Shakespeare's Greco-Roman plays.

1940. University of Toronto. Directed by George Wilson Knight, with Knight as Timon.

1940. Yale Repertory Theatre. Modern dress.

1953. Antioch Area Theatre, Yellow Springs, Ohio. Directed by Mary Morris. Arthur Oshlag as Timon.

1954. The Ensemble, Bijou Theatre, New York.

1955. Oregon Shakespeare Festival, Ashland. Directed by Robert B. Loper. Richard T. Jones as Timon. Outdoor replica Elizabethan stage.

1955. Philadelphia Shakespeare Festival. Directed by David L. German.

1963. Stratford, Ontario. Directed by Michael Langham. John Colicos as Timon. Music by Duke Ellington. Transferred to Chichester (UK) in 1964.

1971. Delacorte Theatre, Central Park, New York. Outdoors. Directed by Gerald Freedman. Shepperd Strudwick as Timon. Musical adaptation. Jonathan Tunick composer.

1974. Colorado Shakespeare Festival, Boulder. Directed by Martha 'Ricky' Weiser, her first production for the Festival. Allen Nause as Timon.

1974. Hartke Theatre, Catholic University of America, Washington, DC. Directed by Gary Jay Williams. Pinkney Venning as Timon.

1975. Champlain Shakespeare Festival, Burlington, Vermont. Directed by Edward J. Feidner. Gerald E. Moses as Timon.

1977. Old Globe Theatre, San Diego National Shakespeare Festival, California. Directed by Eric Christmas. Richard Kneeland as Timon.

1978. Oregon Shakespeare Festival. Directed by Jerry Turner. Michael Kevin as Timon.

1978. Globe Playhouse, Hollywood, California. Directed by Walter Scholz, who also played Apemantus. Lawrence Parks as Timon.

1980. Yale Repertory Theatre. Directed by Lloyd Richards. African-American actor James Earl Jones as Timon.

1982. New Jersey Shakespeare Festival, Drew University Campus, Madison. Directed by Paul Barry, who also played Timon.

1983. Grand Theatre, London, Ontario. Directed by Robin Phillips. William Hutt as Timon.

1987. Washington Square Church, New York. Manhattan Ensemble Company. Directed by Raymond David Marciniak. Glenn Pasch as Timon.

1988. Berkeley Shakespeare Festival, California. James Carpenter as Timon. Directed by Julian López-Morillas.

1988. Old Globe Theatre, San Diego. Directed by Robert Berlinger. Jonathan McMurtry as Timon.

1988. City of New York Parks and Recreation. A Matinee Idyll. Directed by Thomas Caron. Caron as Timon.

1991. Stratford, Ontario. Directed by Michael Langham. Brian Bedford as Timon.

1993. Milwaukee Chamber Theatre. Directed by Montgomery Davis. Jonathan Smoots as Timon.

1993–4. Lyceum, Broadway, New York, National Actors Theatre. Directed by Michael Langham. Adapted from the 1991 Stratford production, with Brian Bedford again playing Timon.

1993. Thick Description, San Francisco. Directed by Tony Kelly, Kelvin Han Yee as Timon, Rhonnie Washington as Apemantus. Text arranged by Karen Amano.

1993. Utah Shakespeare Festival. Directed by Robert Cohen. Sheridan Crist as Timon.

1994. Home for Contemporary Theatre and Art, New York. Ark Ensemble. Directed by Erin B. Mee. Saeed Sayrafiezadeh as Timon.

1995. Outdoor Theatre, New York. American Theatre of Actors. Directed by James Jennings. Tom Bruce as Timon.

1996. Delacorte Theatre, Central Park, New York. Outdoors. Directed by Brian Kulick. Michael Cumpsty as Timon.

1997. Oregon Shakespeare Festival, Ashland. Directed by Penny Metropulos. David Kelly as Timon. Tamu Gray as a female Apemantus.

1997. Chicago Shakespeare Theater. Directed by Michael Bogdanov. Larry Yando as Timon. Designed by Ralph Koltai.

1999. Shakespeare in the Park, Seattle. Directed by Ken Holmes. Erin Day as a female Timon.

2000–1. Shakespeare Theatre, Washington, DC. Directed by Michael Kahn. Philip Goodwin as Timon.

2000. Audio tape. Arkangell Complete Shakespeare series. Alan Howard as Timon. Norman Rodway as Apemantus.

4. Other Regions

1968. University Memorial Theatre, Victoria University, Wellington, New Zealand.

1986. Theatre Group of Beijing Normal University, Beijing, China. National Shakespeare Festival. Directed by Cài Xiāng. Tián Zhigāng as Timon. Evening dress costume and Peking Opera style percussion.

1990. Bet-Zvi Drama School, Ramat-Gan, Israel. Directed by George Miltinano. Translated by Meir Weiseltier.

1996. Shakespeare Theatre Company, Tokyo Globe. Directed by Norio Deguchi. Translated by Yushi Odashima.

2002. Annexe Theatre, University of Tasmania, Launceston, Tasmania, Australia. Directed by Stuart Loone. Jeremy Fee as Timon.

5. Theatrical Adaptations, Offshoots, and Analogues

See 'British Isles' for Shadwell's *The Man-hater* and other early adaptations on the London stage.

1786. Catherine the Great (Catherine II), *The Spendthrift*. Didactic adaptation. Based on Johann Joachim Eschenburg's German translation of Shakespeare (1775–82). Lost and probably not completed. Evidently would have ended with Timon marrying and returning to his place in society.

1828. Ferdinand Raimund, *Der Alpenkönig und der Menschenfeind*. Vienna. Comedy. Analogue.

1908. Adaptation by Émile Fabre. Théâtre Antoine, Paris. In this realist play, Timon has a family; he loses money through expenditure for war, but becomes rich again after joining Alcibiades in the siege of Melos. He now betrays those who refused him help to the enemy, then leaves the city to commit suicide by hanging himself from a tree. See Ruby Cohn, *Modern Shakespeare Offshoots* (1976).

1909. Adaptation, Shimpa style. Misaki-za theatre, Tokyo. Subsequently performed by the Sanekawa Enjaku troupe in Kobe, Kyoto, and Tokyo (Shintomi-za theatre, 1911).

1932. Adaptation by Ferdinand Bruckner (Austrian avant-garde dramatist; nom-de-plume of Theodor Tagger). Burgtheater, Vienna. Directed by Albert Heine. Paul Hartmen as Timon, 'a cultured and peace-loving man in a period of big business speculation that thrives on war'. He forsakes the life of the senses for a life of the mind in the wilderness. See Cohn, *Modern Shakespeare Offshoots*.

1941. George Wilson Knight, 'This Sceptred Isle'. Westminster Theatre in 1941. Included extracts from *Timon of Athens*.

1979. Edward Bond, *The Worlds*. University Theatre, Newcastle-upon-Tyne, and Royal Court Upstairs. Analogue. See Walton.

1991. English National Opera, London Coliseum. Opera version. Composed by Stephen Oliver. Monte Jaffe (bass) as Timon.

INDEX

This is a selective index to the commentary and Introduction. Asterisks identify notes that supplement the information in *OED*. The headnote for a scene is abbreviated 'hn.' Works by Shakespeare and Middleton (see 'Editorial Procedures') are listed by title.

The Anglo-Saxon World

Beowulf

Lancelot of the Lake

The Paston Letters

Sir Gawain and the Green Knight

Tales of the Elders of Ireland

York Mystery Plays

GEOFFREY CHAUCER
The Canterbury Tales
Troilus and Criseyde

HENRY OF HUNTINGDON
The History of the English People
1000–1154

JOCELIN OF BRAKELOND
Chronicle of the Abbey of Bury
St Edmunds

GUILLAUME DE LORRIS
and JEAN DE MEUN
The Romance of the Rose

WILLIAM LANGLAND
Piers Plowman

SIR THOMAS MALORY
Le Morte Darthur

The Oxford World's Classics Website

www.worldsclassics.co.uk

- Information about new titles
- Explore the full range of Oxford World's Classics
- Links to other literary sites and the main OUP webpage
- Imaginative competitions, with bookish prizes
- Peruse the Oxford World's Classics Magazine
- Articles by editors
- Extracts from Introductions
- A forum for discussion and feedback on the series
- Special information for teachers and lecturers

www.worldsclassics.co.uk

American Literature

British and Irish Literature

Children's Literature

Classics and Ancient Literature

Colonial Literature

Eastern Literature

European Literature

History

Medieval Literature

Oxford English Drama

Poetry

Philosophy

Politics

Religion

The Oxford Shakespeare

A complete list of Oxford Paperbacks, including Oxford World's Classics, Oxford Shakespeare, Oxford Drama, and Oxford Paperback Reference, is available in the UK from the Academic Division Publicity Department, Oxford University Press, Great Clarendon Street, Oxford OX2 6DP.

In the USA, complete lists are available from the Paperbacks Marketing Manager, Oxford University Press, 198 Madison Avenue, New York, NY 10016.

Oxford Paperbacks are available from all good bookshops. In case of difficulty, customers in the UK can order direct from Oxford University Press Bookshop, Freepost, 116 High Street, Oxford OX1 4BR, enclosing full payment. Please add 10 per cent of published price for postage and packing.